WARREN MILD

S0-AIC-161

THE LIFE OF
MICHELANGELO
BUONARROTI

The Life of

Michelangelo

Buonarroti

BY

JOHN ADDINGTON
SYMONDS

MODERN LIBRARY · NEW YORK

Random House IS THE PUBLISHER OF

THE MODERN LIBRARY

BENNETT A. CERF · DONALD S. KLOPFER · ROBERT K. HAAS

Manufactured in the United States of America

Printed by Parkway Printing Company   Bound by H. Wolff

CONTENTS

vii

THE LIFE OF
MICHELANGELO BUONARROTI

THE LIFE OF MICHELANGELO

CHAPTER I

I

THE Buonarroti Simoni, to whom Michelangelo belonged, were a Florentine family of ancient burgher nobility. Their arms appear to have been originally "azure two bends or." To this coat was added "a label of four points gules inclosing three fleur-de-lys or." That augmentation, adopted from the shield of Charles of Anjou, occurs upon the scutcheons of many Guelf houses and cities. In the case of the Florentine Simoni, it may be ascribed to the period when Buonarrota di Simone Simoni held office as a captain of the Guelf party (1392). Such, then, was the paternal coat borne by the subject of this Memoir. His brother Buonarroto received a further augmentation in 1515 from Leo X., to wit: "upon a chief or, a pellet azure charged with fleur-de-lys or, between the capital letters L. and X." At the same time he was created Count Palatine. The old and simple bearing of the two bends was then crowded down into the extreme base of the shield, while the Angevine label found room beneath the chief.

According to a vague tradition, the Simoni drew their blood from the high and puissant Counts of Canossa. Michelangelo himself believed in this pedigree, for which there is, however, no foundation in fact, and no heraldic corroboration. According to his friend and biographer Condivi, the sculptor's first Florentine ancestor was a Messer Simone dei Conti di Canossa, who came in 1250 as Podestà to Florence. "The eminent qualities of this man gained for him admission into the burghership of the city, and he

1

was appointed captain of a Sestiere; for Florence in those days was divided into Sestieri, instead of Quartieri, as according to the present usage." Michelangelo's contemporary, the Count Alessandro da Canossa, acknowledged this relationship. Writing on the 9th of October 1520, he addresses the then famous sculptor as "honoured kinsman," and gives the following piece of information: "Turning over my old papers, I have discovered that a Messere Simone da Canossa was Podestà of Florence, as I have already mentioned to the above-named Giovanni da Reggio." Nevertheless, it appears now certain that no Simone da Canossa held the office of Podestà at Florence in the thirteenth century. The family can be traced up to one Bernardo, who died before the year 1228. His grandson was called Buonarrota, and the fourth in descent was Simone. These names recur frequently in the next generations. Michelangelo always addressed his father as "Lodovico di Lionardo di Buonarrota Simoni," or "Louis, the son of Leonard, son of Buonarrota Simoni;" and he used the family surname of Simoni in writing to his brothers and his nephew Lionardo. Yet he preferred to call himself Michelangelo Buonarroti; and after his lifetime Buonarroti became fixed for the posterity of his younger brother. "The reason," says Condivi, "why the family in Florence changed its name from Canossa to Buonarroti was this: Buonarroto continued for many generations to be repeated in their house, down to the time of Michelangelo, who had a brother of that name; and inasmuch as several of these Buonarroti held rank in the supreme magistracy of the republic, especially the brother I have just mentioned, who filled the office of Prior during Pope Leo's visit to Florence, as may be read in the annals of that city, this baptismal name, by force of frequent repetition, became the cognomen of the whole family; the more easily, because it is the custom at Florence, in elections and nominations of officers, to add the Christian names of the father, grandfather, great-grandfather, and sometimes even of remoter ancestors, to that of each citizen. Consequently, through the many Buonarroti who followed one another, and from the Simone who was the first founder of the house in Florence, they gradually came to be called Buonarroti Simoni, which is their present designation." Excluding the legend about Simone da Canossa, this is a pretty accurate account of what really happened. Italian patronymics were formed indeed upon the same rule as those of many Norman families in Great Britain. When the use of Di and Fitz expired, Simoni survived from Di Simone, as did my surname Symonds from Fitz-Symond.

On the 6th of March 1475, according to our present computation, Lodovico di Lionardo Buonarroti Simoni wrote as follows in his private notebook: "I record that on this day, March 6, 1474, a male child was born to me. I gave him the name of Michelangelo, and he was born on a Monday morning four or five hours before daybreak, and he was born while I was Podestà of Caprese, and he was born at Caprese; and the godfathers were those I have named below. He was baptized on the eighth of the same month in the Church of San Giovanni at Caprese. These are the godfathers:—

> Don Daniello di ser Buonaguida of Florence, Rector of San Giovanni at Caprese;
> Don Andrea di . . . . of Poppi, Rector of the Abbey of Diasiano (*i.e.*, Dicciano);
> Jacopo di Francesco of Casurio (?);
> Marco di Giorgio of Caprese;
> Giovanni di Biagio of Caprese;
> Andrea di Biagio of Caprese;
> Francesco di Jacopo del Anduino (?) of Caprese;
> Ser Bartolommeo di Santi del Lanse (?), Notary.

Note that the date is March 6, 1474, according to Florentine usage *ab incarnatione*, and according to the Roman usage, *a nativitate*, it is 1475."

Vasari tells us that the planets were propitious at the moment of Michelangelo's nativity: "Mercury and Venus having entered with benign aspect into the house of Jupiter, which indicated that marvellous and extraordinary works, both of manual art and intellect, were to be expected from him."

II

Caprese, from its beauty and remoteness, deserved to be the birthplace of a great artist. It is not improbable that Lodovico Buonarroti and his wife Francesca approached it from Pontassieve in Valdarno, crossing the little pass of Consuma, descending on the famous battle-field of Campaldino, and skirting the ancient castle of the Conti Guidi at Poppi. Every step in the romantic journey leads over ground hallowed by old historic memories. From Poppi the road descends the Arno to a richly cultivated district, out of which emerges on its hill the prosperous little town of Bibbiena. High up to eastward springs the broken crest of La Vernia, a mass of hard millstone rock (*macigno*) jutting from desolate beds of lime and shale at the height of some 3500 feet above the sea. It was here, among the sombre groves of beech and pine which wave along the ridge, that S. Francis came to found his infant Order, composed the Hymn to the Sun, and received the supreme honour of the stigmata. To this point Dante retired when the death of Henry VII. extinguished his last hopes for Italy. At one extremity of the wedge-like block which forms La Vernia, exactly on the watershed between Arno and Tiber, stands the ruined castle of Chiusi in Casentino. This was one of the two chief places of Lodovico Buonarroti's podesteria. It may be said to crown the valley of the Arno; for the waters gathered here flow downwards toward Arezzo, and eventually wash the city walls of Florence. A few steps farther, travelling south, we pass into the valley of the Tiber, and, after traversing a barren upland region for a couple of hours, reach the verge of the descent upon Caprese. Here the landscape assumes a softer character. Far away stretch blue Apennines, ridge melting into ridge above Perugia in the distance. Gigantic oaks begin to clothe the stony hillsides, and little by little a fertile mountain district of chestnut-woods and vineyards expands before our eyes, equal in charm to those aërial hills and vales above Pontremoli. Caprese has no central commune or head-village. It is an aggregate of scattered hamlets and farmhouses, deeply embosomed in a sea of greenery. Where the valley contracts and the infant Tiber breaks into a gorge, rises a wooded rock crowned with the ruins of an ancient castle. It was here, then, that Michelangelo first saw the light. When we discover that he was a man of more than usually nervous temperament, very different in quality from any of his relatives, we must not forget what a fatiguing journey had been performed by his mother, who was then awaiting her delivery. Even supposing that Lodovico Buonarroti travelled from Florence by Arezzo to Caprese, many miles of rough mountain-roads must have been traversed by her on horseback.

III

Ludovico, who, as we have seen, was Podestà of Caprese and of Chiusi in the Casentino, had already one son by his first wife, Francesca, the daughter of Neri di Miniato del Sera and Bonda Rucellai. This elder brother, Lionardo, grew to manhood, and become a devoted follower of Savonarola. Under the influence of the Ferrarese friar, he determined to abjure the world, and entered the Dominican Order in 1491. We know very little about him, and he is only once mentioned in Michelangelo's correspondence. Even this reference cannot be considered certain. Writing to his father from Rome, July 1, 1497, Michelangelo says: "I let you know that Fra Lionardo returned hither to Rome. He says that he was forced to fly from Viterbo, and that his frock had been taken from him, wherefore he wished to go there (*i.e.*, to Florence). So I gave him a golden ducat, which he asked for; and I think you ought already to have learned this, for he should be there by this time." When Lionardo died is uncertain. We only know that he was in the convent of S. Mark at Florence in the year 1510. Owing to this brother's adoption of the religious life, Michelangelo became, early in his youth, the eldest son of Lodovico's family. It will be seen that during the whole course of his long career he acted as the mainstay of his father, and as father to his younger brothers. The strength and the tenacity of his domestic affections are very remarkable in a man who seems never to have thought of marrying. "Art," he used to say, "is a sufficiently exacting mistress." Instead of seeking to beget children for his own solace, he devoted himself to the interests of his kinsmen.

The office of Podestà lasted only six months, and at the expiration of this term Lodovico returned to Florence. He put the infant Michelangelo out to nurse in the village of Settignano, where the Buonarroti Simoni owned a farm. Most of the people of that district gained their livelihood in the stone-quarries around Settignano and Maiano on the hillside of Fiesole. Michelangelo's foster-mother was the daughter and the wife of stone-cutters. "George," said he in after-years to his friend Vasari, "if I possess anything of good in my mental constitution, it comes from my having been born in your keen climate of Arezzo; just as I drew the chisel and the mallet with which I carve statues in together with my nurse's milk."

When Michelangelo was of age to go to school, his father put him under a grammarian at Florence named Francesco da Urbino. It does not appear, however, that he learned more than reading and writing in Italian, for later on in life we find him complaining that he knew no Latin. The boy's genius attracted him irresistibly to art. He spent all his leisure time in drawing, and frequented the society of youths who were apprenticed to masters in painting and sculpture. Among these he contracted an intimate friendship with Francesco

Granacci, at that time in the workshop of Domenico Ghirlandajo. Granacci used to lend him drawings by Ghirlandajo, and inspired him with the resolution to become a practical artist. Condivi says that "Francesco's influence, combined with the continual craving of his nature, made him at last abandon literary studies. This brought the boy into disfavour with his father and uncles, who often used to beat him severely; for, being insensible to the excellence and nobility of Art, they thought it shameful to give her shelter in their house. Nevertheless, albeit their opposition caused him the greatest sorrow, it was not sufficient to deter him from his steady purpose. On the contrary, growing even bolder he determined to work in colours." Condivi, whose narrative preserves for us Michelangelo's own recollections of his youthful years, refers to this period the painted copy made by the young draughtsman from a copper-plate of Martin Schöngauer. We should probably be right in supposing that the anecdote is slightly antedated. I give it, however, as nearly as possible in the biographer's own words. "Granacci happened to show him a print of S. Antonio tormented by the devils. This was the work of Martino d'Olanda, a good artist for the times in which he lived; and Michelangelo transferred the composition to a panel. Assisted by the same friend with colours and brushes, he treated his subject in so masterly a way that it excited surprise in all who saw it, and even envy, as some say, in Domenico, the greatest painter of his age. In order to diminish the extraordinary impression produced by this picture, Ghirlandajo went about saying that it came out of his own workshop, as though he had some part in the performance. While engaged on this piece, which, beside the figure of the saint, contained many strange forms and diabolical monstrosities, Michelangelo coloured no particular without going first to Nature and comparing her truth with his fancies. Thus he used to frequent the fish-market, and study the shape and hues of fishes' fins, the colour of their eyes, and so forth in the case of every part belonging to them; all of which details he reproduced with the utmost diligence in his painting." Whether this transcript from Schöngauer was made as early as Condivi reports may, as I have said, be reasonably doubted. The anecdote is interesting, however, as showing in what a naturalistic spirit Michelangelo began to work. The unlimited mastery which he acquired over form, and which certainly seduced him at the close of his career into a stylistic mannerism, was based in the first instance upon profound and patient interrogation of reality.

IV

Lodovico perceived at length that it was useless to oppose his son's natural bent. Accordingly, he sent him into Ghirlandajo's workshop. A minute from Ghirlandajo's ledger, under the date 1488, gives information regarding the terms of the apprenticeship. "I record this first of April how I, Lodovico di Lionardo di Buonarrota, bind my son Michelangelo to Domenico and Davit di Tommaso di Currado for the next three ensuing years, under these conditions and contracts: to wit, that the said Michelangelo shall stay with the above-named masters during this time, to learn the art of painting, and to practise the same, and to be at the orders of the above-named; and they, for their part, shall give to him in the course of these three years twenty-four florins (*fiorini di suggello*): to wit, six florins in the first year, eight in the second, ten in the third; making in all the sum of ninety-six pounds (*lire*)." A postscript, dated April 16th of the same year, 1488, records that two florins were paid to Michelangelo upon that day.

It seems that Michelangelo retained no very pleasant memory of his sojourn with the Ghirlandajo brothers. Condivi, in the passage translated above, hints that Domenico was jealous of him. He proceeds as follows: "This jealousy betrayed itself still more when Michelangelo once begged the loan of a certain sketch-book, wherein Domenico had portrayed shepherds with their flocks and watchdogs, landscapes, buildings, ruins, and such-like things. The master refused to lend it; and indeed he had the fame of being somewhat envious; for not only showed he thus scant courtesy toward Michelangelo, but he also treated his brother likewise, sending him into France when he saw that he was making progress and putting forth great promise; and doing this not so much for any profit to David, as that he might himself remain the first of Florentine painters. I have thought fit to mention these things, because I have been told that Domenico's son is wont to ascribe the genius and divinity of Michelangelo in great part to his father's teaching, whereas the truth is that he received no assistance from that master. I ought, however, to add that Michelangelo does not complain: on the contrary, he praises Domenico both as artist and as man."

This passage irritated Vasari beyond measure. He had written his first Life of Michelangelo in 1550. Condivi published his own modest biography in 1553, with the expressed intention of correcting errors and supplying deficiencies made by "others," under which vague word he pointed probably at Vasari. Michelangelo, who furnished Condivi with materials, died in 1564; and Vasari, in 1568, issued a second enlarged edition of the Life, into which he cynically incorporated what he chose to steal from Condivi's sources. The supreme Florentine sculptor being dead and buried, Vasari felt that he was safe in giving the lie direct to this humble rival biographer. Accordingly, he spoke as follows about Michelangelo's relations with Domenico Ghirlandajo: "He was fourteen years of age when he entered that master's service, and inasmuch as one (Condivi), who composed his biography after 1550, when I had published these Lives for the first time, declares that certain persons, from want of familiarity with Michelangelo, have recorded things that did not happen, and have omitted others worthy of relation; and in particular has touched upon the point at issue, accusing Domenico of envy, and saying that he never rendered Michelangelo assistance."——Here Vasari, out of breath with indignation, appeals to the record of Lodovico's contract with the Ghirlandajo brothers. "These minutes," he goes on to say, "I copied from the ledger, in order to show that everything I formerly published, or which will be published at the present time, is truth. Nor am I acquainted with any one who had greater familiarity with Michelangelo than I had, or who served him more faithfully in friendly offices; nor do I believe that a single man could exhibit a larger number of letters written with his own hand, or evincing greater personal affection, than I can."

This contention between Condivi and Vasari, our two contemporary authorities upon the facts of Michelangelo's life, may not seem to be a matter of great moment for his biographer after the lapse of four centuries. Yet the first steps in the art-career of so exceptional a genius possess peculiar interest. It is not insignificant to ascertain, so far as now is possible, what Michelangelo owed to his teachers. In equity, we acknowledge that Lodovico's record on the ledger of the Ghirlandajo brothers proves their willingness to take him as a prentice, and their payment to him of two florins in advance; but the same record does not disprove Condivi's statement, derived from his old master's reminiscences, to the effect that Domenico Ghirlandajo was in no way greatly serviceable to him as an instructor. The fault, in all probability, did not lie with Ghirlandajo alone. Michelangelo, as we shall have occasions in plenty to observe, was difficult to live with; frank in speech to the point of rudeness, ready with criticism, incapable of governing his temper, and at no time apt to work harmoniously with fellow-craftsmen. His extraordinary force and originality of genius made themselves felt, undoubtedly, at the very outset of his career; and Ghirlandajo may be excused if, without being positively jealous of the young eagle settled in his homely nest, he failed to do the utmost for this gifted and rough-natured child of promise. Beethoven's discontent with Haydn as a teacher offers a parallel; and sympathetic students of psychology will perceive that Ghirlandajo and Haydn were almost superfluous in the training of phenomenal natures like Michelangelo and Beethoven.

Vasari, passing from controversy to the gossip of the studio, has sketched a pleasant picture of the young Buonarroti in his master's employ. "The artistic and personal qualities of Michelangelo developed so rapidly that Domenico was astounded by signs of power in him beyond the ordinary scope of youth. He perceived, in short, that he not only surpassed the other students, of whom Ghirlandajo had a large number under his tuition, but also that he often competed on an equality with the master. One of the lads who worked there made a pen-drawing of some women, clothed, from a design of Ghirlandajo. Michelangelo took up the paper, and with a broader nib corrected the outline of a female figure, so as to bring it into perfect truth to life. Wonderful it was to see the difference of the two styles, and to note the judgment and ability of a mere boy, so spirited and bold, who had the courage to chastise his master's handiwork! This drawing I now preserve as a precious relique, since it was given me by Granacci, that it might take a place in my Book of Original Designs, together with others presented to me by Michelangelo. In the year 1550, when I was in Rome, I Giorgio showed it to Michelangelo, who recognised it immediately, and was pleased to see it again, observing modestly that he knew more about the art when he was a child than now in his old age.

"It happened then that Domenico was engaged upon the great Chapel of S. Maria Novella; and being absent one day, Michelangelo set himself to draw from nature the whole scaffolding, with some easels and all the appurtenances of the art, and a few of the young men at work there. When Domenico returned and saw the drawing, he exclaimed: 'This fellow knows more about it than I do,' and remained quite stupefied by the new style and the new method of imitation, which a boy of years so tender had received as a gift from heaven."

Both Condivi and Vasari relate that, during his apprenticeship to Ghirlandajo, Michelangelo demonstrated his technical ability by producing perfect copies of ancient drawings, executing the facsimile with consummate truth of line, and then dirtying the paper so as to pass it off as the original of some old master. "His only object," adds Vasari, "was to keep the originals, by giving copies in exchange; seeing that he admired them as specimens of art, and sought to surpass them by his own handling; and in doing this he acquired great renown." We may pause to doubt whether at the present time——in the case, for instance, of Shelley letters or Rossetti drawings——clever forgeries would be accepted as so virtuous and laudable. But it ought to be remembered that a Florentine workshop at that period contained masses of accumulated designs, all of which were more or less the common property of the painting firm. No single specimen possessed a high market value. It was, in fact, only when art began to expire in Italy, when Vasari published his extensive necrology and formed his famous collection of drawings, that property in a sketch became a topic for moral casuistry.

Of Michelangelo's own work at this early period we possess probably nothing except a rough scrawl on the plaster of a wall at Settignano. Even this does not exist in its original state. The Satyr which is still shown there may, according to Mr. Heath Wilson's suggestion, be a *rifacimento* from the master's hand at a subsequent period of his career.

v

Condivi and Vasari differ considerably in their accounts of Michelangelo's departure from Ghirlandajo's workshop. The former writes as follows: "So then the boy, now drawing one thing and now another, without fixed place or steady line of study, happened one day to be taken by Granacci into the garden of the Medici at San Marco, which garden the magnificent Lorenzo, father of Pope Leo, and a man of the first intellectual distinction, had adorned with antique statues and other reliques of plastic art. When Michelangelo saw these things and felt their beauty, he no longer frequented Domenico's shop, nor did he go elsewhere, but, judging the Medicean gardens to be the best school, spent all his time and faculties in working there." Vasari reports that it was Lorenzo's wish to raise the art of sculpture in Florence to the same level as that of painting; and for this reason he placed Bertoldo, a pupil and follower of Donatello, over his collections, with a special commission to aid and instruct the young men who used them. With the same intention of forming an academy or school of art, Lorenzo went to Ghirlandajo, and begged him to select from his pupils those whom he considered the most promising. Ghirlandajo accordingly drafted off Francesco Granacci and Michelangelo Buonarroti. Since Michelangelo had been formally articled by his father to Ghirlandajo in 1488, he can hardly have left that master in 1489 as unceremoniously as Condivi asserts. Therefore we may, I think, assume that Vasari upon this point has preserved the genuine tradition.

Having first studied the art of design and learned to work in colours under the supervision of Ghirlandajo, Michelangelo now had his native genius directed to sculpture. He began with the rudiments of stone-hewing, blocking out marbles designed for the Library of San Lorenzo, and acquiring that practical skill in the manipulation of the chisel which he exercised all through his life. Condivi and Vasari agree in relating that a copy he made for his own amusement from an antique Faun first brought him into favourable notice with Lorenzo. The boy had begged a piece of refuse marble, and carved a grinning mask, which he was polishing when the Medici passed by. The great man stopped to examine the work, and recognised its merit. At the same time he observed with characteristic geniality: "Oh, you have made this Faun quite old, and yet have left him all his teeth! Do you not know that men of that great age are always wanting in one or two?" Michelangelo took the hint, and knocked a tooth out from the upper jaw. When Lorenzo saw how cleverly he had performed the task, he resolved to provide for the boy's future and to take him into his own household. So, having heard whose son he was, "Go," he said, "and tell your father that I wish to speak with him."

A mask of a grinning Faun may still be seen in the sculpture-gallery of the Bargello at Florence, and the marble is traditionally assigned to Michelangelo. It does not exactly correspond to the account given by Condivi and Vasari; for the mouth shows only two large tusk-like teeth, with the tip of the tongue protruding between them. Still, there is no reason to feel certain that we may not have here Michelangelo's first extant work in marble.

"Michelangelo accordingly went home, and delivered the message of the Magnificent. His father, guessing probably what he was wanted for, could only be persuaded by the urgent prayers of Granacci and other friends to obey the summons. Indeed, he complained loudly that Lorenzo wanted to lead his son astray, abiding firmly by the principle that he would never permit a son of his to be a stone-cutter. Vainly did Granacci explain the difference between a sculptor and a stone-cutter: all his arguments seemed thrown away. Nevertheless, when Lodovico appeared before the Magnificent, and was asked if he would consent to give his son up to the great man's guardianship, he did not know how to refuse. 'In faith,' he added, 'not Michelangelo alone, but all of us, with our lives and all our abilities, are at the pleasure of your Magnificence!' When Lorenzo asked what he desired as a favour to himself, he answered: 'I have never practised any art or trade, but have lived thus far upon my modest income, attending to the little property in land which has come down from my ancestors; and it has been my care not only to preserve these estates, but to increase them so far as I was able by my industry.' The Magnificent then added: 'Well, look about, and see if there be anything in Florence which will suit you. Make use of me, for I will do the utmost that I can for you.' It so happened that a place in the Customs, which could only be filled by a Florentine citizen, fell vacant shortly afterwards. Upon this Lodovico returned to the Magnificent, and begged for it in these words: 'Lorenzo, I am good for nothing but reading and writing. Now, the mate of Marco Pucci in the Customs having died, I should like to enter into this office, feeling myself able to fulfil its duties decently.' The Magnificent laid his hand upon his shoulder, and said with a smile: 'You will always be a poor man;' for he expected him to ask for something far more valuable. Then he added: 'If you care to be the mate of Marco, you can take the post, until such time as a better becomes vacant.' It was worth eight crowns the month, a little more or a little less." A document is extant which shows that Lodovico continued to fill this office at the Customs till 1494, when the heirs of Lorenzo were exiled; for in the year 1512, after the Medici returned to Florence, he applied to Giuliano, Duke of Nemours, to be reinstated in the same.

If it is true, as Vasari asserts, that Michelangelo quitted Ghirlandajo in 1489, and if Condivi is right in saying that he only lived in the Casa Medici for about two years before the death of Lorenzo, April 1492, then he must have spent some twelve months working in the gardens at San Marco before the Faun's mask called attention to his talents. His whole connection with Lorenzo, from the spring of 1489 to the spring of 1492, lasted three years; and, since he was born in March 1475, the space of his life covered by this patronage extended from the commencement of his fifteenth to the commencement of his eighteenth year.

These three years were decisive for the development of his mental faculties and special artistic genius. It is not necessary to enlarge here upon Lorenzo de' Medici's merits and demerits, either as the ruler of Florence or as the central figure in the history of the Italian Renaissance. These have supplied stock topics for discussion by all writers who have devoted their attention to that period of culture. Still we must remember that Michelangelo enjoyed singular privileges under the roof of one who was not only great as diplomatist and politician, and princely in his patronage, but was also a man of original genius in literature, of fine taste in criticism, and of civil urbanity in manners. The palace of the Medici formed a museum, at that period unique, considering the number and value of its art treasures—basreliefs, vases, coins, engraved stones, paintings by the best contemporary masters, statues in bronze and marble by Verocchio and Donatello. Its library contained the costliest manuscripts, collected from all quarters of Europe and the Levant. The guests who assembled in its halls were leaders in that intellectual movement which was destined to spread a new type of culture far and wide over the globe. The young sculptor sat at the same board as Marsilio Ficino, interpreter of Plato; Pico della Mirandola, the phœnix of Oriental erudition; Angelo Poliziano, the unrivalled humanist and melodious Italian poet; Luigi Pulci, the humorous inventor of burlesque romance—with artists, scholars, students innumerable, all in their own departments capable of satisfying a youth's curiosity, by explaining to him the particular virtues of books discussed, or of antique works of art inspected. During those halcyon years, before the invasion of Charles VIII., it seemed as though the peace of Italy might last unbroken. No one foresaw the apocalyptic vials of wrath which were about to be poured forth upon her plains and cities through the next half-century. Rarely, at any period of the world's history, perhaps only in Athens between the Persian and the Peloponnesian wars, has culture, in the highest and best sense of that word, prospered more intelligently and pacifically than it did in the Florence of Lorenzo, through the co-operation and mutual zeal of men of eminence, inspired by common enthusiasms, and labouring in diverse though cognate fields of study and production.

Michelangelo's position in the house was that of an honoured guest or adopted son. Lorenzo not only allowed him five ducats a month by way of pocket-money, together with clothes befitting his station, but he also, says Condivi, "appointed him a good room in the palace, together with all the conveniences he desired, treating him in every respect, as also at his table, precisely like one of his own sons. It was the custom of this household, where men of the noblest birth and highest public rank assembled round the daily board, for the guests to take their places next the master in the order of their arrival; those who were present at the beginning of the meal sat, each according to his degree, next the Magnificent, not moving afterwards for any one who might appear. So it happened that Michelangelo found himself frequently seated above Lorenzo's children and other persons of great consequence, with whom that house continually flourished and abounded. All these illustrious men paid him particular attention, and encouraged him in the honourable art which he had chosen. But the chief to do so was the Magnificent himself, who sent for him oftentimes in a day, in order that he might show him jewels, cornelians, medals, and such-like objects of great rarity, as knowing him to be of excellent parts and judgment in these things." It does not appear that Michelangelo had any duties to perform or services to render. Probably his patron employed him upon some useful work of the kind suggested by Condivi. But the main business of his life in the Casa Medici was to make himself a valiant sculptor, who in after years should confer lustre on the city of the lily and her Medicean masters. What he produced during this period seems to have become his own property, for two pieces of statuary, presently to be described, remained in the possession of his family, and now form a part of the collection in the Casa Buonarroti.

VI

Angelo Poliziano, who was certainly the chief scholar of his age in the new learning, and no less certainly one of its truest poets in the vulgar language, lived as tutor to Lorenzo's children in the palace of the Medici at Florence. Benozzo Gozzoli introduced his portrait, together with the portraits of his noble pupils, in a fresco of the Pisan Campo Santo. This prince of humanists recommended Michelangelo to treat in bas-relief an antique fable, involving the strife of young heroes for some woman's person. Probably he was also able to point out classical examples by which the boyish sculptor might be guided in the undertaking. The subject made enormous demands upon his knowledge of the nude. Adult and youthful figures, in attitudes of vehement attack and resistance, had to be modelled; and the conditions of the myth required that one at least of them should be brought into harmony with equine forms. Michelangelo wrestled vigorously with these difficulties. He produced a work which, though it is imperfect and immature, brings to light the specific qualities of his inherent art-capacity. The bas-relief, still preserved in the Casa Buonarroti at Florence, is, so to speak, in fermentation with powerful half-realised conceptions, audacities of foreshortening, attempts at intricate grouping, violent dramatic action and expression. No previous tradition, unless it was the genius of Greek or Græco-Roman antiquity, supplied Michelangelo with the motive force for this prentice-piece in sculpture. Donatello and other Florentines worked under different sympathies for form, affecting angularity in their treatment of the nude, adhering to literal transcripts from the model or to conventional stylistic schemes. Michelangelo discarded these

limitations, and showed himself an ardent student of reality
in the service of some lofty intellectual ideal. Following
and closely observing Nature, he was also sensitive to the
light and guidance of the classic genius. Yet, at the same
time, he violated the æsthetic laws obeyed by that genius,
displaying his Tuscan proclivities by violent dramatic suggestions, and in loaded, overcomplicated composition. Thus,
in this highly interesting essay, the horoscope of the mightiest Florentine artist was already cast. Nature leads him,
and he follows Nature as his own star bids. But that star is
double, blending classic influence with Tuscan instinct. The
roof of the Sistine was destined to exhibit to an awe-struck
world what wealths of originality lay in the artist thus
gifted, and thus swayed by rival forces. For the present, it
may be enough to remark that, in the geometrical proportions of this bas-relief, which is too high for its length,
Michelangelo revealed imperfect feeling for antique principles; while, in the grouping of the figures, which is more
pictorial than sculpturesque, he already betrayed, what remained with him a defect through life, a certain want of
organic or symmetrical design in compositions which are not
rigidly subordinated to architectural framework or limited
to the sphere of an *intaglio*.

Vasari mentions another bas-relief in marble as belonging
to this period, which, from its style, we may, I think, believe to have been designed earlier than the Centaurs. It is a
seated Madonna with the Infant Jesus, conceived in the
manner of Donatello, but without that master's force and
power over the lines of drapery. Except for the interest attaching to it as an early work of Michelangelo, this piece
would not attract much attention. Vasari praises it for grace
and composition above the scope of Donatello; and certainly
we may trace here the first germ of that sweet and winning
majesty which Buonarroti was destined to develop in his
Pietà of S. Peter, the Madonna at Bruges, and the even
more glorious Madonna of S. Lorenzo. It is also interesting

for the realistic introduction of a Tuscan cottage staircase into the background. This bas-relief was presented to Cosimo de' Medici, first Grand Duke of Tuscany, by Michelangelo's nephew Lionardo. It afterwards came back into the possession of the Buonarroti family, and forms at present an ornament of their house at Florence.

VII

We are accustomed to think of Michelangelo as a self-withdrawn and solitary worker, living for his art, avoiding the conflict of society, immersed in sublime imaginings. On the whole, this is a correct conception of the man. Many passages of his biography will show how little he actively shared the passions and contentions of the stirring times through which he moved. Yet his temperament exposed him to sudden outbursts of scorn and anger, which brought him now and then into violent collision with his neighbours. An incident of this sort happened while he was studying under the patronage of Lorenzo de' Medici, and its consequences marked him physically for life. The young artists whom the Magnificent gathered round him used to practise drawing in the Brancacci Chapel of the Carmine. There Masaccio and his followers bequeathed to us noble examples of the grand style upon the frescoed panels of the chapel walls. It was the custom of industrious lads to make transcripts from those broad designs, some of which Raphael deigned in his latest years to repeat, with altered manner, for the Stanze of the Vatican and the Cartoons. Michelangelo went one day into the Carmine with Piero Torrigiano and other comrades. What ensued may best be reported in the narration which Torrigiano at a later time made to Benvenuto Cellini.

"This Buonarroti and I used, when we were boys, to go into the Church of the Carmine to learn drawing from the chapel of Masaccio. It was Buonarroti's habit to banter all who were drawing there; and one day, when he was annoying me, I got more angry than usual, and, clenching my fist, I gave him such a blow on the nose that I felt bone and cartilage go down like biscuit beneath my knuckles; and this mark of mine he will carry with him to the grave." The portraits of Michelangelo prove that Torrigiano's boast was not a vain one. They show a nose broken in the bridge. But Torrigiano, for this act of violence, came to be regarded by the youth of Florence with aversion, as one who had laid sacrilegious hands upon the sacred ark. Cellini himself would have wiped out the insult with blood. Still Cellini knew that personal violence was not in the line of Michelangelo's character; for Michelangelo, according to his friend and best biographer, Condivi, was by nature, "as is usual with men of sedentary and contemplative habits, rather timorous than otherwise, except when he is roused by righteous anger to resent unjust injuries or wrongs done to himself or others, in which case he plucks up more spirit than those who are esteemed brave; but, for the rest, he is most patient and enduring." Cellini, then, knowing the quality of Michelangelo's temper, and respecting him as a deity of art, adds to his report of Torrigiano's conversation: "These words begat in me such hatred of the man, since I was always gazing at the masterpieces of the divine Michelangelo, that, although I felt a wish to go with him to England, I now could never bear the sight of him."

VIII

The years Michelangelo spent in the Casa Medici were probably the blithest and most joyous of his lifetime. The men of wit and learning who surrounded the Magnificent were not remarkable for piety or moral austerity. Lorenzo himself found it politically useful "to occupy the Florentines with shows and festivals, in order that they might think of their own pastimes and not of his designs, and, growing unused to the conduct of the commonwealth, might leave the reins of government in his hands." Accordingly he de-

vised those Carnival triumphs and processions which filled
the sombre streets of Florence with Bacchanalian revellers,
and the ears of her grave citizens with ill-disguised obscenity.
Lorenzo took part in them himself, and composed several
choruses of high literary merit to be sung by the mas-
queraders. One of these carries a refrain which might be
chosen as a motto for the spirit of that age upon the brink
of ruin:—

> *Youths and maids, enjoy to-day:*
> *Naught ye know about to-morrow!*

He caused the triumphs to be carefully prepared by the best
artists, the dresses of the masquers to be accurately studied,
and their chariots to be adorned with illustrative paintings.
Michelangelo's old friend Granacci dedicated his talents to
these shows, which also employed the wayward fancy of
Piero di Cosimo and Pontormo's power as a colourist. "It
was their wont," says Il Lasca, "to go forth after dinner;
and often the processions paraded through the streets till
three or four hours into the night, with a multitude of
masked men on horseback following, richly dressed, exceeding sometimes three hundred in number, and as many on
foot with lighted torches. Thus they traversed the city, sing-
ing to the accompaniment of music arranged for four, eight,
twelve, or even fifteen voices, and supported by various in-
struments." Lorenzo represented the worst as well as the
best qualities of his age. If he knew how to enslave Florence, it was because his own temperament inclined him to
share the amusements of the crowd, while his genius enabled him to invest corruption with charm. His friend Poliziano entered with the zest of a poet and a pleasure-seeker
into these diversions. He helped Lorenzo to revive the Tuscan Mayday games, and wrote exquisite lyrics to be sung by
girls in summer evenings on the public squares. This giant
of learning, who filled the lecture-rooms of Florence with
students of all nations, and whose critical and rhetorical la-

bours marked an epoch in the history of scholarship, was by nature a versifier, and a versifier of the people. He found nothing easier than to throw aside his professor's mantle and to improvise *ballate* for women to chant as they danced their rounds upon the Piazza di S. Trinità. The frontispiece to an old edition of such lyrics represents Lorenzo surrounded with masquers in quaint dresses, leading the revel beneath the walls of the Palazzo. Another woodcut shows an angle of the Casa Medici in Via Larga, girls dancing the *carola* upon the street below, one with a wreath and thyrsus kneeling, another presenting the Magnificent with a book of love-ditties. The burden of all this poetry was: "Gather ye roses while ye may, cast prudence to the winds, obey your in-stincts."

There is little doubt that Michelangelo took part in these pastimes; for we know that he was devoted to poetry, not always of the gravest kind. An anecdote related by Cellini may here be introduced, since it illustrates the Florentine customs I have been describing, "Luigi Pulci was a young man who possessed extraordinary gifts for poetry, together with sound Latin scholarship. He wrote well, was graceful in manners, and of surpassing personal beauty. While he was yet a lad and living in Florence, it was the habit of folk in certain places of the city to meet together during the nights of summer on the open streets, and he, ranking among the best of the improvisatori, sang there. His recitations were so admirable that the divine Michelangelo, that prince of sculptors and of painters, went, wherever he heard that he would be, with the greatest eagerness and delight to listen to him. There was a man called Piloto, a goldsmith, very able in his art, who, together with myself, joined Buonarroti upon these occasions." In like manner, the young Michelangelo probably attended those nocturnal gatherings upon the steps of the Duomo which have been so graphically de-scribed by Doni: "The Florentines seem to me to take more pleasure in summer airings than any other folk; for they

have, in the square of S. Liberata, between the antique
temple of Mars, now the Baptistery, and that marvellous
work of modern architecture, the Duomo: they have, I say,
certain steps of marble, rising to a broad flat space, upon
which the youth of the city come and lay themselves full
length during the season of extreme heat. The place is fitted
for its purpose, because a fresh breeze is always blowing,
with the blandest of all air, and the flags of white marble
usually retain a certain coolness. There then I seek my
chiefest solace, when, taking my aërial flights, I sail invisibly
above them; see and hear their doings and discourses: and
forasmuch as they are endowed with keen and elevated understanding, they always have a thousand charming things
to relate; as novels, intrigues, fables; they discuss duels,
practical jokes, old stories, tricks played off by men and
women on each other: things, each and all, rare, witty, noble,
decent and in proper taste. I can swear that during all the
hours I spent in listening to their nightly dialogues, I never
heard a word that was not comely and of good repute. Indeed, it seemed to me very remarkable, among such crowds
of young men, to overhear nothing but virtuous conversation."

At the same period, Michelangelo fell under very different influences; and these left a far more lasting impression on his character than the gay festivals and witty
word-combats of the lords of Florence. In 1491 Savonarola,
the terrible prophet of coming woes, the searcher of men's
hearts, and the remorseless denouncer of pleasant vices, began that Florentine career which ended with his martyrdom
in 1498. He had preached in Florence eight years earlier,
but on that occasion he passed unnoticed through the crowd.
Now he took the whole city by storm. Obeying the magic
of his eloquence and the magnetism of his personality, her
citizens accepted this Dominican friar as their political
leader and moral reformer, when events brought about the
expulsion of the Medici in 1494. Michelangelo was one of

his constant listeners at S. Marco and in the Duomo. He witnessed those stormy scenes of religious revival and passionate fanaticism which contemporaries have impressively described. The shorthand-writer to whom we owe the text of Savonarola's sermons at times breaks off with words like these: "Here I was so overcome with weeping that I could not go on." Pico della Mirandola tells that the mere sound of the monk's voice, startling the stillness of the Duomo, thronged through all its space with people, was like a clap of doom; a cold shiver ran through the marrow of his bones, the hairs of his head stood on end while he listened. Another witness reports: "Those sermons caused such terror, alarm, sobbing, and tears, that every one passed through the streets without speaking, more dead than alive."

One of the earliest extant letters of Michelangelo, written from Rome in 1497 to his brother Buonarroto, reveals a vivid interest in Savonarola. He relates the evil rumours spread about the city regarding his heretical opinions, and alludes to the hostility of Fra Mariano da Genezzano; adding this ironical sentence: "Therefore he ought by all means to come and prophesy a little in Rome, when afterwards he will be canonised; and so let all his party be of good cheer." In later years, it is said that the great sculptor read and meditated Savonarola's writings together with the Bible. The apocalyptic thunderings and voices of the Sistine Chapel owe much of their soul-thrilling impressiveness to those studies. Michelet says, not without justice, that the spirit of Savonarola lives again in the frescoes of that vault.

On the 8th of April 1492, Michelangelo lost his friend and patron. Lorenzo died in his villa at Careggi, aged little more than forty-four years. Guicciardini implies that his health and strength had been prematurely broken by sensual indulgences. About the circumstances of his last hours there are some doubts and difficulties; but it seems clear that he expired as a Christian, after a final interview with Savonarola. His death cast a gloom over Italy. Princes and people were growing uneasy with the presentiment of impending disaster; and now the only man who by his diplomatical sagacity could maintain the balance of power had been taken from them. To his friends and dependants in Florence the loss appeared irreparable. Poliziano poured forth his sorrow in a Latin threnody of touching and simple beauty. Two years later both he and Pico della Mirandola followed their master to the grave. Marsilio Ficino passed away in 1499; and a friend of his asserted that the sage's ghost appeared to him. The atmosphere was full of rumours, portents, strange premonitions of revolution and doom. The true golden age of the Italian Renaissance may almost be said to have ended with Lorenzo de' Medici's life.

CHAPTER II

I

AFTER the death of Lorenzo de' Medici, Michelangelo returned to his father's home, and began to work upon a statue of Hercules, which is now lost. It used to stand in the Strozzi Palace until the siege of Florence in 1530, when Giovanni Battista della Palla bought it from the steward of Filippo Strozzi, and sent it into France as a present to the king.

The Magnificent left seven children by his wife Clarice, of the princely Roman house of the Orsini. The eldest, Piero, was married to Alfonsina, of the same illustrious family. Giovanni, the second, had already received a cardinal's hat from his kinsman, Innocent VIII. Guiliano, the third, was destined to play a considerable part in Florentine history under the title of Duke of Nemours. One daughter was married to a Salviati, another to a Ridolfi, a third to the Pope's son, Franceschetto Cybò. The fourth, Luisa, had been betrothed to her distant cousin, Giovanni de' Medici; but the match was broken off, and she remained unmarried.

Piero now occupied that position of eminence and semi-despotic authority in Florence which his father and grand-father had held; but he was made of different stuff, both mentally and physically. The Orsini blood, which he inherited from his mother, mixed but ill in his veins with that of Florentine citizens and bankers. Following the proud and insolent traditions of his maternal ancestors, he began to discard the mask of civil urbanity with which Cosimo and Lorenzo had concealed their despotism. He treated the republic as though it were his own property, and prepared for the coming disasters of his race by the overbearing arrogance of his behaviour. Physically, he was powerful, tall, and active; fond of field-sports, and one of the best pallone-players of his time in Italy. Though he had been a pupil of Poliziano, he displayed but little of his father's interest in learning, art, and literature. Chance brought Michelangelo into personal relations with this man. On the 20th of January 1494 there was a heavy fall of snow in Florence, and Piero sent for the young sculptor to model a colossal snow-man in the courtyard of his palace. Critics have treated this as an insult to the great artist, and a sign of Piero's want of taste; but nothing was more natural than that a previous inmate of the Medicean household should use his talents for the recreation of the family who lived there. Piero upon this occasion begged Michelangelo to return and occupy the room he used to call his own during Lorenzo's lifetime. "And so," writes Condivi, "he remained for some months with the Medici, and was treated by Piero with great kindness; for the latter used to extol two men of his household as persons of rare ability, the one being Michelangelo, the other a Spanish groom, who, in addition to his personal beauty, which was something wonderful, had so good a wind and such agility that when Piero was galloping on horseback he could not outstrip him by a hand's-breadth."

II

At this period of his life Michelangelo devoted himself to anatomy. He had a friend, the Prior of S. Spirito, for whom he carved a wooden crucifix of nearly life-size. This liberal-minded churchman put a room at his disposal, and allowed him to dissect dead bodies. Condivi tells us that the practice of anatomy was a passion with his master. "His prolonged habits of dissection injured his stomach to such an extent that he lost the power of eating or drinking to any profit. It is true, however, that he became so learned in this branch of knowledge that he has often entertained the idea of composing a work for sculptors and painters, which should treat exhaustively of all the movements of the human body, the external aspect of the limbs, the bones, and so forth, adding an ingenious discourse upon the truths discovered by him through the investigations of many years. He would have done this if he had not mistrusted his own power of treating such a subject with the dignity and style of a practised rhetorician. I know well that when he reads Albert Dürer's book, it seems to him of no great value; his own conception being so far fuller and more useful. Truth to tell, Dürer only treats of the measurements and varied aspects of the human form, making his figures straight as stakes; and, what is more important, he says nothing about the attitudes and gestures of the body. Inasmuch as Michelangelo is now advanced in years, and does not count on bringing his ideas to light through composition, he has disclosed to me his theories in their minutest details. He also began to discourse upon the same topic with Messer Realdo Colombo, an anatomist and surgeon of the highest eminence. For the furtherance of such studies this good friend of ours sent him the corpse of a Moor, a young man of incomparable beauty, and admirably adapted for our purpose. It was placed at S. Agata, where I dwelt and still dwell, as being a quarter removed from public observation.

On this corpse Michelangelo demonstrated to me many rare and abstruse things, which perhaps have never yet been fully understood, and all of which I noted down, hoping one day, by the help of some learned man, to give them to the public." Of Michelangelo's studies in anatomy we have one grim but interesting record in a pen-drawing by his hand at Oxford. A corpse is stretched upon a plank and trestles. Two men are bending over it with knives in their hands; and, for light to guide them in their labours, a candle is stuck into the belly of the subject.

As it is not my intention to write the political history of Michelangelo's period, I need not digress here upon the invasion of Italy by Charles VIII., which caused the expulsion of the Medici from Florence, and the establishment of a liberal government under the leadership of Savonarola. Michelangelo appears to have anticipated the catastrophe which was about to overwhelm his patron. He was by nature timid, suspicious, and apt to foresee disaster. Possibly he may have judged that the haughty citizens of Florence would not long put up with Piero's aristocratical insolence. But Condivi tells a story on the subject which is too curious to be omitted, and which he probably set down from Michelangelo's own lips. "In the palace of Piero a man called Cardiere was a frequent inmate. The Magnificent took much pleasure in his society, because he improvised verses to the guitar with marvellous dexterity, and the Medici also practised this art; so that nearly every evening after supper there was music. This Cardiere, being a friend of Michelangelo, confided to him a vision which pursued him, to the following effect. Lorenzo de' Medici appeared to him barely clad in one black tattered robe, and bade him relate to his son Piero that he would soon be expelled and never more return to his home. Now Piero was arrogant and overbearing to such an extent that neither the good-nature of the Cardinal Giovanni, his brother, nor the courtesy and urbanity of Giuliano, was so strong to maintain him in Florence as his own faults to cause his expulsion. Michelangelo encouraged the man to obey Lorenzo and report the matter to his son; but Cardiere, fearing his new master's temper, kept it to himself. On another morning, when Michelangelo was in the courtyard of the palace, Cardiere came with terror and pain written on his countenance. Last night Lorenzo had again appeared to him in the same garb of woe; and while he was awake and gazing with his eyes, the spectre dealt him a blow on the cheek, to punish him for omitting to report his vision to Piero. Michelangelo immediately gave him such a thorough scolding that Cardiere plucked up courage, and set forth on foot for Careggi, a Medicean villa some three miles distant from the city. He had traveled about halfway, when he met Piero, who was riding home; so he stopped the cavalcade, and related all that he had seen and heard. Piero laughed him to scorn, and, beckoning the running footmen, bade them mock the poor fellow. His Chancellor, who was afterwards the Cardinal of Bibbiena, cried out: 'You are a madman! Which do you think Lorenzo loved best, his son or you? If his son, would he not rather have appeared to him than to some one else?' Having thus jeered him, they let him go; and he, when he returned home and complained to Michelangelo, so convinced the latter of the truth of his vision that Michelangelo after two days left Florence with a couple of comrades, dreading that if what Cardiere had predicted should come true, he would no longer be safe in Florence."

This ghost-story bears a remarkable resemblance to what Clarendon relates concerning the apparition of Sir George Villiers. Wishing to warn his son, the Duke of Buckingham, of his coming murder at the hand of Lieutenant Felton, he did not appear to the Duke himself, but to an old man-servant of the family; upon which behaviour of Sir George's ghost the same criticism has been passed as on that of Lorenzo de' Medici.

Michelangelo and his two friends travelled across the Apennines to Bologna, and thence to Venice, where they stopped a few days. Want of money, or perhaps of work there, drove them back upon the road to Florence. When they reached Bologna on the return journey, a curious accident happened to the party. The master of the city, Giovanni Bentivoglio, had recently decreed that every foreigner, on entering the gates, should be marked with a seal of red wax upon his thumb. The three Florentines omitted to obey this regulation, and were taken to the office of the Customs, where they were fined fifty Bolognese pounds. Michelangelo did not possess enough to pay this fine; but it so happened that a Bolognese nobleman called Gianfrancesco Aldovrandi was there, who, hearing that Buonarroti was a sculptor, caused the men to be released. Upon his urgent invitation, Michelangelo went to this gentleman's house, after taking leave of his two friends and giving them all the money in his pocket. With Messer Aldovrandi he remained more than a year, much honoured by his new patron, who took great delight in his genius; "and every evening he made Michelangelo read aloud to him out of Dante or Petrarch, and sometimes Boccaccio, until he went to sleep." He also worked upon the tomb of San Domenico during this first residence at Bologna. Originally designed and carried forward by Niccolò Pisano, this elaborate specimen of mediæval sculpture remained in some points imperfect. There was a San Petronio whose drapery, begun by Niccolò da Bari, was unfinished. To this statue Michelangelo put the last touches; and he also carved a kneeling angel with a candelabrum, the workmanship of which surpasses in delicacy of execution all the other figures on the tomb.

III

Michelangelo left Bologna hastily. It is said that a sculptor who had expected to be employed upon the *arca* of S. Domenic threatened to do him some mischief if he stayed and took the bread out of the mouths of native craftsmen. He returned to Florence some time in 1495. The city was now quiet again, under the rule of Savonarola. Its burghers, in obedience to the friar's preaching, began to assume that air of pietistic sobriety which contrasted strangely with the gay licentiousness encouraged by their former master. Though the reigning branch of the Medici remained in exile, their distant cousins, who were descended from Lorenzo, the brother of Cosimo, Pater Patriæ, kept their place in the republic. They thought it prudent, however, at this time, to exchange the hated name of de' Medici for Popolano. With a member of this section of the Medicean family, Lorenzo di Pierfrancesco, Michelangelo soon found himself on terms of intimacy. It was for him that he made a statue of the young S. John, which was perhaps rediscovered at Pisa in 1874. For a long time this S. Giovannino was attributed to Donatello; and it certainly bears decided marks of resemblance to that master's manner, in the choice of attitude, the close adherence to the model, and the treatment of the hands and feet. Still it has notable affinities to the style of Michelangelo, especially in the youthful beauty of the features, the disposition of the hair, and the sinuous lines which govern the whole composition. It may also be remarked that those peculiarities in the hands and feet which I have mentioned as reminding us of Donatello—a remarkable length in both extremities, owing to the elongation of the metacarpal and metatarsal bones and of the spaces dividing these from the forearm and tibia—are precisely the points which Michelangelo retained through life from his early study of Donatello's work. We notice them particularly in the Dying Slave of the Louvre, which is certainly one of his most characteristic works. Good judges are therefore perhaps justified in identifying this S. Giovannino, which is now in the Berlin Museum, with the statue made for Lorenzo di Pierfrancesco de' Medici.

The next piece which occupied Michelangelo's chisel was

a Sleeping Cupid. His patron thought this so extremely beautiful that he remarked to the sculptor: "If you were to treat it artificially, so as to make it look as though it had been dug up, I would send it to Rome; it would be accepted as an antique, and you would be able to sell it at a far higher price." Michelangelo took the hint. His Cupid went to Rome, and was sold for thirty ducats to a dealer called Messer Baldassare del Milanese, who resold it to Raffaello Riario, the Cardinal di S. Giorgio, for the advanced sum of 200 ducats. It appears from this transaction that Michelangelo did not attempt to impose upon the first purchaser, but that this man passed it off upon the Cardinal as an antique. When the Cardinal began to suspect that the Cupid was the work of a modern Florentine, he sent one of his gentlemen to Florence to inquire into the circumstances. The rest of the story shall be told in Condivi's words.

"This gentleman, pretending to be on the lookout for a sculptor capable of executing certain works in Rome, after visiting several, was addressed to Michelangelo. When he saw the young artist, he begged him to show some proof of his ability; whereupon Michelangelo took a pen (for at that time the crayon [*lapis*] had not come into use), and drew a hand with such grace that the gentleman was stupefied. Afterwards, he asked if he had ever worked in marble, and when Michelangelo said yes, and mentioned among other things a Cupid of such height and in such an attitude, the man knew that he had found the right person. So he related how the matter had gone, and promised Michelangelo, if he would come with him to Rome, to get the difference of price made up, and to introduce him to his patron, feeling sure that the latter would receive him very kindly. Michelangelo, then, partly in anger at having been cheated, and partly moved by the gentleman's account of Rome as the widest field for an artist to display his talents, went with him, and lodged in his house, near the palace of the Cardinal." S. Giorgio compelled Messer Baldassare to refund the 200 ducats, and to take the Cupid back. But Michelangelo got nothing beyond his original price; and both Condivi and Vasari blame the Cardinal for having been a dull and unsympathetic patron to the young artist of genius he had brought from Florence. Still the whole transaction was of vast importance, because it launched him for the first time upon Rome, where he was destined to spend the larger part of his long life, and to serve a succession of Pontiffs in their most ambitious undertakings.

Before passing to the events of his sojourn at Rome, I will wind up the story of the Cupid. It passed first into the hands of Cesare Borgia, who presented it to Guidobaldo di Montefeltro, Duke of Urbino. On the 30th of June 1502, the Marchioness of Mantua wrote a letter to the Cardinal of Este, saying that she should very much like to place this piece, together with an antique statuette of Venus, both of which had belonged to her brother-in-law, the Duke of Urbino, in her own collection. Apparently they had just become the property of Cesare Borgia, when he took and sacked the town of Urbino upon the 20th of June in that year. Cesare Borgia seems to have complied immediately with her wishes; for in a second letter, dated July 22, 1502, she described the Cupid as "without a peer among the works of modern times."

IV

Michelangelo arrived in Rome at the end of June 1496. This we know from the first of his extant letters, which is dated July 2, and addressed to Lorenzo di Pierfrancesco de' Medici. The superscription, however, bears the name of Sandro Botticelli, showing that some caution had still to be observed in corresponding with the Medici, even with those who latterly assumed the name of Popolani. The young Buonarroti writes in excellent spirits: "I only write to inform you that last Saturday we arrived safely, and went at once to visit the Cardinal di San Giorgio; and I presented your letter to him. It appeared to me that he was pleased to see me, and he expressed a wish that I should go immediately to inspect his collection of statues. I spent the whole day there, and for that reason was unable to deliver all your letters. Afterwards, on Sunday, the Cardinal came into the new house, and had me sent for. I went to him, and he asked what I thought about the things which I had seen. I replied by stating my opinion, and certainly I can say with sincerity that there are many fine things in the collection. Then he asked me whether I had the courage to make some beautiful work of art. I answered that I should not be able to achieve anything so great, but that he should see what I could do. We have bought a piece of marble for a life-size statue, and on Monday I shall begin to work."

After describing his reception, Michelangelo proceeds to relate the efforts he was making to regain his Sleeping Cupid from Messer Baldassare: "Afterwards, I gave your letter to Baldassare, and asked him for the child, saying I was ready to refund his money. He answered very roughly, swearing he would rather break it in a hundred pieces; he had bought the child, and it was his property; he possessed writings which proved that he had satisfied the person who sent it to him, and was under no apprehension that he should have to give it up. Then he complained bitterly of you, saying that you had spoken ill of him. Certain of our Florentines sought to accommodate matters, but failed in their attempt. Now I look to coming to terms through the Cardinal; for this is the advice of Baldassare Balducci. What ensues I will report to you." It is clear that Lorenzo di Pierfrancesco, being convinced of the broker's sharp practice, was trying to recover the Sleeping Cupid (the child) at the price originally paid for it, either for himself or for Buonarroti. The Cardinal is mentioned as being the most likely person to secure the desired result.

Whether Condivi is right in saying that S. Giorgio neglected to employ Michelangelo may be doubted. We have seen from this letter to Lorenzo that the Cardinal bought a piece of marble and ordered a life-size statue. But nothing more is heard about the work. Professor Milanesi, however, has pointed out that when the sculptor was thinking of leaving Rome in 1497 he wrote to his father on the 1st of July as follows: "Most revered and beloved father, do not be surprised that I am unable to return, for I have not yet settled my affairs with the Cardinal, and I do not wish to leave until I am properly paid for my labour; and with these great patrons one must go about quietly, since they cannot be compelled. I hope, however, at any rate during the course of next week, to have completed the transaction."

Michelangelo remained at Rome for more than two years after the date of the letter just quoted. We may conjecture, then, that he settled his accounts with the Cardinal, whatever these were, and we know that he obtained other orders. In a second letter to his father, August 19, 1497, he writes thus: "Piero de' Medici gave me a commission for a statue, and I bought the marble. But I did not begin to work upon it, because he failed to perform what he promised. Wherefore I am acting on my own account, and am making a statue for my own pleasure. I bought the marble for five ducats, and it turned out bad. So I threw my money away. Now I have bought another at the same price, and the work I am doing is for my amusement. You will therefore understand that I too have large expenses and many troubles."

During the first year of his residence in Rome (between July 2, 1496, and August 19, 1497) Michelangelo must have made some money, else he could not have bought marble and have worked upon his own account. Vasari asserts that he remained nearly twelve months in the household of the Cardinal, and that he only executed a drawing of S. Francis receiving the stigmata, which was coloured by a barber in S. Giorgio's service, and placed in the Church of S. Pietro a Montorio. Benedetto Varchi describes this picture as having been painted by Buonarroti's own hand. We know nothing more for certain about it. How he earned his money is, therefore, unexplained, except upon the supposition that S. Giorgio, unintelligent as he may have been in his patronage of art, paid him for work performed. I may here add that the Piero de' Medici who gave the commission mentioned in the last quotation was the exiled head of the ruling family. Nothing had to be expected from such a man. He came to Rome in order to be near the Cardinal Giovanni, and to share this brother's better fortunes; but his days and nights were spent in debauchery among the companions and accomplices of shameful riot.

V

Michelangelo, in short, like most young artists, was struggling into fame and recognition. Both came to him by the help of a Roman gentleman and banker, Messer Jacopo Gallo. It so happened that an intimate Florentine friend of Buonarroti, the Baldassare Balducci mentioned at the end of his letter to Lorenzo di Pierfrancesco, was employed in Gallo's house of business. It is probable, therefore, that this man formed the link of connection between the sculptor and his new patron. At all events, Messer Gallo purchased a Bacchus, which now adorns the sculpture-gallery of the Bargello, and a Cupid, which may possibly be the statue at South Kensington.

Condivi says that this gentleman, "a man of fine intelligence, employed him to execute in his own house a marble Bacchus, ten palms in height, the form and aspect of which correspond in all parts to the meaning of ancient authors. The face of the youth is jocund, the eyes wandering and wanton, as is the wont with those who are too much addicted to a taste for wine. In his right hand he holds a cup, lifting it to drink, and gazing at it like one who takes delight in that liquor, of which he was the first discoverer. For this reason, too, the sculptor has wreathed his head with vine-tendrils. On his left arm hangs a tiger-skin, the beast dedicated to Bacchus, as being very partial to the grape. Here the artist chose rather to introduce the skin than the animal itself, in order to hint that sensual indulgence in the pleasure of the grape-juice leads at last to loss of life. With the hand of this arm he holds a bunch of grapes, which a little satyr, crouched below him, is eating on the sly with glad and eager gestures. The child may seem to be seven years, the Bacchus eighteen of age." This description is comparatively correct, except that Condivi is obviously mistaken when he supposes that Michelangelo's young Bacchus faithfully embodies the Greek spirit. The Greeks never forgot, in all their representations of Dionysos, that he was a mystic and enthusiastic deity. Joyous, voluptuous, androgynous, he yet remains the god who brought strange gifts and orgiastic rites to men. His followers, Silenus, Bacchantes, Fauns, exhibit, in their self-abandonment to sensual joy, the operation of his genius. The deity descends to join their revels from his clear Olympian ether, but he is not troubled by the fumes of intoxication. Michelangelo has altered this conception. Bacchus, with him, is a terrestrial young man, upon the verge of toppling over into drunkenness. The value of the work is its realism. The attitude could not be sustained in actual life for a moment without either the goblet spilling its liquor or the body reeling side-ways. Not only are the eyes wavering and wanton, but the muscles of the mouth have relaxed into a tipsy smile; and, instead of the tiger-skin being suspended from the left arm, it has slipped down, and is only kept from falling by the loose grasp of the trembling hand. Nothing, again, could be less godlike than the face of Bacchus. It is the face of a not remarkably good-looking model, and the head is too small both for the body and the heavy crown of leaves. As a study of incipient intoxication, when the whole person is disturbed by drink, but human dignity has not yet yielded to a bestial impulse, this statue proves the energy of Michelangelo's imagination. The physical beauty of his adolescent model in the limbs and body redeems the grossness of the motive by the inalienable charm of health and carnal comeliness. Finally, the technical merits of the work cannot too strongly be insisted on. The modelling of the thorax, the exquisite roundness and fleshiness of the thighs and arms and belly, the smooth skin-surface expressed throughout in marble, will excite admiration in all who are capable of appreciating this aspect of the statuary's art. Michelangelo produced nothing more finished in execution, if we except the Pietà at S. Peter's. His Bacchus alone is sufficient to explode a theory favoured by some critics, that, left to work unhindered, he would still have preferred a certain vagueness, a certain want of polish in his marbles.

Nevertheless, the Bacchus leaves a disagreeable impression on the mind—as disagreeable in its own way as that produced by the Christ of the Minerva. That must be because it is wrong in spiritual conception—brutally materialistic where it ought to have been noble or graceful. In my opinion, the frank, joyous naturalism of Sansovino's Bacchus (also in the Bargello) possesses more of true Greek inspiration than Michelangelo's. If Michelangelo meant to carve a Bacchus, he failed; if he meant to imitate a physically desirable young man in a state of drunkenness, he succeeded.

What Shelley wrote upon this statue may here be introduced, since it combines both points of view in a criticism of much spontaneous vigour.

"The countenance of this figure is the most revolting mistake of the spirit and meaning of Bacchus. It looks drunken, brutal, and narrow-minded, and has an expression of dissoluteness the most revolting. The lower part of the figure is stiff, and the manner in which the shoulders are united to the breast, and the neck to the head, abundantly inharmonious. It is altogether without unity, as was the idea of the deity of Bacchus in the conception of a Catholic. On the other hand, considered merely as a piece of workmanship, it has great merits. The arms are executed in the most perfect and manly beauty; the body is conceived with great energy, and the lines which describe the sides and thighs, and the manner in which they mingle into one another, are of the highest order of boldness and beauty. It wants, as a work of art, unity and simplicity; as a representation of the Greek deity of Bacchus, it wants everything."

Jacopo Gallo is said to have also purchased a Cupid from Michelangelo. It has been suggested, with great plausibility, that this Cupid was the piece which Michelangelo began when Piero de' Medici's commission fell through, and that it therefore preceded the Bacchus in date of execution. It has also been suggested that the so-called Cupid at South Kensington is the work in question. We have no authentic information to guide us in the matter. But the South Kensington Cupid is certainly a production of the master's early manhood. It was discovered some forty years ago, hidden away in the cellars of the Gualfonda (Rucellai) Gardens at Florence, by Professor Miliarini and the famous Florentine sculptor Santarelli. On a cursory inspection they both declared it to be a genuine Michelangelo. The left arm was broken, the right hand damaged, and the hair had never received the sculptor's final touches. Santarelli restored the arm, and the Cupid passed by purchase into the possession of the English nation. This fine piece of sculpture is executed in Michelangelo's proudest, most dramatic manner. The muscular young man of eighteen, a model of superb adolescence, kneels upon his right knee, while the right hand is lowered to lift an arrow from the ground. The left hand is raised above the head, and holds the bow, while the left leg is so placed, with the foot firmly pressed upon the ground, as to indicate that in a moment the youth will rise, fit the shaft to the string, and send it whistling at his adversary. This choice of a momentary attitude is eminently characteristic of Michelangelo's style; and, if we are really to

believe that he intended to portray the god of love, it offers
another instance of his independence of classical tradition.
No Greek would have thus represented Erôs. The lyric poets,
indeed, Ibycus and Anacreon, imaged him as a fierce in-
vasive deity, descending like the whirlwind on an oak, or
striking at his victim with an axe. But these romantic ideas
did not find expression, so far as I am aware, in antique
plastic art. Michelangelo's Cupid is therefore as original
as his Bacchus. Much as critics have written, and with justice, upon the classical tendencies of the Italian Renaissance,
they have failed to point out that the Paganism of the
Cinque Cento rarely involved a servile imitation of the
antique or a sympathetic intelligence of its spirit. Least of
all do we find either of these qualities in Michelangelo.
He drew inspiration from his own soul, and he went straight
to Nature for the means of expressing the conception he had
formed. Unlike the Greeks, he invariably preferred the
particular to the universal, the critical moment of an action
to suggestions of the possibilities of action. He carved an
individual being, not an abstraction or a generalisation of
personality. The Cupid supplies us with a splendid illustration of this criticism. Being a product of his early energy,
before he had formed a certain manneristic way of seeing
Nature and of reproducing what he saw, it not only casts
light upon the spontaneous working of his genius, but it also
shows how the young artist had already come to regard the
inmost passion of the soul. When quite an old man, rhym-
ing those rough platonic sonnets, he always spoke of love
as masterful and awful. For his austere and melancholy
nature, Erôs was no tender or light-winged youngling, but
a masculine tyrant, the tamer of male spirits. Therefore this
Cupid, adorable in the power and beauty of his vigorous
manhood, may well remain for us the myth or symbol of
love as Michelangelo imagined that emotion. In composition, the figure is from all points of view admirable, presenting a series of nobly varied line-harmonies. All we have

to regret is that time, exposure to weather, and vulgar out-rage should have spoiled the surface of the marble.

VI

It is natural to turn from the Cupid to another work belonging to the English nation, which has recently been ascribed to Michelangelo. I mean the Madonna, with Christ, S. John, and four attendant male figures, once in the possession of Mr. H. Labouchere, and now in the National Gallery. We have no authentic tradition regarding this tempera painting, which in my judgment is the most beautiful of the easel pictures attributed to Michelangelo. Internal evidence from style renders its genuineness in the highest degree probable. No one else upon the close of the fifteenth century was capable of producing a composition at once so complicated, so harmonious, and so clear as the group formed by Madonna, Christ leaning on her knee to point a finger at the book she holds, and the young S. John turned round to combine these figures with the exquisitely blended youths behind him. Unfortunately the two angels or genii upon the left hand are unfinished; but had the picture been completed, we should probably have been able to point out another magnificent episode in the composition, determined by the transverse line carried from the hand upon the last youth's shoulder, through the open book and the uplifted arm of Christ, down to the feet of S. John and the last genius on the right side. Florentine painters had been wont to place attendant angels at both sides of their enthroned Madonnas. Fine examples might be chosen from the work of Filippino Lippi and Botticelli. But their angels were winged and clothed like acolytes; the Madonna was seated on a rich throne or under a canopy, with altar-candles, wreaths of roses, flowering lilies. It is characteristic of Michelangelo to adopt a conventional motive, and to treat it with brusque originality. In this picture there are no accessories to the figures, and the attendant angels are Tuscan

lads half draped in succinct tunics. The style is rather that
of a flat relief in stone than of a painting; and though we
may feel something of Ghirlandajo's influence, the spirit
of Donatello and Luca della Robbia are more apparent.
That it was the work of an inexperienced painter is shown
by the failure to indicate pictorial planes. In spite of the
marvellous and intricate beauty of the line-composition, it
lacks that effect of graduated distances which might perhaps
have been secured by execution in bronze or marble. The
types have not been chosen with regard to ideal loveliness
or dignity, but accurately studied from living models. This
is very obvious in the heads of Christ and S. John. The two
adolescent genii on the right hand possess a high degree of
natural grace. Yet even here what strikes one most is the
charm of their attitude, the lovely interlacing of their arms
and breasts, the lithe alertness of the one lad contrasted
with the thoughtful leaning languor of his comrade. Only
perhaps in some drawings of combined male figures made by
Ingres for his picture of the Golden Age have lines of equal
dignity and simple beauty been developed. I do not think that
this Madonna, supposing it to be a genuine piece by Michelangelo, belongs to the period of his first residence in Rome.
In spite of its immense intellectual power, it has an air of
immaturity. Probably Heath Wilson was right in assigning
it to the time spent at Florence after Lorenzo de' Medici's
death, when the artist was about twenty years of age.

I may take this occasion for dealing summarily with the
Entombment in the National Gallery. The picture, which
is half finished, has no pedigree. It was bought out of the
collection of Cardinal Fesch, and pronounced to be a Michelangelo by the Munich painter Cornelius. Good judges have
adopted this attribution, and to differ from them requires
some hardihood. Still it is painful to believe that at any
period of his life Michelangelo could have produced a composition so discordant, so unsatisfactory in some anatomical
details, so feelingless and ugly. It bears indubitable traces

of his influence; that is apparent in the figure of the dead
Christ. But this colossal nude, with the massive chest and
attenuated legs, reminds us of his manner in old age;
whereas the rest of the picture shows no trace of that
manner. I am inclined to think that the Entombment was
the production of a second-rate craftsman, working upon
some design made by Michelangelo at the advanced period
when the Passion of our Lord occupied his thoughts in
Rome. Even so, the spirit of the drawing must have been
imperfectly assimilated; and, what is more puzzling, the
composition does not recall the style of Michelangelo's old
age. The colouring, so far as we can understand it, rather
suggests Pontormo.

VII

Michelangelo's good friend, Jacopo Gallo, was again
helpful to him in the last and greatest work which he produced during this Roman residence. The Cardinal Jean
de la Groslaye de Villiers François, Abbot of S. Denys,
and commonly called by Italians the Cardinal di San Dionigi, wished to have a specimen of the young sculptor's handiwork. Accordingly articles were drawn up to the following effect on August 26, 1498: "Let it be known and
manifest to whoso shall read the ensuing document, that
the most Rev. Cardinal of S. Dionigi has thus agreed with
the master Michelangelo, sculptor of Florence, to wit, that
the said master shall make a Pietà of marble at his own cost;
that is to say, a Virgin Mary clothed, with the dead Christ in
her arms, of the size of a proper man, for the price of 450
golden ducats of the Papal mint, within the term of one
year from the day of the commencement of the work."
Next follow clauses regarding the payment of the money,
whereby the Cardinal agrees to disburse sums in advance.
The contract concludes with a guarantee and surety given
by Jacopo Gallo. "And I, Jacopo Gallo, pledge my word to
his most Rev. Lordship that the said Michelangelo will finish

the said work within one year, and that it shall be the finest work in marble which Rome to-day can show, and that no master of our days shall be able to produce a better. And, in like manner, on the other side, I pledge my word to the said Michelangelo that the most Rev. Card. will disburse the payments according to the articles above engrossed. To witness which, I, Jacopo Gallo, have made this present writing with my own hand, according to the date of year, month, and day as above."

The Pietà raised Michelangelo at once to the highest place among the artists of his time, and it still remains unrivalled for the union of sublime æsthetic beauty with profound religious feeling. The mother of the dead Christ is seated on a stone at the foot of the cross, supporting the body of her son upon her knees, gazing sadly at his wounded side, and gently lifting her left hand, as though to say, "Behold and see!" She has the small head and heroic torso used by Michelangelo to suggest immense physical force. We feel that such a woman has no difficulty in holding a man's corpse upon her ample lap and in her powerful arms. Her face, which differs from the female type he afterwards preferred, resembles that of a young woman. For this he was rebuked by critics who thought that her age should correspond more naturally to that of her adult son. Condivi reports that Michelangelo explained his meaning in the following words: "Do you not know that chaste women maintain their freshness far longer than the unchaste? How much more would this be the case with a virgin, into whose breast there never crept the least lascivious desire which could affect the body? Nay, I will go further, and hazard the belief that this unsullied bloom of youth, besides being maintained in her by natural causes, may have been miraculously wrought to convince the world of the virginity and perpetual purity of the Mother. This was not necessary for the Son. On the contrary, in order to prove that the Son of God took upon himself, as in very truth he did take, a human body, and became subject to all that an ordinary man is subject to, with the exception of sin; the human nature of Christ, instead of being superseded by the divine, was left to the operation of natural laws, so that his person revealed the exact age to which he had attained. You need not, therefore, marvel if, having regard to these considerations, I made the most Holy Virgin, Mother of God, much younger relatively to her Son than women of her years usually appear, and left the Son such as his time of life demanded." "This reasoning," adds Condivi, "was worthy of some learned theologian, and would have been little short of marvellous in most men, but not in him, whom God and Nature fashioned, not merely to be peerless in his handiwork, but also capable of the divinest concepts, as innumerable discourses and writings which we have of his make clearly manifest."

The Christ is also somewhat youthful, and modelled with the utmost delicacy; suggesting no lack of strength, but subordinating the idea of physical power to that of a refined and spiritual nature. Nothing can be more lovely than the hands, the feet, the arms, relaxed in slumber. Death becomes immortally beautiful in that recumbent figure, from which the insults of the scourge, the cross, the brutal lance have been erased. Michelangelo did not seek to excite pity or to stir devotion by having recourse to those mediæval ideas which were so passionately expressed in S. Bernard's hymn to the Crucified. The æsthetic tone of his dead Christ is rather that of some sweet solemn strain of cathedral music, some motive from a mass of Palestrina or a Passion of Sebastian Bach. Almost involuntarily there rises to the memory that line composed by Bion for the genius of earthly loveliness bewailed by everlasting beauty—

E'en as a corpse he is fair, fair corpse as fallen aslumber.

It is said that certain Lombards passing by and admiring the Pietà ascribed it to Christoforo Solari of Milan, sur-

named Il Gobbo. Michelangelo, having happened to overhear them, shut himself up in the chapel, and engraved the
belt upon the Madonna's breast with his own name. This he
never did with any other of his works.

This masterpiece of highest art combined with pure religious feeling was placed in the old Basilica of S. Peter's,
in a chapel dedicated to Our Lady of the Fever, Madonna
della Febbre. Here, on the night of August 19, 1503, it
witnessed one of those horrid spectacles which in Italy at
that period so often intervened to interrupt the rhythm of
romance and beauty and artistic melody. The dead body of
Roderigo Borgia, Alexander VI., lay in state from noon on-
wards in front of the high altar; but since "it was the most
repulsive, monstrous, and deformed corpse which had ever
yet been seen, without any form or figure of humanity,
shame compelled them to partly cover it." "Late in the evening it was transferred to the chapel of Our Lady of the
Fever, and deposited in a corner by six hinds or porters and
two carpenters, who had made the coffin too narrow and too
short. Joking and jeering, they stripped the tiara and the
robes of office from the body, wrapped it up in an old car-
pet, and then with force of fists and feet rammed it down
into the box, without torches, without a ministering priest,
without a single person to attend and bear a consecrated
candle." Of such sort was the vigil kept by this solemn
statue, so dignified in grief and sweet in death, at the ignoble
obsequies of him who, occupying the loftiest throne of Christendom, incarnated the least erected spirit of his age. The
ivory-smooth white corpse of Christ in marble, set over
against that festering corpse of his Vicar on earth, "black
as a piece of cloth or the blackest mulberry," what a hideous
contrast!

VIII

It may not be inappropriate to discuss the question of the
Bruges Madonna here. This is a marble statue, well placed

in a chapel of Notre Dame, relieved against a black marble niche, with excellent illumination from the side. The style is undoubtedly Michelangelesque, the execution careful, the surface-finish exquisite, and the type of the Madonna extremely similar to that of the Pietà at S. Peter's. She is seated in an attitude of almost haughty dignity, with the left foot raised upon a block of stone. The expression of her features is marked by something of sternness, which seems inherent in the model. Between her knees stands, half reclining, half as though wishing to step downwards from the throne, her infant Son. One arm rests upon his mother's knee; the right hand is thrown round to clasp her left. This attitude gives grace of rhythm to the lines of his nude body. True to the realism which controlled Michelangelo at the commencement of his art career, the head of Christ, who is but a child, slightly overloads his slender figure. Physically he resembles the Infant Christ of our National Gallery picture, but has more of charm and sweetness. All these indications point to a genuine product of Michelangelo's first Roman manner; and the position of the statue in a chapel ornamented by the Bruges family of Mouscron renders the attribution almost certain. However, we have only two authentic records of the work among the documents at our disposal. Condivi, describing the period of Michelangelo's residence in Florence (1501–1504), says: "He also cast in bronze a Madonna with the Infant Christ, which certain Flemish merchants of the house of Mouscron, a most noble family in their own land, bought for two hundred ducats, and sent to Flanders." A letter addressed under date August 4, 1506, by Giovanni Balducci in Rome to Michelangelo at Florence, proves that some statue which was destined for Flanders remained among the sculptor's property at Florence. Balducci uses the feminine gender in writing about this work, which justifies us in thinking that it may have been a Madonna. He says that he has found a trustworthy agent to convey it to Viareggio, and to ship it thence to Bruges, where it will be delivered into the hands of the heir of John and Alexander Mouscron and Co., "as being their property." This statue, in all probability, is the "Madonna in marble" about which Michelangelo wrote to his father from Rome on the 31st of January 1507, and which he begged his father to keep hidden in their dwelling. It is difficult to reconcile Condivi's statement with Balducci's letter. The former says that the Madonna bought by the Mouscron family was cast in bronze at Florence. The Madonna in the Mouscron Chapel at Notre Dame is a marble. I think we may assume that the Bruges Madonna is the piece which Michelangelo executed for the Mouscron brothers, and that Condivi was wrong in believing it to have been cast in bronze. That the statue was sent some time after the order had been given, appears from the fact that Balducci consigned it to the heir of John and Alexander, "as being their property;" but it cannot be certain at what exact date it was begun and finished.

IX

While Michelangelo was acquiring immediate celebrity and immortal fame by these three statues, so different in kind and hitherto unrivalled in artistic excellence, his family lived somewhat wretchedly at Florence. Lodovico had lost his small post at the Customs after the expulsion of the Medici; and three sons, younger than the sculptor, were now growing up. Buonarroto, born in 1477, had been put to the cloth-trade, and was serving under the Strozzi in their warehouse at the Porta Rossa. Giovan-Simone, two years younger (he was born in 1479), after leading a vagabond life for some while, joined Buonarroto in a cloth-business provided for them by Michelangelo. He was a worthless fellow, and gave his eldest brother much trouble. Sigismondo, born in 1481, took to soldiering; but at the age of forty he settled down upon the paternal farm at Settignano, and annoyed his brother by sinking into the condition of a common peasant.

The constant affection felt for these not very worthy relatives by Michelangelo is one of the finest traits in his character. They were continually writing begging letters, grumbling and complaining. He supplied them with funds, stinting himself in order to maintain them decently and to satisfy their wishes. But the more he gave, the more they demanded; and on one or two occasions, as we shall see in the course of this biography, their rapacity and ingratitude roused his bitterest indignation. Nevertheless, he did not swerve from the path of filial and brotherly kindness which his generous nature and steady will had traced. He remained the guardian of their interests, the custodian of their honour, and the builder of their fortunes to the end of his long life. The correspondence with his father and these brothers and a nephew, Lionardo, was published in full for the first time in 1875. It enables us to comprehend the true nature of the man better than any biographical notice; and I mean to draw largely upon this source, so as gradually, by successive stipplings, as it were, to present a miniature portrait of one who was both admirable in private life and incomparable as an artist.

This correspondence opens in the year 1497. From a letter addressed to Lodovico under the date August 19, we learn that Buonarroto had just arrived in Rome, and informed his brother of certain pecuniary difficulties under which the family was labouring. Michelangelo gave advice, and promised to send all the money he could bring together. "Although, as I have told you, I am out of pocket myself, I will do my best to get money, in order that you may not have to borrow from the Monte, as Buonarroto says is possible. Do not wonder if I have sometimes written irritable letters; for I often suffer great distress of mind and temper, owing to matters which must happen to one who is away from home. . . . In spite of all this, I will send you what you ask for, even should I have to sell myself into slavery."

Buonarroto must have paid a second visit to Rome; for

we possess a letter from Lodovico to Michelangelo, under date December 19, 1500, which throws important light upon the latter's habits and designs. The old man begins by saying how happy he is to observe the love which Michelangelo bears his brothers. Then he speaks about the cloth-business which Michelangelo intends to purchase for them. Afterwards, he proceeds as follows: "Buonarroto tells me that you live at Rome with great economy, or rather penuriousness. Now economy is good, but penuriousness is evil, seeing that it is a vice displeasing to God and men, and moreover injurious both to soul and body. So long as you are young, you will be able for a time to endure these hardships; but when the vigour of youth fails, then diseases and infirmities make their appearance; for these are caused by personal discomforts, mean living, and penurious habits. As I said, economy is good; but, above all things, shun stinginess. Live discreetly well, and see you have what is needful. Whatever happens, do not expose yourself to physical hardships; for in your profession, if you were once to fall ill (which God forbid), you would be a ruined man. Above all things, take care of your head, and keep it moderately warm, and see that you never wash: have yourself rubbed down, but do not wash." This sordid way of life became habitual with Michelangelo. When he was dwelling at Bologna in 1506, he wrote home to his brother Buonarroto: "With regard to Giovan-Simone's proposed visit, I do not advise him to come yet awhile, for I am lodged here in one wretched room, and have bought a single bed, in which we all four of us (*i.e.*, himself and his three workmen) sleep." And again: "I am impatient to get away from this place, for my mode of life here is so wretched, that if you only knew what it is, you would be miserable." The summer was intensely hot at Bologna, and the plague broke out. In these circumstances it seems miraculous that the four sculptors in one bed escaped contagion. Michelangelo's parsimonious habits were not occasioned by poverty or avarice. He accumulated large sums of money by his labour, spent it freely on his family, and exercised bountiful charity for the welfare of his soul. We ought rather to ascribe them to some constitutional peculiarity, affecting his whole temperament, and tinging his experience with despondency and gloom. An absolute insensibility to merely decorative details, to the loveliness of jewels, stuffs, and natural objects, to flowers and trees and pleasant landscapes, to everything, in short, which delighted the Italians of that period, is a main characteristic of his art. This abstraction and aridity, this ascetic devotion of his genius to pure ideal form, this almost mathematical conception of beauty, may be ascribed, I think, to the same psychological qualities which determined the dreary conditions of his home-life. He was no niggard either of money or of ideas; nay, even profligate of both. But melancholy made him miserly in all that concerned personal enjoyment; and he ought to have been born under that leaden planet Saturn rather than Mercury and Venus in the house of Jove. Condivi sums up his daily habits thus: "He has always been extremely temperate in living, using food more because it was necessary than for any pleasure he took in it; especially when he was engaged upon some great work; for then he usually confined himself to a piece of bread, which he ate in the middle of his labour. However, for some time past, he has been living with more regard to health, his advanced age putting this constraint upon his natural inclination. Often have I heard him say: 'Ascanio, rich as I may have been, I have always lived like a poor man.' And this abstemiousness in food he has practised in sleep also; for sleep, according to his own account, rarely suits his constitution, since he continually suffers from pains in the head during slumber, and any excessive amount of sleep deranges his stomach. While he was in full vigour, he generally went to bed with his clothes on, even to the tall boots, which he has always worn, because of a chronic tendency to cramp, as well as for other reasons. At certain seasons he has kept these boots on for such a length of time, that when he drew them off the skin came away together with the leather, like that of a sloughing snake. He was never stingy of cash, nor did he accumulate money, being content with just enough to keep him decently; wherefore, though innumerable lords and rich folk have made him splendid offers for some specimen of his craft, he rarely complied, and then, for the most part, more out of kindness and friendship than with any expectation of gain." In spite of all this, or rather because of his temperance in food and sleep and sexual pleasure, together with his manual industry, he preserved excellent health into old age.

I have thought it worth while to introduce this general review of Michelangelo's habits, without omitting some details which may seem repulsive to the modern reader, at an early period of his biography, because we ought to carry with us through the vicissitudes of his long career and many labours an accurate conception of our hero's personality. For this reason it may not be unprofitable to repeat what Condivi says about his physical appearance in the last years of his life. "Michelangelo is of a good complexion; more muscular and bony than fat or fleshy in his person: healthy above all things, as well by reason of his natural constitution as of the exercise he takes, and habitual continence in food and sexual indulgence. Nevertheless, he was a weakly child, and has suffered two illnesses in manhood. His countenance always showed a good and wholesome colour. Of stature he is as follows: height middling; broad in the shoulders; the rest of the body somewhat slender in proportion. The shape of his face is oval, the space above the ears being one sixth higher than a semicircle. Consequently the temples project beyond the ears, and the ears beyond the cheeks, and these beyond the rest; so that the skull, in relation to the whole head, must be called large. The forehead, seen in front, is square; the nose, a little flattened—not by nature, but because, when he was a young boy, Torrigiano de' Torrigiani a brutal and insolent fellow, smashed in the cartilage with his fist. Michelangelo was carried home half dead on this occasion; and Torrigiano, having been exiled from Florence for his violence, came to a bad end. The nose, however, being what it is, bears a proper proportion to the forehead and the rest of the face. The lips are thin, but the lower is slightly thicker than the upper; so that, seen in profile, it projects a little. The chin is well in harmony with the features I have described. The forehead, in a side-view, almost hangs over the nose; and this looks hardly less than broken, were it not for a trifling proturberance in the middle. The eyebrows are not thick with hair; the eyes may even be called small, of a colour like horn, but speckled and stained with spots of bluish yellow. The ears in good proportion; hair of the head black, as also the beard, except that both are now grizzled by old age; the beard double-forked, about five inches long, and not very bushy, as may partly be observed in his portrait."

We have no contemporary account of Michelangelo in early manhood; but the tenor of his life was so even, and, unlike Cellini, he moved so constantly upon the same lines and within the same sphere of patient self-reserve, that it is not difficult to reconstruct the young and vigorous sculptor out of this detailed description by his loving friend and servant in old age. Few men, notably few artists, have preserved that continuity of moral, intellectual, and physical development in one unbroken course which is the specific characterisation of Michelangelo. As years advanced, his pulses beat less quickly and his body shrank. But the man did not alter. With the same lapse of years, his style grew drier and more abstract, but it did not alter in quality or depart from its ideal. He seems to me in these respects to be like Milton: wholly unlike the plastic and assimilative genius of a Raphael.

CHAPTER III

I

MICHELANGELO returned to Florence in the spring of 1501. Condivi says that domestic affairs compelled him to leave Rome, and the correspondence with his father makes this not improbable. He brought a heightened reputation back to his native city. The Bacchus and the Madonna della Febbre had placed him in advance of any sculptor of his time. Indeed, in these first years of the sixteenth century he may be said to have been the only Tuscan sculptor of commanding eminence. Ghiberti, Della Quercia, Brunelleschi, Donatello, all had joined the majority before his birth. The second group of distinguished craftsmen—Verocchio, Luca della Robbia, Rossellino, Da Maiano, Civitali, Desiderio da Settignano—expired at the commencement of the century. It seemed as though a gap in the ranks of plastic artists had purposely been made for the entrance of a predominant and tyrannous personality. Jacopo Tatti, called Sansovino, was the only man who might have disputed the place of pre-eminence with Michelangelo, and Sansovino chose Venice for the theatre of his life-labours. In these circumstances, it is not singular that commissions speedily began to overtax the busy sculptor's power of execution. I do not mean to assert that the Italians, in the year 1501, were conscious of Michelangelo's unrivalled qualities, or sensitive to the corresponding limitations which rendered these qualities eventually baneful to the evolution of the arts; but they could not help feeling that in this young man of twenty-six they possessed a first-rate craftsman, and one who had no peer among contemporaries.

The first order of this year came from the Cardinal Francesco Piccolomini, who was afterwards elected Pope in 1503, and who died after reigning three weeks with the title of Pius III. He wished to decorate the Piccolomini

Chapel in the Duomo of Siena with fifteen statues of male
saints. A contract was signed on June 5, by which Michelangelo agreed to complete these figures within the space of
three years. One of them, a S. Francis, had been already
begun by Piero Torrigiano; and this, we have some reason
to believe, was finished by the master's hand. Accounts differ
about his share in the remaining fourteen statues; but the
matter is of no great moment, seeing that the style of the
work is conventional, and the scale of the figures disagreeably squat and dumpy. It seems almost impossible that these
ecclesiastical and tame pieces should have been produced at
the same time as the David by the same hand. Neither Vasari
nor Condivi speaks about them, although it is certain that
Michelangelo was held bound to his contract during several
years. Upon the death of Pius III., he renewed it with the
Pope's heirs, Jacopo and Andrea Piccolomini, by a deed
dated September 15, 1504; and in 1537 Anton Maria Piccolomini, to whom the inheritance succeeded, considered
himself Michelangelo's creditor for the sum of a hundred
crowns, which had been paid beforehand for work not
finished by the sculptor.

A far more important commission was intrusted to
Michelangelo in August of the same year, 1501. Condivi,
after mentioning his return to Florence, tells the history of
the colossal David in these words: "Here he stayed some time,
and made the statue which stands in front of the great door
of the Palace of the Signory, and is called the Giant by all
people. It came about in this way. The Board of Works at
S. Maria del Fiore owned a piece of marble nine cubits in
height, which had been brought from Carrara some hundred
years before by a sculptor insufficiently acquainted with his
art. This was evident, inasmuch as, wishing to convey it
more conveniently and with less labour, he had it blocked
out in the quarry, but in such a manner that neither he nor
any one else was capable of extracting a statue from the
block, either of the same size, or even on a much smaller

scale. The marble being, then, useless for any good purpose, Andrea del Monte San Savino thought that he might get possession of it from the Board, and begged them to make him a present of it, promising that he would add certain pieces of stone and carve a statue from it. Before they made up their minds to give it, they sent for Michelangelo; then, after explaining the wishes and the views of Andrea, and considering his own opinion that it would be possible to extract a good thing from the block, they finally offered it to him. Michelangelo accepted, added no pieces, and got the statue out so exactly, that, as any one may see, in the top of the head and at the base some vestiges of the rough surface of the marble still remain. He did the same in other works, as, for instance, in the Contemplative Life upon the tomb of Julius; indeed, it is a sign left by masters on their work, proving them to be absolute in their art. But in the David it was much more remarkable, for this reason, that the difficulty of the task was not overcome by adding pieces; and also he had to contend with an ill-shaped marble. As he used to say himself, it is impossible, or at least extraordinarily difficult in statuary to set right the faults of the blocking out. He received for this work 400 ducats, and carried it out in eighteen months."

The sculptor who had spoiled this block of marble is called "Maestro Simone" by Vasari; but the abundant documents in our possession, by aid of which we are enabled to trace the whole history of Michelangelo's David with minuteness, show that Vasari was misinformed. The real culprit was Agostino di Antonio di Duccio, or Guccio, who had succeeded with another colossal statue for the Duomo. He is honourably known in the history of Tuscan sculpture by his reliefs upon the façade of the Duomo at Modena, describing episodes in the life of S. Gemignano, by the romantically charming reliefs in marble, with terracotta settings, on the Oratory of S. Bernardino at Perugia, and by a large amount of excellent surface-work in stone upon the chapels of S. Francesco at Rimini. We gather from one of the contracts with Agostino that the marble was originally blocked out for some prophet. But Michelangelo resolved to make a David; and two wax models, now preserved in the Museo Buonarroti, neither of which corresponds exactly with the statue as it exists, show that he felt able to extract a colossal figure in various attitudes from the damaged block. In the first contract signed between the Consuls of the Arte della Lana, the Operai del Duomo, and the sculptor, dated August 16, 1501, the terms are thus settled: "That the worthy master Michelangelo, son of Lodovico Buonarroti, citizen of Florence, has been chosen to fashion, complete, and finish to perfection that male statue called the Giant, of nine cubits in height, now existing in the workshop of the cathedral, blocked out aforetime by Master Agostino of Florence, and badly blocked; and that the work shall be completed within the term of the next ensuing two years, dating from September, at a salary of six golden florins per month; and that what is needful for the accomplishment of this task, as workmen, timbers, &c., which he may require, shall be supplied him by the Operai; and when the statue is finished, the Consuls and Operai who shall be in office shall estimate whether he deserve a larger recompense, and this shall be left to their consciences."

II

Michelangelo began to work on Monday morning, September 13, in a wooden shed erected for the purpose, not far from the cathedral. On the 28th of February 1502, the statue, which is now called for the first time "the Giant, or David," was brought so far forward that the judges declared it to be half finished, and decided that the sculptor should be paid in all 400 golden florins, including the stipulated salary. He seems to have laboured assiduously during the next two years, for by a minute of the 25th of January 1504 the David is said to be almost entirely finished. On this date a solemn council of the most important artists resident in Florence was convened at the Opera del Duomo to consider where it should be placed.

We possess full minutes of this meeting, and they are so curious that I shall not hesitate to give a somewhat detailed account of the proceedings. Messer Francesco Filarete, the chief herald of the Signory, and himself an architect of some pretensions, opened the discussion in a short speech to this effect: "I have turned over in my mind those suggestions which my judgment could afford me. You have two places where the statue may be set up: the first, that where the Judith stands; the second, in the middle of the courtyard where the David is. The first might be selected, because the Judith is an omen of evil, and no fit object where it stands, we having the cross and lily for our ensign; besides, it is not proper that the woman should kill the male; and, above all, this statue was erected under an evil constellation, since you have gone continually from bad to worse since then. Pisa has been lost too. The David of the courtyard is imperfect in the right leg; and so I should counsel you to put the Giant in one of these places, but I give the preference myself to that of the Judith." The herald, it will be perceived, took for granted that Michelangelo's David would be erected in the immediate neighbourhood of the Palazzo Vecchio. The next speaker, Francesco Monciatto, a wood-carver, advanced the view that it ought to be placed in front of the Duomo, where the Colossus was originally meant to be put up. He was immediately followed, and his resolution was seconded, by no less personages than the painters Cosimo Rosselli and Sandro Botticelli. Then Giuliano da San Gallo, the illustrious architect, submitted a third opinion to the meeting. He began his speech by observing that he agreed with those who wished to choose the steps of the Duomo, but due consideration caused him to alter his mind. "The imperfection of the marble, which is softened by exposure to the air, rendered the durability of the statue doubtful. He therefore voted for the middle of the Loggia dei Lanzi, where the David would be under cover." Messer Angelo di Lorenzo Manfidi, second herald of the Signory, rose to state a professional objection. "The David, if erected under the middle arch of the Loggia, would break the order of the ceremonies practised there by the Signory and other magistrates. He therefore proposed that the arch facing the Palazzo (where Donatello's Judith is now) should be chosen." The three succeeding speakers, people of no great importance, gave their votes in favour of the chief herald's resolution. Others followed San Gallo, among whom was the illustrious Lionardo da Vinci. He thought the statue could be placed under the middle arch of the Loggia without hindrance to ceremonies of state. Salvestro, a jeweller, and Filippino Lippi, the painter, were of opinion that the neighbourhood of the Palazzo should be adopted, but that the precise spot should be left to the sculptor's choice. Gallieno, an embroiderer, and David Ghirlandajo, the painter, suggested a new place —namely, where the lion or Marzocco stood on the Piazza. Antonio da San Gallo, the architect, and Michelangelo, the goldsmith, father of Baccio Bandinelli, supported Giuliano da San Gallo's motion. Then Giovanni Piffero—that is, the father of Benvenuto Cellini—brought the discussion back to the courtyard of the palace. He thought that in the Loggia the statue would be only partly seen, and that it would run risks of injury from scoundrels. Giovanni delle Corniole, the incomparable gem-cutter, who has left us the best portrait of Savonarola, voted with the two San Galli, "because he hears the stone is soft." Piero di Cosimo, the painter, and teacher of Andrea del Sarto, wound up the speeches with a strong recommendation that the choice of the exact spot should be left to Michelangelo Buonarroti. This was eventually decided on, and he elected to have his David set up in the place preferred by the chief herald—that is to say, upon the steps of the Palazzo Vecchio, on the right side of the entrance.

The next thing was to get the mighty mass of sculptured marble safely moved from the Duomo to the Palazzo. On the 1st of April, Simone del Pollajuolo, called Il Cronaca, was commissioned to make the necessary preparations; but later on, upon the 30th, we find Antonio da San Gallo, Baccio d'Agnolo, Bernardo della Ciecha, and Michelangelo associated with him in the work of transportation. An enclosure of stout beams and planks was made and placed on movable rollers. In the middle of this the statue hung suspended, with a certain liberty of swaying to the shocks and lurches of the vehicle. More than forty men were employed upon the windlasses which drew it slowly forward. In a contemporary record we possess a full account of the transit: "On the 14th of May 1504, the marble Giant was taken from the Opera. It came out at 24 o'clock, and they broke the wall above the gateway enough to let it pass. That night some stones were thrown at the Colossus with intent to harm it. Watch had to be kept at night; and it made way very slowly, bound as it was upright, suspended in the air with enormous beams and intricate machinery of ropes. It took four days to reach the Piazza, arriving on the 18th at the hour of 12. More than forty men were employed to make it go; and there were fourteen rollers joined beneath it, which were changed from hand to hand. Afterwards, they worked until the 8th of June 1504 to place it on the platform (*ringhiera*) where the Judith used to stand. The Judith was removed and set upon the ground within the palace. The said Giant was the work of Michelangelo Buonarroti."

Where the masters of Florence placed it, under the direction of its maker, Michelangelo's great white David stood for more than three centuries uncovered, open to all injuries of frost and rain, and to the violence of citizens, until, for the better preservation of this masterpiece of modern art, it was removed in 1873 to a hall of the Accademia delle

Belle Arti. On the whole, it has suffered very little. Weather has slightly worn away the extremities of the left foot; and in 1527, during a popular tumult, the left arm was broken by a huge stone cast by the assailants of the palace. Giorgio Vasari tells us how, together with his friend Cecchino Salviati, he collected the scattered pieces, and brought them to the house of Michelangelo Salviati, the father of Cecchino. They were subsequently put together by the care of the Grand Duke Cosimo, and restored to the statue in the year 1543.

III

In the David Michelangelo first displayed that quality of *terribilità*, of spirit-quailing, awe-inspiring force, for which he afterwards became so famous. The statue imposes, not merely by its size and majesty and might, but by something vehement in the conception. He was, however, far from having yet adopted those systematic proportions for the human body which later on gave an air of monotonous impressiveness to all his figures. On the contrary, this young giant strongly recalls the model; still more strongly indeed than the Bacchus did. Wishing perhaps to adhere strictly to the Biblical story, Michelangelo studied a lad whose frame was not developed. The David, to state the matter frankly, is a colossal hobbledehoy. His body, in breadth of the thorax, depth of the abdomen, and general stoutness, has not grown up to the scale of the enormous hands and feet and heavy head. We feel that he wants at least two years to become a fully developed man, passing from adolescence to the maturity of strength and beauty. This close observance of the imperfections of the model at a certain stage of physical growth is very remarkable, and not altogether pleasing in a statue more than nine feet high. Both Donatello and Verocchio had treated their Davids in the same realistic manner, but they were working on a small scale and in bronze. I insist upon this point, because students of Michelangelo have been apt to overlook his extreme sincerity and naturalism in the first stages of his career.

Having acknowledged that the head of David is too massive and the extremities too largely formed for ideal beauty, hypercriticism can hardly find fault with the modelling and execution of each part. The attitude selected is one of great dignity and vigour. The heroic boy, quite certain of victory, is excited by the coming contest. His brows are violently contracted, the nostrils tense and quivering, the eyes fixed keenly on the distant Philistine. His larynx rises visibly, and the sinews of his left thigh tighten, as though the whole spirit of the man were braced for a supreme endeavour. In his right hand, kept at a just middle point between the hip and knee, he holds the piece of wood on which his sling is hung. The sling runs round his back, and the centre of it, where the stone bulges, is held with the left hand, poised upon the left shoulder, ready to be loosed. We feel that the next movement will involve the right hand straining to its full extent the sling, dragging the stone away, and whirling it into the air; when, after it has sped to strike Goliath in the forehead, the whole lithe body of the lad will have described a curve, and recovered its perpendicular position on the two firm legs. Michelangelo invariably chose some decisive moment in the action he had to represent; and though he was working here under difficulties, owing to the limitations of the damaged block at his disposal, he contrived to suggest the imminence of swift and sudden energy which shall disturb the equilibrium of his young giant's pose. Critics of this statue, deceived by its superficial resemblance to some Greek athletes at rest, have neglected the candid realism of the momentary act foreshadowed. They do not understand the meaning of the sling. Even Heath Wilson, for instance, writes: "The massive shoulders are thrown back, the right arm is pendent, and *the right hand grasps resolutely the stone* with which the adversary is to be slain." This entirely falsifies the sculptor's motive, misses the meaning of the sling, renders the broad strap behind the back superfluous, and changes into mere plastic symbolism what Michelangelo intended to be a moment caught from palpitating life.

It has often been remarked that David's head is modelled upon the type of Donatello's S. George at Orsanmichele. The observation is just; and it suggests a comment on the habit Michelangelo early formed of treating the face idealistically, however much he took from study of his models. Vasari, for example, says that he avoided portraiture, and composed his faces by combining several individuals. We shall see a new ideal type of the male head emerge in a group of statues, among which the most distinguished is Giuliano de' Medici at San Lorenzo. We have already seen a female type created in the Madonnas of S. Peter's and Notre Dame at Bruges. But this is not the place to discuss Michelangelo's theory of form in general. That must be reserved until we enter the Sistine Chapel, in order to survey the central and the crowning product of his genius in its prime.

We have every reason to believe that Michelangelo carved his David with no guidance but drawings and a small wax model about eighteen inches in height. The inconvenience of this method, which left the sculptor to wreak his fury on the marble with mallet and chisel, can be readily conceived. In a famous passage, disinterred by M. Mariette from a French scholar of the sixteenth century, we have this account of the fiery master's system: "I am able to affirm that I have seen Michelangelo, at the age of more than sixty years, and not the strongest for his time of life, knock off more chips from an extremely hard marble in one quarter of an hour than three young stone-cutters could have done in three or four—a thing quite incredible to one who has not seen it. He put such impetuosity and fury into his work that I thought the whole must fly to pieces; hurling to the ground at one blow great fragments three or four inches thick, shaving the line so closely that if he had overpassed it by a hair's-breadth he ran the risk of losing all, since one cannot mend a marble afterwards or repair mistakes, as one does with figures of clay and stucco." It is said that, owing to this violent way of attacking his marble, Michelangelo sometimes bit too deep into the stone, and had to abandon a promising piece of sculpture. This is one of the ways of accounting for his numerous unfinished statues. Accordingly a myth has sprung up representing the great master as working in solitude upon huge blocks, with nothing but a sketch in wax before him. Fact is always more interesting than fiction; and, while I am upon the topic of his method, I will introduce what Cellini has left written on this subject. In his treatise on the Art of Sculpture, Cellini lays down the rule that sculptors in stone ought first to make a little model two palms high, and after this to form another as large as the statue will have to be. He illustrates this by a critique of his illustrious predecessors. "Albeit many able artists rush boldly on the stone with the fierce force of mallet and chisel, relying on the little model and a good design, yet the result is never found by them to be so satisfactory as when they fashion the model on a large scale. This is proved by our Donatello, who was a Titan in the art, and afterwards by the stupendous Michelangelo, who worked in both ways. Discovering latterly that the small models fell far short of what his excellent genius demanded, he adopted the habit of making most careful models exactly of the same size as the marble statue was to be. This we have seen with our own eyes in the Sacristy of S. Lorenzo. Next, when a man is satisfied with his full-sized model, he must take charcoal, and sketch out the main view of his figure on the marble in such wise that it shall be distinctly traced; for he who has not previously settled his design may sometimes find himself deceived by the chiselling irons. Michelangelo's method in this matter was the best. He used first to sketch in the principal aspect, and then to begin work by removing the surface stone upon that side, just as if he intended to fashion a figure in half-relief; and thus he went on gradually uncovering the rounded form."

Vasari, speaking of four rough-hewn Captives, possibly the figures now in a grotto of the Boboli Gardens, says: They are well adapted for teaching a beginner how to extract statues from the marble without injury to the stone. The safe method which they illustrate may be described as follows. You first take a model in wax or some other hard material, and place it lying in a vessel full of water. The water, by its nature, presents a level surface; so that, if you gradually lift the model, the higher parts are first exposed, while the lower parts remain submerged; and, proceeding thus, the whole round shape at length appears above the water. Precisely in the same way ought statues to be hewn out from the marble with the chisel; first uncovering the highest surfaces, and proceeding to disclose the lowest. This method was followed by Michelangelo while blocking out the Captives, and therefore his Excellency the Duke was fain to have them used as models by the students in his Academy." It need hardly be remarked that the ingenious process of "pointing the marble" by means of the "pointing machine" and "scale-stones," which is at present universally in use among sculptors, had not been invented in the sixteenth century.

IV

I cannot omit a rather childish story which Vasari tells about the David. After it had been placed upon its pedestal before the palace, and while the scaffolding was still there, Piero Soderini, who loved and admired Michelangelo, told him that he thought the nose too large. The sculptor immediately ran up the ladder till he reached a point upon the level of the giant's shoulder. He then took his hammer and chisel, and, having concealed some dust of marble in the hollow of his hand, pretended to work off a portion from the surface of the nose. In reality he left it as he found it; but

Soderini, seeing the marble dust fall scattering through the air, thought that his hint had been taken. When, therefore, Michelangelo called down to him, "Look at it now!" Soderini shouted up in reply, "I am far more pleased with it; you have given life to the statue."

At this time Piero Soderini, a man of excellent parts and sterling character, though not gifted with that mixture of audacity and cunning which impressed the Renaissance imagination, was Gonfalonier of the Republic. He had been elected to the supreme magistracy for life, and was practically Doge of Florence. His friendship proved on more than one occasion of some service to Michelangelo, and while the gigantic David was in progress he gave the sculptor a new commission, the history of which must now engage us. The Florentine envoys to France had already written in June 1501 from Lyons, saying that Pierre de Rohan, Maréchal de Gié, who stood high in favour at the court of Louis XII., greatly desired a copy of the bronze David by Donatello in the courtyard of the Palazzo Vecchio. He appeared willing to pay for it, but the envoys thought that he expected to have it as a present. The French alliance was a matter of the highest importance to Florence, and at this time the Republic was heavily indebted to the French crown. Soderini, therefore, decided to comply with the Marshal's request, and on the 12th of August 1502 Michelangelo undertook to model a David of two cubits and a quarter within six months. In the bronze-casting he was assisted by a special master, Benedetto da Rovezzano. During the next two years a brisk correspondence was kept up between the envoys and the Signory about the statue, showing the Marshal's impatience. Meanwhile De Rohan became Duke of Nemours in 1503 by his marriage with a sister of Louis d'Armagnac, and shortly afterwards he fell into disgrace. Nothing more was to be expected from him at the court of Blois. But the statue was in progress, and the question arose to whom it should be given. The choice of the Signory fell on Florimond Robertet, secretary of finance, whose favour would be useful to the Florentines in their pecuniary transactions with the King. A long letter from the envoy, Francesco Pandolfini, in September 1505, shows that Robertet's mind had been sounded on the subject; and we gather from a minute of the Signory, dated November 6, 1508, that at last the bronze David, weighing about 800 pounds, had been "packed in the name of God" and sent to Signa on its way to Leghorn. Robertet received it in due course, and placed it in the courtyard of his château of Bury, near Blois. Here it remained for more than a century, when it was removed to the château of Villeroy. There it disappeared. We possess, however, a fine pen-and-ink drawing by the hand of Michelangelo, which may well have been a design for this second David. The muscular and naked youth, not a mere lad like the colossal statue, stands firmly posed upon his left leg with the trunk thrown boldly back. His right foot rests on the gigantic head of Goliath, and his left hand, twisted back upon the buttock, holds what seems meant for the sling. We see here what Michelangelo's conception of an ideal David would have been when working under conditions more favourable than the damaged block afforded. On the margin of the page the following words may be clearly traced: "Davicte cholla fromba e io chollarcho Michelagniolo,"—David with the sling, and I with the bow.

Meanwhile Michelangelo received a still more important commission on the 24th of April 1503. The Consuls of the Arte della Lana and the Operai of the Duomo ordered twelve Apostles, each 4¼ cubits high, to be carved out of Carrara marble and placed inside the church. The sculptor undertook to furnish one each year, the Board of Works defraying all expenses, supplying the costs of Michelangelo's living and his assistants, and paying him two golden florins a month. Besides this, they had a house built for him in the Borgo Pinti after Il Cronaca's design. He occupied this house free of charges while he was in Florence, until it became manifest that the contract of 1503 would never be carried out. Later on, in March 1508, the tenement was let on lease to him and his heirs. But he only held it a few months; for on the 15th of June the lease was cancelled, and the house transferred to Sigismondo Martelli.

The only trace surviving of these twelve Apostles is the huge blocked-out S. Matteo, now in the courtyard of the Accademia. Vasari writes of it as follows: "He also began a statue in marble of S. Matteo, which, though it is but roughly hewn, shows perfection of design, and teaches sculptors how to extract figures from the stone without exposing them to injury, always gaining ground by removing the superfluous material, and being able to withdraw or change in case of need." This stupendous sketch or shadow of a mighty form is indeed instructive for those who would understand Michelangelo's method. It fully illustrates the passages quoted above from Cellini and Vasari, showing how a design of the chief view of the statue must have been chalked upon the marble, and how the unfinished figure gradually emerged into relief. Were we to place it in a horizontal position on the ground, that portion of a rounded form which has been disengaged from the block would emerge just in the same way as a model from a bath of water not quite deep enough to cover it. At the same time we learn to appreciate the observations of Vigenere while we study the titanic chisel-marks, grooved deeply in the body of the stone, and carried to the length of three or four inches. The direction of these strokes proves that Michelangelo worked equally with both hands, and the way in which they are hatched and crossed upon the marble reminds one of the pen-drawing of a bold draughtsman. The mere surface-handling of the stone has remarkable affinity in linear effect to a pair of the master's pen-designs for a naked man, now in the Louvre. On paper he seems to hew with the pen, on marble to sketch with the chisel. The saint appears literally to be growing out of his stone prison, as though he were alive and enclosed there waiting to be liberated. This recalls Michelangelo's fixed opinion regarding sculpture, which he defined as the art "that works by force of taking away." In his writings we often find the idea expressed that a statue, instead of being a human thought invested with external reality by stone, is more truly to be regarded as something which the sculptor seeks and finds inside his marble—a kind of marvellous discovery. Thus he says in one of his poems: "Lady, in hard and craggy stone the mere removal of the surface gives being to a figure, which ever grows the more the stone is hewn away." And again-

> *The best of artists hath no thought to show*
> *Which the rough stone in its superfluous shell*
> *Doth not include: to break the marble spell*
> *Is all the hand that serves the brain can do.*

S. Matthew seems to palpitate with life while we scrutinise the amorphous block; and yet there is little there more tangible than some such form as fancy loves to image in the clouds.

To conclude what I have said in this section about Michelangelo's method of working on the marble, I must confirm what I have stated about his using both left and right hand while chiselling. Raffaello da Montelupo, who was well acquainted with him personally, informs us of the fact: "Here I may mention that I am in the habit of drawing with my left hand, and that once, at Rome, while I was sketching the Arch of Trajan from the Colosseum, Michelangelo and Sebastiano del Piombo, both of whom were naturally left-handed (although they did not work with the left hand excepting when they wished to use great strength), stopped to see me, and expressed great wonder, no sculptor or painter ever having done so before me, as far as I know."

V

If Vasari can be trusted, it was during this residence at Florence, when his hands were so fully occupied, that Michelangelo found time to carve the two *tondi*, Madonnas in relief enclosed in circular spaces, which we still possess. One of them, made for Taddeo Taddei, is now at Burlington House, having been acquired by the Royal Academy through the medium of Sir George Beaumont. This ranks among the best things belonging to that Corporation. The other, made for Bartolommeo Pitti, will be found in the Palazzo del Bargello at Florence. Of the two, that of our Royal Academy is the more ambitious in design, combining singular grace and dignity in the Madonna with action playfully suggested in the infant Christ and little S. John. That of the Bargello is simpler, more tranquil, and more stately. The one recalls the motive of the Bruges Madonna, the other almost anticipates the Delphic Sibyl. We might fancifully call them a pair of native pearls or uncut gems, lovely by reason even of their sketchiness. Whether by intention, as some critics have supposed, or for want of time to finish, as I am inclined to believe, these two reliefs are left in a state of incompleteness which is highly suggestive. Taking the Royal Academy group first, the absolute roughness of the groundwork supplies an admirable background to the figures, which seem to emerge from it as though the whole of them were there, ready to be disentangled. The most important portions of the composition—Madonna's head and throat, the drapery of her powerful breast, on which the child Christ reclines, and the naked body of the boy—are wrought to a point which only demands finish. Yet parts of these two figures remain undetermined. Christ's feet are still imprisoned in the clinging marble; His left arm and hand are only indicated, and His right hand is resting on a mass of broken stone, which hides a portion of His mother's drapery, but leaves the position of her hand uncertain. The infant S. John, upright upon his feet, balancing the chief group, is hazily subordinate. The whole of his form looms blurred through the veil of stone, and what his two hands and arms are doing with the hidden right arm and hand of the Virgin may hardly be conjectured. It is clear that on this side of the composition the marble was to have been more deeply cut, and that we have the highest surfaces of the relief brought into prominence at those points where, as I have said, little is wanting but the finish of the graver and the file. The Bargello group is simpler and more intelligible. Its composition by masses being quite apparent, we can easily construct the incomplete figure of S. John in the background. What results from the study of these two circular sketches in marble is that, although Michelangelo believed all sculpture to be imperfect in so far as it approached the style of painting, yet he did not disdain to labour in stone with various planes of relief which should produce the effect of chiaroscuro. Furthermore, they illustrate what Cellini and Vasari have already taught us about his method. He refused to work by piecemeal, but began by disengaging the first, the second, then the third surfaces, following a model and a drawing which controlled the cutting. Whether he preferred to leave off when his idea was sufficiently indicated, or whether his numerous engagements prevented him from excavating the lowest surfaces, and lastly polishing the whole, is a question which must for ever remain undecided. Considering the exquisite elaboration given to the Pietà of the Vatican, the Madonna at Bruges, the Bacchus and the David, the Moses and parts of the Medicean monuments, I incline to think that, with time enough at his disposal, he would have carried out these rounds in all their details. A criticism he made on Donatello, recorded for us by Condivi, to the effect that this great master's works lost their proper effect on close inspection through a want of finish, confirms my opinion. Still there is no doubt that he must have been pleased, as all true lovers of art are, with the picturesque effect—an effect as of things half seen in dreams or emergent from primeval substances—which the imperfection of the craftsman's labour leaves upon the memory.

At this time Michelangelo's mind seems to have been much occupied with circular compositions. He painted a large Holy Family of this shape for his friend Angelo Doni, which may, I think, be reckoned the only easel-picture attributable with absolute certainty to his hand. Condivi simply says that he received seventy ducats for this fine work. Vasari adds one of his prattling stories to the effect that Doni thought forty sufficient; whereupon Michelangelo took the picture back, and said he would not let it go for less than a hundred: Doni then offered the original sum of seventy, but Michelangelo replied that if he was bent on bargaining he should not pay less than 140. Be this as it may, one of the most characteristic products of the master's genius came now into existence. The Madonna is seated in a kneeling position on the ground; she throws herself vigorously backward, lifting the little Christ upon her right arm, and presenting him to a bald-headed old man, S. Joseph, who seems about to take him in his arms. This group, which forms a tall pyramid, is balanced on both sides by naked figures of young men reclining against a wall at some distance, while a remarkably ugly little S. John can be discerned in one corner. There is something very powerful and original in the composition of this sacred picture, which, as in the case of all Michelangelo's early work, develops the previous traditions of Tuscan art on lines which no one but himself could have discovered. The central figure of the Madonna, too, has always seemed to me a thing of marvellous beauty, and of stupendous power in the strained attitude and nobly modelled arms. It has often been asked what the male nudes have got to do with the subject. Probably Michelangelo intended in this episode to surpass a Madonna by Luca Signorelli, with whose genius he obviously was in sympathy, and who felt, like him, the supreme beauty of the naked adolescent form. Signorelli had painted a circular Madonna with two nudes in the landscape distance for Lorenzo de' Medici. The picture is hung now in the gallery of the Uffizi. It is enough perhaps to remark that Michelangelo needed these figures for his scheme, and for filling the space at his disposal. He was either unable or unwilling to compose a background of trees, meadows, and pastoral folk in the manner of his predecessors. Nothing but the infinite variety of human forms upon a barren stage of stone or arid earth would suit his haughty sense of beauty. The nine persons who make up the picture are all carefully studied from the life, and bear a strong Tuscan stamp. S. John is literally ignoble, and Christ is a commonplace child. The Virgin Mother is a magnificent *contadina* in the plenitude of adult womanhood. Those, however, who follow Mr. Ruskin in blaming Michelangelo for carelessness about the human face and head, should not fail to notice what sublime dignity and grace he has communicated to his model here. In technical execution the Doni Madonna is faithful to old Florentine usage, but lifeless and unsympathetic. We are disagreeably reminded by every portion of the surface that Lionardo's subtle play of tones and modulated shades, those *sfumature*, as Italians call them, which transfer the mystic charm of nature to the canvas, were as yet unknown to the great draughtsman. There is more of atmosphere, of colour suggestion, and of chiaroscuro in the marble *tondi* described above. Moreover, in spite of very careful modelling, Michelangelo has failed to make us feel the successive planes of his composition. The whole seems flat, and each distance, instead of being graduated, starts forward to the eye. He required, at this period of his career, the relief of sculpture in order to express the roundness of the human form and the relative depth of objects placed in a receding order. If anything were needed to make us believe the story of his saying to Pope Julius II. that sculpture and not painting was his trade, this superb design, so deficient in the essential qualities of painting proper, would suffice. Men infinitely inferior to himself in genius and sense of form, a Perugino, a Francia, a Fra Bartolommeo, an Albertinelli, possessed more of the magic which evokes pictorial beauty. Nevertheless, with all its aridity, rigidity, and almost repulsive hardness of colour, the Doni Madonna ranks among the great pictures of the world. Once seen it will never be forgotten: it tyrannises and dominates the imagination by its titanic power of drawing. No one, except perhaps Lionardo, could draw like that, and Lionardo would not have allowed his linear scheme to impose itself so remorselessly upon the mind.

VI

Just at this point of his development, Michelangelo was brought into competition with Lionardo da Vinci, the only living rival worthy of his genius. During the year 1503 Piero Soderini determined to adorn the hall of the Great Council in the Palazzo Vecchio with huge mural frescoes, which should represent scenes in Florentine history. Documents regarding the commencement of these works and the contracts made with the respective artists are unfortunately wanting. But it appears that Da Vinci received a commission for one of the long walls in the autumn of that year. We have items of expenditure on record which show that the Municipality of Florence assigned him the Sala del Papa at S. Maria Novella before February 1504, and were preparing the necessary furniture for the construction of his Cartoon. It seems that he was hard at work upon the 1st of April, receiving fifteen golden florins a month for his labour. The subject which he chose to treat was the battle of Anghiari in 1440, when the Florentine mercenaries entirely routed the troops of Filippo Maria Visconti, led by Niccolò Piccinino, one of the greatest generals of his age. In August 1504 Soderini commissioned Michelangelo to prepare Cartoons for the opposite wall of the great Sala, and assigned to him a workshop in the Hospital of the Dyers at S. Onofrio. A minute of expenditure, under date October 31, 1504, shows that the paper for the Cartoon had been already provided; and Michelangelo continued to work upon it until his call to Rome at the beginning of 1505. Lionardo's battle-piece consisted of two groups on horseback engaged in a fierce struggle for a standard. Michelangelo determined to select a subject which should enable him to display all his power as the supreme draughtsman of the nude. He chose an episode from the war with Pisa, when, on the 28th of July 1364, a band of 400 Florentine soldiers were surprised bathing by Sir John Hawkwood and his English riders. It goes by the name of the Battle of Pisa, though the event really took place at Cascina on the Arno, some six miles above that city.

We have every reason to regard the composition of this Cartoon as the central point in Michelangelo's life as an artist. It was the watershed, so to speak, which divided his earlier from his later manner; and if we attach any value to the critical judgment of his enthusiastic admirer, Cellini, even the roof of the Sistine fell short of its perfection. Important, however, as it certainly is in the history of his development, I must defer speaking of it in detail until the end of the next chapter. For some reason or other, unknown to us, he left his work unfinished early in 1505, and went, at the Pope's invitation, to Rome. When he returned, in the ensuing year, to Florence, he resumed and completed the design. Some notion of its size may be derived from what we know about the material supplied for Lionardo's Cartoon. This, say Crowe and Cavalcaselle, "was made up of one ream and twenty-nine quires, or about 288 square feet of royal folio paper, the mere pasting of which necessitated a consumption of eighty-eight pounds of flour, the mere lining of which required three pieces of Florentine linen."

Condivi, summing up his notes of this period spent by Michelangelo at Florence, says: "He stayed there some time without working to much purpose in his craft, having taken to the study of poets and rhetoricians in the vulgar tongue, and to the composition of sonnets for his pleasure." It is difficult to imagine how Michelangelo, with all his engagements, found the leisure to pursue these literary amusements. But Condivi's biography is the sole authentic source which we possess for the great master's own recollections of his past life. It is, therefore, not improbable that in the sentence I have quoted we may find some explanation of the want of finish observable in his productions at this point. Michelangelo was, to a large extent, a dreamer; and this single phrase throws light upon the expanse of time, the barren spaces, in his long laborious life. The poems we now possess by his pen are clearly the wreck of a vast multitude; and most of those accessible in manuscript and print belong to a later stage of his development. Still the fact remains that in early manhood he formed the habit of conversing with writers of Italian and of fashioning his own thoughts into rhyme. His was a nature capable indeed of vehement and fiery activity, but by constitution somewhat saturnine and sluggish, only energetic when powerfully stimulated; a meditative man, glad enough to be inert when not spurred forward on the path of strenuous achievement. And so, it seems, the literary bent took hold upon him as a relief from labour, as an excuse for temporary inaction. In his own art, the art of design, whether this assumed the form of sculpture or of painting or of architecture, he did nothing except at the highest pressure. All his accomplished work shows signs of the intensest cerebration. But he tried at times to slumber, sunk in a wise passiveness. Then he communed with the poets, the prophets, and the prose-writers of his country. We can well imagine, therefore, that, tired with the labours of the chisel or the brush, he gladly gave himself to composition, leaving half finished on his easel things which had for him their adequate accomplishment.

I think it necessary to make these suggestions, because, in

my opinion, Michelangelo's inner life and his literary proclivities have been hitherto too much neglected in the scheme
of his psychology. Dazzled by the splendour of his work,
critics are content to skip spaces of months and years, during
which the creative genius of the man smouldered. It is, as
I shall try to show, in those intervals, dimly revealed to us
by what remains of his poems and his correspondence, that
the secret of this man, at once so tardy and so energetic, has
to be discovered.

A great master of a different temperament, less solitary,
less saturnine, less sluggish, would have formed a school, as
Raffaello did. Michelangelo formed no school, and was incapable of confiding the execution of his designs to any
subordinates. This is also a point of the highest importance
to insist upon. Had he been other than he was—a gregarious
man, contented with the *à peu près* in art—he might have
sent out all those twelve Apostles for the Duomo from his
workshop. Raffaello would have done so; indeed, the work
which bears his name in Rome could not have existed except
under these conditions. Now nothing is left to us of the
twelve Apostles except a rough-hewn sketch of S. Matthew.
Michelangelo was unwilling or unable to organise a band of
craftsmen fairly interpretative of his manner. When his
own hand failed, or when he lost the passion for his labour,
he left the thing unfinished. And much of this incompleteness in his life-work seems to me due to his being what I
called a dreamer. He lacked the merely business faculty,
the power of utilising hands and brains. He could not bring
his genius into open market, and stamp inferior productions
with his countersign. Willingly he retired into the solitude
of his own self, to commune with great poets and to meditate upon high thoughts, while he indulged the emotions arising from forms of strength and beauty presented to his gaze
upon the pathway of experience.

CHAPTER IV

I

AMONG the many nephews whom Sixtus IV. had raised to eminence, the most distinguished was Giuliano della Rovere, Cardinal of S. Pietro in Vincoli, and Bishop of Ostia. This man possessed a fiery temper, indomitable energy, and the combative instinct which takes delight in fighting for its own sake. Nature intended him for a warrior; and, though circumstances made him chief of the Church, he discharged his duties as a Pontiff in the spirit of a general and a conqueror. When Julius II. was elected in November 1503, it became at once apparent that he intended to complete what his hated predecessors, the Borgias, had begun, by reducing to his sway all the provinces over which the See of Rome had any claims, and creating a central power in Italy. Unlike the Borgias, however, he entertained no plan of raising his own family to sovereignty at the expense of the Papal power. The Della Roveres were to be contented with their Duchy of Urbino, which came to them by inheritance from the Montefeltri. Julius dreamed of Italy for the Italians, united under the hegemony of the Supreme Pontiff, who from Rome extended his spiritual authority and political influence over the whole of Western Europe. It does not enter into the scheme of this book to relate the series of wars and alliances in which this belligerent Pope involved his country, and the final failure of his policy, so far as the liberation of Italy from the barbarians was concerned. Suffice it to say, that at the close of his stormy reign he had reduced the States of the Church to more or less complete obedience, bequeathing to his successors an ecclesiastical kingdom which the enfeebled condition of the peninsula at large enabled them to keep intact.

There was nothing petty or mean in Julius II.; his very faults bore a grandiose and heroic aspect. Turbulent, impatient, inordinate in his ambition, reckless in his choice of means, prolific of immense projects, for which a lifetime would have been too short, he filled the ten years of his pontificate with a din of incoherent deeds and vast schemes half accomplished. Such was the man who called Michelangelo to Rome at the commencement of 1505. Why the sculptor was willing to leave his Cartoon unfinished, and to break his engagement with the Operai del Duomo, remains a mystery. It is said that the illustrious architect, Giuliano da San Gallo, who had worked for Julius while he was cardinal, and was now his principal adviser upon matters of art, suggested to the Pope that Buonarroti could serve him admirably in his ambitious enterprises for the embellishment of the Eternal City. We do not know for certain whether Julius, when he summoned Michelangelo from Florence, had formed the design of engaging him upon a definite piece of work. The first weeks of his residence in Rome are said to have been spent in inactivity, until at last Julius proposed to erect a huge monument of marble for his own tomb.

Thus began the second and longest period of Michelangelo's art-industry. Henceforth he was destined to labour for a series of Popes, following their whims with distracted energies and a lamentable waste of time. The incompleteness which marks so much of his performance was due to the rapid succession of these imperious masters, each in turn careless about the schemes of his predecessor, and bent on using the artist's genius for his own profit. It is true that nowhere but in Rome could Michelangelo have received commissions on so vast a scale. Nevertheless we cannot but regret the fate which drove him to consume years of hampered industry upon what Condivi calls "the tragedy of Julius's tomb," upon quarrying and road-making for Leo X., upon the abortive plans at S. Lorenzo, and upon architectural and engineering works, which were not strictly within his province. At first it seemed as though fortune was about to smile on him. In Julius he found a patron who could understand and appreciate his powers. Between the two men there existed a strong bond of sympathy due to community of temperament. Both aimed at colossal achievements in their respective fields of action. The imagination of both was fired by large and simple rather than luxurious and subtle thoughts. Both were *uomini terribili*, to use a phrase denoting vigour of character and energy of genius, made formidable by an abrupt, uncompromising spirit. Both worked with what the Italians call fury, with the impetuosity of dæmonic natures; and both left the impress of their individuality stamped indelibly upon their age. Julius, in all things grandiose, resolved to signalise his reign by great buildings, great sculpture, great pictorial schemes. There was nothing of the dilettante and collector about him. He wanted creation at a rapid rate and in enormous quantities. To indulge this craving, he gathered round him a band of demigods and Titans, led by Bramante, Raffaello, Michelangelo, and enjoyed the spectacle of a new world of art arising at his bidding through their industry of brain and hand.

II

What followed upon Michelangelo's arrival in Rome may be told in Condivi's words: "Having reached Rome, many months elapsed before Julius decided on what great work he would employ him. At last it occurred to him to use his genius in the construction of his own tomb. The design furnished by Michelangelo pleased the Pope so much that he sent him off immediately to Carrara, with commission to quarry as much marble as was needful for that undertaking. Two thousand ducats were put to his credit with Alamanni Salviati at Florence for expenses. He remained more than eight months among those mountains, with two servants and a horse, but without any salary except his keep. One day, while inspecting the locality, the fancy took him to convert a hill which commands the sea-shore into a Colossus, visible by mariners afar. The shape of the huge rock, which lent itself admirably to such a purpose, attracted him; and he was further moved to emulate the ancients, who, sojourning in the place peradventure with the same object as himself, in order to while away the time, or for some other motive, have left certain unfinished and rough-hewn monuments, which give a good specimen of their craft. And assuredly he would have carried out this scheme, if time enough had been at his disposal, or if the special purpose of his visit to Carrara had permitted. I one day heard him lament bitterly that he had not done so. Well, then, after quarrying and selecting the blocks which he deemed sufficient, he had them brought to the sea, and left a man of his to ship them off. He returned to Rome, and having stopped some days in Florence on the way, when he arrived there, he found that part of the marble had already reached the Ripa. There he had them disembarked, and carried to the Piazza of S. Peter's behind S. Caterina, where he kept his lodging, close to the corridor connecting the Palace with the Castle of S. Angelo. The quantity of stone was enormous, so that, when it was all spread out upon the square, it stirred amazement in the minds of most folk, but joy in the Pope's. Julius indeed began to heap favours upon Michelangelo; for when he had begun to work, the Pope used frequently to betake himself to his house, conversing there with him about the tomb, and about other works which he proposed to carry out in concert with one of his brothers. In order to arrive more conveniently at Michelangelo's lodgings, he had a drawbridge thrown across from the corridor, by which he might gain privy access."

The date of Michelangelo's return to Rome is fixed approximately by a contract signed at Carrara between him and two shipowners of Lavagna. This deed is dated November 12, 1505. It shows that thirty-four cartloads of marble were then ready for shipment, together with two figures weighing fifteen cartloads more. We have a right to assume that Michelangelo left Carrara soon after completing this transaction. Allowing, then, for the journey and the halt at Florence, he probably reached Rome in the last week of that month.

III

The first act in the tragedy of the sepulchre had now begun, and Michelangelo was embarked upon one of the mightiest undertakings which a sovereign of the stamp of Julius ever intrusted to a sculptor of his titanic energy. In order to form a conception of the magnitude of the enterprise, I am forced to enter into a discussion regarding the real nature of the monument. This offers innumerable difficulties, for we only possess imperfect notices regarding the original design, and two doubtful drawings belonging to an uncertain period. Still it is impossible to understand those changes in the Basilica of S. Peter's which were occasioned by the project of Julius, or to comprehend the immense annoyances to which the tomb exposed Michelangelo, without grappling with its details. Condivi's text must serve for guide. This, in fact, is the sole source of any positive value. He describes the tomb, as he believed it to have been first planned, in the following paragraph:—

"To give some notion of the monument, I will say that it was intended to have four faces: two of eighteen cubits, serving for the sides, and two of twelve for the ends, so that the whole formed one great square and a half. Surrounding it externally were niches to be filled with statues, and between each pair of niches stood terminal figures, to the front of which were attached on certain consoles projecting from the wall another set of statues bound like prisoners. These represented the Liberal Arts, and likewise Painting, Sculpture, Architecture, each with characteristic emblems, rendering their identification easy. The intention was to show that all the talents had been taken captive by death, together with Pope Julius, since never would they find another patron to cherish and encourage them as he had done. Above these figures ran a cornice, giving unity to the whole work. Upon the flat surface formed by this cornice were to be four large statues, one of which, that is, the Moses, now exists at S. Pietro ad Vincula. And so, arriving at the summit, the tomb ended in a level space, whereon were two angels who supported a sarcophagus. One of them appeared to smile, rejoicing that the soul of the Pope had been received among the blessed spirits; the other seemed to weep, as sorrowing that the world had been robbed of such a man. From one of the ends, that is, by the one which was at the head of the monument, access was given to a little chamber like a chapel, enclosed within the monument, in the midst of which was a marble chest, wherein the corpse of the Pope was meant to be deposited. The whole would have been executed with stupendous finish. In short, the sepulchre included more than forty statues, not counting the histories in half-reliefs, made of bronze, all of them pertinent to the general scheme and representative of the mighty Pontiff's actions."

Vasari's account differs in some minor details from Condivi's, but it is of no authoritative value. Not having appeared in the edition of 1550, we may regard it as a *réchauffée* of Condivi, with the usual sauce provided by the Aretine's imagination. The only addition I can discover which throws light upon Condivi's narrative is that the statues in the niches were meant to represent provinces conquered by Julius. This is important, because it leads us to conjecture that Vasari knew a drawing now preserved in the Uffizi, and sought, by its means, to add something to his predecessor's description. The drawing will occupy our attention shortly; but it may here be remarked that in 1505, the date of the first project, Julius was only entering upon his conquests. It would have been a gross act of flattery on the part of the sculptor, a flying in the face of Nemesis on the part of his patron, to design a sepulchre anticipating length of life and luck sufficient for these triumphs.

What then Condivi tells us about the first scheme is, that it was intended to stand isolated in the tribune of S. Peter's; that it formed a rectangle of a square and half a square; that the podium was adorned with statues in niches flanked by projecting dadoes supporting captive arts, ten in number; that at each corner of the platform above the podium a seated statue was placed, one of which we may safely identify with the Moses; and that above this, surmounting the whole monument by tiers, arose a second mass, culminating in a sarcophagus supported by two angels. He further adds that the tomb was entered at its extreme end by a door, which led to a little chamber where lay the body of the Pope, and that bronze bas-reliefs formed a prominent feature of the total scheme. He reckons that more than forty statues would have been required to complete the whole design, although he has only mentioned twenty-two of the most prominent.

More than this we do not know about the first project. We have no contracts and no sketches that can be referred to the date 1505. Much confusion has been introduced into the matter under consideration by the attempt to reconcile Condivi's description with the drawing I have just alluded to. Heath Wilson even used that drawing to impugn Condivi's accuracy with regard to the number of the captives and the seated figures on the platform. The drawing in question, as we shall presently see, is of great importance for the subsequent history of the monument; and I believe that it to some extent preserves the general aspect which the tomb, as first designed, was intended to present. Two points about it, however, prevent our taking it as a true guide to Michelangelo's original conception. One is that it is clearly only part of a larger scheme of composition. The other is that it shows a sarcophagus, not supported by angels, but posed upon the platform. Moreover, it corresponds to the declaration appended in 1513 by Michelangelo to the first extant document we possess about the tomb.

Julius died in February 1513, leaving, it is said, to his

executors directions that his sepulchre should not be carried out upon the first colossal plan. If he did so, they seem at the beginning of their trust to have disregarded his intentions. Michelangelo expressly states in one of his letters that the Cardinal of Agen wished to proceed with the tomb, but on a larger scale. A deed dated May 6, 1513, was signed, at the end of which Michelangelo specified the details of the new design. It differed from the former in many important respects, but most of all in the fact that now the structure was to be attached to the wall of the church. I cannot do better than translate Michelangelo's specifications. They run as follows: "Let it be known to all men that I, Michelangelo, sculptor of Florence, undertake to execute the sepulchre of Pope Julius in marble, on the commission of the Cardinal of Agens and the Datary (Pucci), who, after his death, have been appointed to complete this work, for the sum of 16,500 golden ducats of the Camera; and the composition of the said sepulchre is to be in the form ensuing: A rectangle visible from three of its sides, the fourth of which is attached to the wall and cannot be seen. The front face, that is, the head of this rectangle, shall be twenty palms in breadth and fourteen in height, the other two, running up against the wall, shall be thirty-five palms long and likewise fourteen palms in height. Each of these three sides shall contain two tabernacles, resting on a basement which shall run round the said space, and shall be adorned with pilasters, architrave, frieze, and cornice, as appears in the little wooden model. In each of the said six tabernacles will be placed two figures about one palm taller than life (i.e., 6¾ feet), twelve in all; and in front of each pilaster which flanks a tabernacle shall stand a figure of similar size, twelve in all. On the platform above the said rectangular structure stands a sarcophagus with four feet, as may be seen in the model, upon which will be Pope Julius sustained by two angels at his head, with two at his feet; making five figures on the sarcophagus, all larger than life, that is, about twice the size. Round about the said sarcophagus will be placed six dadoes or pedestals, on which six figures of the same dimensions will sit. Furthermore, from the platform, where it joins the wall, springs a little chapel about thirty-five palms high (26 feet 3 inches), which shall contain five figures larger than all the rest, as being farther from the eye. Moreover, there shall be three histories, either of bronze or of marble, as may please the said executors, introduced on each face of the tomb between one tabernacle and another." All this Michelangelo undertook to execute in seven years for the stipulated sum.

The new project involved thirty-eight colossal statues; and, fortunately for our understanding of it, we may be said with almost absolute certainty to possess a drawing intended to represent it. Part of this is a pen-and-ink sketch at the Uffizi, which has frequently been published, and part is a sketch in the Berlin Collection. These have been put together by Professor Middleton of Cambridge, who has also made out a key-plan of the tomb. With regard to its proportions and dimensions as compared with Michelangelo's specification, there remain some difficulties, with which I cannot see that Professor Middleton has grappled. It is perhaps not improbable, as Heath Wilson suggested, that the drawing had been thrown off as a picturesque forecast of the monument without attention to scale. Anyhow, there is no doubt that in this sketch, so happily restored by Professor Middleton's sagacity and tact, we are brought close to Michelangelo's conception of the colossal work he never was allowed to execute. It not only answers to the description translated above from the sculptor's own appendix to the contract, but it also throws light upon the original plan of the tomb designed for the tribune of S. Peter's. The basement of the podium has been preserved, we may assume, in its more salient features. There are the niches spoken of by Condivi, with Vasari's conquered provinces prostrate at the feet of winged Victories. These are flanked by the terminal figures, against which, upon projecting consoles, stand the bound captives. At the right hand facing us, upon the upper platform, is seated Moses, with a different action of the hands, it is true, from that which Michelangelo finally adopted. Near him is a female figure, and the two figures grouped upon the left angle seem to be both female. To some extent these statues bear out Vasari's tradition that the platform in the first design was meant to sustain figures of the contemplative and active life of the soul—Dante's Leah and Rachel.

This great scheme was never carried out. The fragments which may be safely assigned to it are the Moses at S. Pietro in Vincoli and the two bound captives of the Louvre; the Madonna and Child, Leah and Rachel, and two seated statues also at S. Pietro in Vincoli, belong to the plan, though these have undergone considerable alterations. Some other scattered fragments of the sculptor's work may possibly be connected with its execution. Four male figures roughly hewn, which are now wrought into the rock-work of a grotto in the Boboli Gardens, together with the young athlete trampling on a prostrate old man (called the Victory) and the Adonis of the Museo Nazionale at Florence, have all been ascribed to the sepulchre of Julius in one or other of its stages. But these attributes are doubtful, and will be criticised in their proper place and time. Suffice it now to say that Vasari reports, beside the Moses, Victory, and two Captives at the Louvre, eight figures for the tomb blocked out by Michelangelo at Rome, and five blocked out at Florence.

Continuing the history of this tragic undertaking, we come to the year 1516. On the 8th of July in that year, Michelangelo signed a new contract, whereby the previous deed of 1513 was annulled. Both of the executors were alive and parties to this second agreement. "A model was made, the width of which is stated at twenty-one feet, after the monument had been already sculptured of a width of almost twenty-three feet. The architectural design was adhered to with the same pedestals and niches and the same crowning cornice of the first story. There were to be six statues in front, but the conquered provinces were now dispensed with. There was also to be one niche only on each flank, so that the projection of the monument from the wall was reduced more than half, and there were to be only twelve statues beneath the cornice and one relief, instead of twenty-four statues and three reliefs. On the summit of this basement a shrine was to be erected, within which was placed the effigy of the Pontiff on his sarcophagus, with two heavenly guardians. The whole of the statues described in this third contract amount to nineteen." Heath Wilson observes, with much propriety, that the most singular fact about these successive contracts is the departure from certain fixed proportions both of the architectural parts and the statues, involving a serious loss of outlay and of work. Thus the two Captives of the Louvre became useless, and, as we know, they were given away to Ruberto Strozzi in a moment of generosity by the sculptor. The sitting figures detailed in the deed of 1516 are shorter than the Moses by one foot. The standing figures, now at S. Pietro in Vincoli, correspond to the specifications. What makes the matter still more singular is, that after signing the contract under date July 8, 1516, Michelangelo in November of the same year ordered blocks of marble from Carrara with measurements corresponding to the specifications of the deed of 1513.

The miserable tragedy of the sepulchre dragged on for another sixteen years. During this period the executors of Julius passed away, and the Duke Francesco Maria della Rovere replaced them. He complained that Michelangelo neglected the tomb, which was true, although the fault lay not with the sculptor, but with the Popes, his taskmasters. Legal proceedings were instituted to recover a large sum of money, which, it was alleged, had been disbursed without due work delivered by the master. Michelangelo had recourse to Clement VII., who, being anxious to monopolise his labour, undertook to arange matters with the Duke. On the 29th of April 1532 a third and solemn contract was signed at Rome in presence of the Pope, witnessed by a number of illustrious personages. This third contract involved a fourth design for the tomb, which Michelangelo undertook to furnish, and at the same time to execute six statues with his own hand. On this occasion the notion of erecting it in S. Peter's was finally abandoned. The choice lay between two other Roman churches, that of S. Maria del Popolo, where monuments to several members of the Della Rovere family existed, and that of S. Pietro in Vincoli, from which Julius II. had taken his cardinal's title. Michelangelo decided for the latter, on account of its better lighting. The six statues promised by Michelangelo are stated in the contract to be "begun and not completed, extant at the present date in Rome or in Florence." Which of the several statues blocked out for the monument were to be chosen is not stated; and as there are no specifications in the document, we cannot identify them with exactness. At any rate, the Moses must have been one; and it is possible that the Leah and Rachel, Madonna, and two seated statues, now at S. Pietro, were the other five.

It might have been thought that at last the tragedy had dragged on to its conclusion. But no; there was a fifth act, a fourth contract, a fifth design. Paul III. succeeded to Clement VII., and, having seen the Moses in Michelangelo's workshop, declared that this one statue was enough for the deceased Pope's tomb. The Duke Francesco Maria della Rovere died in 1538, and was succeeded by his son, Guidobaldo II. The new Duke's wife was a granddaughter of Paul III., and this may have made him amenable to the Pope's influence. At all events, upon the 20th of August 1542 a final contract was signed, stating that Michelangelo had been prevented "by just and legitimate impediments from carrying out" his engagement under date April 29, 1532, releasing him from the terms of the third deed, and establishing new conditions. The Moses, finished by the hand of Michelangelo, takes the central place in this new monument. Five other statues are specified: "to wit, a Madonna with the child in her arms, which is already finished; a Sibyl, a Prophet, an Active Life and a Contemplative Life, blocked out and nearly completed by the said Michelangelo." These four were given to Raffaello da Montelupo to finish. The reclining portrait-statue of Julius, which was carved by Maso del Bosco, is not even mentioned in this contract. But a deed between the Duke's representative and the craftsmen Montelupo and Urbino exists, in which the latter undertakes to see that Michelangelo shall retouch the Pope's face.

Thus ended the tragedy of the tomb of Pope Julius II. It is supposed to have been finally completed in 1545, and was set up where it still remains uninjured at S. Pietro in Vincoli.

IV

I judged it needful to anticipate the course of events by giving this brief history of a work begun in 1505, and carried on with so many hindrances and alterations through forty years of Michelangelo's life. We shall often have to return to it, since the matter cannot be lightly dismissed. The tomb of Julius empoisoned Michelangelo's manhood, hampered his energy, and brought but small if any profit to his purse. In one way or another it is always cropping up, and may be said to vex his biographers and the students of his life as much as it annoyed himself. We may now return to those early days in Rome, when the project had still a fascination both for the sculptor and his patron.

The old Basilica of S. Peter on the Vatican is said to have been built during the reign of Constantine, and to have been consecrated in 324 A.D. It was one of the largest of those Roman buildings, measuring 435 feet in length from the great door to the end of the tribune. A spacious open square or atrium, surrounded by a cloister-portico, gave access to the church. This, in the Middle Ages, gained the name of the Paradiso. A kind of tabernacle, in the centre of the square, protected the great bronze fir-cone, which was formerly supposed to have crowned the summit of Hadrian's Mausoleum, the Castle of S. Angelo. Dante, who saw it in the courtyard of S. Peter's, used it as a standard for his giant Nimrod. He says—

> *La faccia sua mi parea lunga e grossa,*
> *Come la pina di San Pietro a Roma.*
> —(*Inf.* xxxi. 58.)

This mother-church of Western Christendom was adorned inside and out with mosaics in the style of those which may still be seen at Ravenna. Above the lofty row of columns which flanked the central aisle ran processions of saints and sacred histories. They led the eye onward to what was called the Arch of Triumph, separating this portion of the building from the transept and the tribune. The concave roof of the tribune itself was decorated with a colossal Christ, enthroned between S. Peter and S. Paul, surveying the vast spaces of his house: the lord and master, before whom pilgrims from all parts of Europe came to pay tribute and to perform acts of homage. The columns were of precious marbles, stripped from Pagan palaces and temples; and the roof was tiled with plates of gilded bronze, torn in the age of Heraclius from the shrine of Venus and of Roma on the Sacred Way.

During the eleven centuries which elapsed between its consecration and the decree for its destruction, S. Peter's had been gradually enriched with a series of monuments, inscriptions, statues, frescoes, upon which were written the annals of successive ages of the Church. Giotto worked there under Benedict II. in 1340. Pope after Pope was buried there. In the early period of Renaissance sculpture, Mino da Fiesole, Pollaiuolo, and Filarete added works in bronze and marble, which blent the grace of Florentine religious tradition with quaint neo-pagan mythologies. These treasures, priceless for the historian, the antiquary, and the artist, were now going to be ruthlessly swept away at a pontiff's bidding, in order to make room for his haughty and self-laudatory monument. Whatever may have been the artistic merits of Michelangelo's original conception for the tomb, the spirit was in no sense Christian. Those rows of captive Arts and Sciences, those Victories exulting over prostrate cities, those allegorical colossi symbolising the mundane virtues of a mighty ruler's character, crowned by the portrait of the Pope, over whom Heaven rejoiced while Cybele deplored his loss—all this pomp of power and parade of ingenuity harmonised but little with the humility of a contrite soul returning to its Maker and its Judge. The new temple, destined to supersede the old basilica, embodied an aspect of Latin Christianity which had very little indeed in common with the piety of the primitive Church. S. Peter's, as we see it now, represents the majesty of Papal Rome, the spirit of a secular monarchy in the hands of priests; it is the visible symbol of that schism between the Teutonic and the Latin portions of the Western Church which broke out soon after its foundation, and became irreconcilable before the cross was placed upon its cupola. It seemed as though in sweeping away the venerable traditions of eleven hundred years, and replacing Rome's time-honoured Mother-Church with an edifice bearing the brand-new stamp of hybrid neo-pagan architecture, the Popes had wished to signalise that rupture with the past and that atrophy of real religious life which marked the counter-reformation.

Julius II. has been severely blamed for planning the entire reconstruction of his cathedral. It must, however, be urged in his defence that the structure had already, in 1447, been pronounced insecure. Nicholas V. ordered his architects, Bernardo Rossellini and Leo Battista Alberti, to prepare plans for its restoration. It is, of course, impossible for us to say for certain whether the ancient fabric could have

been preserved, or whether its dilapidation had gone so far
as to involve destruction. Bearing in mind the recklessness
of the Renaissance and the passion which the Popes had for
engaging in colossal undertakings, one is inclined to suspect
that the unsound state of the building was made a pretext
for beginning a work which flattered the architectural tastes
of Nicholas, but was not absolutely necessary. However this
may have been, foundations for a new tribune were laid
outside the old apse, and the wall rose some feet above the
ground before the Pope's death. Paul II. carried on the
building; but during the pontificates of Sixtus, Innocent,
and Alexander it seems to have been neglected. Meanwhile
nothing had been done to injure the original basilica; and
when Julius announced his intention of levelling it to the
ground, his cardinals and bishops entreated him to refrain
from an act so sacrilegious. The Pope was not a man to take
advice or make concessions. Accordingly, turning a deaf
ear to these entreaties, he had plans prepared by Giuliano da
San Gallo and Bramante. Those eventually chosen were
furnished by Bramante; and San Gallo, who had hitherto
enjoyed the fullest confidence of Julius, is said to have left
Rome in disgust. For reasons which will afterwards appear,
he could not have done so before the summer months
of 1506.

It is not yet the proper time to discuss the building of S.
Peter's. Still, with regard to Bramante's plan, this much may
here be said. It was designed in the form of a Greek cross,
surmounted with a huge circular dome and flanked by two
towers. Bramante used to boast that he meant to raise the
Pantheon in the air; and the plan, as preserved for us by
Serlio, shows that the cupola would have been constructed
after that type. Competent judges, however, declare that in-
superable difficulties must have arisen in carrying out this
design, while the piers constructed by Bramante were found
in effect to be wholly insufficient for their purpose. For the
æsthetic beauty and the commodiousness of his building we

have the strongest evidence in a letter written by Michelangelo, who was by no means a partial witness. "It cannot be denied," he says, "that Bramante's talent as an architect was equal to that of any one from the times of the ancients until now. He laid the first plan of S. Peter's, not confused, but clear and simple, full of light and detached from surrounding buildings, so that it interfered with no part of the palace. It was considered a very fine design, and indeed any one can see with his own eyes now that it is so. All the architects who departed from Bramante's scheme, as did Antonio da San Gallo, have departed from the truth." Though Michelangelo gave this unstinted praise to Bramante's genius as a builder, he blamed him severely both for his want of honesty as a man, and also for his vandalism in dealing with the venerable church he had to replace. "Bramante," says Condivi, "was addicted, as everybody knows, to every kind of pleasure. He spent enormously, and, though the pension granted him by the Pope was large, he found it insufficient for his needs. Accordingly he made profit out of the works committed to his charge, erecting the walls of poor material, and without regard for the substantial and enduring qualities which fabrics on so huge a scale demanded. This is apparent in the buildings at S. Peter's, the Corridore of the Belvedere, the Convent of San Pietro ad Vincula, and other of his edifices, which have had to be strengthened and propped up with buttresses and similar supports in order to prevent them tumbling down." Bramante, during his residence in Lombardy, developed a method of erecting piers with rubble enclosed by hewn stone or plaster-covered brickwork. This enabled an unconscientious builder to furnish bulky architectural masses, which presented a specious aspect of solidity and looked more costly than they really were. It had the additional merit of being easy and rapid in execution. Bramante was thus able to gratify the whims and caprices of his impatient patron, who desired to see the works of art he ordered rise like the fabric of Aladdin's lamp before his very eyes. Michelangelo is said to have exposed the architect's trickeries to the Pope; what is more, he complained with just and bitter indignation of the wanton ruthlessness with which Bramante set about his work of destruction. I will again quote Condivi here, for the passage seems to have been inspired by the great sculptor's verbal reminiscences: "The worst was, that while he was pulling down the old S. Peter's, he dashed those marvellous antique columns to the ground, without paying the least attention, or caring at all when they were broken into fragments, although he might have lowered them gently and preserved their shafts intact. Michelangelo pointed out that it was an easy thing enough to erect piers by placing brick on brick, but that to fashion a column like one of these taxed all the resources of art."

On the 18th of April 1506, Julius performed the ceremony of laying the foundation-stone of the new S. Peter's. The place chosen was the great sustaining pier of the dome, near which the altar of S. Veronica now stands. A deep pit had been excavated, into which the aged Pope descended fearlessly, only shouting to the crowd above that they should stand back and not endanger the falling in of the earth above him. Coins and medals were duly deposited in a vase, over which a ponderous block of marble was lowered, while Julius, bareheaded, sprinkled the stone with holy water and gave the pontifical benediction. On the same day he wrote a letter to Henry VII. of England, informing the King that "by the guidance of our Lord and Saviour Jesus Christ he had undertaken to restore the old basilica which was perishing through age."

V

The terms of cordial intimacy which subsisted between Julius and Michelangelo at the close of 1505 were destined to be disturbed. The Pope intermitted his visits to the sculptor's workshop, and began to take but little interest in the

monument. Condivi directly ascribes this coldness to the intrigues of Bramante, who whispered into the Pontiff's ear
that it was ill-omened for a man to construct his own tomb
in his lifetime. It is not at all improbable that he said something of the sort, and Bramante was certainly no good friend
to Michelangelo. A manœuvring and managing individual,
entirely unscrupulous in his choice of means, condescending
to flattery and lies, he strove to stand as patron between the
Pope and subordinate craftsmen. Michelangelo had come to
Rome under San Gallo's influence, and Bramante had just
succeeded in winning the commission to rebuild S. Peter's
over his rival's head. It was important for him to break up
San Gallo's party, among whom the sincere and uncompromising Michelangelo threatened to be very formidable.
The jealousy which he felt for the man was envenomed by
a fear lest he should speak the truth about his own dishonesty.
To discredit Michelangelo with the Pope, and, if possible,
to drive him out of Rome, was therefore Bramante's interest: more particularly as his own nephew, Raffaello da
Urbino, had now made up his mind to join him there. We
shall see that he succeeded in expelling both San Gallo and
Buonarroti during the course of 1506, and that in their absence he reigned, together with Raffaello, almost alone in
the art-circles of the Eternal City.

I see no reason, therefore, to discredit the story told by
Condivi and Vasari regarding the Pope's growing want of
interest in his tomb. Michelangelo himself, writing from
Rome in 1542, thirty-six years after these events, says that
"all the dissensions between Pope Julius and me arose from
the envy of Bramante and Raffaello da Urbino, and this
was the cause of my not finishing the tomb in his lifetime.
They wanted to ruin me. Raffaello indeed had good reason;
for all he had of art he owed to me." But, while we are
justified in attributing much to Bramante's intrigues, it must
be remembered that the Pope at this time was absorbed in his
plans for conquering Bologna. Overwhelmed with business

and anxious about money, he could not have had much leisure to converse with sculptors.

Michelangelo was still in Rome at the end of January. On the 31st of that month he wrote to his father, complaining that the marbles did not arrive quickly enough, and that he had to keep Julius in good humour with promises. At the same time he begged Lodovico to pack up all his drawings, and to send them, well secured against bad weather, by the hand of a carrier. It is obvious that he had no thoughts of leaving Rome, and that the Pope was still eager about the monument. Early in the spring he assisted at the discovery of the Laocoon. Francesco, the son of Giuliano da San Gallo, describes how Michelangelo was almost always at his father's house; and coming there one day, he went, at the architect's invitation, down to the ruins of the Palace of Titus. "We set off, all three together; I on my father's shoulders. When we descended into the place where the statue lay, my father exclaimed at once, 'That is the Laocoon, of which Pliny speaks.' The opening was enlarged, so that it could be taken out; and after we had sufficiently admired it, we went home to breakfast." Julius bought the marble for 500 crowns, and had it placed in the Belvedere of the Vatican. Scholars praised it in Latin lines of greater or lesser merit, Sadoleto writing even a fine poem; and Michelangelo is said, but without trustworthy authority, to have assisted in its restoration.

This is the last glimpse we have of Michelangelo before his flight from Rome. Under what circumstances he suddenly departed may be related in the words of a letter addressed by him to Giuliano da San Gallo in Rome upon the 2nd of May 1506, after his return to Florence.

"GIULIANO,—Your letter informs me that the Pope was angry at my departure, as also that his Holiness is inclined to proceed with the works agreed upon between us, and that I may return and not be anxious about anything.

"About my leaving Rome, it is a fact that on Holy Saturday I heard the Pope, in conversation with a jeweller at table and with the Master of Ceremonies, say that he did not mean to spend a farthing more on stones, small or great. This caused me no little astonishment. However, before I left his presence, I asked for part of the money needed to carry on the work. His Holiness told me to return on Monday. I did so, and on Tuesday, and on Wednesday, and on Thursday, as the Pope saw. At last, on Friday morning, I was sent away, or plainly turned out of doors. The man who did this said he knew me, but that such were his orders. I, who had heard the Pope's words on Saturday, and now perceived their result in deeds, was utterly cast down. This was not, however, quite the only reason of my departure; there was something else, which I do not wish to communicate; enough that it made me think that, if I stayed in Rome, that city would be my tomb before it was the Pope's. And this was the cause of my sudden departure.

"Now you write to me at the Pope's instance. So I beg you to read him this letter, and inform his Holiness that I am even more than ever disposed to carry out the work."

Further details may be added from subsequent letters of Michelangelo. Writing in January 1524 to his friend Giovanni Francesco Fattucci, he says: "When I had finished paying for the transport of these marbles, and all the money was spent, I furnished the house I had upon the Piazza di S. Pietro with beds and utensils at my own expense, trusting to the commission of the tomb, and sent for workmen from Florence, who are still alive, and paid them in advance out of my own purse. Meanwhile Pope Julius changed his mind about the tomb, and would not have it made. Not knowing this, I applied to him for money, and was expelled from the chamber. Enraged at such an insult, I left Rome on the moment. The things with which my house was stocked went to the dogs. The marbles I had brought to Rome lay till the date of Leo's creation on the Piazza, and both lots were injured and pillaged."

Again, a letter of October 1542, addressed to some prelate, contains further particulars. We learn he was so short of money that he had to borrow about 200 ducats from his friend Baldassare Balducci at the bank of Jacopo Gallo. The episode at the Vatican and the flight to Poggibonsi are related thus:—

"To continue my history of the tomb of Julius: I say that when he changed his mind about building it in his lifetime, some ship-loads of marble came to the Ripa, which I had ordered a short while before from Carrara; and as I could not get money from the Pope to pay the freightage, I had to borrow 150 or 200 ducats from Baldassare Balducci, that is, from the bank of Jacopo Gallo. At the same time workmen came from Florence, some of whom are still alive; and I furnished the house which Julius gave me behind S. Caterina with beds and other furniture for the men, and what was wanted for the work of the tomb. All this being done without money, I was greatly embarrassed. Accordingly, I urged the Pope with all my power to go forward with the business, and he had me turned away by a groom one morning when I came to speak upon the matter. A Lucchese bishop, seeing this, said to the groom: 'Do you not know who that man is?' The groom replied to me: 'Excuse me, gentleman; I have orders to do this.' I went home, and wrote as follows to the Pope: 'Most blessed Father, I have been turned out of the palace to-day by your orders; wherefore I give you notice that from this time forward, if you want me, you must look for me elsewhere than at Rome.' I sent this letter to Messer Agostino, the steward, to give it to the Pope. Then I sent for Cosimo, a carpenter, who lived with me and looked after household matters, and a stone-heaver, who is still alive, and said to them: 'Go for a Jew, and sell everything in the house, and come to Florence.' I went, took the post, and travelled towards Florence. The Pope, when he had read my letter, sent five horsemen after me, who reached me at Poggi-

bonsi about three hours after nightfall, and gave me a letter
from the Pope to this effect: 'When you have seen these
present, come back at once to Rome, under penalty of our
displeasure.' The horsemen were anxious I should answer,
in order to prove that they had overtaken me. I replied then
to the Pope, that if he would perform the conditions he
was under with regard to me, I would return; but otherwise
he must not expect to have me again. Later on, while I was
at Florence, Julius sent three briefs to the Signory. At last
the latter sent for me and said: 'We do not want to go
to war with Pope Julius because of you. You must return;
and if you do so, we will write you letters of such authority
that, should he do you harm, he will be doing it to this
Signory.' Accordingly I took the letters, and went back to
the Pope, and what followed would be long to tell."

These passages from Michelangelo's correspondence confirm Condivi's narrative of the flight from Rome, showing
that he had gathered his information from the sculptor's
lips. Condivi differs only in making Michelangelo send a
verbal message, and not a written letter, to the Pope. "Enraged by this repulse, he exclaimed to the groom: 'Tell the
Pope that if henceforth he wants me, he must look for me
elsewhere.' "

It is worth observing that only the first of these letters,
written shortly after the event, and intended for the Pope's
ear, contains a hint of Michelangelo's dread of personal
violence if he remained in Rome. His words seem to point
at poison or the dagger. Cellini's autobiography yields sufficient proof that such fears were not unjustified by practical
experience; and Bramante, though he preferred to work by
treachery of tongue, may have commanded the services of
assassins, *uomini arditi e facinorosi*, as they were somewhat euphemistically called. At any rate, it is clear that
Michelangelo's precipitate departure and vehement refusal
to return were occasioned by more pungent motives than the
Pope's frigidity. This has to be noticed, because we learn

from several incidents of the same kind in the master's life
that he was constitutionally subject to sudden fancies and
fears of imminent danger to his person from an enemy. He
had already quitted Bologna in haste from dread of assassination or maltreatment at the hands of native sculptors.

VI

The negotiations which passed between the Pope and the
Signory of Florence about what may be called the extradition of Michelangelo form a curious episode in his biography, throwing into powerful relief the importance he had
already acquired among the princes of Italy. I propose to
leave these for the commencement of my next chapter, and
to conclude the present with an account of his occupations
during the summer months at Florence.

Signor Gotti says that he passed three months away from
Julius in his native city. Considering that he arrived before
the end of April, and reached Bologna at the end of November 1506, we have the right to estimate this residence
at about seven months. A letter written to him from Rome
on the 4th of August shows that he had not then left
Florence upon any intermediate journey of importance.
Therefore there is every reason to suppose that he enjoyed
a period of half a year of leisure, which he devoted to finishing his Cartoon for the Battle of Pisa.

It had been commenced, as we have seen, in a workshop
at the Spedale dei Tintori. When he went to Bologna in the
autumn, it was left, exposed presumably to public view, in
the Sala del Papa at S. Maria Novella. It had therefore
been completed; but it does not appear that Michelangelo
had commenced his fresco in the Sala del Gran Consiglio.

Lionardo began to paint his Battle of the Standard in
March 1505. The work advanced rapidly; but the method
he adopted, which consisted in applying oil colours to a fat
composition laid thickly on the wall, caused the ruin of his
picture. He is said to have wished to reproduce the encaustic

process of the ancients, and lighted fires to harden the surface of the fresco. This melted the wax in the lower portions of the paste, and made the colours run. At any rate,
no traces of the painting now remain in the Sala del Gran
Consiglio, the walls of which are covered by the mechanical
and frigid brush-work of Vasari. It has even been suggested
that Vasari knew more about the disappearance of his predecessor's masterpiece than he has chosen to relate. Lionardo's
Cartoon has also disappeared, and we know the Battle of
Anghiari only by Edelinck's engraving from a drawing of
Rubens, and by some doubtful sketches.

The same fate was in store for Michelangelo's Cartoon.
All that remains to us of that great work is the chiaroscuro
transcript at Holkham, a sketch for the whole composition
in the Albertina Gallery at Vienna, which differs in some
important details from the Holkham group, several interesting pen-and-chalk drawings by Michelangelo's own hand,
also in the Albertina Collection, and a line-engraving by
Marcantonio Raimondi, commonly known as "Les Grim-
peurs."

We do not know at what exact time Michelangelo finished his Cartoon in 1506. He left it, says Condivi, in the
Sala del Papa. Afterwards it must have been transferred
to the Sala del Gran Consiglio; for Albertini, in his
Memoriale, or Guide-Book to Florence, printed in 1510,
speaks of both "the works of Lionardo da Vinci and the
designs of Michelangelo" as then existing in that hall.
Vasari asserts that it was taken to the house of the Medici,
and placed in the great upper hall, but gives no date. This
may have taken place on the return of the princely family
in 1512. Cellini confirms this view, since he declares that
when he was copying the Cartoon, which could hardly
have happened before 1513, the Battle of Pisa was at the
Palace of the Medici, and the Battle of Anghiari at the
Sala del Papa. The way in which it finally disappeared is
involved in some obscurity, owing to Vasari's spite and

mendacity. In the first, or 1550, edition of the "Lives of
the Painters," he wrote as follows: "Having become a regular object of study to artists, the Cartoon was carried to
the house of the Medici, into the great upper hall; and this
was the reason that it came with too little safeguard into
the hands of those said artists: inasmuch as, during the
illness of the Duke Giuliano, when no one attended to such
matters, it was torn in pieces by them and scattered abroad,
so that fragments may be found in many places, as is proved
by those existing now in the house of Uberto Strozzi, a
gentleman of Mantua, who holds them in great respect."
When Vasari published his second edition, in 1568, he repeated this story of the destruction of the Cartoon, but
with a very significant alteration. Instead of saying "it was
torn in pieces *by them*," he now printed "it was torn in
pieces, *as hath been told elsewhere*." Now Bandinelli, Vasari's mortal enemy, and the scapegoat for all the sins of
his generation among artists, died in 1559, and Vasari felt
that he might safely defame his memory. Accordingly he
introduced a Life of Bandinelli into the second edition of
his work, containing the following passage: "Baccio was
in the habit of frequenting the place where the Cartoon
stood more than any other artists, and had in his possession
a false key; what follows happened at the time when Piero
Soderini was deposed in 1512, and the Medici returned.
Well, then, while the palace was in tumult and confusion
through this revolution, Baccio went alone, and tore the
Cartoon into a thousand fragments. Why he did so was not
known; but some surmised that he wanted to keep certain
pieces of it by him for his own use; some, that he wished
to deprive young men of its advantages in study; some, that
he was moved by affection for Lionardo da Vinci, who
suffered much in reputation by this design; some, perhaps
with sharper intuition, believed that the hatred he bore to
Michelangelo inspired him to commit the act. The loss of
the Cartoon to the city was no slight one, and Baccio de-

served the blame he got, for everybody called him envious and spiteful." This second version stands in glaring contradiction to the first, both as regards the date and the place where the Cartoon was destroyed. It does not, I think, deserve credence, for Cellini, who was a boy of twelve in 1512, could hardly have drawn from it before that date; and if Bandinelli was so notorious for his malignant vandalism as Vasari asserts, it is most improbable that Cellini, while speaking of the Cartoon in connection with Torrigiano, should not have taken the opportunity to cast a stone at the man whom he detested more than any one in Florence. Moreover, if Bandinelli had wanted to destroy the Cartoon for any of the reasons above assigned to him, he would not have dispersed fragments to be treasured up with reverence. At the close of this tedious summary I ought to add that Condivi expressly states: "I do not know by what ill-fortune it subsequently came to ruin." He adds, however, that many of the pieces were found about in various places, and that all of them were preserved like sacred objects. We have, then, every reason to believe that the story told in Vasari's first edition is the literal truth. Copyists and engravers used their opportunity, when the palace of the Medici was thrown into disorder by the severe illness of the Duke of Nemours, to take away portions of Michelangelo's Cartoon for their own use in 1516.

Of the Cartoon and its great reputation, Cellini gives us this account: "Michelangelo portrayed a number of footsoldiers, who, the season being summer, had gone to bathe in the Arno. He drew them at the very moment the alarm is sounded, and the men all naked run to arms; so splendid is their action, that nothing survives of ancient or of modern art, which touches the same lofty point of excellence; and, as I have already said, the design of the great Lionardo was itself most admirably beautiful. These two Cartoons stood, one in the palace of the Medici, the other in the hall of the Pope. So long as they remained intact, they were the school of the world. Though the divine Michelangelo in later life finished that great chapel of Pope Julius (the Sistine), he never rose halfway to the same pitch of power; his genius never afterwards attained to the force of those first studies." Allowing for some exaggeration due to enthusiasm for things enjoyed in early youth, this is a very remarkable statement. Cellini knew the frescoes of the Sistine well, yet he maintains that they were inferior in power and beauty to the Battle of Pisa. It seems hardly credible; but, if we believe it, the legend of Michelangelo's being unable to execute his own designs for the vault of that chapel falls to the ground.

VII

The great Cartoon has become less even than a memory, and so, perhaps, we ought to leave it in the limbo of things inchoate and unaccomplished. But this it was not, most emphatically. Decidedly it had its day, lived and sowed seeds for good or evil through its period of brief existence: so many painters of the grand style took their note from it; it did so much to introduce the last phase of Italian art, the phase of efflorescence, the phase deplored by critics steeped in mediæval feeling. To recapture something of its potency from the description of contemporaries is therefore our plain duty, and for this we must have recourse to Vasari's text. He says: "Michelangelo filled his canvas with nude men, who, bathing at the time of summer heat in Arno, were suddenly called to arms, the enemy assailing them. The soldiers swarmed up from the river to resume their clothes; and here you could behold depicted by the master's godlike hands one hurrying to clasp his limbs in steel and give assistance to his comrades, another buckling on the cuirass, and many seizing this or that weapon, with cavalry in squadrons giving the attack. Among the multitude of figures, there was an old man, who wore upon his head an ivy wreath for shade. Seated on the ground, in act to draw his hose up, he was hampered by the wetness of his legs; and while he heard the clamour of the soldiers, the cries, the rumbling of the drums, he pulled with all his might; all the muscles and sinews of his body were seen in strain; and what was more, the contortion of his mouth showed what agony of haste he suffered, and how his whole frame laboured to the toe-tips. Then there were drummers and men with flying garments, who ran stark naked toward the fray. Strange postures too: this fellow upright, that man kneeling, or bent down, or on the point of rising; all in the air foreshortened with full conquest over every difficulty. In addition, you discovered groups of figures sketched in various methods, some outlined with charcoal, some etched with strokes, some shadowed with the stump, some relieved in white-lead; the master having sought to prove his empire over all materials of draughtsmanship. The craftsmen of design remained therewith astonished and dumbfounded, recognising the furthest reaches of their art revealed to them by this unrivalled masterpiece. Those who examined the forms I have described, painters who inspected and compared them with works hardly less divine, affirm that never in the history of human achievement was any product of a man's brain seen like to them in mere supremacy. And certainly we have the right to believe this; for when the Cartoon was finished, and carried to the Hall of the Pope, amid the acclamation of all artists, and to the exceeding fame of Michelangelo, the students who made drawings from it, as happened with foreigners and natives through many years in Florence, became men of mark in several branches. This is obvious, for Aristotele da San Gallo worked there, as did Ridolfo Ghirlandajo, Raffaello Sanzio da Urbino, Francesco Granaccio, Baccio Bandinelli, and Alonso Berughetta, the Spaniard; they were followed by Andrea del Sarto, Franciabigio, Jacopo Sansovino, Rosso, Maturino, Lorenzetto, Tribolo, then a boy, Jacopo da

Pontormo, and Pierin del Vaga: all of them first-rate masters of the Florentine school."

It does not appear from this that Vasari pretended to have seen the great Cartoon. Born in 1512, he could not indeed have done so; but there breathes through his description a gust of enthusiasm, an afflatus of concurrent witnesses to its surpassing grandeur. Some of the details raise a suspicion that Vasari had before his eyes the transcript *en grisaille* which he says was made by Aristotele da San Gallo, and also the engraving by Marcantonio Raimondi. The prominence given to the ivy-crowned old soldier troubled by his hose confirms the accuracy of the Holkham picture and the Albertina drawing. But none of these partial transcripts left to us convey that sense of multitude, space, and varied action which Vasari's words impress on the imagination. The fullest, that at Holkham, contains nineteen figures, and these are schematically arranged in three planes, with outlying subjects in foreground and background. Reduced in scale, and treated with the arid touch of a feeble craftsman, the linear composition suggests no large æsthetic charm. It is simply a bas-relief of carefully selected attitudes and vigorously studied movements—nineteen men, more or less unclothed, put together with the scientific view of illustrating possibilities and conquering difficulties in postures of the adult male body. The extraordinary effect, as of something superhuman, produced by the Cartoon upon contemporaries, and preserved for us in Cellini's and Vasari's narratives, must then have been due to unexampled qualities of strength in conception, draughtsmanship, and execution. It stung to the quick an age of artists who had abandoned the representation of religious sentiment and poetical feeling for technical triumphs and masterly solutions of mechanical problems in the treatment of the nude figure. We all know how much more than this Michelangelo had in him to give, and how unjust it would be to judge a masterpiece from his hand by the miserable relics now at our disposal. Still I cannot refrain from thinking that the Cartoon for the Battle of Pisa, taken up by him as a field for the display of his ability, must, by its very brilliancy, have accelerated the ruin of Italian art. Cellini, we saw, placed it above the frescoes of the Sistine. In force, veracity, and realism it may possibly have been superior to those sublime productions. Everything we know about the growth of Michelangelo's genius leads us to suppose that he departed gradually but surely from the path of Nature. He came, however, to use what he had learned from Nature as means for the expression of soul-stimulating thoughts. This, the finest feature of his genius, no artist of the age was capable of adequately comprehending. Accordingly, they agreed in extolling a cartoon which displayed his faculty of dealing with *un bel corpo ignudo* as the climax of his powers.

As might be expected, there was no landscape in the Cartoon. Michelangelo handled his subject wholly from the point of view of sculpture. A broken bank and a retreating platform, a few rocks in the distance and a few waved lines in the foreground, showed that the naked men were by a river. Michelangelo's unrelenting contempt for the many-formed and many-coloured stage on which we live and move—his steady determination to treat men and women as nudities posed in the void, with just enough of solid substance beneath their feet to make their attitudes intelligible—is a point which must over and over again be insisted on. In the psychology of the master, regarded from any side one likes to take, this constitutes his leading characteristic. It gives the key, not only to his talent as an artist, but also to his temperament as a man.

Marcantonio seems to have felt and resented the aridity of composition, the isolation of plastic form, the tyranny of anatomical science, which even the most sympathetic of us feel in Michelangelo. This master's engraving of three lovely nudes, the most charming memento preserved to us from the Cartoon, introduces a landscape of grove and farm, field and distant hill, lending suavity to the muscular male body and restoring it to its proper place among the sinuous lines and broken curves of Nature. That the land-scape was adapted from a copper-plate of Lucas van Leyden signifies nothing. It serves the soothing purpose which sensitive nerves, irritated by Michelangelo's aloofness from all else but thought and naked flesh and posture, gratefully acknowledge.

While Michelangelo was finishing his Cartoon, Lionardo da Vinci was painting his fresco. Circumstances may have brought the two chiefs of Italian art frequently together in the streets of Florence. There exists an anecdote of one encounter, which, though it rests upon the credit of an anonymous writer, and does not reflect a pleasing light upon the hero of this biography, cannot be neglected. "Lionardo," writes our authority, "was a man of fair presence, well-proportioned, gracefully endowed, and of fine aspect. He wore a tunic of rose-colour, falling to his knees; for at that time it was the fashion to carry garments of some length; and down to the middle of his breast there flowed a beard beautifully curled and well arranged. Walking with a friend near S. Trinità, where a company of honest folk were gathered, and talk was going on about some passage from Dante, they called to Lionardo, and begged him to explain its meaning. It so happened that just at this moment Michelangelo went by, and, being hailed by one of them, Lionardo answered: 'There goes Michelangelo; he will interpret the verses you require.' Whereupon Michelangelo, who thought he spoke in this way to make fun of him, replied in anger: 'Explain them yourself, you who made the model of a horse to cast in bronze, and could not cast it, and to your shame left it in the lurch.' With these words, he turned his back to the group, and went his way. Lionardo remained standing there, red in the face for the reproach cast at him; and Michelangelo, not satisfied, but wanting to sting him to the quick, added: 'And those Milanese capons believed in your ability to do it!' "

We can only take anecdotes for what they are worth, and that may perhaps be considered slight when they are anonymous. This anecdote, however, in the original Florentine diction, although it betrays a partiality for Lionardo, bears the aspect of truth to fact. Moreover, even Michelangelo's admirers are bound to acknowledge that he had a rasping tongue, and was not incapable of showing his bad temper by rudeness. From the period of his boyhood, when Torrigiano smashed his nose, down to the last years of his life in Rome, when he abused his nephew Lionardo and hurt the feelings of his best and oldest friends, he discovered signs of a highly nervous and fretful temperament. It must be admitted that the dominant qualities of nobility and generosity in his nature were alloyed by suspicion bordering on littleness, and by petulant yieldings to the irritation of the moment which are incompatible with the calm of an Olympian genius.

CHAPTER V

I

WHILE Michelangelo was living and working at Florence, Bramante had full opportunity to poison the Pope's mind in Rome. It is commonly believed, on the faith of a sentence in Condivi, that Bramante, when he dissuaded Julius from building the tomb in his own lifetime, suggested the painting of the Sistine Chapel. We are told that he proposed Michelangelo for this work, hoping his genius would be hampered by a task for which he was not fitted. There are many improbabilities in this story; not the least being our certainty that the fame of the Cartoon must have reached Bramante before Michelangelo's arrival in the first months of 1505. But the Cartoon did not prove that

Buonarroti was a practical wall-painter or colourist; and we have reason to believe that Julius had himself conceived the notion of intrusting the Sistine to his sculptor. A good friend of Michelangelo, Pietro Rosselli, wrote this letter on the subject, May 6, 1506: "Last Saturday evening, when the Pope was at supper, I showed him some designs which Bramante and I had to test; so, after supper, when I had displayed them, he called for Bramante, and said: 'San Gallo is going to Florence to-morrow, and will bring Michelangelo back with him.' Bramante answered: 'Holy Father, he will not be able to do anything of the kind. I have conversed much with Michelangelo, and he has often told me that he would not undertake the chapel, which you wanted to put upon him; and that, you notwithstanding, he meant only to apply himself to sculpture, and would have nothing to do with painting.' To this he added: 'Holy Father, I do not think he has the courage to attempt the work, because he has small experience in painting figures, and these will be raised high above the line of vision, and in foreshortening (*i.e.*, because of the vault). That is something different from painting on the ground.' The Pope replied: 'If he does not come, he will do me wrong; and so I think that he is sure to return.' Upon this I up and gave the man a sound rating in the Pope's presence, and spoke as I believe you would have spoken for me; and for the time he was struck dumb, as though he felt that he had made a mistake in talking as he did. I proceeded as follows: 'Holy Father, that man never exchanged a word with Michelangelo, and if what he has just said is the truth, I beg you to cut my head off, for he never spoke to Michelangelo; also I feel sure that he is certain to return, if your Holiness requires it.'"

This altercation throws doubt on the statement that Bramante originally suggested Michelangelo as painter of the Sistine. He could hardly have turned round against his own recommendation; and, moreover, it is likely that he would have wished to keep so great a work in the hands of his own set, Raffaello, Peruzzi, Sodoma, and others.

Meanwhile, Michelangelo's friends in Rome wrote, encouraging him to come back. They clearly thought that he was hazarding both profit and honour if he stayed away. But Michelangelo, whether the constitutional timidity of which I have spoken, or other reasons damped his courage, felt that he could not trust to the Pope's mercies. What effect San Gallo may have had upon him, supposing this architect arrived in Florence at the middle of May, can only be conjectured. The fact remains that he continued stubborn for a time. In the lengthy autobiographical letter written to some prelate in 1542, Michelangelo relates what followed: "Later on, while I was at Florence, Julius sent three briefs to the Signory. At last the latter sent for me and said: 'We do not want to go to war with Pope Julius because of you. You must return; and if you do so, we will write you letters of such authority that, should he do you harm, he will be doing it to this Signory.' Accordingly I took the letters, and went back to the Pope."

Condivi gives a graphic account of the transaction which ensued. "During the months he stayed in Florence three papal briefs were sent to the Signory, full of threats, commanding that he should be sent back by fair means or by force. Piero Soderini, who was Gonfalonier for life at that time, had sent him against his own inclination to Rome when Julius first asked for him. Accordingly, when the first of these briefs arrived, he did not compel Michelangelo to go, trusting that the Pope's anger would calm down. But when the second and the third were sent, he called Michelangelo and said: 'You have tried a bout with the Pope on which the King of France would not have ventured; therefore you must not go on letting yourself be prayed for. We do not wish to go to war on your account with him, and put our state in peril. Make your mind up to return.' Michelangelo, seeing himself brought to this pass, and still fearing the anger of the Pope, bethought him of taking refuge in the East. The Sultan indeed besought him with most liberal promises, through the means of certain Franciscan friars, to come and construct a bridge from Constantinople to Pera, and to execute other great works. When the Gonfalonier got wind of this intention he sent for Michelangelo and used these arguments to dissuade him: 'It were better to choose death with the Pope than to keep in life by going to the Turk. Nevertheless, there is no fear of such an ending; for the Pope is well disposed, and sends for you because he loves you, not to do you harm. If you are afraid, the Signory will send you with the title of ambassador; forasmuch as public personages are never treated with violence, since this would be done to those who send them.' "

We only possess one brief from Julius to the Signory of Florence. It is dated Rome, July 8, 1506, and contains this passage: "Michelangelo the sculptor, who left us without reason, and in mere caprice, is afraid, as we are informed, of returning, though we for our part are not angry with him, knowing the humours of such men of genius. In order, then, that he may lay aside all anxiety, we rely on your loyalty to convince him in our name, that if he returns to us, he shall be uninjured and unhurt, retaining our apostolic favour in the same measure as he formerly enjoyed it." The date, July 8, is important in this episode of Michelangelo's life. Soderini sent back an answer to the Pope's brief within a few days, affirming that "Michelangelo the sculptor is so terrified that, notwithstanding the promise of his Holiness, it will be necessary for the Cardinal of Pavia to write a letter signed by his own hand to us, guaranteeing his safety and immunity. We have done, and are doing, all we can to make him go back; assuring your Lordship that, unless he is gently handled, he will quit Florence, as he has already twice wanted to do." This letter is followed by another addressed to the Cardinal of Volterra under date July 28. Soderini repeats that Michel-angelo will not budge, because he has as yet received no definite safe-conduct. It appears that in the course of August the negotiations had advanced to a point at which Michel-angelo was willing to return. On the last day of the month the Signory drafted a letter to the Cardinal of Pavia in which they say that "Michelangelo Buonarroti, sculptor, citizen of Florence, and greatly loved by us, will exhibit these letters present, having at last been persuaded to repose confidence in his Holiness." They add that he is coming in good spirits and with good-will. Something may have hap-pened to renew his terror, for this despatch was not de-livered, and nothing more is heard of the transaction till toward the close of November. It is probable, however, that Soderini suddenly discovered how little Michelangelo was likely to be wanted; Julius, on the 27th of August, having started on what appeared to be his mad campaign against Perugia and Bologna. On the 21st of November following the Cardinal of Pavia sent an autograph letter from Bologna to the Signory, urgently requesting that they would despatch Michelangelo immediately to that town, inasmuch as the Pope was impatient for his arrival, and wanted to employ him on important works. Six days later, November 27, Soderini writes two letters, one to the Cardinal of Pavia and one to the Cardinal of Volterra, which finally con-clude the whole business. The epistle to Volterra begins thus: "The bearer of these present will be Michelangelo, the sculptor, whom we send to please and satisfy his Holi-ness. We certify that he is an excellent young man, and in his own art without peer in Italy, perhaps also in the universe. We cannot recommend him more emphatically. His nature is such, that with good words and kindness, if these are given him, he will do everything; one has to show him love and treat him kindly, and he will perform things which will make the whole world wonder." The letter to

Pavia is written more familiarly, reading like a private introduction. In both of them Soderini enhances the service he is rendering the Pope by alluding to the magnificent design for the Battle of Pisa which Michelangelo must leave unfinished.

Before describing his reception at Bologna, it may be well to quote two sonnets here which throw an interesting light upon Michelangelo's personal feeling for Julius and his sense of the corruption of the Roman Curia. The first may well have been written during this residence at Florence; and the autograph of the second has these curious words added at the foot of the page: "*Vostro Michelagniolo*, in Turchia." Rome itself, the Sacred City, has become a land of infidels, and Michelangelo, whose thoughts are turned to the Levant, implies that he would find himself no worse off with the Sultan than the Pope.

> *My Lord! if ever ancient saw spake sooth,*
>   *Hear this which saith: Who can doth never will.*
>   *Lo, thou hast lent thine ear to fables still,*
>   *Rewarding those who hate the name of truth.*
> *I am thy drudge, and have been from my youth—*
>   *Thine, like the rays which the sun's circle fill;*
>   *Yet of my dear time's waste thou think'st no ill:*
>   *The more I toil, the less I move thy ruth.*
> *Once 'twas my hope to raise me by thy height;*
>   *But 'tis the balance and the powerful sword*
>   *Of Justice, not false Echo, that we need.*
> *Heaven, as it seems, plants virtue in despite*
>   *Here on the earth, if this be our reward—*
>   *To seek for fruit on trees too dry to breed.*

> *Here helms and swords are made of chalices:*
>   *The blood of Christ is sold so much the quart:*
>   *His cross and thorns are spears and shields; and short*
>   *Must be the time ere even His patience cease.*

Nay, let Him come no more to raise the fees.
  Of this foul sacrilege beyond report:
  For Rome still flays and sells Him at the court,
  Where paths are slosed to virtue's fair increase.
Now were fit time for me to scrape a treasure,
  Seeing that work and gain are gone; while he
  Who wears the robe, is my Medusa still.
God welcomes poverty perchance with pleasure:
  But of that better life what hope have we,
  When the blessed banner leads to nought but ill?

While Michelangelo was planning frescoes and venting his bile in sonnets, the fiery Pope had started on his perilous career of conquest. He called the Cardinals together, and informed them that he meant to free the cities of Perugia and Bologna from their tyrants. God, he said, would protect His Church; he could rely on the support of France and Florence. Other Popes had stirred up wars and used the services of generals; he meant to take the field in person. Louis XII. is reported to have jeered among his courtiers at the notion of a high-priest riding to the wars. A few days afterwards, on the 27th of August, the Pope left Rome attended by twenty-four cardinals and 500 men-at-arms. He had previously secured the neutrality of Venice and a promise of troops from the French court. When Julius reached Orvieto, he was met by Gianpaolo Baglioni, the bloody and licentious despot of Perugia. Notwithstanding Baglioni knew that Julius was coming to assert his supremacy, and notwithstanding the Pope knew that this might drive to desperation a man so violent and stained with crime as Baglioni, they rode together to Perugia, where Gianpaolo paid homage and supplied his haughty guest with soldiers. The rashness of this act of Julius sent a thrill of admiration throughout Italy, stirring that sense of *terribilità* which fascinated the imagination of the Renaissance. Machiavelli, commenting upon the action of the Baglioni, remarks that the event proved how difficult it is for a man to be perfectly and scientifically wicked. Gianpaolo, he says, murdered his relations, oppressed his subjects, and boasted of being a father by his sister; yet, when he got his worst enemy into his clutches, he had not the spirit to be magnificently criminal, and murder or imprison Julius. From Perugia the Pope crossed the Apennines, and found himself at Imola upon the 20th of October. There he received news that the French governor of Milan, at the order of his king, was about to send him a reinforcement of 600 lances and 3000 foot-soldiers. This announcement, while it cheered the heart of Julius, struck terror into the Bentivogli, masters of Bologna. They left their city and took refuge in Milan, while the people of Bologna sent envoys to the Pope's camp, surrendering their town and themselves to his apostolic clemency. On the 11th of November, S. Martin's day, Giuliano della Rovere made his triumphal entry into Bologna, having restored two wealthy provinces to the states of the Church by a stroke of sheer audacity, unparalleled in the history of any previous pontiff. Ten days afterwards we find him again renewing negotiations with the Signory for the extradition of Michelangelo.

II

"Arriving then one morning at Bologna, and going to hear Mass at S. Petronio, there met him the Pope's grooms of the stable, who immediately recognised him, and brought him into the presence of his Holiness, then at table in the Palace of the Sixteen. When the Pope beheld him, his face clouded with anger, and he cried: 'It was your duty to come to seek us, and you have waited till we came to seek you;' meaning thereby that his Holiness having travelled to Bologna, which is much nearer to Florence than Rome, he had come to find him out. Michelangelo knelt, and prayed for pardon in a loud voice, pleading in his excuse that he had not erred through frowardness, but through great distress of mind, having been unable to endure the expulsion he received. The Pope remained holding his head low and answering nothing, evidently much agitated; when a certain prelate, sent by Cardinal Soderini to put in a good word for Michelangelo, came forward and said: 'Your Holiness might overlook his fault; he did wrong through ignorance: these painters, outside their art, are all like this.' Thereupon the Pope answered in a fury: 'It is you, not I, who are insulting him. It is you, not he, who are the ignoramus and the rascal. Get hence out of my sight, and bad luck to you!' When the fellow did not move, he was cast forth by the servants, as Michelangelo used to relate, with good round kicks and thumpings. So the Pope, having spent the surplus of his bile upon the bishop, took Michelangelo apart and pardoned him. Not long afterwards he sent for him and said: 'I wish you to make my statue on a large scale in bronze. I mean to place it on the façade of San Petronio.' When he went to Rome in course of time, he left 1000 ducats at the bank of Messer Antonmaria da Lignano for this purpose. But before he did so Michelangelo had made the clay model. Being in some doubt how to manage the left hand, after making the Pope give the benediction with the right, he asked Julius, who had come to see the statue, if he would like it to hold a book. 'What book?' replied he: 'a sword! I know nothing about letters, not I.' Jesting then about the right hand, which was vehement in action, he said with a smile to Michelangelo: 'That statue of yours, is it blessing or cursing?' To which the sculptor replied: 'Holy Father, it is threatening this people of Bologna if they are not prudent.' "

Michelangelo's letter to Fattucci confirms Condivi's narrative. "When Pope Julius went to Bologna the first time, I was forced to go there with a rope round my neck to beg his pardon. He ordered me to make his portrait in bronze, sitting, about seven cubits (14 feet) in height. When he asked what it would cost, I answered that I thought I could cast it for 1000 ducats; but that this was not my trade, and that I did not wish to undertake it. He answered: 'Go to work; you shall cast it over and over again till it succeeds; and I will give you enough to satisfy your wishes.' To put it briefly, I cast the statue twice; and at the end of two years, at Bologna, I found that I had four and a half ducats left. I never received anything more for this job; and all the moneys I paid out during the said two years were the 1000 ducats with which I promised to cast it. These were disbursed to me in instalments by Messer Antonio Maria da Legnano, a Bolognese."

The statue must have been more than thrice life-size, if it rose fourteen feet in a sitting posture. Michelangelo worked at the model in a hall called the Stanza del Pavaglione behind the Cathedral. Three experienced workmen were sent, at his request, from Florence, and he began at once upon the arduous labour. His domestic correspondence, which at this period becomes more copious and interesting, contains a good deal of information concerning his residence at Bologna. His mode of life, as usual, was miserable and penurious in the extreme. This man, about whom popes and cardinals and gonfaloniers had been corresponding, now hired a single room with one bed in it, where, as we have seen, he slept together with his three assistants. There can be no doubt that such eccentric habits prevented Michelangelo from inspiring his subordinates with due respect. The want of control over servants and workmen, which is a noticeable feature of his private life, may in part be attributed to this cause. And now, at Bologna, he soon got into trouble with the three craftsmen he had engaged to help him. They were Lapo d'Antonio di Lapo, a sculptor at the Opera del Duomo; Lodovico del Buono, surnamed Lotti, a metal-caster and founder of cannon; and Pietro Urbano, a craftsman who continued long in his service. Lapo boasted that he was executing the statue in partnership with Michelangelo and upon equal terms, which did not seem incredible considering their association in a single bedroom. Beside this, he intrigued and cheated in money matters. The master felt that he must get rid of him, and send the fellow back to Florence. Lapo, not choosing to go alone, lest the truth of the affair should be apparent, persuaded Lodovico to join him; and when they reached home, both began to calumniate their master. Michelangelo, knowing that they were likely to do so, wrote to his brother Buonarroto on the 1st of February 1507: "I inform you further how on Friday morning I sent away Lapo and Lodovico, who were in my service. Lapo, because he is good for nothing and a rogue, and could not serve me. Lodovico is better, and I should have been willing to keep him another two months, but Lapo, in order to prevent blame falling on himself alone, worked upon the other so that both went away together. I write you this, not that I regard them, for they are not worth three farthings, the pair of them, but because if they come to talk to Lodovico (Buonarroti) he must not be surprised at what they say. Tell him by no means to lend them his ears; and if you want to be informed about them, go to Messer Angelo, the herald of the Signory; for I have written the whole story to him, and he will, out of his kindly feeling, tell you just what happened."

In spite of these precautions, Lapo seems to have gained the ear of Michelangelo's father, who wrote a scolding letter in his usual puzzle-headed way. Michelangelo replied in a tone of real and ironical humility, which is exceedingly characteristic: "Most revered father, I have received a letter from you to-day, from which I learn that you have been informed by Lapo and Lodovico. I am glad that you should rebuke me, because I deserve to be rebuked as a ne'er-do-well and sinner as much as any one, or perhaps more. But you must know that I have not been guilty in the affair for which you take me to task now, neither as regards them nor any one else, except it be in doing more than was my duty."

After this exordium he proceeds to give an elaborate explanation of his dealings with Lapo, and the man's roguery.

The correspondence with Buonarroto turns to a considerable extent upon a sword-hilt which Michelangelo designed for the Florentine, Pietro Aldobrandini. It was the custom then for gentlemen to carry swords and daggers with hilt and scabbard wonderfully wrought by first-rate artists. Some of these, still extant, are among the most exquisite specimens of sixteenth-century craft. This little affair gave Michelangelo considerable trouble. First of all, the man who had to make the blade was long about it. From the day when the Pope came to Bologna, he had more custom than all the smiths in the city were used in ordinary times to deal with. Then, when the weapon reached Florence, it turned out to be too short. Michelangelo affirmed that he had ordered it exactly to the measure sent, adding that Aldobrandini was "probably not born to wear a dagger at his belt." He bade his brother present it to Filippo Strozzi, as a compliment from the Buonarroti family; but the matter was bungled. Probably Buonarroto tried to get some valuable equivalent; for Michelangelo writes to say that he is sorry "he behaved so scurvily toward Filippo in so trifling an affair."

Nothing at all transpires in these letters regarding the company kept by Michelangelo at Bologna. The few stories related by tradition which refer to this period are not much to the sculptor's credit for courtesy. The painter Francia, for instance, came to see the statue, and made the commonplace remark that he thought it very well cast and of excellent bronze. Michelangelo took this as an insult to his design, and replied: "I owe the same thanks to Pope Julius who supplied the metal, as you do to the colourmen who sell you paints." Then, turning to some gentlemen present there, he added that Francia was "a blockhead." Francia had a son remarkable for youthful beauty. When Michelangelo first saw him he asked whose son he was, and, on being informed, uttered this caustic compliment: "Your father makes handsomer living figures than he paints them." On some other occasion, a stupid Bolognese gentleman asked whether he thought his statue or a pair of oxen were the bigger. Michelangelo replied: "That is according to the oxen. If Bolognese, oh! then with a doubt ours of Florence are smaller." Possibly Albrecht Dürer may have met him in the artistic circles of Bologna, since he came from Venice on a visit during these years; but nothing is known about their intercourse.

III

Julius left Bologna on the 22nd of February 1507. Michelangelo remained working diligently at his model. In less than three months it was nearly ready to be cast. Accordingly, the sculptor, who had no practical knowledge of bronze-founding, sent to Florence for a man distinguished in that craft, Maestro dal Ponte of Milan. During the last three years he had been engaged as Master of the Ordnance under the Republic. His leave of absence was signed upor. the 15th of May 1507.

Meanwhile the people of Bologna were already planning revolution. The Bentivogli retained a firm hereditary hold on their affections, and the government of priests is never popular, especially among the nobles of a state. Michelangelo writes to his brother Giovan Simone (May 2) describing the bands of exiles who hovered round the city and kept its burghers in alarm: "The folk are stifling in their coats of mail; for during four days past the whole county is under arms, in great confusion and peril, especially the party of the Church." The Papal Legate, Francesco Alidosi, Cardinal of Pavia, took such prompt measures that the attacking troops were driven back. He also executed some of the citizens who had intrigued with the exiled family. The summer was exceptionally hot, and plague hung about; all articles of food were dear and bad. Michelangelo felt miserable, and fretted to be free; but the statue kept him hard at work.

When the time drew nigh for the great operation, he wrote in touching terms to Buonarroto: "Tell Lodovico (their father) that in the middle of next month I hope to cast my figure without fail. Therefore, if he wishes to offer prayers or aught else for its good success, let him do so betimes, and say that I beg this of him." Nearly the whole of June elapsed, and the business still dragged on. At last, upon the 1st of July, he advised his brother thus: "We have cast my figure, and it has come out so badly that I verily believe I shall have to do it all over again. I reserve details, for I have other things to think of. Enough that it has gone wrong. Still I thank God, because I take everything for the best." From the next letter we learn that only the lower half of the statue, up to the girdle, was properly cast. The metal for the rest remained in the furnace, probably in the state of what Cellini called a cake. The furnace had to be pulled down and rebuilt, so as to cast the upper half. Michelangelo adds that he does not know whether Master Bernardino mismanaged the matter from ignorance or bad luck. "I had such faith in him that I thought he could have cast the statue without fire. Nevertheless, there is no denying that he is an able craftsman, and that he worked with good-will. Well, he has failed, to my loss and also to his own, seeing he gets so much blame that he dares not lift his head up in Bologna." The second casting must have taken place about the 8th of July; for on the 10th Michelangelo writes that it is done, but the clay is too hot for the result to be reported, and Bernardino left yesterday. When the statue was uncovered, he was able to reassure his brother: "My affair might have turned out much better, and also much worse. At all events, the whole is there, so far as I can see; for it is not yet quite disengaged. I shall want, I think, some months to work it up with file and hammer, because it has come out rough. Well, well, there is much to thank God for; as I said, it might have been worse." On making further discoveries, he finds that the cast is far less bad than he expected; but the labour of cleaning it with polishing tools proved longer and more irksome than he expected: "I am exceedingly anxious to get away home, for here I pass my life in huge discomfort and with extreme fatigue. I work night and day, do nothing else; and the labour I am forced to undergo is such, that if I had to begin the whole thing over again, I do not think I could survive it. Indeed, the undertaking has been one of enormous difficulty; and if it had been in the hand of another man, we should have fared but ill with it. However, I believe that the prayers of some one have sustained and kept me in health, because all Bologna thought I should never bring it to a proper end." We can see that Michelangelo was not unpleased with the result; and the statue must have been finished soon after the New Year. However, he could not leave Bologna. On the 18th of February 1508 he writes to Buonarroto that he is kicking his heels, having received orders from the Pope to stay until the bronze was placed. Three days later—that is, upon the 21st of February—the Pope's portrait was hoisted to its pedestal above the great central door of S. Petronio.

It remained there rather less than three years. When the Papal Legate fled from Bologna in 1511, and the party of the Bentivogli gained the upper hand, they threw the mighty mass of sculptured bronze, which had cost its maker so much trouble, to the ground. That happened on the 30th of December. The Bentivogli sent it to the Duke Alfonso d'Este of Ferrara, who was a famous engineer and gunsmith. He kept the head intact, but cast a huge cannon out of part of the material, which took the name of La Giulia. What became of the head is unknown. It is said to have weighed 600 pounds.

So perished another of Michelangelo's masterpieces; and all we know for certain about the statue is that Julius was seated, in full pontificals, with the triple tiara on his head, raising the right hand to bless, and holding the keys of S. Peter in the left.

Michelangelo reached Florence early in March. On the 18th of that month he began again to occupy his house at Borgo Pinti, taking it this time on hire from the Operai del Duomo. We may suppose, therefore, that he intended to recommence work on the Twelve Apostles. A new project seems also to have been started by his friend Soderini —that of making him erect a colossal statue of Hercules subduing Cacus opposite the David. The Gonfalonier was in correspondence with the Marquis of Carrara on the 10th of May about a block of marble for this giant; but Michelangelo at that time had returned to Rome, and of the Cacus we shall hear more hereafter.

IV

When Julius received news that his statue had been duly cast and set up in its place above the great door of S. Petronio, he began to be anxious to have Michelangelo once more near his person. The date at which the sculptor left Florence again for Rome is fixed approximately by the fact that Lodovico Buonarroti emancipated his son from parental control upon the 13th of March 1508. According to Florentine law, Michelangelo was not of age, nor master over his property and person, until this deed had been executed.

In the often-quoted letter to Fattucci he says: "The Pope was still unwilling that I should complete the tomb, and ordered me to paint the vault of the Sistine. We agreed for 3000 ducats. The first design I made for this work had twelve apostles in the lunettes, the remainder being a certain space filled in with ornamental details, according to the usual manner. After I had begun, it seemed to me that this would turn out rather meanly; and I told the Pope that the Apostles alone would yield a poor effect, in my opinion. He asked me why. I answered, 'Because they too were poor.'

Then he gave me commission to do what I liked best, and promised to satisfy my claims for the work, and told me to paint down the pictured histories upon the lower row."

There is little doubt that Michelangelo disliked beginning this new work, and that he would have greatly preferred to continue the sepulchral monument, for which he had made such vast and costly preparations. He did not feel certain how he should succeed in fresco on a large scale, not having had any practice in that style of painting since he was a prentice under Ghirlandajo. It is true that the Cartoon for the Battle of Pisa had been a splendid success; still this, as we have seen, was not coloured, but executed in various methods of outline and chiaroscuro. Later on, while seriously engaged upon the Sistine, he complains to his father: "I am still in great distress of mind, because it is now a year since I had a farthing from the Pope; and I do not ask, because my work is not going forward in a way that seems to me to deserve it. That comes from its difficulty, and also *from this not being my trade*. And so I waste my time without results. God help me."

We may therefore believe Condivi when he asserts that "Michelangelo, who had not yet practised colouring, and knew that the painting of a vault is very difficult, endeavoured by all means to get himself excused, putting Raffaello forward as the proper man, and pleading that this was not his trade, and that he should not succeed." Condivi states in the same chapter that Julius had been prompted to intrust him with the Sistine by Bramante, who was jealous of his great abilities, and hoped he might fail conspicuously when he left the field of sculpture. I have given my reasons above for doubting the accuracy of this tradition; and what we have just read of Michelangelo's own hesitation confirms the statement made by Bramante in the Pope's presence, as recorded by Rosselli. In fact, although we may assume the truth of Bramante's hostility, it is difficult to form an exact conception of the intrigues he carried on against Buonarroti.

Julius would not listen to any arguments. Accordingly, Michelangelo made up his mind to obey the patron whom he nicknamed his Medusa. Bramante was commissioned to erect the scaffolding, which he did so clumsily, with beams suspended from the vault by huge cables, that Michelangelo asked how the holes in the roof would be stopped up when his painting was finished. The Pope allowed him to take down Bramante's machinery, and to raise a scaffold after his own design. The rope alone which had been used, and now was wasted, enabled a poor carpenter to dower his daughter. Michelangelo built his own scaffold free from the walls, inventing a method which was afterwards adopted by all architects for vault-building. Perhaps he remembered the elaborate drawing he once made of Ghirlandajo's assistants at work upon the ladders and wooden platforms at S. Maria Novella.

Knowing that he should need helpers in so great an undertaking, and also mistrusting his own ability to work in fresco, he now engaged several excellent Florentine painters. Among these, says Vasari, were his friends Francesco Granacci and Giuliano Bugiardini, Bastiano da San Gallo surnamed Aristotele, Angelo di Donnino, Jacopo di Sandro, and Jacopo surnamed l'Indaco. Vasari is probably accurate in his statement here; for we shall see that Michelangelo, in his *Ricordi*, makes mention of five assistants, two of whom are proved by other documents to have been Granacci and Indaco. We also possess two letters from Granacci which show that Bugiardini, San Gallo, Angelo di Donnino, and Jacopo l'Indaco were engaged in July. The second of Granacci's letters refers to certain disputes and hagglings with the artists. This may have brought Michelangelo to Florence, for he was there upon the 11th of August 1508, as appears from the following deed of renunciation: "In the year of our Lord 1508, on the 11th day of August, Michelangelo, son of Lodovico di Lionardo di Buonarrota, repudiated the inheritance of his uncle Francesco by an instrument drawn up by the hand of Ser Giovanni di Guasparre da Montevarchi, notary of Florence, on the 27th of July 1508." When the assistants arrived at Rome is not certain. It must, however, have been after the end of July. The extracts from Michelangelo's notebooks show that he had already sketched an agreement as to wages several weeks before. "I record how on this day, the 10th of May 1508, I, Michelangelo, sculptor, have received from the Holiness of our Lord Pope Julius II. 500 ducats of the Camera, the which were paid me by Messer Carlino, chamberlain, and Messer Carlo degli Albizzi, on account of the painting of the vault of the Sistine Chapel, on which I begin to work to-day, under the conditions and contracts set forth in a document written by his Most Reverend Lordship of Pavia, and signed by my hand.

"For the painter-assistants who are to come from Florence, who will be five in number, twenty gold ducats of the Camera apiece, on this condition; that is to say, that when they are here and are working in harmony with me, the twenty ducats shall be reckoned to each man's salary; the said salary to begin upon the day they leave Florence. And if they do not agree with me, half of the said money shall be paid them for their travelling expenses, and for their time."

On the strength of this *Ricordo*, it has been assumed that Michelangelo actually began to paint the Sistine on the 10th of May 1508. That would have been physically and literally impossible. He was still at Florence, agreeing to rent his house in Borgo Pinti, upon the 18th of March. Therefore he had no idea of going to Rome at that time. When he arrived there, negotiations went on, as we have seen, between him and Pope Julius. One plan for the decoration of the roof was abandoned, and another on a grander scale had to be designed. To produce working Cartoons for that immense scheme in less than two months would have been beyond the capacities of any human brain and hands. But there are many indications that the vault was not prepared for painting, and the materials for fresco not accumulated, till a much later date. For instance, we possess a series of receipts by Piero Rosselli, acknowledging several disbursements for the plastering of the roof between May 11 and July 27. We learn from one of these that Granacci was in Rome before June 3; and Michelangelo writes for fine blue colours to a certain Fra Jacopo Gesuato at Florence upon the 13th of May. All is clearly in the air as yet, and on the point of preparation. Michelangelo's phrase, "on which I begin work to-day," will have to be interpreted, therefore, in the widest sense, as implying that he was engaging assistants, getting the architectural foundation ready, and procuring a stock of necessary articles. The whole summer and autumn must have been spent in taking measurements and expanding the elaborate design to the proper scale of working drawings; and, if Michelangelo had toiled alone without his Florentine helpers, it would have been impossible for him to have got through with these preliminary labours in so short a space of time.

Michelangelo's method in preparing his Cartoons seems to have been the following. He first made a small-scale sketch of the composition, sometimes including a large variety of figures. Then he went to the living models, and studied portions of the whole design in careful transcripts from Nature, using black and red chalk, pen, and sometimes bistre. Among the most admirable of his drawings left to us are several which were clearly executed with a view to one or other of these great Cartoons. Finally, returning to the first composition, he repeated that, or so much of it as could be transferred to a single sheet, on the exact scale of the intended fresco. These enlarged drawings were applied to the wet surface of the plaster, and their outlines pricked in with dots to guide the painter in his brush-work. When we reflect upon the extent of the Sistine vault (it is estimated at more than 10,000 square feet of surface), and the difficulties presented by its curves, lunettes, spandrels, and pendentives; when we remember that this enormous space is alive with 343 figures in every conceivable attitude, some of them twelve feet in height, those seated as prophets and sibyls measuring nearly eighteen feet when upright, all animated with extraordinary vigour, presenting types of the utmost variety and vivid beauty, imagination quails before the intellectual energy which could first conceive a scheme so complex, and then carry it out with mathematical precision in its minutest details.

The date on which Michelangelo actually began to paint the fresco is not certain. Supposing he worked hard all the summer, he might have done so when his Florentine assistants arrived in August; and, assuming that the letter to his father above quoted (*Lettere*, x.) bears a right date, he must have been in full swing before the end of January 1509. In that letter he mentions that Jacopo, probably l'Indaco, "the painter whom I brought from Florence, returned a few days ago; and as he complained about me here in Rome, it is likely that he will do so there. Turn a deaf ear to him; he is a thousandfold in the wrong, and I could say much about his bad behaviour toward me." Vasari informs us that these assistants proved of no use; whereupon, he destroyed all they had begun to do, refused to see them, locked himself up in the chapel, and determined to complete the work in solitude. It seems certain that the painters were sent back to Florence. Michelangelo had already provided for the possibility of their not being able to co-operate with him; but what the cause of their failure was we can only conjecture. Trained in the methods of the old Florentine school of fresco-painting, incapable of entering into the spirit of a style so supereminently noble and so astoundingly original as Michelangelo's, it is probable that they spoiled his designs in their attempts to colour them. Harford pithily remarks: "As none of the suitors of Penelope could bend the bow of Ulysses, so one hand alone was capable of wielding the pencil of Buonarroti." Still it must not be imagined that

Michelangelo ground his own colours, prepared his daily measure of wet plaster, and executed the whole series of frescoes with his own hand. Condivi and Vasari imply, indeed, that this was the case; but, beside the physical impossibility, the fact remains that certain portions are obviously executed by inferior masters. Vasari's anecdotes, moreover, contradict his own assertion regarding Michelangelo's single-handed labour. He speaks about the caution which the master exercised to guard himself against any treason of his workmen in the chapel. Nevertheless, far the larger part, including all the most important figures, and especially the nudes, belongs to Michelangelo.

These troubles with his assistants illustrate a point upon which I shall have to offer some considerations at a future time. I allude to Michelangelo's inaptitude for forming a school of intelligent fellow-workers, for fashioning inferior natures into at least a sympathy with his aims and methods, and finally for living long on good terms with hired subordinates. All those qualities which the facile and genial Raffaello possessed in such abundance, and which made it possible for that young favourite of heaven and fortune to fill Rome with so much work of mixed merit, were wanting to the stern, exacting, and sensitive Buonarroti.

But the assistants were not the only hindrance to Michelangelo at the outset. Condivi says that "he had hardly begun painting, and had finished the picture of the Deluge, when the work began to throw out mould to such an extent that the figures could hardly be seen through it. Michelangelo thought that this excuse might be sufficient to get him relieved of the whole job. So he went to the Pope and said: 'I already told your Holiness that painting is not my trade; what I have done is spoiled; if you do not believe it, send to see.' The Pope sent San Gallo, who, after inspecting the fresco, pronounced that the lime-basis had been put on too wet, and that water oozing out produced this mouldy surface. He told Michelangelo what the cause was, and bade him proceed with the work. So the excuse helped him nothing." About the fresco of the Deluge Vasari relates that, having begun to paint this compartment first, he noticed that the figures were too crowded, and consequently changed his scale in all the other portions of the ceiling. This is a plausible explanation of what is striking—namely, that the story of the Deluge is quite differently planned from the other episodes upon the vaulting. Yet I think it must be rejected, because it implies a total change in all the working Cartoons, as well as a remarkable want of foresight.

Condivi continues: "While he was painting, Pope Julius used oftentimes to go and see the work, climbing by a ladder, while Michelangelo gave him a hand to help him on to the platform. His nature being eager and impatient of delay, he decided to have the roof uncovered, although Michelangelo had not given the last touches, and had only completed the first half—that is, from the door to the middle of the vault." Michelangelo's letters show that the first part of his work was executed in October. He writes thus to his brother Buonarroto: "I am remaining here as usual, and shall have finished my painting by the end of the week after next—that is, the portion of it which I began; and when it is uncovered, I expect to be paid, and shall also try to get a month's leave to visit Florence."

v

The uncovering took place upon November 1, 1509. All Rome flocked to the chapel, feeling that something stupendous was to be expected after the long months of solitude and seclusion during which the silent master had been working. Nor were they disappointed. The effect produced by only half of the enormous scheme was overwhelming. As Vasari says, "This chapel lighted up a lamp for our art which casts abroad lustre enough to illuminate the world, drowned for so many centuries in darkness." Painters saw at a glance that the genius which had revolutionised sculpture was now destined to introduce a new style and spirit into their art. This was the case even with Raffaello, who, in the frescoes he executed at S. Maria della Pace, showed his immediate willingness to learn from Michelangelo, and his determination to compete with him. Condivi and Vasari are agreed upon this point, and Michelangelo himself, in a moment of hasty indignation, asserted many years afterwards that what Raffaello knew of art was derived from him. That is, of course, an over-statement; for, beside his own exquisite originality, Raffaello formed a composite style successively upon Perugino, Fra Bartolommeo, and Lionardo. He was capable not merely of imitating, but of absorbing and assimilating to his lucid genius the excellent qualities of all in whom he recognised superior talent. At the same time, Michelangelo's influence was undeniable, and we cannot ignore the testimony of those who conversed with both great artists—of Julius himself, for instance, when he said to Sebastian del Piombo: "Look at the work of Raffaello, who, after seeing the masterpieces of Michelangelo, immediately abandoned Perugino's manner, and did his utmost to approach that of Buonarroti."

Condivi's assertion that the part uncovered in November 1509 was the first half of the whole vault, beginning from the door and ending in the middle, misled Vasari, and Vasari misled subsequent biographers. We now know for certain that what Michelangelo meant by "the portion I began" was the whole central space of the ceiling—that is to say, the nine compositions from Genesis, with their accompanying genii and architectural surroundings. That is rendered clear by a statement in Albertini's Roman Handbook, to the effect that the "upper portion of the whole vaulted roof" had been uncovered when he saw it in 1509. Having established this error in Condivi's narrative, what he proceeds to relate may obtain some credence. "Raffaello, when he beheld the new and marvellous style of Michelangelo's work, being extraordinarily apt at imitation, sought,

by Bramante's means, to obtain a commission for the rest."
Had Michelangelo ended at a line drawn halfway across
the breadth of the vault, leaving the Prophets and Sibyls,
the lunettes and pendentives, all finished so far, it would
have been a piece of monstrous impudence even in Bramante, and an impossible discourtesy in gentle Raffaello, to
have begged for leave to carry on a scheme so marvellously
planned. But the history of the Creation, Fall, and Deluge,
when first exposed, looked like a work complete in itself.
Michelangelo, who was notoriously secretive, had almost
certainly not explained his whole design to painters of Bramante's following; and it is also improbable that he had as
yet prepared his working Cartoons for the lower and larger
portion of the vault. Accordingly, there remained a large
vacant space to cover between the older frescoes by Signorelli, Perugino, Botticelli, and other painters, round the
walls below the windows, and that new miracle suspended
in the air. There was no flagrant impropriety in Bramante's
thinking that his nephew might be allowed to carry the
work downward from that altitude. The suggestion may
have been that the Sistine Chapel should become a Museum
of Italian art, where all painters of eminence could deposit
proofs of their ability, until each square foot of wall was
covered with competing masterpieces. But when Michelangelo heard of Bramante's intrigues, he was greatly disturbed in spirit. Having begun his task unwillingly, he now
felt an equal or greater unwillingness to leave the stupendous conception of his brain unfinished. Against all expectation of himself and others, he had achieved a decisive
victory, and was placed at one stroke, Condivi says, "above
the reach of envy." His hand had found its cunning for
fresco as for marble. Why should he be interrupted in the
full swing of triumphant energy? "Accordingly, he sought
an audience with the Pope, and openly laid bare all the per-
secutions he had suffered from Bramante, and discovered
the numerous misdoings of the man." It was on this oc-

casion, according to Condivi, that Michelangelo exposed Bramante's scamped work and vandalism at S. Peter's. Julius, who was perhaps the only man in Rome acquainted with his sculptor's scheme for the Sistine vault, brushed the cobwebs of these petty intrigues aside, and left the execution of the whole to Michelangelo.

There is something ignoble in the task of recording rivalries and jealousies between artists and men of letters. Genius, however, like all things that are merely ours and mortal, shuffles along the path of life, half flying on the wings of inspiration, half hobbling on the feet of interest, the crutches of commissions. Michelangelo, although he made the David and the Sistine, had also to make money. He was entangled with shrewd men of business, and crafty spendthrifts, ambitious intriguers, folk who used undoubted talents, each in its kind excellent and pure, for baser purposes of gain or getting on. The art-life of Rome seethed with such blood-poison; and it would be sentimental to neglect what entered so deeply and so painfully into the daily experience of our hero. Raffaello, kneaded of softer and more facile clay than Michelangelo, throve in this environment, and was somehow able—so it seems—to turn its venom to sweet uses. I like to think of the two peers, moving like stars on widely separated orbits, with radically diverse temperaments, proclivities, and habits, through the turbid atmosphere enveloping but not obscuring their lucidity. Each, in his own way, as it seems to me, contrived to keep himself unspotted by the world; and if they did not understand one another and make friends, this was due to the different conceptions they were framed to take of life, the one being the exact antipodes to the other.

VI

Postponing descriptive or æsthetic criticism of the Sistine frescoes, I shall proceed with the narration of their gradual completion.

We have few documents to guide us through the period of time which elapsed between the first uncovering of Michelangelo's work on the roof of the Sistine (November 1, 1509) and its ultimate accomplishment (October 1512). His domestic correspondence is abundant, and will be used in its proper place; but nothing transpires from those pages of affection, anger, and financial negotiation to throw light upon the working of the master's mind while he was busied in creating the sibyls and prophets, the episodes and idyls, which carried his great Bible of the Fate of Man downwards through the vaulting to a point at which the Last Judgment had to be presented as a crowning climax. For the anxious student of his mind and life-work, nothing is more desolating than the impassive silence he maintains about his doings as an artist. He might have told us all we want to know, and never shall know here about them. But while he revealed his personal temperament and his passions with singular frankness, he locked up the secret of his art, and said nothing.

Eventually we must endeavour to grasp Michelangelo's work in the Sistine as a whole, although it was carried out at distant epochs of his life. For this reason I have thrown these sentences forward, in order to embrace a wide span of his artistic energy (from May 10, 1508, to perhaps December 1541). There is, to my mind, a unity of conception between the history depicted on the vault, the prophets and forecomers on the pendentives, the types selected for the spandrels, and the final spectacle of the day of doom. Living, as he needs must do, under the category of time, Michelangelo was unable to execute his stupendous picture-book of human destiny in one sustained manner. Years passed over him of thwarted endeavour and distracted energies—years of quarrying and sculpturing, of engineering and obeying the vagaries of successive Popes. Therefore, when he came at last to paint the Last Judgment, he was a worn man, exhausted in services of many divers sorts. And, what is most perplexing to the reconstructive critic, nothing in his correspondence remains to indicate the stages of his labour. The letters tell plenty about domestic anxieties, annoyances in his poor craftsman's household, purchases of farms, indignant remonstrances with stupid brethren; but we find in them, as I have said, no clue to guide us through that mental labyrinth in which the supreme artist was continually walking, and at the end of which he left to us the Sistine as it now is.

VII

The old reckoning of the time consumed by Michelangelo in painting the roof of the Sistine, and the traditions concerning his mode of work there, are clearly fabulous. Condivi says: "He finished the whole in twenty months, without having any assistance whatsoever, not even of a man to grind his colours." From a letter of September 7, 1510, we learn that the scaffolding was going to be put up again, and that he was preparing to work upon the lower portion of the vaulting. Nearly two years elapse before we hear of it again. He writes to Buonarroto on the 24th of July 1512: "I am suffering greater hardships than ever man endured, ill, and with overwhelming labour; still I put up with all in order to reach the desired end." Another letter on the 21st of August shows that he expects to complete his work at the end of September; and at last, in October, he writes to his father: "I have finished the chapel I was painting. The Pope is very well satisfied." On the calculation that he began the first part on May 10, 1508, and finished the whole in October 1512, four years and a half were employed upon the work. A considerable part of this time was of course taken up with the preparation of Cartoons; and the nature of fresco-painting rendered the winter months not always fit for active labour. The climate of Rome is not so mild but that wet plaster might often freeze and crack during December, January, and February. Besides, with all his superhuman energy, Michelangelo could not have painted straight on daily without rest or stop. It seems, too, that the master was often in need of money, and that he made two journeys to the Pope to beg for supplies. In the letter to Fattucci he says: "When the vault was nearly finished, the Pope was again at Bologna; whereupon, I went twice to get the necessary funds, and obtained nothing, and lost all that time until I came back to Rome. When I reached Rome, I began to make Cartoons—that is, for the ends and sides of the said chapel, hoping to get money at last and to complete the work. I never could extract a farthing; and when I complained one day to Messer Bernardo da Bibbiena and to Atalante, representing that I could not stop longer in Rome, and that I should be forced to go away with God's grace, Messer Bernardo told Atalante he must bear this in mind, for that he wished me to have money, whatever happened." When we consider, then, the magnitude of the undertaking, the arduous nature of the preparatory studies, and the waste of time in journeys and through other hindrances, four and a half years are not too long a period for a man working so much alone as Michelangelo was wont to do.

We have reason to believe that, after all, the frescoes of the Sistine were not finished in their details. "It is true," continues Condivi, "that I have heard him say he was not suffered to complete the work according to his wish. The Pope, in his impatience, asked him one day when he would be ready with the Chapel, and he answered: 'When I shall be able.' To which his Holiness replied in a rage: 'You want to make me hurl you from that scaffold!' Michelangelo heard and remembered, muttering: 'That you shall not do to me.' So he went straightway, and had the scaffolding taken down. The frescoes were exposed to view on All Saints' day, to the great satisfaction of the Pope, who went that day to service there, while all Rome flocked together to admire them. What Michelangelo felt forced to leave undone was the retouching of certain parts with ultramarine upon dry ground, and also some gilding, to give the whole a richer effect. Giulio, when his heat cooled down, wanted Michelangelo to make these last additions; but he, considering the trouble it would be to build up all that scaffolding afresh, observed that what was missing mattered little. 'You ought at least to touch it up with gold,' replied the Pope; and Michelangelo, with that familiarity he used toward his Holiness, said carelessly: 'I have not observed that men wore gold.' The Pope rejoined: 'It will look poor.' Buonarroti added: 'Those who are painted there were poor men.' So the matter turned into pleasantry, and the frescoes have remained in their present state." Condivi goes on to state that Michelangelo received 3000 ducats for all his expenses, and that he spent as much as twenty or twenty-five ducats on colours alone. Upon the difficult question of the moneys earned by the great artist in his life-work, I shall have to speak hereafter, though I doubt whether any really satisfactory account can now be given of them.

VIII

Michelangelo's letters to his family in Florence throw a light at once vivid and painful over the circumstances of his life during these years of sustained creative energy. He was uncomfortable in his bachelor's home, and always in difficulties with his servants. "I am living here in discontent, not thoroughly well, and undergoing great fatigue, without money, and with no one to look after me." Again, when one of his brothers proposed to visit him in Rome, he writes: "I hear that Gismondo means to come hither on his affairs. Tell him not to count on me for anything; not because I do not love him as a brother, but because I am not in the position to assist him. I am bound to care for myself first, and I cannot provide myself with necessaries. I live here in great distress and the utmost bodily fatigue, have no friends, and seek none. I have not even time enough

to eat what I require. Therefore let no additional burdens
be put upon me, for I could not bear another ounce." In
the autumn of 1509 he corresponded with his father about
the severe illness of an assistant workman whom he kept,
and also about a boy he wanted sent from Florence. "I
should be glad if you could hear of some lad at Florence,
the son of good parents and poor, used to hardships, who
would be willing to come and live with me here, to do the
work of the house, buy what I want, and go around on
messages; in his leisure time he could learn. Should such a boy
be found, please let me know; because there are only rogues
here, and I am in great need of some one." All through his
life, Michelangelo adopted the plan of keeping a young
fellow to act as general servant, and at the same time to
help in art-work. Three of these servants are interwoven
with the chief events of his later years, Pietro Urbano,
Antonio Mini, and Francesco d'Amadore, called Urbino,
the last of whom became his faithful and attached friend
till death parted them. Women about the house he could
not bear. Of the serving-maids at Rome he says: "They are
all strumpets and swine." Well, it seems that Lodovico
found a boy, and sent him off to Rome. What followed is
related in the next letter. "As regards the boy you sent
me, that rascal of a muleteer cheated me out of a ducat for
his journey. He swore that the bargain had been made for
two broad golden ducats, whereas all the lads who come
here with the muleteers pay only ten carlins. I was more
angry at this than if I had lost twenty-five ducats, because
I saw that his father had resolved to send him on mule-
back like a gentleman. Oh, I had never such good luck,
not I! Then both the father and the lad promised that he
would do everything, attend to the mule, and sleep upon
the ground, if it was wanted. And now I am obliged to look
after him. As if I needed more worries than the one I have
had ever since I arrived here! My apprentice, whom I left
in Rome, has been ill from the day on which I returned

until now. It is true that he is getting better; but he lay for about a month in peril of his life, despaired of by the doctors, and I never went to bed. There are other annoyances of my own; and now I have the nuisance of this lad, who says that he does not want to waste time, that he wants to study, and so on. At Florence he said he would be satisfied with two or three hours a day. Now the whole day is not enough for him, but he must needs be drawing all the night. It is all the fault of what his father tells him. If I complained, he would say that I did not want him to learn. I really require some one to take care of the house; and if the boy had no mind for this sort of work, they ought not to have put me to expense. But they are good-for-nothing, and are working toward a certain end of their own. Enough, I beg you to relieve me of the boy; he has bored me so that I cannot bear it any longer. The muleteer has been so well paid that he can very well take him back to Florence. Besides, he is a friend of the father. Tell the father to send for him home. I shall not pay another farthing. I have no money. I will have patience till he sends; and if he does not send, I will turn the boy out of doors. I did so already on the second day of his arrival, and other times also, and the father does not believe it.

"*P.S.*—If you talk to the father of the lad, put the matter to him nicely: as that he is a good boy, but too refined, and not fit for my service, and say that he had better send for him home."

The repentant postscript is eminently characteristic of Michelangelo. He used to write in haste, apparently just as the thoughts came. Afterwards he read his letter over, and softened its contents down, if he did not, as sometimes happened, feel that his meaning required enforcement; in that case he added a stinging tail to the epigram. How little he could manage the people in his employ is clear from the last notice we possess about the unlucky lad from Florence. "I wrote about the boy, to say that his father

ought to send for him, and that I would not disburse more
money. This I now confirm. The driver is paid to take
him back. At Florence he will do well enough, learning his
trade and dwelling with his parents. Here he is not worth
a farthing, and makes me toil like a beast of burden; and
my other apprentice has not left his bed. It is true that
I have not got him in the house; for when I was so tired
out that I could not bear it, I sent him to the room of a
brother of his. I have no money."

These household difficulties were a trifle, however, compared with the annoyances caused by the stupidity of his
father and the greediness of his brothers. While living like
a poor man in Rome, he kept continually thinking of their
welfare. The letters of this period are full of references
to the purchase of land, the transmission of cash when it
was to be had, and the establishment of Buonarroto in a
draper's business. They, on their part, were never satisfied,
and repaid his kindness with ingratitude. The following
letter to Giovan Simone shows how terrible Michelangelo
could be when he detected baseness in a brother:—

"GIOVAN SIMONE,—It is said that when one does good
to a good man, he makes him become better, but that a bad
man becomes worse. It is now many years that I have been
endeavouring with words and deeds of kindness to bring
you to live honestly and in peace with your father and the
rest of us. You grow continually worse. I do not say that
you are a scoundrel; but you are of such sort that you have
ceased to give satisfaction to me or anybody. I could read
you a long lesson on your ways of living; but they would
be idle words, like all the rest that I have wasted. To cut
the matter short, I will tell you as a fact beyond all question that you have nothing in the world: what you spend
and your house-room, I give you, and have given you these
many years, for the love of God, believing you to be my
brother like the rest. Now, I am sure that you are not my

brother, else you would not threaten my father. Nay, you are a beast; and as a beast I mean to treat you. Know that he who sees his father threatened or roughly handled is bound to risk his own life in this cause. Let that suffice. I repeat that you have nothing in the world; and if I hear the least thing about your ways of going on, I will come to Florence by the post, and show you how far wrong you are, and teach you to waste your substance, and set fire to houses and farms you have not earned. Indeed you are not where you think yourself to be. If I come, I will open your eyes to what will make you weep hot tears, and recognise on what false grounds you base your arrogance.

"I have something else to say to you, which I have said before. If you will endeavour to live rightly, and to honour and revere your father, I am willing to help you like the rest, and will put it shortly within your power to open a good shop. If you act otherwise, I shall come and settle your affairs in such a way that you will recognise what you are better than you ever did, and will know what you have to call your own, and will have it shown to you in every place where you may go. No more. What I lack in words I will supply with deeds.

"MICHELANGELO *in Rome*.

"I cannot refrain from adding a couple of lines. It is as follows. I have gone these twelve years past drudging about through Italy, borne every shame, suffered every hardship, worn my body out in every toil, put my life to a thousand hazards, and all with the sole purpose of helping the fortunes of my family. Now that I have begun to raise it up a little, you only, you alone, choose to destroy and bring to ruin in one hour what it has cost me so many years and such labour to build up. By Christ's body this shall not be; for I am the man to put to the rout ten thousand of your sort, whenever it be needed. Be wise in time, then, and do not try the patience of one who has other things to vex him."

Even Buonarroto, who was the best of the brothers and dearest to his heart, hurt him by his graspingness and want of truth. He had been staying at Rome on a visit, and when he returned to Florence it appears that he bragged about his wealth, as if the sums expended on the Buonarroti farms were not part of Michelangelo's earnings. The consequence was that he received a stinging rebuke from his elder brother. "The said Michele told me you mentioned to him having spent about sixty ducats at Settignano. I remember your saying here too at table that you had disbursed a large sum out of your own pocket. I pretended not to understand, and did not feel the least surprise, because I know you. I should like to hear from your ingratitude out of what money you gained them. If you had enough sense to know the truth, you would not say: 'I spent so and so much of my own;' also you would not have come here to push your affairs with me, seeing how I have always acted toward you in the past, but would have rather said: 'Michelangelo remembers what he wrote to us, and if he does not now do what he promised, he must be prevented by something of which we are ignorant,' and then have kept your peace; because it is not well to spur the horse that runs as fast as he is able, and more than he is able. But you have never known me, and do not know me. God pardon you; for it is He who granted me the grace to bear what I do bear and have borne, in order that you might be helped. Well, you will know me when you have lost me."

Michelangelo's angry moods rapidly cooled down. At the bottom of his heart lay a deep and abiding love for his family. There is something caressing in the tone with which he replies to grumbling letters from his father. "Do not vex yourself. God did not make us to abandon us." "If you want me, I will take the post, and be with you in two days. Men are worth more than money." His warm affection transpires even more clearly in the two following documents: "I should like you to be thoroughly convinced that all the labours I have ever undergone have not been more for myself than for your sake. What I have bought, I bought to be yours so long as you live. If you had not been here, I should have bought nothing. Therefore, if you wish to let the house and farm, do so at your pleasure. This income, together with what I shall give you, will enable you to live like a lord." At a time when Lodovico was much exercised in his mind and spirits by a lawsuit, his son writes to comfort the old man. "Do not be discomfited, nor give yourself an ounce of sadness. Remember that losing money is not losing one's life. I will more than make up to you what you must lose. Yet do not attach too much value to worldly goods, for they are by nature untrustworthy. Thank God that this trial, if it was bound to come, came at a time when you have more resources than you had in years past. Look to preserving your life and health, but let your fortunes go to ruin rather than suffer hardships; for I would sooner have you alive and poor; if you were dead, I should not care for all the gold in the world. If those chatterboxes or any one else reprove you, let them talk, for they are men without intelligence and without affection."

References to public events are singularly scanty in this correspondence. Much as Michelangelo felt the woes of Italy—and we know he did so by his poems—he talked but little, doing his work daily like a wise man all through the dust and din stirred up by Julius and the League of Cambrai. The lights and shadows of Italian experience at that time are intensely dramatic. We must not altogether forget the vicissitudes of war, plague, and foreign invasion, which exhausted the country, while its greatest men continued to produce immortal masterpieces. Aldo Manuzio was quietly printing his complete edition of Plato, and Michelangelo was transferring the noble figure of a prophet or a sibyl to the plaster of the Sistine, while young Gaston de Foix was dying at the point of victory upon the bloody shores of the Ronco. Sometimes, however, the disasters of his country touched Michelangelo so nearly that he had to write or speak about them. After the battle of Ravenna, on the 11th of April 1512, Raimondo de Cardona and his Spanish troops brought back the Medici to Florence. On their way, the little town of Prato was sacked with a barbarity which sent a shudder through the whole peninsula. The Cardinal Giovanni de' Medici, who entered Florence on the 14th of September, established his nephews as despots in the city, and intimidated the burghers by what looked likely to be a reign of terror. These facts account for the uneasy tone of a letter written by Michelangelo to Buonarroto. Prato had been taken by assault upon the 30th of August, and was now prostrate after those hideous days of torment, massacre, and outrage indescribable which followed. In these circumstances Michelangelo advises his family to "escape into a place of safety, abandoning their household gear and property; for life is far more worth than money." If they are in need of cash, they may draw upon his credit with the Spedalingo of S. Maria Novella. The constitutional liability to panic which must be recognised in Michelangelo emerges at the close of the letter. "As to public events, do not meddle with them either by deed or word. Act as though the plague were raging. Be the first to fly." The Buonarroti did not take his advice, but remained at Florence, enduring agonies of terror. It was a time when disaffection toward the Medicean princes exposed men to risking life and limb. Rumours reached Lodovico that his son had talked imprudently at Rome. He wrote to inquire what truth there was in the report, and Michelangelo replied: "With regard to the Medici, I have never spoken a single word against them, except in the way that everybody talks—as, for instance, about the sack of Prato; for if the stones could have cried out, I think they would have spoken. There have been many other things said since then, to which, when I heard them, I have answered: 'If they are really acting in this way, they are doing wrong;' not that I believed the reports; and God grant they are not true. About a month ago, some one who makes a show of friendship for me spoke very evilly about their deeds. I rebuked him, told him that it was not well to talk so, and begged him not to do so again to me. However, I should like Buonarroto quietly to find out how the rumour arose of my having calumniated the Medici; for if it is some one who pretends to be my friend, I ought to be upon my guard."

The Buonarroti family, though well affected toward Savonarola, were connected by many ties of interest and old association with the Medici, and were not powerful enough to be the mark of violent political persecution. Nevertheless, a fine was laid upon them by the newly restored Government. This drew forth the following epistle from Michelangelo:—

"DEAREST FATHER,—Your last informs me how things are going on at Florence, though I already knew something. We must have patience, commit ourselves to God, and repent of our sins; for these trials are solely due to them, and more particularly to pride and ingratitude. I never conversed with a people more ungrateful and puffed up than the Florentines. Therefore, if judgment comes, it is but right and reasonable. As for the sixty ducats you tell me you are fined, I think this a scurvy trick, and am exceedingly annoyed. However, we must have patience as long as it pleases God. I will write and enclose two lines to Giuliano de' Medici. Read them, and if you like to present them to him, do so; you will see whether they are likely to be of any use. If not, consider whether we can sell our property and go to live elsewhere. . . . Look to your life and health; and if you cannot share the honours of the land like other burghers, be contented that bread does not

fail you, and live well with Christ, and poorly, as I do here;
for I live in a sordid way, regarding neither life nor
honours—that is, the world—and suffer the greatest hardships and innumerable anxieties and dreads. It is now about
fifteen years since I had a single hour of well-being, and
all that I have done has been to help you, and you have
never recognised this nor believed it. God pardon us all!
I am ready to go on doing the same so long as I live, if only
I am able."

We have reason to believe that the petition to Giuliano
proved effectual, for in his next letter he congratulates his
father upon their being restored to favour. In the same
communication he mentions a young Spanish painter whom
he knew in Rome, and whom he believes to be ill at Florence. This was probably the Alonso Berughetta who made
a copy of the Cartoon for the Battle of Pisa. In July 1508
Michelangelo wrote twice about a Spaniard who wanted
leave to study the Cartoon; first begging Buonarroto to
procure the keys for him, and afterwards saying that he is
glad to hear that the permission was refused. It does not
appear certain whether this was the same Alonso; but it is
interesting to find that Michelangelo disliked his Cartoon
being copied. We also learn from these letters that the
Battle of Pisa then remained in the Sala del Papa.

IX

I will conclude this chapter by translating a sonnet addressed to Giovanni da Pistoja, in which Michelangelo
humorously describes the discomforts he endured while engaged upon the Sistine. Condivi tells us that from painting
so long in a strained attitude, gazing up at the vault, he
lost for some time the power of reading except when he
lifted the paper above his head and raised his eyes. Vasari
corroborates the narrative from his own experience in the
vast halls of the Medicean palace.

I've grown a goitre by dwelling in this den—
As cats from stagnant streams in Lombardy,
Or in what other land they hap to be—
Which drives the belly close beneath the chin:
My beard turns up to heaven; my nape falls in,
Fixed on my spine: my breast-bone visibly
Grows like a harp: a rich embroidery
Bedews my face from brush-drops thick and thin.
My loins into my paunch like levers grind:
My buttock like a crupper bears my weight;
My feet unguided wander to and fro;
In front my skin grows loose and long; behind,
By bending it becomes more taut and strait;
Crosswise I strain me like a Syrian bow:
Whence false and quaint, I know,
Must be the fruit of squinting brain and eye;
For ill can aim the gun that bends awry.
Come then, Giovanni, try
To succour my dead pictures and my fame,
Since foul I fare and painting is my shame.

CHAPTER VI

I

THE Sistine Chapel was built in 1473 by Baccio Pontelli, a Florentine architect, for Pope Sixtus IV. It is a simple barn-like chamber, 132 feet in length, 44 in breadth, and 68 in height from the pavement. The ceiling consists of one expansive flattened vault, the central portion of which offers a large plane surface, well adapted to fresco decoration. The building is lighted by twelve windows, six upon each side of its length. These are placed high up, their rounded arches running parallel with the first spring of the vaulting. The ends of the chapel are closed by flat walls, against the western of which is raised the altar.

When Michelangelo was called to paint here, he found both sides of the building, just below the windows, decorated in fresco by Perugino, Cosimo Rosselli, Sandro Botticelli, Luca Signorelli, and Domenico Ghirlandajo. These masters had depicted, in a series of twelve subjects, the history of Moses and the life of Jesus. Above the lines of fresco, in the spaces between the windows and along the eastern end at the same height, Botticelli painted a row of twenty-eight Popes. The spaces below the frescoed histories, down to the seats which ran along the pavement, were blank, waiting for the tapestries which Raffaello afterwards supplied from cartoons now in possession of the English Crown. At the west end, above the altar, shone three decorative frescoes by Perugino, representing the Assumption of the Virgin, between the finding of Moses and the Nativity. The two last of these pictures opened respectively the history of Moses and the life of Christ, so that the Old and New Testaments were equally illustrated upon the Chapel walls. At the opposite, or eastern end, Ghirlandajo painted the Resurrection, and there was a corresponding picture of Michael contending with Satan for the body of Moses.

Such was the aspect of the Sistine Chapel when Michelangelo began his great work. Perugino's three frescoes on the west wall were afterwards demolished to make room for his Last Judgment. The two frescoes on the east wall are now poor pictures by very inferior masters; but the twelve Scripture histories and Botticelli's twenty-eight Popes remain from the last years of the fifteenth century.

Taken in their aggregate, the wall-paintings I have described afforded a fair sample of Umbrian and Tuscan art in its middle or *quattrocento* age of evolution. It remained for Buonarroti to cover the vault and the whole western end with masterpieces displaying what Vasari called the "modern" style in its most sublime and imposing manifestation. At the same time he closed the cycle of the

figurative arts, and rendered any further progress on the
same lines impossible. The growth which began with Niccolò of Pisa and with Cimabue, which advanced through
Giotto and his school, Perugino and Pinturicchio, Piero della
Francesca and Signorelli, Fra Angelico and Benozzo Gozzoli, the Ghirlandajo brothers, the Lippi and Botticelli,
effloresced in Michelangelo, leaving nothing for after-
comers but manneristic imitation.

II

Michelangelo, instinctively and on principle, reacted
against the decorative methods of the fifteenth century. If
he had to paint a biblical or mythological subject, he avoided
landscapes, trees, flowers, birds, beasts, and subordinate
groups of figures. He eschewed the arabesques, the labyrinths
of foliage and fruit enclosing pictured panels, the candelabra and gay bands of variegated patterns, which enabled
a *quattrocento* painter, like Gozzoli or Pinturicchio, to produce brilliant and harmonious general effects at a small
expenditure of intellectual energy. Where the human body
struck the keynote of the music in a work of art, he judged
that such simple adjuncts and naïve concessions to the
pleasure of the eye should be avoided. An architectural
foundation for the plastic forms to rest on, as plain in
structure and as grandiose in line as could be fashioned,
must suffice. These principles he put immediately to the test
in his first decorative undertaking. For the vault of the
Sistine he designed a mighty architectural framework in
the form of a hypæthral temple, suspended in the air on
jutting pilasters, with bold cornices, projecting brackets, and
ribbed arches flung across the void of heaven. Since the
whole of this ideal building was painted upon plaster, its
inconsequence, want of support, and disconnection from the
ground-plan of the chapel do not strike the mind. It is felt
to be a mere basis for the display of pictorial art, the theatre
for a thousand shapes of dignity and beauty.

I have called this imaginary temple hypæthral, because the master left nine openings in the flattened surface of the central vault. They are unequal in size, five being short parallelograms, and four being spaces of the same shape but twice their length. Through these the eye is supposed to pierce the roof and discover the unfettered region of the heavens. But here again Michelangelo betrayed the inconsequence of his invention. He filled the spaces in question with nine dominant paintings, representing the history of the Creation, the Fall, and the Deluge. Taking our position at the west end of the chapel and looking upwards, we see in the first compartment God dividing light from darkness; in the second, creating the sun and the moon and the solid earth; in the third, animating the ocean with His brooding influence; in the fourth, creating Adam; in the fifth, creating Eve. The sixth represents the temptation of our first parents and their expulsion from Paradise. The seventh shows Noah's sacrifice before entering the ark; the eighth depicts the Deluge, and the ninth the drunkenness of Noah. It is clear that, between the architectural conception of a roof opening on the skies and these pictures of events which happened upon earth, there is no logical connection. Indeed, Michelangelo's new system of decoration bordered dangerously upon the barocco style, and contained within itself the germs of a vicious mannerism.

It would be captious and unjust to push this criticism home. The architectural setting provided for the figures and the pictures of the Sistine vault is so obviously conventional, every point of vantage has been so skilfully appropriated to plastic uses, every square inch of the ideal building becomes so naturally, and without confusion, a pedestal for the human form, that we are lost in wonder at the synthetic imagination which here for the first time combined the arts of architecture, sculpture, and painting in a single organism. Each part of the immense composition, down to the smallest detail, is necessary to the total effect. We are in the presence of a most complicated yet mathematically ordered scheme, which owes life and animation to one master-thought. In spite of its complexity and scientific precision, the vault of the Sistine does not strike the mind as being artificial or worked out by calculation, but as being pedestined to existence, inevitable, a cosmos instinct with vitality.

On the pendentives between the spaces of the windows, running up to the ends of each of the five lesser pictures, Michelangelo placed alternate prophets and sibyls upon firm projecting consoles. Five sibyls and five prophets run along the side-walls of the chapel. The end-walls sustain each of them a prophet. These twelve figures are introduced as heralds and pioneers of Christ the Saviour, whose presence on the earth is demanded by the fall of man and the renewal of sin after the Deluge. In the lunettes above the windows and the arched recesses or spandrels over them are depicted scenes setting forth the genealogy of Christ and of His Mother. At each of the four corner-spandrels of the ceiling, Michelangelo painted, in spaces of a very peculiar shape and on a surface of embarrassing inequality, one magnificent subject symbolical of man's redemption. The first is the raising of the Brazen Serpent in the wilderness; the second, the punishment of Haman; the third, the victory of David over Goliath; the fourth, Judith with the head of Holofernes.

Thus, with a profound knowledge of the Bible, and with an intense feeling for religious symbolism, Michelangelo unrolled the history of the creation of the world and man, the entrance of sin into the human heart, the punishment of sin by water, and the reappearance of sin in Noah's family. Having done this, he intimated, by means of four special mercies granted to the Jewish people—types and symbols of God's indulgence—that a Saviour would arise to redeem the erring human race. In confirmation of this promise, he called twelve potent witnesses, seven of the

Hebrew prophets and five of the Pagan sibyls. He made appeal to history, and set around the thrones on which these witnesses are seated scenes detached from the actual lives of our Lord's human ancestors.

The intellectual power of this conception is at least equal to the majesty and sublime strength of its artistic presentation. An awful sense of coming doom and merited damnation hangs in the thunderous canopy of the Sistine vault, tempered by a solemn and sober expectation of the Saviour. It is much to be regretted that Christ, the Desired of all Nations, the Redeemer and Atoner, appears nowhere adequately represented in the Chapel. When Michelangelo resumed his work there, it was to portray him as an angered Hercules, hurling curses upon helpless victims. The august rhetoric of the ceiling loses its effective value when we can nowhere point to Christ's life and work on earth; when there is no picture of the Nativity, none of the Crucifixion, none of the Resurrection; and when the feeble panels of a Perugino and a Cosimo Rosselli are crushed into insignificance by the terrible Last Judgment. In spite of Buonarroti's great creative strength, and injuriously to his real feeling as a Christian, the piecemeal production which governs all large art undertakings results here in a maimed and onesided rendering of what theologians call the Scheme of Salvation.

III

So much has been written about the pictorial beauty, the sublime imagination, the dramatic energy, the profound significance, the exact science, the shy graces, the terrible force, and finally the vivid powers of characterisation displayed in these frescoes, that I feel it would be impertinent to attempt a new discourse upon a theme so time-worn. I must content myself with referring to what I have already published, which will, I hope, be sufficient to demonstrate that I do not avoid the task for want of enthusiasm. The study of much rhetorical criticism makes me feel strongly that, in front of certain masterpieces, silence is best, or, in lieu of silence, some simple pregnant sayings, capable of rousing folk to independent observation.

These convictions need not prevent me, however, from fixing attention upon a subordinate matter, but one which has the most important bearing upon Michelangelo's genius. After designing the architectural theatre which I have attempted to describe, and filling its main spaces with the vast religious drama he unrolled symbolically in a series of primeval scenes, statuesque figures, and countless minor groups contributing to one intellectual conception, he proceeded to charge the interspaces—all that is usually left for facile decorative details—with an army of passionately felt and wonderfully executed nudes, forms of youths and children, naked or half draped, in every conceivable posture and with every possible variety of facial type and expression. On pedestals, cornices, medallions, tympanums, in the angles made by arches, wherever a vacant plane or unused curve was found, he set these vivid transcripts from humanity in action. We need not stop to inquire what he intended by that host of plastic shapes evoked from his imagination. The triumphant leaders of the crew, the twenty lads who sit upon their consoles, sustaining medallions by ribands which they lift, have been variously and inconclusively interpreted. In the long row of Michelangelo's creations, those young men are perhaps the most significant—athletic adolescents, with faces of feminine delicacy and poignant fascination. But it serves no purpose to inquire what they symbolise. If we did so, we should have to go further, and ask, What do the bronze figures below them, twisted into the boldest attitudes the human frame can take, or the twinned children on the pedestals, signify? In this region, the region of pure plastic play, when art drops the wand of the interpreter and allows physical beauty to be a law unto itself, Michelangelo demonstrated that no decorative element in the hand of a really supreme master is equal to the nude.

Previous artists, with a strong instinct for plastic as opposed to merely picturesque effect, had worked upon the same line. Donatello revelled in the rhythmic dance and stationary grace of children. Luca Signorelli initiated the plan of treating complex ornament by means of the mere human body; and for this reason, in order to define the position of Michelangelo in Italian art-history, I shall devote the next section of this chapter to Luca's work at Orvieto. But Buonarroti in the Sistine carried their suggestions to completion. The result is a mapped-out chart of living figures—a vast pattern, each detail of which is a masterpiece of modelling. After we have grasped the intellectual content of the whole, the message it was meant to inculcate, the spiritual meaning present to the maker's mind, we discover that, in the sphere of artistic accomplishment, as distinct from intellectual suggestion, one rhythm of purely figurative beauty has been carried throughout—from God creating Adam to the boy who waves his torch above the censer of the Erythrean sibyl.

IV

Of all previous painters, only Luca Signorelli deserves to be called the forerunner of Michelangelo, and his Chapel of S. Brizio in the Cathedral at Orvieto in some remarkable respects anticipates the Sistine. This eminent master was commissioned in 1499 to finish its decoration, a small portion of which had been begun by Fra Angelico. He completed the whole Chapel within the space of two years; so that the young Michelangelo, upon one of his journeys to or from Rome, may probably have seen the frescoes in their glory. Although no visit to Orvieto is recorded by his biographers, the fame of these masterpieces by a man whose work at Florence had already influenced his youthful genius must certainly have attracted him to a city which lay on the direct route from Tuscany to the Campagna.

The four walls of the Chapel of S. Brizio are covered with paintings setting forth events immediately preceding and following the day of judgment. A succession of panels, differing in size and shape, represent the preaching of Antichrist, the destruction of the world by fire, the resurrection of the body, the condemnation of the lost, the reception of saved souls into bliss, and the final states of heaven and hell. These main subjects occupy the upper spaces of each wall, while below them are placed portraits of poets, surrounded by rich and fanciful arabesques, including various episodes from Dante and antique mythology. Obeying the spirit of the fifteenth century, Signorelli did not aim at what may be termed an architectural effect in his decoration of this building. Each panel of the whole is treated separately, and with very unequal energy, the artist seeming to exert his strength chiefly in those details which made demands on his profound knowledge of the human form and his enthusiasm for the nude. The men and women of the Resurrection, the sublime angels of Heaven and of the Judgment, the discoloured and degraded fiends of Hell, the magnificently foreshortened clothed figures of the Fulminati, the portraits in the preaching of Antichrist, reveal Luca's specific quality as a painter, at once impressively imaginative and crudely realistic. There is something in his way of regarding the world and of reproducing its aspects which dominates our fancy, does violence to our sense of harmony and beauty, leaves us broken and bewildered, resentful and at the same moment enthralled. He is a power which has to be reckoned with; and the reason for speaking about him at length here is that, in this characteristic blending of intense vision with impassioned realistic effort after truth to fact, this fascination mingled with repulsion, he anticipated Michelangelo. Deep at the root of all Buonarroti's artistic qualities lie these contradictions. Studying Signorelli, we study a parallel psychological problem. The chief difference between the two masters lies in the command of æsthetic synthesis, the constructive sense of harmony, which belonged to the younger, but which might, we feel, have been granted in like measure to the elder, had Luca been born, as Michelangelo was, to complete the evolution of Italian figurative art, instead of marking one of its most important intermediate moments.

The decorative methods and instincts of the two men were closely similar. Both scorned any element of interest or beauty which was not strictly plastic—the human body supported by architecture or by rough indications of the world we live in. Signorelli invented an intricate design for arabesque pilasters, one on each side of the door leading from his chapel into the Cathedral. They are painted *en grisaille*, and are composed exclusively of nudes, mostly male, perched or grouped in a marvellous variety of attitudes upon an ascending series of slender-stemmed vases, which build up gigantic candelabra by their aggregation. The naked form is treated with audacious freedom. It appears to be elastic in the hands of the modeller. Some dead bodies carried on the backs of brawny porters are even awful by the contrast of their wet-clay limpness with the muscular energy of brutal life beneath them. Satyrs giving drink to one another, fauns whispering in the ears of stalwart women, centaurs trotting with corpses flung across their cruppers, combatants trampling in frenzy upon prostrate enemies, men sunk in self-abandonment to sloth or sorrow—such are the details of these incomparable columns, where our sense of the grotesque and vehement is immediately corrected by a perception of rare energy in the artist who could play thus with his plastic puppets.

We have here certainly the preludings to Michelangelo's serener, more monumental work in the Sistine Chapel. The leading motive is the same in both great masterpieces. It consists in the use of the simple body, if possible the nude body, for the expression of thought and emotion, the telling of a tale, the delectation of the eye by ornamental details. It consists also in the subordination of the female to the male nude as the symbolic unit of artistic utterance. Buonarroti is greater than Signorelli chiefly through that larger and truer perception of æsthetic unity which seems to be the final outcome of a long series of artistic effort. The arabesques, for instance, with which Luca wreathed his portraits of the poets, are monstrous, bizarre, in doubtful taste. Michelangelo, with a finer instinct for harmony, a deeper grasp on his own dominant ideal, excluded this element of *quattrocento* decoration from his scheme. Raffaello, with the graceful tact essential to the style, developed its crude rudiments into the choice forms of fanciful delightfulness which charm us in the Loggie.

Signorelli loved violence. A large proportion of the circular pictures painted *en grisaille* on these walls represent scenes of massacre, assassination, torture, ruthless outrage. One of them, extremely spirited in design, shows a group of three executioners hurling men with millstones round their necks into a raging river from the bridge which spans it. The first victim flounders half merged in the flood; a second plunges head foremost through the air; the third stands bent upon the parapet, his shoulders pressed down by the varlets on each side, at the very point of being flung to death by drowning. In another of these pictures a man seated upon the ground is being tortured by the breaking of his teeth, while a furious fellow holds a club suspended over him, in act to shatter his thigh-bones. Naked soldiers wrestle in mad conflict, whirl staves above their heads, fling stones, displaying their coarse muscles with a kind of frenzy. Even the classical subjects suffer from extreme dramatic energy of treatment. Ceres, seeking her daughter through the plains of Sicily, dashes frantically on a car of dragons, her hair dishevelled to the winds, her cheeks gashed by her own crooked fingers. Eurydice struggles in the clutch of bestial devils; Pluto, like a mediæval Satan, frowns above the scene of fiendish riot; the violin of Orpheus thrills faintly through the infernal tumult. Gazing on the spasms and convulsions of these grim subjects, we are inclined to credit a legend preserved at Orvieto to the effect that the painter depicted his own unfaithful mistress in the naked woman who is being borne on a demon's back through the air to hell.

No one who has studied Michelangelo impartially will deny that in this preference for the violent he came near to Signorelli. We feel it in his choice of attitude, the strain he puts upon the lines of plastic composition, the stormy energy of his conception and expression. It is what we call his *terribilità*. But here again that dominating sense of harmony, that instinct for the necessity of subordinating each artistic element to one strain of architectonic music, which I have already indicated as the leading note of difference between him and the painter of Cortona, intervened to elevate his terribleness into the region of sublimity. The violence of Michelangelo, unlike that of Luca, lay not so much in the choice of savage subjects (cruelty, ferocity, extreme physical and mental torment) as in a forceful, passionate, tempestuous way of handling all the themes he treated. The angels of the Judgment, sustaining the symbols of Christ's Passion, wrestle and bend their agitated limbs like athletes. Christ emerges from the sepulchre, not in victorious tranquillity, but with the clash and clangour of an irresistible energy set free. Even in the Crucifixion, one leg has been wrenched away from the nail which pierced its foot, and writhes round the knee of the other still left riven to the cross. The loves of Leda and the Swan, of Ixion and Juno, are spasms of voluptuous pain; the sleep of the Night is troubled with fantastic dreams, and the Dawn starts into consciousness with a shudder of prophetic anguish. There is not a hand, a torso, a simple nude, sketched by this extraordinary master, which does not vibrate with nervous tension, as though the fingers that grasped the pen were clenched and the eyes that viewed the model glowed beneath knit brows. Michelangelo, in fact, saw nothing, felt nothing, interpreted nothing, on exactly the same lines as any one who had preceded or who followed him. His imperious personality he stamped upon the smallest trifle of his work.

Luca's frescoes at Orvieto, when compared with Michelangelo's in the Sistine, mark the transition from the art of the fourteenth, through the art of the fifteenth, to that of the sixteenth century, with broad and trenchant force. They are what Marlowe's dramas were to Shakespeare's. They retain much of the mediæval tradition both as regards form and sentiment. We feel this distinctly in the treatment of Dante, whose genius seems to have exerted at least as strong an influence over Signorelli's imagination as over that of Michelangelo. The episodes from the Divine Comedy are painted in a rude Gothic spirit. The spirits of Hell seem borrowed from grotesque bas-reliefs of the Pisan school. The draped, winged, and armed angels of Heaven are posed with a ceremonious research of suavity or grandeur. These and other features of his work carry us back to the period of Giotto and Niccolò Pisano. But the true force of the man, what made him a commanding master of the middle period, what distinguished him from all his fellows of the *quattrocento*, is the passionate delight he took in pure humanity—the nude, the body studied under all its aspects and with no repugnance for its coarseness— man in his crudity made the sole sufficient object for figura- tive art, anatomy regarded as the crowning and supreme end of scientific exploration. It is this in his work which carries us on toward the next age, and justifies our calling Luca "the morning-star of Michelangelo."

It would be wrong to ascribe too much to the immediate influence of the elder over the younger artist—at any rate in so far as the frescoes of the Chapel of S. Brizio may have determined the creation of the Sistine. Yet Vasari left on record that "even Michelangelo followed the manner of Signorelli, as any one may see." Undoubtedly, Buonarroti, while an inmate of Lorenzo de' Medici's palace at Florence, felt the power of Luca's Madonna with the naked figures in the background; the leading motive of which he transcended in his Doni Holy Family. Probably at an early period he had before his eyes the bold nudities, uncompromising designs, and awkward composition of Luca's so-called School of Pan. In like manner, we may be sure that during his first visit to Rome he was attracted by Signorelli's solemn fresco of Moses in the Sistine. These things were sufficient to establish a link of connection between the painter of Cortona and the Florentine sculptor. And when Michelangelo visited the Chapel of S. Brizio, after he had fixed and formed his style (exhibiting his innate force of genius in the Pietà, the Bacchus, the Cupid, the David, the statue of Julius, the Cartoon for the Battle of Pisa), that early bond of sympathy must have been renewed and enforced. They were men of a like temperament, and governed by kindred æsthetic instincts. Michelangelo brought to its perfection that system of working wholly through the human form which Signorelli initiated. He shared his violence, his *terribilità*, his almost brutal candour. In the fated evolution of Italian art, describing its parabola of vital energy, Michelangelo softened, sublimed, and harmonised his predecessor's qualities. He did this by abandoning Luca's naïvetés and crudities; exchanging his savage transcripts from coarse life for profoundly studied idealisations of form; subordinating his rough and casual design to schemes of balanced composition, based on architectural relations; penetrating the whole accomplished work, as he intended it should be, with a solemn and severe strain of unifying intellectual melody.

Viewed in this light, the vault of the Sistine and the later fresco of the Last Judgment may be taken as the final outcome of all previous Italian art upon a single line of creative energy, and that line the one anticipated by Luca Signorelli. In like manner, the Stanze and Loggie of the Vatican were the final outcome of the same process upon another line, suggested by Perugino and Fra Bartolommeo.

Michelangelo adapted to his own uses and bent to his own genius motives originated by the Pisani, Giotto, Giacopo della Quercia, Donatello, Masaccio, while working in the spirit of Signorelli. He fused and recast the antecedent materials of design in sculpture and painting, producing a quintessence of art beyond which it was impossible to advance without breaking the rhythm, so intensely strung, and without contradicting too violently the parent inspiration. He strained the chord of rhythm to its very utmost, and made incalculable demands upon the religious inspiration of its predecessors. His mighty talent was equal to the task of transfusion and remodelling which the exhibition of the supreme style demanded. But after him there remained nothing for successors except mechanical imitation, soulless rehandling of themes he had exhausted by reducing them to his imperious imagination in a crucible of fiery intensity.

V

No critic with a just sense of phraseology would call Michelangelo a colourist in the same way as Titian and Rubens were colourists. Still it cannot be denied with justice that the painter of the Sistine had a keen perception of what his art required in this region, and of how to attain it. He planned a comprehensive architectural scheme, which served as setting and support for multitudes of draped and undraped human figures. The colouring is kept deliberately low and subordinate to the two main features of the design —architecture, and the plastic forms of men and women. Flesh-tints, varying from the strong red tone of Jonah's athletic manhood, through the glowing browns of the seated

Genii, to the delicate carnations of Adam and the paler hues of Eve; orange and bronze in draperies, medallions, decorative nudes, russets like the tints of dead leaves; lilacs, cold greens, blue used sparingly; all these colours are dominated and brought into harmony by the greys of the architectural setting. It may indeed be said that the different qualities of flesh-tints, the architectural greys, and a dull bronzed yellow strike the chord of the composition. Reds are conspicuous by their absence in any positive hue. There is no vermilion, no pure scarlet or crimson, but a mixed tint verging upon lake. The yellows are brought near to orange, tawny, bronze, except in the hair of youthful personages, a large majority of whom are blonde. The only colour which starts out staringly is ultramarine, owing of course to this mineral material resisting time and change more perfectly than the pigments with which it is associated. The whole scheme leaves a grave harmonious impression on the mind, thoroughly in keeping with the sublimity of the thoughts expressed. No words can describe the beauty of the flesh-painting, especially in the figures of the Genii, or the technical delicacy with which the modelling of limbs, the modulation from one tone to another, have been carried from silvery transparent shades up to the strongest accents.

VI

Mr. Ruskin has said, and very justly said, that "the highest art can do no more than rightly represent the human form." This is what the Italians of the Renaissance meant when, through the mouths of Ghiberti, Buonarroti, and Cellini, they proclaimed that the perfect drawing of a fine nude, "un bel corpo ignudo," was the final test of mastery in plastic art. Mr. Ruskin develops his text in sentences which have peculiar value from his lips. "This is the simple test, then, of a perfect school—that it has represented the human form so that it is impossible to conceive of its being better done. And that, I repeat, has been accomplished twice only: once in Athens, once in Florence. And so narrow is the excellence even of these two exclusive schools, that it cannot be said of either of them that they represented the entire human form. The Greeks perfectly drew and perfectly moulded the body and limbs, but there is, so far as I am aware, no instance of their representing the face as well as any great Italian. On the other hand, the Italian painted and carved the face insuperably; but I believe there is no instance of his having perfectly represented the body, which, by command of his religion, it became his pride to despise and his safety to mortify."

We need not pause to consider whether the Italian's inferiority to the Greek's in the plastic modelling of human bodies was due to the artist's own religious sentiment. That seems a far-fetched explanation for the shortcomings of men so frankly realistic and so scientifically earnest as the masters of the Cinque Cento were. Michelangelo's magnificent cartoon of Leda and the Swan, if it falls short of some similar subject in some *gabinetto segreto* of antique fresco, does assuredly not do so because the draughtsman's hand faltered in pious dread or pious aspiration. Nevertheless, Ruskin is right in telling us that no Italian modelled a female nude equal to the Aphrodite of Melos, or a male nude equal to the Apoxyomenos of the Braccio Nuovo. He is also right in pointing out that no Greek sculptor approached the beauty of facial form and expression which we recognise in Raffaello's Madonna di San Sisto, in Sodoma's S. Sebastian, in Guercino's Christ at the Corsini Palace, in scores of early Florentine sepulchral monuments and pictures, in Umbrian saints and sweet strange portrait-fancies by Da Vinci.

The fact seems to be that Greek and Italian plastic art followed different lines of development, owing to the difference of dominant ideas in the races, and to the difference of social custom. Religion naturally played a foremost part in the art-evolution of both epochs. The anthropomorphic

Greek mythology encouraged sculptors to concentrate their attention upon what Hegel called "the sensuous manifestation of the idea," while Greek habits rendered them familiar with the body frankly exhibited. Mediæval religion withdrew Italian sculptors and painters from the problems of purely physical form, and obliged them to study the expression of sentiments and aspirations which could only be rendered by emphasising psychical qualities revealed through physiognomy. At the same time, modern habits of life removed the naked body from their ken.

We may go further, and observe that the conditions under which Greek art flourished developed what the Germans call "Allgemeinheit," a tendency to generalise, which was inimical to strongly marked facial expression or characterisation. The conditions of Italian art, on the other hand, favoured an opposite tendency—to particularise, to enforce detail, to emphasise the artist's own ideal or the model's quality. When the type of a Greek deity had been fixed, each successive master varied this within the closest limits possible. For centuries the type remained fundamentally unaltered, undergoing subtle transformations, due partly to the artist's temperament, and partly to changes in the temper of society. Consequently those aspects of the human form which are capable of most successful generalisation, the body and the limbs, exerted a kind of conventional tyranny over Greek art. And Greek artists applied to the face the same rules of generalisation which were applicable to the body.

The Greek god or goddess was a sensuous manifestation of the idea, a particle of universal godhood incarnate in a special fleshly form, corresponding to the particular psychological attributes of the deity whom the sculptor had to represent. No deviation from the generalised type was possible. The Christian God, on the contrary, is a spirit; and all the emanations from this spirit, whether direct, as in the person of Christ, or derived, as in the persons of the saints, owe their sensuous form and substance to the exigencies of mortal existence, which these persons temporarily and phenomenally obeyed. Since, then, the sensuous manifestation has now become merely symbolic, and is no longer an indispensable investiture of the idea, it may be altered at will in Christian art without irreverence. The utmost capacity of the artist is now exerted, not in enforcing or refining a generalised type, but in discovering some new facial expression which shall reveal psychological quality in a particular being. Doing so, he inevitably insists upon the face; and having formed a face expressive of some defined quality, he can hardly give to the body that generalised beauty which belongs to a Greek nymph or athlete.

What we mean by the differences between Classic and Romantic art lies in the distinctions I am drawing. Classicism sacrifices character to breadth. Romanticism sacrifices breadth to character. Classic art deals more triumphantly with the body, because the body gains by being broadly treated. Romantic art deals more triumphantly with the face, because the features lose by being broadly treated.

This brings me back to Mr. Ruskin, who, in another of his treatises, condemns Michelangelo for a want of variety, beauty, feeling, in his heads and faces. Were this the case, Michelangelo would have little claim to rank as one of the world's chief artists. We have admitted that the Italians did not produce such perfectly beautiful bodes and limbs as the Greeks did, and have agreed that the Greeks produced less perfectly beautiful faces than the Italians. Suppose, then, that Michelangelo failed in his heads and faces, he, being an Italian, and therefore confessedly inferior to the Greeks in his bodies and limbs, must, by the force of logic, emerge less meritorious than we thought him.

VII

To many of my readers the foregoing section will appear superfluous, polemical, sophistic—three bad things. I wrote it, and I let it stand, however, because it serves as preface to what I have to say in general about Michelangelo's ideal of form. He was essentially a Romantic as opposed to a Classic artist. That is to say, he sought invariably for character—character in type, character in attitude, character in every action of each muscle, character in each extravagance of pose. He applied the Romantic principle to the body and the limbs, exactly to that region of the human form which the Greeks had conquered as their province. He did so with consummate science and complete mastery of physiological law. What is more, he compelled the body to become expressive, not, as the Greeks had done, of broad general conceptions, but of the most intimate and poignant personal emotions. This was his main originality. At the same time, being a Romantic, he deliberately renounced the main tradition of that manner. He refused to study portraiture, as Vasari tells us, and as we see so plainly in the statues of the Dukes at Florence. He generalised his faces, composing an ideal cast of features out of several types. In the rendering of the face and head, then, he chose to be a Classic, while in the treatment of the body he was vehemently modern. In all his work which is not meant to be dramatic—that is, excluding the damned souls in the Last Judgment, the bust of Brutus, and some keen psychological designs—character is sacrificed to a studied ideal of form, so far as the face is concerned. That he did this wilfully, on principle, is certain. The proof remains in the twenty heads of those incomparable genii of the Sistine, each one of whom possesses a beauty and a quality peculiar to himself alone. They show that, if he had so chosen, he could have played upon the human countenance with the same facility as on the human body, varying its expressiveness *ad infinitum*.

Why Michelangelo preferred to generalise the face and to particularise the body remains a secret buried in the abysmal deeps of his personality. In his studies from the model, unlike Lionardo, he almost always left the features vague, while working out the trunk and limbs with strenuous passion. He never seems to have been caught and fascinated by the problem offered by the eyes and features of a male or female. He places masks or splendid commonplaces upon frames palpitant and vibrant with vitality in pleasure or in anguish.

In order to guard against an apparent contradiction, I must submit that, when Michelangelo particularised the body and the limbs, he strove to make them the symbols of some definite passion or emotion. He seems to have been more anxious about the suggestions afforded by their pose and muscular employment than he was about the expression of the features. But we shall presently discover that, so far as pure physical type is concerned, he early began to generalise the structure of the body, passing finally into what may not unjustly be called a mannerism of form.

These points may be still further illustrated by what a competent critic has recently written upon Michelangelo's treatment of form. "No one," says Professor Brücke, "ever knew so well as Michelangelo Buonarroti how to produce powerful and strangely harmonious effects by means of figures in themselves open to criticism, simply by his mode of placing and ordering them, and of distributing their lines. For him a figure existed only in his particular representation of it; how it would have looked in any other position was a matter of no concern to him." We may even go further, and maintain that Michelangelo was sometimes wilfully indifferent to the physical capacities of the human body in his passionate research of attitudes which present picturesque and novel beauty. The ancients worked on quite a different method. They created standard types which, in every conceivable posture, would exhibit the grace and symmetry belonging to well-proportioned frames. Michelangelo looked to the effect of a particular posture. He may have been seduced by his habit of modelling figures in clay in-

stead of going invariably to the living subject, and so may
have handled nature with unwarrantable freedom. Anyhow,
we have here another demonstration of his romanticism.

VIII

The true test of the highest art is that it should rightly
represent the human form. Agreed upon this point, it remains for us to consider in what way Michelangelo conceived and represented the human form. If we can discover
his ideal, his principles, his leading instincts in this decisive
matter, we shall unlock, so far as that is possible, the secret
of his personality as man and artist. The psychological
quality of every great master must eventually be determined
by his mode of dealing with the phenomena of sex.

In Pheidias we find a large impartiality. His men and
women are cast in the same mould of grandeur, inspired
with equal strength and sweetness, antiphonal notes in dual
harmony. Praxiteles leans to the female, Lysippus to the
male; and so, through all the gamut of the figurative craftsmen, we discover more or less affinity for man or woman.
One is swayed by woman and her gracefulness, the other by
man and his vigour. Few have realised the Pheidian perfection of doing equal justice.

Michelangelo emerges as a mighty master who was
dominated by the vision of male beauty, and who saw the
female mainly through the fascination of the other sex.
The defect of his art is due to a certain constitutional cal-
lousness, a want of sensuous or imaginative sensibility for
what is specifically feminine.

Not a single woman carved or painted by the hand of
Michelangelo has the charm of early youth or the grace of
virginity. The Eve of the Sistine, the Madonna of S.
Peter's, the Night and Dawn of the Medicean Sacristy, are
female in the anatomy of their large and grandly modelled
forms, but not feminine in their sentiment. This proposition
requires no proof. It is only needful to recall a Madonna by

Raphael, a Diana by Correggio, a Leda by Lionardo, a Venus by Titian, a S. Agnes by Tintoretto. We find ourselves immediately in a different region—the region of artists who loved, admired, and comprehended what is feminine in the beauty and the temperament of women. Michelangelo neither loved, nor admired, nor yielded to the female sex. Therefore he could not deal plastically with what is best and loveliest in the female form. His plastic ideal of the woman is masculine. He builds a colossal frame of muscle, bone, and flesh, studied with supreme anatomical science. He gives to Eve the full pelvis and enormous haunches of an adult matron. It might here be urged that he chose to symbolise the fecundity of her who was destined to be the mother of the human race. But if this was his meaning, why did he not make Adam a corresponding symbol of fatherhood? Adam is an adolescent man, colossal in proportions, but beardless, hairless; the attributes of sex in him are developed, but not matured by use. The Night, for whom no symbolism of maternity was needed, is a woman who has passed through many pregnancies. Those deeply delved wrinkles on the vast and flaccid abdomen sufficiently indicate this. Yet when we turn to Michelangelo's sonnets on Night, we find that he habitually thought of her as a mysterious and shadowy being, whose influence, though potent for the soul, disappeared before the frailest of all creatures bearing light. The Dawn, again, in her deep lassitude, has nothing of vernal freshness. Built upon the same type as the Night, she looks like Messalina dragging herself from heavy slumber, for once satiated as well as tired, stricken for once with the conscience of disgust. When he chose to depict the acts of passion or of sensual pleasure, a similar want of sympathy with what is feminine in womanhood leaves an even more discordant impression on the mind. I would base the proof of this remark upon the marble Leda of the Bargello Museum, and an old engraving of Ixion clasping the phantom of Juno under the form of a cloud. In neither case do we possess Michelangelo's own handiwork; he must not, therefore, be credited with the revolting expression, as of a drunken profligate, upon the face of Leda. Yet in both cases he is indubitably responsible for the general design, and for the brawny carnality of the repulsive woman. I find it difficult to resist the conclusion that Michelangelo felt himself compelled to treat women as though they were another and less graceful sort of males. The sentiment of woman, what really distinguishes the sex, whether voluptuously or passionately or poetically apprehended, emerges in no eminent instance of his work. There is a Cartoon at Naples for a Bacchante, which Bronzino transferred to canvas and coloured. This design illustrates the point on which I am insisting. An athletic circus-rider of mature years, with abnormally developed muscles, might have posed as model for this female votary of Dionysus. Before he made this drawing, Michelangelo had not seen those frescoes of the dancing Bacchantes from Pompeii; nor had he perhaps seen the Mænads on Greek bas-reliefs tossing wild tresses backwards, swaying virginal lithe bodies to the music of the tambourine. We must not, therefore, compare his concept with those masterpieces of the later classical imagination. Still, many of his contemporaries, vastly inferior to him in penetrative insight, a Giovanni da Udine, a Perino del Vaga, a Primaticcio, not to speak of Raffaello or of Lionardo, felt what the charm of youthful womanhood upon the revel might be. He remained insensible to the melody of purely feminine lines; and the only reason why his transcripts from the female form are not gross like those of Flemish painters, repulsive like Rembrandt's, fleshly like Rubens's, disagreeable like the drawings made by criminals in prisons, is that they have little womanly about them.

Lest these assertions should appear too dogmatic, I will indicate the series of works in which I recognise Michelangelo's sympathy with genuine female quality. All the domestic groups, composed of women and children, which fill the lunettes and groinings between the windows in the Sistine Chapel, have a charming twilight sentiment of family life or maternal affection. They are among the loveliest and most tranquil of his conceptions. The Madonna above the tomb of Julius II. cannot be accused of masculinity, nor the ecstatic figure of the Rachel beneath it. Both of these statues represent what Goethe called "das ewig Weibliche" under a truly felt and natural aspect. The Delphian and Erythrean Sibyls are superb in their majesty. Again, in those numerous designs for Crucifixions, Depositions from the Cross, and Pietàs, which occupied so much of Michelangelo's attention during his old age, we find an intense and pathetic sympathy with the sorrows of Mary, expressed with noble dignity and a pious sense of godhead in the human mother. It will be remarked that throughout the cases I have reserved as exceptions, it is not woman in her plastic beauty and her radiant charm that Michelangelo has rendered, but woman in her tranquil or her saddened and sorrow-stricken moods. What he did not comprehend and could not represent was woman in her girlishness, her youthful joy, her physical attractiveness, her magic of seduction.

Michelangelo's women suggest demonic primitive beings, composite and undetermined products of the human race in evolution, before the specific qualities of sex have been eliminated from a general predominating mass of masculinity. At their best, they carry us into the realm of Lucretian imagination. He could not have incarnated in plastic form Shakespeare's Juliet and Imogen, Dante's Francesca da Rimini, Tasso's Erminia and Clorinda; but he might have supplied a superb illustration to the opening lines of the Lucretian epic, where Mars lies in the bed of Venus, and the goddess spreads her ample limbs above her Roman lover. He might have evoked images tallying the vision of primal passion in the fourth book of that poem. As I have

elsewhere said, writing about Lucretius: "There is something almost tragic in these sighs and pantings and pleasure-
throes, these incomplete fruitions of souls pent within their
frames of flesh. We seem to see a race of men and women
such as never lived, except perhaps in Rome or in the
thought of Michelangelo, meeting in leonine embracements
that yield pain, whereof the climax is, at best, relief from
rage and respite for a moment from consuming fire. There
is a life elemental rather than human in those mighty limbs;
and the passion that twists them on the marriage-bed has in
it the stress of storms, the rampings and roarings of leopards
at play. Take this single line:—

et Venus in silvis jungebat corpora amantum.

What a picture of primeval breadth and vastness! The
forest is the world, and the bodies of the lovers are things
natural and unashamed, and Venus is the tyrannous instinct
that controls the blood in spring."

What makes Michelangelo's crudity in his plastic treatment of the female form the more remarkable is that in his
poetry he seems to feel the influence of women mystically.
I shall have to discuss this topic in another place. It is
enough here to say that, with very few exceptions, we remain in doubt whether he is addressing a woman at all.
There are none of those spontaneous utterances by which a
man involuntarily expresses the outgoings of his heart to
a beloved object, the throb of irresistible emotion, the physical ache, the sense of wanting, the joys and pains, the hopes
and fears, the ecstasies and disappointments, which belong
to genuine passion. The woman is, for him, an allegory,
something he has not approached and handled. Of her personality we learn nothing. Of her bodily presentment, the
eyes alone are mentioned; and the eyes are treated as the
path to Paradise for souls which seek emancipation from the
flesh. Raffaello's few and far inferior sonnets vibrate with
an intense and potent sensibility to this woman or to that.

Michelangelo's "donna" might just as well be a man; and indeed the poems he addressed to men, though they have nothing sensual about them, reveal a finer touch in the emotion of the writer. It is difficult to connect this vaporous incorporeal "donna" of the poems with those brawny colossal adult females of the statues, unless we suppose that Michelangelo remained callous both to the physical attractions and the emotional distinction of woman as she actually is.

I have tried to demonstrate that, plastically, he did not understand women, and could not reproduce their form in art with sympathetic feeling for its values of grace, suavity, virginity, and frailty. He imported masculine qualities into every female theme he handled. The case is different when we turn to his treatment of the male figure. It would be impossible to adduce a single instance, out of the many hundreds of examples furnished by his work, in which a note of femininity has been added to the masculine type. He did not think enough of women to reverse the process, and create hermaphroditic beings like the Apollino of Praxiteles or the S. Sebastian of Sodoma. His boys and youths and adult men remain, in the truest and the purest sense of the word, virile. Yet with what infinite variety, with what a deep intelligence of its resources, with what inexhaustible riches of enthusiasm and science, he played upon the lyre of the male nude! How far more fit for purposes of art he felt the man to be than the woman is demonstrated, not only by his approaching woman from the masculine side, but also by his close attention to none but male qualities in men. I need not insist or enlarge upon this point. The fact is apparent to every one with eyes to see. It would be futile to expound Michelangelo's fertility in dealing with the motives of the male figure as minutely as I judged it necessary to explain the poverty of his inspiration through the female. But it ought to be repeated that, over the whole gamut of the scale, from the grace of boyhood, through the multiform delightfulness of adolescence into the firm force of early manhood, and the sterner virtues of adult age, one severe and virile spirit controls his fashioning of plastic forms. He even exaggerates what is masculine in the male, as he caricatures the female by ascribing impossible virility to her. But the exaggeration follows here a line of mental and moral rectitude. It is the expression of his peculiar sensibility to physical structure.

IX

When we study the evolution of Michelangelo's ideal of form, we find at the beginning of his life a very short period in which he followed the traditions of Donatello and imitated Greek work. The seated Madonna in bas-relief and the Giovannino belong to this first stage. So does the bas-relief of the Centaurs. It soon becomes evident, however, that Michelangelo was not destined to remain a continuator of Donatello's manner or a disciple of the classics. The next period, which includes the Madonna della Febbre, the Bruges Madonna, the Bacchus, the Cupid, and the David, is marked by an intense search after the truth of Nature. Both Madonnas might be criticised for unreality, owing to the enormous development of the thorax and something artificial in the type of face. But all the male figures seem to have been studied from the model. There is an individuality about the character of each, a naturalism, an aiming after realistic expression, which separate this group from previous and subsequent works by Buonarroti. Traces of Donatello's influence survive in the treatment of the long large hands of David, the cast of features selected for that statue, and the working of the feet. Indeed it may be said that Donatello continued through life to affect the genius of Michelangelo by a kind of sympathy, although the elder master's naïveté was soon discarded by the younger.

The second period culminated in the Cartoon for the Battle of Pisa. This design appears to have fixed the style now known to us as Michelangelesque, and the loss of it is therefore irreparable. It exercised the consummate science which he had acquired, his complete mastery over the male nude. It defined his firm resolve to treat linear design from the point of view of sculpture rather than of painting proper. It settled his determination to work exclusively through and by the human figure, rejecting all subordinate elements of decoration. Had we possessed this epoch-making masterpiece, we should probably have known Michelangelo's genius in its flower-period of early ripeness, when anatomical learning was still combined with a sustained dependence upon Nature. The transition from the second to the third stage in this development of form-ideal remains imperfectly explained, because the bathers in the Arno were necessary to account for the difference between the realistic David and the methodically studied genii of the Sistine.

The vault of the Sistine shows Michelangelo's third manner in perfection. He has developed what may be called a scheme of the human form. The apparently small head, the enormous breadth of shoulder, the thorax overweighing the whole figure, the finely modelled legs, the large and powerful extremities, which characterise his style henceforward, culminate in Adam, repeat themselves throughout the genii, govern the prophets. But Nature has not been neglected. Nothing is more remarkable in that vast decorative mass of figures than the variety of types selected, the beauty and animation of the faces, the extraordinary richness, elasticity, and freshness of the attitudes presented to the eye. Every period of life has been treated with impartial justice, and both sexes are adequately handled. The Delphian, Erythrean, and Libyan Sibyls display a sublime sense of facial beauty. The Eve of the Temptation has even something of positively feminine charm. This is probably due to the fact that Michelangelo here studied expression and felt the necessity of dramatic characterisation in this part of his work. He struck each chord of what may be called the poetry of figurative art, from the epic cantos of

Creation, Fall, and Deluge, through the tragic odes uttered by prophets and sibyls, down to the lyric notes of the genii, and the sweet idyllic strains of the groups in the lunettes and spandrels.

It cannot be said that even here Michelangelo · felt the female nude as sympathetically as he felt the male. The women in the picture of the Deluge are colossal creatures, scarcely distinguishable from the men except by their huge bosoms. His personal sense of beauty finds fullest expression in the genii. The variations on one theme of youthful love-liness and grace are inexhaustible; the changes rung on atti-tude, and face, and feature are endless. The type, as I have said, has already become schematic. It is adolescent, but the adolescence is neither that of the Greek athlete nor that of the nude model. Indeed, it is hardly natural; nor yet is it ideal in the Greek sense of that term. The physical grace-fulness of a slim ephebus was never seized by Michelangelo. His Ganymede displays a massive trunk and brawny thighs. Compare this with the Ganymede of Titian. Compare the Cupid at South Kensington with the Praxitelean Genius of the Vatican—the Adonis and the Bacchus of the Bargello with Hellenic statues. The bulk and force of maturity are combined with the smoothness of boyhood and with a deli-cacy of face that borders on the feminine.

It is an arid region, the region of this mighty master's spirit. There are no heavens and no earth or sea in it; no living creatures, forests, flowers; no bright colours, brilliant lights, or cavernous darks. In clear grey twilight appear a multitude of naked forms, both male and female, yet neither male nor female of the actual world; rather the brood of an inventive intellect, teeming with preoccupations of abiding thoughts and moods of feeling, which become for it incarnate in these stupendous figures. It is as though Michelangelo worked from the image in his brain outwards to a physical presentment supplied by his vast knowledge of life, creating forms proper to his own specific concept.

Nowhere else in plastic art does the mental world peculiar to the master press in so immediately, without modification and without mitigation, upon our sentient imagination. I sometimes dream that the inhabitants of the moon may be like Michelangelo's men and women, as I feel sure its landscape resembles his conception of the material universe.

What I have called Michelangelo's third manner, the purest manifestation of which is to be found in the vault of the Sistine, sustained itself for a period of many years. The surviving fragments of sculpture for the tomb of Julius, especially the Captives of the Louvre and the statues in the Sacristy at S. Lorenzo, belong to this stage. A close and intimate *rapport* with Nature can be perceived in all the work he designed and executed during the pontificates of Leo and Clement. The artist was at his fullest both of mental energy and physical vigour. What he wrought now bears witness to his plenitude of manhood. Therefore, although the type fixed for the Sistine prevailed——I mean that generalisation of the human form in certain wilfully selected proportions, conceived to be ideally beautiful or necessary for the grand style in vast architectonic schemes of decoration——still it is used with an exquisite sensitiveness to the pose and structure of the natural body, a delicate tact in the definition of muscle and articulation, an acute feeling for the qualities of flesh and texture. None of the creations of this period, moreover, are devoid of intense animating emotions and ideas.

Unluckily, during all the years which intervened between the Sistine vault and the Last Judgment, Michelangelo was employed upon architectural problems and engineering projects, which occupied his genius in regions far removed from that of figurative art. It may, therefore, be asserted, that although he did not retrograde from want of practice, he had no opportunity of advancing further by the concentration of his genius on design. This accounts, I think, for the change in his manner which we notice when he began to paint in Rome under Pope Paul III. The fourth stage in his development of form is reached now. He has lost nothing of his vigour, nothing of his science. But he has drifted away from Nature. All the innumerable figures of the Last Judgment, in all their varied attitudes, with divers moods of dramatic expression, are diagrams wrought out imaginatively from the stored-up resources of a lifetime It may be argued that it was impossible to pose models, in other words, to appeal to living men and women, for the foreshortenings of falling or soaring shapes in that huge drift of human beings. This is true; and the strongest testimony to the colossal powers of observation possessed by Michelangelo is that none of all those attitudes are wrong. We may verify them, if we take particular pains to do so, by training the sense of seeing to play the part of a detective camera. Michelangelo was gifted with a unique faculty for seizing momentary movements, fixing them upon his memory, and transferring them to fresco by means of his supreme acquaintance with the bony structure and the muscular capacities of the human frame. Regarded from this point of view, the Last Judgment was an unparallelel success. As such the contemporaries of Buonarroti hailed it. Still, the breath of life has exaled from all those bodies, and the tyranny of the schematic ideal of form is felt in each of them. Without meaning to be irreverent, we might fancy that two elastic lay-figures, one male, the other female, both singularly similar in shape, supplied the materials for the total composition. Of the dramatic intentions and suggestions underlying these plastic and elastic shapes I am not now speaking. It is my present business to establish the phases through which my master's sense of form passed from its cradle to its grave.

In the frescoes of the Cappella Paolina, so ruined at this day that we can hardly value them, the mechanic manner of the fourth stage seems to reach its climax. Ghosts of their former selves, they still reveal the poverty of creative and spontaneous inspiration which presided over their nativity.

Michelangelo's fourth manner might be compared with that of Milton in "Paradise Regained" and "Samson Agonistes." Both of these great artists in old age exaggerate the defects of their qualities. Michelangelo's ideal of line and proportion in the human form becomes stereotyped and strained, as do Milton's rhythms and his Latinisms. The generous wine of the Bacchus and of "Comus," so intoxicating in its newness, the same wine in the Sistine and "Paradise Lost," so overwhelming in its mature strength, has acquired an austere aridity. Yet, strange to say, amid these autumn stubbles of declining genius we light upon oases more sweet, more tenderly suggestive, than aught the prime produced. It is not my business to speak of Milton here. I need not recall his "Knights of Logres and of Lyonesse," or resume his Euripidean garlands showered on Samson's grave. But, for my master Michelangelo, it will suffice to observe that all the grace his genius held, refined, of earthly grossness quit, appeared, under the dominance of this fourth manner, in the mythological subjects he composed for Tommaso Cavalieri, and, far more nobly, in his countless studies for the celebration of Christ's Passion. The designs bequeathed to us from this period are very numerous. They were never employed in the production of any monumental work of sculpture or of painting. For this very reason, because they were occasional improvisations, preludes, dreams of things to be, they preserve the finest bloom, the Indian summer of his fancy. Lovers of Michelangelo must dedicate their latest and most loving studies to this phase of his fourth manner.

X

If we seek to penetrate the genius of an artist, not merely forming a correct estimate of his technical ability and science, but also probing his personality to the core, as near as this is possible for us to do, we ought to give our undivided study to his drawings. It is there, and there alone, that we come face to face with the real man, in his unguarded moments, in his hours of inspiration, in the laborious effort to solve a problem of composition, or in the happy flow of genial improvisation. Michelangelo was wont to maintain that all the arts are included in the art of design. Sculpture, painting, architecture, he said, are but subordinate branches of draughtsmanship. And he went so far as to assert that the mechanical arts, with engineering and fortification, nay, even the minor arts of decoration and costume, owe their existence to design. The more we reflect upon this apparent paradox, the more shall we feel it to be true. At any rate, there are no products of human thought and feeling capable of being expressed by form which do not find their common denominator in a linear drawing. The simplicity of a sketch, the comparative rapidity with which it is produced, the concentration of meaning demanded by its rigid economy of means, render it more symbolical, more like the hieroglyph of its maker's mind, than any finished work can be. We may discover a greater mass of interesting objects in a painted picture or a carved statue; but we shall never find exactly the same thing, never the involuntary revelation of the artist's soul, the irrefutable witness to his mental and moral qualities, to the mysteries of his genius and to its limitations.

If this be true of all artists, it is in a peculiar sense true of Michelangelo. Great as he was as sculptor, painter, architect, he was only perfect and impeccable as draughtsman. Inadequate realisation, unequal execution, fatigue, satiety, caprice of mood, may sometimes be detected in his frescoes and his statues; but in design we never find him faulty, hasty, less than absolute master over the selected realm of thought. His most interesting and instructive work remains what he performed with pen and chalk in hand. Deeply, therefore, must we regret the false modesty which made him destroy masses of his drawings, while we have reason to be thankful for those marvellous photographic processes which nowadays have placed the choicest of his masterpieces within the reach of every one.

The following passages from Vasari's and Condivi's Lives deserve attention by those who approach the study of Buonarroti's drawings. Vasari says: "His powers of imagination were such, that he was frequently compelled to abandon his purpose, because he could not express by the hand those grand and sublime ideas which he had conceived in his mind; nay, he has spoiled and destroyed many works for this cause; and I know, too, that some short time before his death he burnt a large number of his designs, sketches, and cartoons, that none might see the labours he had endured, and the trials to which he had subjected his spirit, in his resolve not to fall short of perfection. I have myself secured some drawings by his hand, which were found in Florence, and are now in my book of designs, and these, although they give evidence of his great genius, yet prove also that the hammer of Vulcan was necessary to bring Minerva from the head of Jupiter. He would construct an ideal shape out of nine, ten and even twelve different heads, for no other purpose than to obtain a certain grace of harmony and composition which is not to be found in the natural form, and would say that the artist must have his measuring tools, not in the hand, but in the eye, because the hands do but operate, it is the eye that judges; he pursued the same idea in architecture also." Condivi adds some information regarding his extraordinary fecundity and variety of invention: "He was gifted with a most tenacious memory, the power of which was such that, though he painted so many thousands of figures, as any one can see, he never made one exactly like another or posed in the same attitude. Indeed, I have heard him say that he never draws a line without remembering whether he has drawn it before; erasing any repetition, when the design was meant to be exposed to public view. His force of imagination is also most extraordinary. This has been the chief reason why he was never quite satisfied with his own work, and always depreciated its quality, esteeming that his hand failed to attain the idea which he had formed within his brain."

XI

The four greatest draughtsmen of this epoch were Lionardo da Vinci, Michelangelo, Raffaello, and Andrea del Sarto. They are not to be reckoned as equals; for Lionardo and Michelangelo outstrip the other two almost as much as these surpass all lesser craftsmen. Each of the four men expressed his own peculiar vision of the world with pen, or chalk, or metal point, finding the unique inevitable line, the exact touch and quality of stroke, which should present at once a lively transcript from real Nature, and a revelation of the artist's particular way of feeling Nature. In Lionardo it is a line of subtlety and infinite suggestiveness; in Michelangelo it compels attention, and forcibly defines the essence of the object; in Raffaello it carries melody, the charm of an unerring rhythm; in Andrea it seems to call for tone, colour, atmosphere, and makes their presence felt. Raffaello was often faulty: even in the wonderful pen-drawing of two nudes he sent to Albrecht Dürer as a sample of his skill, we blame the knees and ankles of his models. Lionardo was sometimes wilful, whimsical, seduced by dreamland, like a god born amateur. Andrea allowed his facility to lead him into languor, and lacked passion. Michelangelo's work shows none of these shortcomings; it is always technically faultness, instinct with passion, supereminent in force. But we crave more of grace, of sensuous delight, of sweetness, than he chose, or perhaps was able, to communicate. We should welcome a little more of human weakness if he gave a little more of divine suavity.

Michelangelo's style of design is that of a sculptor, Andrea's of a colourist, Lionardo's of a curious student, Raffaello's of a musician and improvisatore. These distinctions are not merely fanciful, nor based on what we know about the men in their careers. We feel similar distinctions in the case of all great draughtsmen. Titian's chalk-studies, Fra Bartolommeo's, so singularly akin to Andrea del Sarto's, Giorgione's pen-and-ink sketch for a Lucretia, are seen at once by their richness and blurred outlines to be the work of colourists. Signorelli's transcripts from the nude, remarkably similar to those of Michelangelo, reveal a sculptor rather than a painter. Botticelli, with all his Florentine precision, shows that, like Lionardo, he was a seeker and a visionary in his anxious feeling after curve and attitude. Mantegna seems to be graving steel or cutting into marble. It is easy to apply this analysis in succession to any draughtsman who has style. To do so would, however, be superfluous: we should only be enforcing what is a truism to all intelligent students of art—namely, that each individual stamps his own specific quality upon his handiwork; reveals even in the neutral region of design his innate preference for colour or pure form as a channel of expression; betrays the predominance of mental energy or sensuous charm, of scientific curiosity or plastic force, of passion or of tenderness, which controls his nature. This inevitable and unconscious revelation of the man in art-work strikes us as being singularly modern. We do not apprehend it to at all the same extent in the sculpture of the ancients, whether it be that our sympathies are too remote from Greek and Roman ways of feeling, or whether the ancients really conceived art more collectively in masses, less individually as persons.

No master exhibits this peculiarly modern quality more decisively than Michelangelo, and nowhere is the personality of his genius, what marks him off and separates him from all fellow-men, displayed with fuller emphasis than in his drawings. To use the words of a penetrative critic, from whom it is a pleasure to quote: "The thing about Michelangelo is this; he is not, so to say, at the head of a class, but he stands apart by himself: he is not possessed of a skill which renders him unapproached or unapproachable; but rather, he is of so unique an order, that no other artist whatever seems to suggest comparison with him." Mr. Selwyn Image goes on to define in what a true sense the words "creator" and "creative" may be applied to him: how the shows and appearances of the world were for him but hieroglyphs of underlying ideas, with which his soul was familiar, and from which he worked again outward; "his learning and skill in the arts supplying to his hand such large and adequate symbols of them as are otherwise beyond attainment." This, in a very difficult and impalpable region of æsthetic criticism, is finely said, and accords with Michelangelo's own utterances upon art and beauty in his poems. Dwelling like a star apart, communing with the eternal ideas, the permanent relations of the universe, uttering his inmost thoughts about these mysteries through the vehicles of science and of art, for which he was so singularly gifted, Michelangelo, in no loose or trivial sense of that phrase, proved himself to be a creator. He introduces us to a world seen by no eyes except his own, compels us to become familiar with forms unapprehended by our senses, accustoms us to breathe a rarer and more fiery atmosphere than we were born into.

The vehicles used by Michelangelo in his designs were mostly pen and chalk. He employed both a sharp-nibbed pen of some kind, and a broad flexible reed, according to the exigencies of his subject or the temper of his mood. The chalk was either red or black, the former being softer than the latter. I cannot remember any instances of those chiaroscuro washes which Raffaello handled in so masterly a manner, although Michelangelo frequently combined bistre shading with pen outlines. In like manner he does not seem to have favoured the metal point upon prepared paper, with which Lionardo produced unrivalled masterpieces. Some drawings, where the yellow outline bites into a parchment paper, blistering at the edges, suggest a rusty metal in the instrument. We must remember, however, that the inks of that period were frequently corrosive, as is proved by the state of many documents now made illegible through the gradual attrition of the paper by mineral acids. It is also not impossible that artists may have already invented what we call steel pens. Sarpi, in the seventeenth century, thanks a correspondent for the gift of one of these mechanical devices. Speaking broadly, the reed and the quill, red and black chalk, or *matita*, were the vehicles of Michelangelo's expression as a draughtsman. I have seen very few examples of studies heightened with white chalk, and none produced in the fine Florentine style of Ghirlandajo by white chalk alone upon a dead-brown surface. In this matter it is needful to speak with diffidence; for the sketches of our master are so widely scattered that few students can have examined the whole of them; and photographic reproductions, however admirable in their fidelity to outline, do not always give decisive evidence regarding the materials employed.

One thing seems manifest. Michelangelo avoided those mixed methods with which Lionardo, the magician, wrought wonders. He preferred an instrument which could be freely, broadly handled, inscribing form in strong plain strokes upon the candid paper. The result attained, whether wrought by bold lines, or subtly hatched, or finished with the utmost delicacy of modulated shading, has always been traced out conscientiously and firmly, with one pointed stylus (pen, chalk, or matita), chosen for the purpose. As I have said, it is the work of a sculptor, accustomed to wield chisel and mallet upon marble, rather than that of a painter, trained to secure effects by shadows and glazings.

It is possible, I think, to define, at least with some approximation to precision, Michelangelo's employment of his favourite vehicles for several purposes and at different periods of his life. A broad-nibbed pen was used almost invariably in making architectural designs of cornices, pilasters, windows, also in plans for military engineering. Sketches of tombs and edifices, intended to be shown to patrons, were partly finished with the pen; and here we find a subordinate and very limited use of the brush in shading. Such performances may be regarded as products of the workshop rather than as examples of the artist's mastery. The style of them is often conventional, suggesting the intrusion of a pupil or the deliberate adoption of an office mannerism. The pen plays a foremost part in all the greatest and most genial creations of his fancy when it worked energetically in preparation for sculpture or for fresco. The Louvre is rich in masterpieces of this kind—the fiery study of a David; the heroic figures of two male nudes, hatched into stubborn salience like pieces of carved wood; the broad conception of the Madonna at S. Lorenzo in her magnificent repose and passionate cascade of fallen draperies; the repulsive but superabundantly powerful profile of a goat-like faun. These, and the stupendous studies of the Albertina Collection at Vienna, including the supine man with thorax violently raised, are worked with careful hatchings, stroke upon stroke, effecting a suggestion of plastic roundness. But we discover quite a different use of the pen in some large simple outlines of seated female figures at the Louvre; in thick, almost muddy, studies at Vienna, where the form emerges out of oft-repeated sodden blotches; in the grim light and shade, the rapid suggestiveness of the dissection scene at Oxford. The pen in the hand of Michelangelo was the tool by means of which he realised his most trenchant conceptions and his most picturesque impressions. In youth and early manhood, when his genius was still vehement, it seems to have been his favourite vehicle.

The use of chalk grew upon him in later life, possibly because he trusted more to his memory now, and loved the dreamier softer medium for uttering his fancies. Black chalk was employed for rapid notes of composition, and also for the more elaborate productions of his pencil. To this material we owe the head of Horror which he gave to Gherardo Perini (in the Uffizi), the Phaethon, the Tityos, the Ganymede he gave to Tommaso Cavalieri (at Windsor). It is impossible to describe the refinements of modulated shading and the precision of predetermined outlines by means of which these incomparable drawings have been produced. They seem to melt and to escape inspection, yet they remain fixed on the memory as firmly as forms in carven basalt.

The whole series of designs for Christ's Crucifixion and Deposition from the Cross are executed in chalk, sometimes black, but mostly red. It is manifest, upon examination, that they are not studies from the model, but thoughts evoked and shadowed forth on paper. Their perplexing multiplicity and subtle variety—as though a mighty improvisatore were preluding again and yet again upon the clavichord to find his theme, abandoning the search, renewing it, altering the key, changing the accent—prove that this continued seeking with the crayon after form and composition was carried on in solitude and abstract moments. Incomplete as the designs may be, they reveal Michelangelo's loftiest dreams and purest visions. The nervous energy, the passionate grip upon the subject, shown in the pen-drawings, are absent here. These qualities are replaced by meditation and an air of rapt devotion. The drawings for the Passion might be called the prayers and pious thoughts of the stern master.

Red chalk he used for some of his most brilliant conceptions. It is not necessary to dwell upon the bending woman's head at Oxford, or the torso of the lance-bearer at Vienna. Let us confine our attention to what is perhaps the most pleasing and most perfect of all Michelangelo's designs— the "Bersaglio," or the "Arcieri," in the Queen's collection at Windsor.

It is a group of eleven naked men and one woman, fiercely footing the air, and driving shafts with all their might to pierce a classical terminal figure, whose face, like that of Pallas, and broad breast are guarded by a spreading shield. The draughtsman has indicated only one bow, bent with fury by an old man in the background. Yet all the actions proper to archery are suggested by the violent gestures

and strained sinews of the crowd. At the foot of the terminal
statue, Cupid lies asleep upon his wings, with idle bow and
quiver. Two little genii of love, in the background, are lighting up a fire, puffing its flames, as though to drive the arch-
ers onward. Energy and ardour, impetuous movement and
passionate desire, could not be expressed with greater force,
nor the tyranny of some blind impulse be more imaginatively felt. The allegory seems to imply that happiness is not
to be attained, as human beings mostly strive to seize it, by
the fierce force of the carnal passions. It is the contrast between celestial love asleep in lustful souls, and vulgar love
inflaming tyrannous appetites:—

> *The one love soars, the other downward tends;*
> *The soul lights this, while that the senses stir,*
> *And still lust's arrow at base quarry flies.*

This magnificent design was engraved during Buonarroti's lifetime, or shortly afterwards, by Niccolò Beatrizet.
Some follower of Raffaello used the print for a fresco in
the Palazzo Borghese at Rome. It forms one of the series
in which Raffaello's marriage of Alexander and Roxana is
painted. This has led some critics to ascribe the drawing itself to the Urbinate. Indeed, at first sight, one might almost
conjecture that the original chalk study was a genuine work
of Raffaello, aiming at rivalry with Michelangelo's manner. The calm beauty of the statue's classic profile, the
refinement of all the faces, the exquisite delicacy of the
adolescent forms, and the dominant veiling of strength
with grace, are not precisely Michelangelesque. The technical execution of the design, however, makes its attribution
certain. Well as Raffaello could draw, he could not draw
like this. He was incapable of rounding and modelling the
nude with those soft stipplings and granulated shadings
which bring the whole surface out like that of a bas-relief
in polished marble. His own drawing for Alexander and
Roxana, in red chalk, and therefore an excellent subject

for comparison with the Arcieri, is hatched all over in straight lines; a method adopted by Michelangelo when working with the pen, but, so far as I am aware, never, or very rarely, used when he was handling chalk. The style of this design and its exquisite workmanship correspond exactly with the finish of the Cavalieri series at Windsor. The paper, moreover, is indorsed in Michelangelo's handwriting with a memorandum bearing the date April 12, 1530. We have then in this masterpiece of draughtsmanship an example, not of Raffaello in a Michelangelising mood, but of Michelangelo for once condescending to surpass Raffaello on his own ground of loveliness and rhythmic grace.

CHAPTER VII

I

JULIUS died upon the 21st of February 1513. "A prince," says Guicciardini, "of inestimable courage and tenacity, but headlong, and so extravagant in the schemes he formed, that his own prudence and moderation had less to do with shielding him from ruin than the discord of sovereigns and the circumstances of the times in Europe: worthy, in all truth, of the highest glory had he been a secular potentate, or if the pains and anxious thought he employed in augmenting the temporal greatness of the Church by war had been devoted to her spiritual welfare in the arts of peace."

Italy rejoiced when Giovanni de' Medici was selected to succeed him, with the title of Leo X. "Venus ruled in Rome with Alexander, Mars with Julius, now Pallas enters on her reign with Leo." Such was the tenor of the epigrams which greeted Leo upon his triumphal progress to the Lateran. It was felt that a Pope of the house of Medici would be a patron of arts and letters, and it was hoped that the son of Lorenzo the Magnificent might restore the equilibrium of power in Italy. Leo X. has enjoyed a greater fame than he deserved. Extolled as an Augustus in his lifetime, he left his name to what is called the golden age of Italian culture. Yet he cannot be said to have raised any first-rate men of genius, or to have exercised a very wise patronage over those whom Julius brought forward. Michelangelo and Raffaello were in the full swing of work when Leo claimed their services. We shall see how he hampered the rare gifts of the former by employing him on uncongenial labours; and it was no great merit to give a free rein to the inexhaustible energy of Raffaello. The project of a new S. Peter's belonged to Julius. Leo only continued the scheme, using such assistants as the times provided after Bramante's death in 1514. Julius instinctively selected men of soaring and audacious genius, who were capable of planning on a colossal scale. Leo delighted in the society of clever people, poetasters, petty scholars, lutists, and buffoons. Rome owes no monumental work to his inventive brain, and literature no masterpiece to his discrimination. Ariosto, the most brilliant poet of the Renaissance, returned in disappointment from the Vatican. "When I went to Rome and kissed the foot of Leo," writes the ironical satirist, "he bent down from the holy chair, and took my hand and saluted me on both cheeks. Besides, he made me free of half the stamp-dues I was bound to pay; and then, breast full of hope, but smirched with mud, I retired and took my supper at the Ram."

The words which Leo is reported to have spoken to his brother Giuliano when he heard the news of his election, express the character of the man and mark the difference between his ambition and that of Julius. "Let us enjoy the Papacy, since God has given it us." To enjoy life, to squander the treasures of the Church on amusements, to feed a rabble of flatterers, to contract enormous debts, and to disturb the peace of Italy, not for some vast scheme of ecclesiastical aggrandisement, but in order to place the princes of his family on thrones, that was Leo's conception of the Papal privileges and duties. The portraits of the two Popes, both from the hand of Raffaello, are eminently characteristic. Julius, bent, white-haired, and emaciated, has the nervous glance of a passionate and energetic temperament. Leo, heavy-jawed, dull-eyed, with thick lips and a brawny jowl, betrays the coarser fibre of a sensualist.

II

We have seen already that Julius, before his death, provided for his monument being carried out upon a reduced scale. Michelangelo entered into a new contract with the executors, undertaking to finish the work within the space of seven years from the date of the deed, May 6, 1513. He received in several payments, during that year and the years 1514, 1515, 1516, the total sum of 6100 golden ducats. This proves that he must have pushed the various operations connected with the tomb vigorously forward, employing numerous workpeople, and ordering supplies of marble. In fact, the greater part of what remains to us of the unfinished monument may be ascribed to this period of comparatively uninterrupted labour. Michelangelo had his workshop in the Macello de' Corvi, but we know very little about the details of his life there. His correspondence happens to be singularly scanty between the years 1513 and 1516. One letter, however, written in May 1518, to the Capitano of Cortona throws a ray of light upon this barren tract of time, and introduces an artist of eminence, whose intellectual affinity to Michelangelo will always remain a matter of interest. "While I was at Rome, in the first year of Pope Leo, there came the Master Luca Signorelli of Cortona, painter. I met him one day near Monte Giordano, and he told me that he was come to beg something from the Pope, I forget what: he had run the risk of losing life and limb for his devotion to the house of Medici, and now it seemed they did not recognise him: and so forth, saying many things I have forgotten. After these discourses, he asked me for forty giulios [a coin equal in value to the more modern paolo, and worth perhaps eight shillings of present money], and told me where to send them to, at the house of a shoemaker, his lodgings. I not having the money about me, promised to send it, and did so by the hand of a young man in my service, called Silvio, who is still alive and in Rome, I believe. After the lapse of some days, perhaps because his business with the Pope had failed, Messer Luca came to my house in the Macello de' Corvi, the same where I live now, and found me working on a marble statue, four cubits in height, which has the hands bound behind the back, and bewailed himself with me, and begged another forty, saying that he wanted to leave Rome. I went up to my bedroom, and brought the money down in the presence of a Bolognese maid I kept, and I think the Silvio above mentioned was also there. When Luca got the cash, he went away, and I have never seen him since; but I remember complaining to him, because I was out of health and could not work, and he said: 'Have no fear, for the angels from heaven will come to take you in their arms and aid you.'" This is in several ways an interesting document. It brings vividly before our eyes magnificent expensive Signorelli and his meanly living comrade, each of them mighty masters of a terrible and noble style, passionate lovers of the nude, devoted to masculine types of beauty, but widely and profoundly severed by differences in their personal tastes and habits. It also gives us a glimpse into Michelangelo's workshop at the moment when he was blocking out one of the bound Captives at the Louvre. It seems from what follows in the letter that Michelangelo had attempted to recover the money through his brother Buonarroto, but that Signorelli refused to acknowledge his debt. The Capitano wrote that he was sure it had been discharged. "That," adds Michelangelo, "is the same as calling me the biggest blackguard; and so I should be, if I wanted to get back what had been already paid. But let your Lordship think what you like about it, I am bound to get the money, and so I swear." The remainder of the autograph is torn and illegible; it seems to wind up with a threat.

The records of this period are so scanty that every detail acquires a certain importance for Michelangelo's biographer. By a deed executed on the 14th of June 1514, we find that he contracted to make a figure of Christ in marble, "life-sized, naked, erect, with a cross in his arms, and in such attitude as shall seem best to Michelangelo." The persons who ordered the statue were Bernardo Cencio (a Canon of S. Peter's), Mario Scappucci, and Metello Varj dei Porcari, a Roman of ancient blood. They undertook to pay 200 golden ducats for the work; and Michelangelo promised to finish it within the space of four years, when it was to be placed in the Church of S. Maria sopra Minerva. Metello Varj, though mentioned last in the contract, seems to have been the man who practically gave the commission, and to whom Michelangelo was finally responsible for its performance. He began to hew it from a block, and discovered black veins in the working. This, then, was thrown aside, and a new marble had to be attacked. The statue, now visible at the Minerva, was not finished until the year 1521, when we shall have to return to it again.

There is a point of some interest in the wording of this contract, on which, as facts to dwell upon are few and far between at present, I may perhaps allow myself to digress. The master is here described as *Michelangelo* (*di Lodovico*) *Simoni, Scultore.* Now Michelangelo always signed his own letters Michelangelo Buonarroti, although he addressed the members of his family by the surname of Simoni. This proves that the patronymic usually given to the house at large was still Simoni, and that Michelangelo himself acknowledged that name in a legal document. The adoption of Buonarroti by his brother's children and descendants may therefore be ascribed to usage ensuing from the illustration of their race by so renowned a man. It should also be observed that at this time Michelangelo is always described in deeds as sculptor, and that he frequently signs with *Michelangelo, Scultore*. Later on in life he changed his views. He wrote in 1548 to his nephew Lionardo: "Tell the priest not to write to me again as *Michelangelo the sculptor*, for I am not known here except as Michelangelo Buonarroti. Say, too, that if a citizen of Florence wants to have an altar-piece painted, he must find some painter; for I was never either sculptor or painter in the way of one who keeps a shop. I have always avoided that, for the honour of my father and my brothers. True, I have served three Popes; but that was a matter of necessity." Earlier, in 1543, he had written to the same effect: "When you correspond with me, do not use the superscription *Michelangelo Simoni*, nor *sculptor*; it is enough to put *Michelangelo Buonarroti*, for that is how I am known here." On another occasion, advising his nephew what surname the latter ought to adopt, he says: "I should certainly use *Simoni*, and if the whole (that is, the whole list of patronymics in use at Florence) is too long, those who cannot read it may leave it alone." These communications prove that, though he had come to be known as Buonarroti, he did not wish the family to drop their old surname of Simoni. The reason was that he believed in their legendary descent from the Counts of Canossa through a Podestà of Florence, traditionally known as Simone da Canossa. This opinion had been confirmed in 1520, as we have seen above, by a letter he received from the Conte Alessandro da Canossa, addressing him as "Honoured kinsman." In the correspondence with Lionardo, Michelangelo alludes to this act of recognition: "You will find a letter from the Conte Alessandro da Canossa in the book of contracts. He came to visit me at Rome, and treated me like a relative. Take care of it." The dislike expressed by Michelangelo to be called *sculptor*, and addressed upon the same terms as other artists, arose from a keen sense of his nobility. The feeling emerges frequently in his letters between 1540 and 1550. I will give a specimen: "As to the purchase of a house, I repeat that you ought to buy one of honourable condition, at 1500 or 2000 crowns; and it ought to be in our quarter (Santa Croce), if possible. I say this, because an honourable mansion in the city does a family great credit. It makes more impression than farms in the country; and we are truly burghers, who claim a very noble ancestry. I always strove my utmost to resuscitate our house, but I had not brothers able to assist me. Try then to do what I write you, and make Gismondo come back to live in Florence, so that I may not endure the shame of hearing it said here that I have a brother at Settignano who trudges after oxen. One day, when I find the time, I will tell you all about our origin, and whence we sprang, and when we came to Florence. Perhaps you know nothing about it; still we ought not to rob ourselves of what God gave us." The same feeling runs through the letters he wrote Lionardo about the choice of a wife. One example will suffice: "I believe that in Florence there are many noble and poor families with whom it would be a charity to form connections. If there were no dower, there would also be no arrogance. Pay no heed should people say you want to ennoble yourself, since it is notorious that we are ancient citizens of Florence, and as noble as any other house."

Michelangelo, as we know now, was mistaken in accepting his supposed connection with the illustrious Counts of Canossa, whose castle played so conspicuous a part in the struggle between Hildebrand and the Empire, and who were imperially allied through the connections of the Countess Matilda. Still he had tradition to support him, confirmed by the assurance of the head of the Canossa family. Nobody could accuse him of being a snob or parvenu. He lived like a poor man, indifferent to dress, establishment, and personal appearances. Yet he prided himself upon his ancient birth; and since the Simoni had been indubitably noble for several generations, there was nothing despicable in his desire to raise his kinsfolk to their proper station. Almost culpably careless in all things that concerned his health and comfort, he spent his earnings for the welfare of his brothers, in order that an honourable posterity might carry on the name he bore, and which he made illustrious. We may smile at his peevishness in repudiating the title of *sculptor* after bearing it through so many years of glorious labour; but when he penned the letter I have quoted, he was the supreme artist of Italy, renowned as painter, architect, military engineer; praised as poet; befriended with the best and greatest of his contemporaries; recognised as unique, not only in the art of sculpture. If he felt some pride of race, we cannot blame the plain-liver and high-thinker, who, robbing himself of luxuries and necessaries even, enabled his kinsmen to maintain their rank among folk gently born and nobly nurtured.

III

In June 1515 Michelangelo was still working at the tomb of Julius. But a letter to Buonarroto shows that he was already afraid of being absorbed for other purposes by Leo: "I am forced to put great strain upon myself this summer in order to complete my undertaking; for I think that I shall soon be obliged to enter the Pope's service. For this reason, I have bought some twenty migliaia [measure of weight] of brass to cast certain figures." The monument then was so far advanced that, beside having a good number of the marble statues nearly finished, he was on the point of executing the bronze reliefs which filled their interspaces. We have also reason to believe that the architectural basis forming the foundation of the sepulchre had been brought well forward, since it is mentioned in the next ensuing contracts.

Just at this point, however, when two or three years of steady labour would have sufficed to terminate this mount of sculptured marble, Leo diverted Michelangelo's energies from the work, and wasted them in schemes that came to nothing. When Buonarroti penned that sonnet in which he called the Pope his Medusa, he might well have been thinking of Leo, though the poem ought probably to be referred to the earlier pontificate of Julius. Certainly the Medici did more than the Della Rovere to paralyse his power and turn the life within him into stone. Writing to Sebastiano del Piombo in 1521, Michelangelo shows how fully he was aware of this. He speaks of "the three years I have lost."

A meeting had been arranged for the late autumn of 1515 between Leo X. and Francis I. at Bologna. The Pope left Rome early in November, and reached Florence on the 30th. The whole city burst into a tumult of jubilation, shouting the Medicean cry of "*Palle*" as Leo passed slowly through the streets, raised in his pontifical chair upon the shoulders of his running footmen. Buonarroto wrote a long and interesting account of this triumphal entry to his brother in Rome. He describes how a procession was formed by the Pope's court and guard and the gentlemen of Florence. "Among the rest, there went a bevy of young men, the noblest in our commonwealth, all dressed alike with doublets of violet satin, holding gilded staves in their hands. They paced before the Papal chair, a brave sight to see. And first there marched his guard, and then his grooms, who carried him aloft beneath a rich canopy of brocade, which was sustained by members of the College, while round about the chair walked the Signory." The procession moved onward to the Church of S. Maria del Fiore, where the Pope stayed to perform certain ceremonies at the high altar, after which he was carried to his apartments at S. Maria Novella. Buonarroto was one of the Priors during this month, and accordingly he took an official part in all the entertainments and festivities, which continued for three days. On the 3rd of December Leo left Florence for

Bologna, where Francis arrived upon the 11th. Their conference lasted till the 15th, when Francis returned to Milan. On the 18th Leo began his journey back to Florence, which he re-entered on the 22nd. On Christmas day (Buonarroto writes *Pasqua*) a grand Mass was celebrated at S. Maria Novella, at which the Signory attended. The Pope celebrated in person, and, according to custom on high state occasions, the water with which he washed his hands before and during the ceremony had to be presented by personages of importance. "This duty," says Buonarroto, "fell first to one of the Signori, who was Giannozzo Salviati; and as I happened that morning to be Proposto, I went the second time to offer water to his Holiness; the third time, this was done by the Duke of Camerino, and the fourth time by the Gonfalonier of Justice." Buonarroto remarks that "he feels pretty certain it will be all the same to Michelangelo whether he hears or does not hear about these matters. Yet, from time to time, when I have leisure, I scribble a few lines."

Buonarroto himself was interested in this event; for, having been one of the Priors, he received from Leo the title of Count Palatine, with reversion to all his posterity. Moreover, for honourable addition to his arms, he was allowed to bear a chief charged with the Medicean ball and fleur-de-lys, between the capital letters L. and X.

Whether Leo conceived the plan of finishing the façade of S. Lorenzo at Florence before he left Rome, or whether it occurred to him during this visit, is not certain. The church had been erected by the Medici and other magnates from Brunelleschi's designs, and was perfect except for the façade. In its sacristy lay the mortal remains of Cosimo, Lorenzo the Magnificent, and many other members of the Medicean family. Here Leo came on the first Sunday in Advent to offer up prayers, and the Pope is said to have wept upon his father's tomb. It may possibly have been on this occasion that he adopted the scheme so fatal to the happiness of the great sculptor. Condivi clearly did not know what led to Michelangelo's employment on the façade of S. Lorenzo, and Vasari's account of the transaction is involved. Both, however, assert that he was wounded, even to tears, at having to abandon the monument of Julius, and that he prayed in vain to be relieved of the new and uncongenial task.

IV

Leo at first intended to divide the work between several masters, giving Buonarroti the general direction of the whole. He ordered Giuliano da San Gallo, Raffaello da Urbino, Baccio d'Agnolo, Andrea and Jacopo Sansovino to prepare plans. While these were in progress, Michelangelo also thought that he would try his hand at a design. As ill-luck ruled, Leo preferred his sketch to all the rest. Vasari adds that his unwillingness to be associated with any other artist in the undertaking, and his refusal to follow the plans of an architect, prevented the work from being executed, and caused the men selected by Leo to return in desperation to their ordinary pursuits. There may be truth in the report; for it is certain that, after Michelangelo had been forced to leave the tomb of Julius and to take part in the façade, he must have claimed to be sole master of the business. The one thing we know about his mode of operation is, that he brooked no rival near him, mistrusted collaborators, and found it difficult to co-operate even with the drudges whom he hired at monthly wages.

Light is thrown upon these dissensions between Michelangelo and his proposed assistants by a letter which Jacopo Sansovino wrote to him at Carrara on the 30th of June 1517. He betrays his animus at the commencement by praising Baccio Bandinelli, to mention whom in the same breath with Buonarroti was an insult. Then he proceeds: "The Pope, the Cardinal, and Jacopo Salviati are men who when they say yes, it is a written contract, inasmuch as they are true to their word, and not what you pretend them to be. You measure them with your own rod; for neither contracts nor plighted troth avail with you, who are always saying nay and yea, according as you think it profitable. I must inform you, too, that the Pope promised me the sculptures, and so did Salviati; and they are men who will maintain me in my right to them. In what concerns you, I have done all I could to promote your interests and honour, not having earlier perceived that you never conferred a benefit on any one, and that, beginning with myself, to expect kindness from you, would be the same as wanting water not to wet. I have reason for what I say, since we have often met together in familiar converse, and may the day be cursed on which you ever said any good about anybody on earth." How Michelangelo answered this intemperate and unjust invective is not known to us. In some way or other the quarrel between the two sculptors must have been made up—probably through a frank apology on Sansovino's part. When Michelangelo, in 1524, supplied the Duke of Sessa with a sketch for the sepulchral monument to be erected for himself and his wife, he suggested that Sansovino should execute the work, proving thus by acts how undeserved the latter's hasty words had been.

The Church of S. Lorenzo exists now just as it was before the scheme for its façade occurred to Leo. Not the smallest part of that scheme was carried into effect, and large masses of the marbles quarried for the edifice lay wasted on the Tyrrhene sea-shore. We do not even know what design Michelanglo adopted. A model may be seen in the Accademia at Florence ascribed to Baccio d'Agnolo, and there is a drawing of a façade in the Uffizi attributed to Michelangelo, both of which have been supposed to have some connection with S. Lorenzo. It is hardly possible, however, that Buonarroti's competitors could have been beaten from the field by things so spiritless and ugly. A pen-and-ink drawing at the Museo Buonarroti possesses greater merit,

and may perhaps have been a first rough sketch for the
façade. It is not drawn to scale or worked out in the manner of practical architects; but the sketch exhibits features
which we know to have existed in Buonarroti's plan—masses
of sculpture, with extensive bas-reliefs in bronze. In form
the façade would not have corresponded to Brunelleschi's
building. That, however, signified nothing to Italian architects, who were satisfied when the frontispiece to a church
or palace agreeably masked what lay behind it. As a frame
for sculpture, the design might have served its purpose,
though there are large spaces difficult to account for; and
spiteful folk were surely justified in remarking to the Pope
that no one life sufficed for the performance of the whole.

Nothing testifies more plainly to the ascendancy which
this strange man acquired over the imagination of his contemporaries, while yet comparatively young, than the fact
that Michelangelo had to relinquish work for which he was
pre-eminently fitted (the tomb of Julius) for work to
which his previous studies and his special inclinations in no-
wise called him. He undertook the façade of S. Lorenzo
reluctantly, with tears in his eyes and dolour in his bosom,
at the Pope Medusa's bidding. He was compelled to recommence art at a point which hitherto possessed for him no
practical importance. The drawings of the tomb, the sketch
of the façade, prove that in architecture he was still a novice.
Hitherto, he regarded building as the background to sculpture, or the surface on which frescoes might be limned. To
achieve anything great in this new sphere implied for him a
severe course of preliminary studies. It depends upon our
final estimate of Michelangelo as an architect whether we regard the three years spent in Leo's service for S. Lorenzo as
wasted. Being what he was, it is certain that, when the commission had been given, and he determined to attack his task
alone, the man set himself down to grasp the principles of
construction. There was leisure enough for such studies in
the years during which we find him moodily employed

among Tuscan quarries. The question is whether this strain
upon his richly gifted genius did not come too late. When
called to paint the Sistine, he complained that painting was
no art of his. He painted, and produced a masterpiece; but
sculpture still remained the major influence in all he
wrought there. Now he was bidden to quit both sculpture
and painting for another field, and, as Vasari hints, he
would not work under the guidance of men trained to architecture. The result was that Michelangelo applied himself to
building with the full-formed spirit of a figurative artist.
The obvious defects and the salient qualities of all he afterwards performed as architect seem due to the forced diversion of his talent at this period to a type of art he had not
properly assimilated. Architecture was not the natural mistress of his spirit. He bent his talents to her service at a Pontiff's word, and, with the honest devotion to work which
characterised the man, he produced renowned monuments
stamped by his peculiar style. Nevertheless, in building, he
remains a sublime amateur, aiming at scenical effect, subordinating construction to decoration, seeking ever back toward opportunities for sculpture or for fresco, and occasionally (as in the cupola of S. Peter's) hitting upon a thought
beyond the reach of inferior minds.

The paradox implied in this diversion of our hero from
the path he ought to have pursued may be explained in three
ways. First, he had already come to be regarded as a man of
unique ability, from whom everything could be demanded.
Next, it was usual for the masters of the Renaissance, from
Leo Battista Alberti down to Raffaello da Urbino and
Lionardo da Vinci, to undertake all kinds of technical work
intrusted to their care by patrons. Finally, Michelangelo,
though he knew that sculpture was his goddess, and never
neglected her first claim upon his genius, felt in him that
burning ambition for greatness, that desire to wrestle with
all forms of beauty and all depths of science, which tempted
him to transcend the limits of a single art and try his powers

in neighbour regions. He was a man born to aim at all, to dare all, to embrace all, to leave his personality deep-trenched on all the provinces of art he chose to traverse.

V

The whole of 1516 and 1517 elapsed before Leo's plans regarding S. Lorenzo took a definite shape. Yet we cannot help imagining that when Michelangelo cancelled his first contract with the executors of Julius, and adopted a reduced plan for the monument, he was acting under Papal pressure. This was done at Rome in July, and much against the will of both parties. Still it does not appear that any one contemplated the abandonment of the scheme; for Buonarroti bound himself to perform his new contract within the space of nine years, and to engage "in no work of great importance which should interfere with its fulfilment." He spent a large part of the year 1516 at Carrara, quarrying marbles, and even hired the house of a certain Francesco Pelliccia in that town. On the 1st of November he signed an agreement with the same Pelliccia involving the purchase of a vast amount of marble, whereby the said Pelliccia undertook to bring down four statues of 4½ cubits each and fifteen of 4¼ cubits from the quarries where they were being rough-hewn. It was the custom to block out columns, statues, &c., on the spot where the stone had been excavated, in order, probably, to save weight when hauling. Thus the blocks arrived at the sea-shore with rudely adumbrated outlines of the shape they were destined to assume under the artist's chisel. It has generally been assumed that the nineteen figures in question were intended for the tomb. What makes this not quite certain, however, is that the contract of July specifies a greatly reduced quantity and scale of statues. Therefore they may have been intended for the façade. Anyhow, the contract above-mentioned with Francesco Pelliccia was cancelled on the 7th of April following, for reasons which will presently appear.

During the month of November 1516 Michelangelo received notice from the Pope that he was wanted in Rome. About the same time news reached him from Florence of his father's severe illness. On the 23rd he wrote as follows to Buonarroto: "I gathered from your last that Lodovico was on the point of dying, and how the doctor finally pronounced that if nothing new occurred he might be considered out of danger. Since it is so, I shall not prepare to come to Florence, for it would be very inconvenient. Still, if there is danger, I should desire to see him, come what might, before he died, if even I had to die together with him. I have good hope, however, that he will get well, and so I do not come. And if he should have a relapse—from which may God preserve him and us—see that he lacks nothing for his spiritual welfare and the sacraments of the Church, and find out from him if he wishes us to do anything for his soul. Also, for the necessaries of the body, take care that he lacks nothing; for I have laboured only and solely for him, to help him in his needs before he dies. So bid your wife look with loving-kindness to his household affairs. I will make everything good to her and all of you, if it be necessary. Do not have the least hesitation, even if you have to expend all that we possess."

We may assume that the subsequent reports regarding Lodovico's health were satisfactory; for on the 5th of December Michelangelo set out for Rome. The executors of Julius had assigned him free quarters in a house situated in the Trevi district, opposite the public road which leads to S. Maria del Loreto. Here, then, he probably took up his abode. We have seen that he had bound himself to finish the monument of Julius within the space of nine years, and to engage "in no work of great moment which should interfere with its performance." How this clause came to be inserted in a deed inspired by Leo is one of the difficulties with which the whole tragedy of the sepulchre bristles. Perhaps we ought to conjecture that the Pope's intentions with regard to the façade of S. Lorenzo only became settled in the late autumn. At any rate, he had now to transact with the executors of Julius, who were obliged to forego the rights over Michelangelo's undivided energies which they had acquired by the clause I have just cited. They did so with extreme reluctance, and to the bitter disappointment of the sculptor, who saw the great scheme of his manhood melting into air, dwindling in proportions, becoming with each change less capable of satisfactory performance.

Having at last definitely entered the service of Pope Leo, Michelangelo travelled to Florence, and intrusted Baccio d'Agnolo with the construction of the model of his façade. It may have been upon the occasion of this visit that one of his father's whimsical fits of temper called out a passionate and sorry letter from his son. It appears that Pietro Urbano, Michelangelo's trusty henchman at this period, said something which angered Lodovico, and made him set off in a rage to Settignano:—

"DEAREST FATHER,—I marvelled much at what had happened to you the other day, when I did not find you at home. And now, hearing that you complain of me, and say that I have turned you out of doors, I marvel much the more, inasmuch as I know for certain that never once from the day that I was born till now had I a single thought of doing anything or small or great which went against you; and all this time the labours I have undergone have been for the love of you alone. Since I returned from Rome to Florence, you know that I have always cared for you, and you know that all that belongs to me I have bestowed on you. Some days ago, then, when you were ill, I promised solemnly never to fail you in anything within the scope of my whole faculties so long as my life lasts; and this I again affirm. Now I am amazed that you should have forgotten everything so soon. And yet you have learned to know me by experience these thirty years, you and your sons, and are well aware that I have always thought and acted, so far as I was able, for your good. How can you go about saying I have turned you out of doors? Do you not see what a reputation you have given me by saying I have turned you out? Only this was wanting to complete my tale of troubles, all of which I suffer for your love. You repay me well, forsooth. But let it be as it must: I am willing to acknowledge that I have always brought shame and loss on you, and on this supposition I beg your pardon. Reckon that you are pardoning a son who has lived a bad life and done you all the harm which it is possible to do. And so I once again implore you to pardon me, scoundrel that I am, and not bring on me the reproach of having turned you out of doors; for that matters more than you imagine to me. After all, I am your son."

From Florence Michelangelo proceeded again to Carrara for the quarrying of marble. This was on the last day of December. From his domestic correspondence we find that he stayed there until at least the 13th of March 1517; but he seems to have gone to Florence just about that date, in order to arrange matters with Baccio d'Agnolo about the model. A fragmentary letter to Buonarroto, dated March 13, shows that he had begun a model of his own at Carrara, and that he no longer needed Baccio's assistance. On his arrival at Florence he wrote to Messer Buoninsegni, who acted as intermediary at Rome between himself and the Pope in all things that concerned the façade: "Messer Domenico, I have come to Florence to see the model which Baccio has finished, and find it a mere child's plaything. If you think it best to have it sent, write to me. I leave again to-morrow for Carrara, where I have begun to make a model in clay with Grassa [a stone-hewer from Settignano]." Then he adds that, in the long run, he believes that he shall have to make the model himself, which distresses him on account of the Pope and the Cardinal Giulio. Lastly, he informs his correspondent that he has contracted with two separate companies for two hundred cartloads of Carrara marble.

An important letter to the same Domenico Buoninsegni, dated Carrara, May 2, 1517, proves that Michelangelo had become enthusiastic about his new design. "I have many things to say to you. So I beg you to take some patience when you read my words, because it is a matter of moment. Well, then, I feel it in me to make this façade of S. Lorenzo such that it shall be a mirror of architecture and of sculpture to all Italy. But the Pope and the Cardinal must decide at once whether they want to have it done or not. If they desire it, then they must come to some definite arrangement, either intrusting the whole to me on contract, and leaving me a free hand, or adopting some other plan which may occur to them, and about which I can form no idea." He proceeds at some length to inform Buoninsegni of various transactions regarding the purchase of marble, and the difficulties he encounters in procuring perfect blocks. His estimate for the costs of the whole façade is 35,000 golden ducats, and he offers to carry the work through for that sum in six years. Meanwhile he peremptorily demands an immediate settlement of the business, stating that he is anxious to leave Carrara. The vigorous tone of this document is unmistakable. It seems to have impressed his correspondents; for Buoninsegni replies upon the 8th of May that the Cardinal expressed the highest satisfaction at "the great heart he had for conducting the work of the façade." At the same time the Pope was anxious to inspect the model.

Leo, I fancy, was always more than half-hearted about the façade. He did not personally sympathise with Michelangelo's character; and, seeing what his tastes were, it is impossible that he can have really appreciated the quality of his genius. Giulio de' Medici, afterwards Pope Clement VII., was more in sympathy with Buonarroti both as artist and as man. To him we may with probability ascribe the impulse given at this moment to the project. After several visits to

Florence during the summer, and much correspondence with
the Medici through their Roman agent, Michelangelo went
finally, upon the 31st of August, to have the model completed under his own eyes by a workman in his native city.
It was carefully constructed of wood, showing the statuary
in wax-relief. Nearly four months were expended on this
miniature. The labour was lost, for not a vestige of it now
remains. Near the end of December he despatched his servant, Pietro Urbano, with the finished work to Rome. On
the 29th of that month, Urbano writes that he exposed the
model in Messer Buoninsegni's apartment, and that the Pope
and Cardinal were very well pleased with it. Buoninsegni
wrote to the same effect, adding, however, that folk said it
could never be finished in the sculptor's lifetime, and suggesting that Michelangelo should hire assistants from Milan,
where he, Buoninsegni, had seen excellent stonework in
progress at the Duomo.

Some time in January 1518, Michelangelo travelled to
Rome, conferred with Leo, and took the façade of S. Lorenzo on contract. In February he returned by way of Florence to Carrara, where the quarry-masters were in open
rebellion against him, and refused to carry out their contracts. This forced him to go to Genoa, and hire ships there
for the transport of his blocks. Then the Carraresi corrupted the captains of these boats, and drove Michelangelo to
Pisa (April 7), where he finally made an arrangement with
a certain Francesco Peri to ship the marbles lying on the
sea-shore at Carrara.

The reason of this revolt against him at Carrara may be
briefly stated. The Medici determined to begin working the
old marble quarries of Pietra Santa, on the borders of the
Florentine domain, and this naturally aroused the commer-
cial jealousy of the folk at Carrara. "Information," says
Condivi, "was sent to Pope Leo that marbles could be found
in the high-lands above Pietra Santa, fully equal in quality
and beauty to those of Carrara. Michelangelo, having been

sounded on the subject, chose to go on quarrying at Carrara
rather than to take those belonging to the State of Florence.
This he did because he was befriended with the Marchese
Alberigo, and lived on a good understanding with him. The
Pope wrote to Michelangelo, ordering him to repair to Pietra
Santa, and see whether the information he had received
from Florence was correct. He did so, and ascertained that
the marbles were very hard to work, and ill-adapted to their
purpose; even had they been of the proper kind, it would be
difficult and costly to convey them to the sea. A road of
many miles would have to be made through the mountains
with pick and crowbar, and along the plain on piles, since
the ground there was marshy. Michelangelo wrote all this to
the Pope, who preferred, however, to believe the persons
who had written to him from Florence. So he ordered him
to construct the road." The road, it may parenthetically be
observed, was paid for by the wealthy Wool Corporation of
Florence, who wished to revive this branch of Florentine
industry. "Michelangelo, carrying out the Pope's commands,
had the road laid down, and transported large quantities of
marbles to the sea-shore. Among these were five columns of
the proper dimensions, one of which may be seen upon the
Piazza di S. Lorenzo. The other four, forasmuch as the
Pope changed his mind and turned his thoughts elsewhere,
are still lying on the sea-beach. Now the Marquis of Carrara, deeming that Michelangelo had developed the quarries
at Pietra Santa out of Florentine patriotism, became his
enemy, and would not suffer him to return to Carrara for
certain blocks which had been excavated there: all of which
proved the source of great loss to Michelangelo."

When the contract with Francesco Pellicia was cancelled,
April 7, 1517, the project for developing the Florentine
stone-quarries does not seem to have taken shape. We must
assume, therefore, that the motive for this step was the
abandonment of the tomb. The *Ricordi* show that Michelangelo was still buying marbles and visiting Carrara down to

the end of February 1518. His correspondence from Pietra Santa and Serravezza, where he lived when he was opening the Florentine quarries of Monte Altissimo, does not begin, with any certainty, until March 1518. We have indeed one letter written to Girolamo del Bardella of Porto Venere upon the 6th of August, without date of year. This was sent from Serravezza, and Milanesi, when he first made use of it, assigned it to 1517. Gotti, following that indication, asserts that Michelangelo began his operations at Monte Altissimo in July 1517; but Milanesi afterwards changed his opinion, and assigned it to the year 1519. I believe he was right, because the first letter, bearing a certain date from Pietra Santa, was written in March 1518 to Pietro Urbano. It contains the account of Michelangelo's difficulties with the Carraresi, and his journey to Genoa and Pisa. We have, therefore, every reason to believe that he finally abandoned Carrara for Pietra Santa at the end of February 1518.

Pietra Santa is a little city on the Tuscan seaboard; Serravezza is a still smaller fortress-town at the foot of the Carrara mountains. Monte Altissimo rises above it; and on the flanks of that great hill lie the quarries Della Finocchiaja, which Michelangelo opened at the command of Pope Leo. It was not without reluctance that Michelangelo departed from Carrara, offending the Marquis Malaspina, breaking his contracts, and disappointing the folk with whom he had lived on friendly terms ever since his first visit in 1505. A letter from the Cardinal Giulio de' Medici shows that great pressure was put upon him. It runs thus: "We have received yours, and shown it to our Lord the Pope. Considering that all your doings are in favour of Carrara, you have caused his Holiness and us no small astonishment. What we heard from Jacopo Salviati contradicts your opinion. He went to examine the marble-quarries at Pietra Santa, and informed us that there are enormous quantities of stone, excellent in quality and easy to bring down. This being the case, some suspicion has arisen in our minds that you, for your own interests, are too partial to the quarries of Carrara, and want to depreciate those of Pietra Santa. This, of a truth, would be wrong in you, considering the trust we have always reposed in your honesty. Wherefore we inform you that, regardless of any other consideration, his Holiness wills that all the work to be done at S. Peter's or S. Reparata, or on the façade of S. Lorenzo, shall be carried out with marbles supplied from Pietra Santa, and no others, for the reasons above written. Moreover, we hear that they will cost less than those of Carrara; but, even should they cost more, his Holiness is firmly resolved to act as I have said, furthering the business of Pietra Santa for the public benefit of the city. Look to it, then, that you carry out in detail all that we have ordered without fail; for if you do otherwise, it will be against the expressed wishes of his Holiness and ourselves, and we shall have good reason to be seriously wroth with you. Our agent Domenico (Buoninsegni) is bidden to write to the same effect. Reply to him how much money you want, and quickly, banishing from your mind every kind of obstinacy."

Michelangelo began to work with his usual energy at roadmaking and quarrying. What he learned of practical business as engineer, architect, master of works, and paymaster during these years among the Carrara mountains must have been of vast importance for his future work. He was preparing himself to organise the fortifications of Florence and the Leonine City, and to crown S. Peter's with the cupola. Quarrying, as I have said, implied cutting out and rough-hewing blocks exactly of the right dimensions for certain portions of a building or a piece of statuary. The master was therefore obliged to have his whole plan perfect in his head before he could venture to order marble. Models, drawings made to scale, careful measurements, were necessary at each successive step. Day and night Buonarroti was at work; in the saddle early in the morning, among stone-cutters and road-makers; in the evening, studying, projecting, calculating, settling up accounts by lamplight.

VI

The narrative of Michelangelo's personal life and movements must here be interrupted in order to notice an event in which he took no common interest. The members of the Florentine Academy addressed a memorial to Leo X., requesting him to authorise the translation of Dante Alighieri's bones from Ravenna to his native city. The document was drawn up in Latin, and dated October 20, 1518. Among the names and signatures appended, Michelangelo's alone is written in Italian: "I, Michelangelo, the sculptor, pray the like of your Holiness, offering my services to the divine poet for the erection of a befitting sepulchre to him in some honourable place in this city." Nothing resulted from this petition, and the supreme poet's remains still rest beneath "the little cupola, more neat than solemn," guarded by Pietro Lombardi's half-length portrait.

Of Michelangelo's special devotion to Dante and the "Divine Comedy" we have plenty of proof. In the first place, there exist the two fine sonnets to his memory, which were celebrated in their author's lifetime, and still remain among the best of his performances in verse. It does not appear when they were composed. The first is probably earlier than the second; for below the autograph of the latter is written, "Messer Donato, you ask of me what I do not possess." The Donato is undoubtedly Donato Giannotti, with whom Michelangelo lived on very familiar terms at Rome about 1545. I will here insert my English translation of these sonnets:—

From heaven his spirit came, and, robed in clay,
  The realms of justice and of mercy trod:
  Then rose a living man to gaze on God,
  That he might make the truth as clear as day.

For that pure star, that brightened with his ray
   The undeserving nest where I was born,
   The whole wide world would be a prize to scorn;
   None but his Maker can due guerdon pay.
I speak of Dante, whose high work remains
   Unknown, unhonoured by that thankless brood,
   Who only to just men deny their wage.
Were I but he! Born for like lingering pains,
   Against his exile coupled with his good
   I'd gladly change the world's best heritage!

No tongue can tell of him what should be told,
   For on blind eyes his splendour shines too strong;
   'T were easier to blame those who wrought him wrong,
   Than sound his least praise with a mouth of gold.
He to explore the place of pain was bold,
   Then soared to God, to teach our souls by song;
   The gates heaven oped to bear his feet along,
   Against his just desire his country rolled.
Thankless I call her, and to her own pain
   The nurse of fell mischance; for sign take this,
   That ever to the best she deals more scorn;
Among a thousand proofs let one remain;
   Though ne'er was fortune more unjust than his,
   His equal or his better ne'er was born.

The influence of Dante over Buonarroti's style of composition impressed his contemporaries. Benedetto Varchi, in the proemium to a lecture upon one of Michelangelo's poems, speaks of it as "a most sublime sonnet, full of that antique purity and Dantesque gravity." Dante's influence over the great artist's pictorial imagination is strongly marked in the fresco of the Last Judgment, where Charon's boat, and Minos with his twisted tail, are borrowed direct from the *Inferno*. Condivi, moreover, informs us that the statues of the Lives Contemplative and Active upon the tomb of Julius were suggested by the Rachel and Leah of the *Purgatorio*. We also know that he filled a book with drawings illustrative of the "Divine Comedy." By a miserable accident this most precious volume, while in the possession of Antonio Montauti, the sculptor, perished at sea on a journey from Livorno to Rome.

But the strongest proof of Michelangelo's reputation as a learned student of Dante is given in Donato Giannotti's Dialogue upon the number of days spent by the poet during his journey through Hell and Purgatory. Luigi del Riccio, who was a great friend of the sculptor's, is supposed to have been walking one day toward the Lateran with Antonio Petreo. Their conversation fell upon Cristoforo Landino's theory that the time consumed by Dante in this transit was the whole of the night of Good Friday, together with the following day. While engaged in this discussion, they met Donato Giannotti taking the air with Michelangelo. The four friends joined company, and Petreo observed that it was a singular good fortune to have fallen that morning upon two such eminent Dante scholars. Donato replied: "With regard to Messer Michelangelo, you have abundant reason to say that he is an eminent Dantista, since I am acquainted with no one who understands him better and has a fuller mastery over his works." It is not needful to give a detailed account of Buonarroti's Dantesque criticism, reported in these dialogues, although there are good grounds for supposing them in part to represent exactly what Giannotti heard him say. This applies particularly to his able interpretation of the reason why Dante placed Brutus and Cassius in hell—not as being the murderers of a tyrant, but as having laid violent hands upon the sacred majesty of the Empire in the person of Cæsar. The narrative of Dante's journey through Hell and Purgatory, which is put into Michelangelo's mouth, if we are to believe that he really made it extempore and without book, shows a most minute knowledge of the *Inferno*.

VII

Michelangelo's doings at Serravezza can be traced with some accuracy during the summers of 1518 and 1519. An important letter to Buonarroto, dated April 2, 1518, proves that the execution of the road had not yet been decided on. He is impatient to hear whether the Wool Corporation has voted the necessary funds and appointed him to engineer it. "With regard to the construction of the road here, please tell Jacopo Salviati that I shall carry out his wishes, and he will not be betrayed by me. I do not look after any interests of my own in this matter, but seek to serve my patrons and my country. If I begged the Pope and Cardinal to give me full control over the business, it was that I might be able to conduct it to those places where the best marbles are. Nobody here knows anything about them. I did not ask for the commission in order to make money; nothing of the sort is in my head." This proves conclusively that much which has been written about the waste of Michelangelo's abilities on things a lesser man might have accomplished is merely sentimental. On the contrary, he was even accused of begging for the contract from a desire to profit by it. In another letter, of April 18, the decision of the Wool Corporation was still anxiously expected. Michelangelo gets impatient. "I shall mount my horse, and go to find the Pope and Cardinal, tell them how it is with me, leave the business here, and return to Carrara. The folk there pray for my return as one is wont to pray to Christ." Then he complains of the worthlessness and disloyalty of the stone-hewers he brought from Florence, and winds up with an angry postscript: "Oh, cursed a thousand times the day and hour when I left Carrara! This is the cause of my utter ruin. But I shall go back there soon. Nowadays it is a sin to do one's duty." On the 22nd of April the Wool Corporation assigned to Michelangelo a contract for the quarries, leaving him free to act as he thought best. Complaints follow about his workmen.

One passage is curious: "Sandro, he too has gone away from here. He stopped several months with a mule and a little mule in grand style, doing nothing but fish and make love. He cost me a hundred ducats to no purpose; has left a certain quantity of marble, giving me the right to take the blocks that suit my purpose. However, I cannot find among them what is worth twenty-five ducats, the whole being a jumble of rascally work. Either maliciously or through ignorance, he has treated me very ill."

Upon the 17th April 1517, Michelangelo had bought a piece of ground in Via Mozza, now Via S. Zanobi, at Florence, from the Chapter of S. Maria del Fiore, in order to build a workshop there. He wished, about the time of the last letter quoted, to get an additional lot of land, in order to have larger space at his command for the finishing of marbles. The negotiations went on through the summer of 1518, and on the 24th of November he records that the purchase was completed. Premises adapted to the sculptor's purpose were erected, which remained in Michelangelo's possession until the close of his life.

In August 1518 he writes to a friend at Florence that the road is now as good as finished, and that he is bringing down his columns. The work is more difficult than he expected. One man's life had been already thrown away, and Michelangelo himself was in great danger. "The place where we have to quarry is exceedingly rough, and the workmen are very stupid at their business. For some months I must make demands upon my powers of patience until the mountains are tamed and the men instructed. Afterwards we shall proceed more quickly. Enough, that I mean to do what I promised, and shall produce the finest thing that Italy has ever seen, if God assists me."

There is no want of heart and spirit in these letters. Irritable at moments, Michelangelo was at bottom enthusiastic, and, like Napoleon Buonaparte, felt capable of conquering the world with his sole arm.

In September we find him back again at Florence, where he seems to have spent the winter. His friends wanted him to go to Rome; they thought that his presence there was needed to restore the confidence of the Medici and to overpower calumniating rivals. In reply to a letter of admonition written in this sense by his friend Lionardo di Compagno, the saddle-maker, he writes: "Your urgent solicitations are to me so many stabs of the knife. I am dying of annoyance at not being able to do what I should like to do, through my ill-luck." At the same time he adds that he has now arranged an excellent workshop, where twenty statues can be set up together. The drawback is that there are no means of covering the whole space in and protecting it against the weather. This yard, encumbered with the marbles for S. Lorenzo, must have been in the Via Mozza.

Early in the spring he removed to Serravezza, and resumed the work of bringing down his blocked-out columns from the quarries. One of these pillars, six of which he says were finished, was of huge size, intended probably for the flanks to the main door at S. Lorenzo. It tumbled into the river, and was smashed to pieces. Michelangelo attributed the accident solely to the bad quality of iron which a rascally fellow had put into the lewis-ring by means of which the block was being raised. On this occasion he again ran considerable risk of injury, and suffered great annoyance. The following letter of condolence, written by Jacopo Salviati, proves how much he was grieved, and also shows that he lived on excellent terms with the Pope's right-hand man and counsellor: "Keep up your spirits and proceed gallantly with your great enterprise, for your honour requires this, seeing you have commenced the work. Confide in me; nothing will be amiss with you, and our Lord is certain to compensate you for far greater losses than this. Have no doubt upon this point, and if you want one thing more than another, let me know, and you shall be served immediately. Remember that your undertaking a work of such magnitude will lay our city under the deepest obligation, not only to yourself, but also to your family for ever. Great men, and of courageous spirit, take heart under adversities, and become more energetic."

A pleasant thread runs through Michelangelo's correspondence during these years. It is the affection he felt for his workman Pietro Urbano. When he leaves the young man behind him at Florence, he writes frequently, giving him advice, bidding him mind his studies, and also telling him to confess. It happened that Urbano fell ill at Carrara toward the end of August. Michelangelo, on hearing the news, left Florence and travelled by post to Carrara. Thence he had his friend transported on the backs of men to Serravezza, and after his recovery sent him to pick up strength in his native city of Pistoja. In one of the *Ricordi* he reckons the cost of all this at 33½ ducats.

While Michelangelo was residing at Pietra Santa in 1518, his old friend and fellow-worker, Pietro Rosselli, wrote to him from Rome, asking his advice about a tabernacle of marble which Pietro Soderini had ordered. It was to contain the head of S. John the Baptist, and to be placed in the Church of the Convent of S. Silvestro. On the 7th of June Soderini wrote upon the same topic, requesting a design. This Michelangelo sent in October, the execution of the shrine being intrusted to Federigo Frizzi. The incident would hardly be worth mentioning, except for the fact that it brings to mind one of Michelangelo's earliest patrons, the good-hearted Gonfalonier of Justice, and anticipates the coming of the only woman he is known to have cared for, Vittoria Colonna. It was at S. Silvestro that she dwelt, retired in widowhood, and here occurred those Sunday morning conversations of which Francesco d'Olanda has left us so interesting a record.

During the next year, 1519, a certain Tommaso di Dolfo invited him to visit Adrianople. He reminded him how, coming together in Florence, when Michelangelo lay there in hiding from Pope Julius, they had talked about the East, and he had expressed a wish to travel into Turkey. Tommaso di Dolfo dissuaded him on that occasion, because the ruler of the province was a man of no taste and careless about the arts. Things had altered since, and he thought there was a good opening for an able sculptor. Things, however, had altered in Italy also, and Buonarroti felt no need to quit the country where his fame was growing daily.

Considerable animation is introduced into the annals of Michelangelo's life at this point by his correspondence with jovial Sebastiano del Piombo. We possess one of this painter's letters, dating as early as 1510, when he thanks Buonarroti for consenting to be godfather to his boy Luciano; a second of 1512, which contains the interesting account of his conversation with Pope Julius about Michelangelo and Raffaello; and a third, of 1518, turning upon the rivalry between the two great artists. But the bulk of Sebastiano's gossipy and racy communications belongs to the period of thirteen years between 1520 and 1533; then it suddenly breaks off, owing to Michelangelo's having taken up his residence at Rome during the autumn of 1533. A definite rupture at some subsequent period separated the old friends. These letters are a mine of curious information respecting artistic life at Rome. They prove, beyond the possibility of doubt, that, whatever Buonarroti and Sanzio may have felt, their flatterers, dependants, and creatures cherished the liveliest hostility and lived in continual rivalry. It is somewhat painful to think that Michelangelo could have lent a willing ear to the malignant babble of a man so much inferior to himself in nobleness of nature—have listened when Sebastiano taunted Raffaello as "Prince of the Synagogue," or boasted that a picture of his own was superior to "the tapestries just come from Flanders." Yet Sebastiano was not the only friend to whose idle gossip the great sculptor indulgently stooped. Lionardo, the saddle-maker, was even more offensive. He writes, for instance, upon New Year's Day,

1519, to say that the Resurrection of Lazarus, for which Michelangelo had contributed some portion of the design, was nearly finished, and adds: "Those who understand art rank it far above Raffaello. The vault, too, of Agostino Chigi has been exposed to view, and is a thing truly disgraceful to a great artist, far worse than the last hall of the Palace. Sebastiano has nothing to fear."

We gladly turn from these quarrels to what Sebastiano teaches us about Michelangelo's personal character. The general impression in the world was that he was very difficult to live with. Julius, for instance, after remarking that Raffaello changed his style in imitation of Buonarroti, continued: " 'But he is terrible, as you see; one cannot get on with him.' I answered to his Holiness that your terribleness hurt nobody, and that you only seem to be terrible because of your passionate devotion to the great works you have on hand." Again, he relates Leo's estimate of his friend's character: "I know in what esteem the Pope holds you, and when he speaks of you, it would seem that he were talking about a brother, almost with tears in his eyes; for he has told me you were brought up together as boys" (Giovanni de' Medici and the sculptor were exactly of the same age), "and shows that he knows and loves you. But you frighten everybody, even Popes!" Michelangelo must have complained of this last remark, for Sebastiano, in a letter dated a few days later, reverts to the subject: "Touching what you reply to me about your terribleness, I, for my part, do not esteem you terrible; and if I have not written on this subject do not be surprised, seeing you do not strike me as terrible, except only in art—that is to say, in being the greatest master who ever lived: that is my opinion; if I am in error, the loss is mine." Later on, he tells us what Clement VII. thought: "One letter to your friend (the Pope) would be enough; you would soon see what fruit it bore; because I know how he values you. He loves you, knows your nature, adores your work, and tastes its quality as much as it is possible for man to do. Indeed, his appreciation is miraculous, and such as ought to give great satisfaction to an artist. He speaks of you so honourably, and with such loving affection, that a father could not say of a son what he does of you. It is true that he has been grieved at times by buzzings in his ear about you at the time of the siege of Florence. He shrugged his shoulders and cried, 'Michelangelo is in the wrong; I never did him any injury.'" It is interesting to find Sebastiano, in the same letter, complaining of Michelangelo's sensitiveness. "One favour I would request of you, that is, that you should come to learn your worth, and not stoop as you do to every little thing, and remember that eagles do not prey on flies. Enough! I know that you will laugh at my prattle; but I do not care; Nature has made me so, and I am not Zuan da Rezzo."

VIII

The year 1520 was one of much importance for Michelangelo. A *Ricordo* dated March 10 gives a brief account of the last four years, winding up with the notice that "Pope Leo, perhaps because he wants to get the façade at S. Lorenzo finished quicker than according to the contract made with me, and I also consenting thereto, sets me free . . . and so he leaves me at liberty, under no obligation of accounting to any one for anything which I have had to do with him or others upon his account." It appears from the draft of a letter without date that some altercation between Michelangelo and the Medici preceded this rupture. He had been withdrawn from Serravezza to Florence in order that he might plan the new buildings at S. Lorenzo; and the workmen of the Opera del Duomo continued the quarrying business in his absence. Marbles which he had excavated for S. Lorenzo were granted by the Cardinal de' Medici to the custodians of the cathedral, and no attempt was made to settle accounts. Michelangelo's indignation was roused by this indifference to his interests, and he complains in terms of extreme bitterness. Then he sums up all that he has lost, in addition to expected profits. "I do not reckon the wooden model for the said façade, which I made and sent to Rome; I do not reckon the period of three years wasted in this work; I do not reckon that I have been ruined (in health and strength perhaps) by the undertaking; I do not reckon the enormous insult put on me by being brought here to do the work, and then seeing it taken away from me, and for what reason I have not yet learned; I do not reckon my house in Rome, which I left, and where marbles, furniture and blocked-out statues have suffered to upwards of 500 ducats. Omitting all these matters, out of the 2300 ducats I received, only 500 remain in my hands."

When he was an old man, Michelangelo told Condivi that Pope Leo changed his mind about S. Lorenzo. In the often-quoted letter to the prelate he said: "Leo, not wishing me to work at the tomb of Julius, *pretended that he wanted to complete* the façade of S. Lorenzo at Florence." What was the real state of the case can only be conjectured. It does not seem that the Pope took very kindly to the façade; so the project may merely have been dropped through carelessness. Michelangelo neglected his own interests by not going to Rome, where his enemies kept pouring calumnies into the Pope's ears. The Marquis of Carrara, as reported by Lionardo, wrote to Leo that "he had sought to do you honour, and had done so to his best ability. It was your fault if he had not done more—the fault of your sordidness, your quarrelsomeness, your eccentric conduct." When, then, a dispute arose between the Cardinal and the sculptor about the marbles, Leo may have felt that it was time to break off from an artist so impetuous and irritable. Still, whatever faults of temper Michelangelo may have had, and however difficult he was to deal with, nothing can excuse the Medici for their wanton waste of his physical and mental energies at the height of their development.

On the 6th of April 1520 Raffaello died, worn out with

labour and with love, in the flower of his wonderful young manhood. It would be rash to assert that he had already given the world the best he had to offer, because nothing is so incalculable as the evolution of genius. Still we perceive now that his latest manner, both as regards style and feeling, and also as regards the method of execution by assistants, shows him to have been upon the verge of intellectual decline. While deploring Michelangelo's impracticability— that solitary, self-reliant, and exacting temperament which made him reject collaboration, and which doomed so much of his best work to incompleteness—we must remember that to the very end of his long life he produced nothing (except perhaps in architecture) which does not bear the seal and superscription of his fervent self. Raffaello, on the contrary, just before his death, seemed to be exhaling into a nebulous mist of brilliant but unsatisfactory performances. Diffusing the rich and facile treasures of his genius through a host of lesser men, he had almost ceased to be a personality. Even his own work, as proved by the Transfiguration, was deteriorating. The blossom was overblown, the bubble on the point of bursting; and all those pupils who had gathered round him, drawing like planets from the sun their lustre, sank at his death into frigidity and insignificance. Only Giulio Romano burned with a torrid sensual splendour all his own. Fortunately for the history of the Renaissance, Giulio lived to evoke the wonder of the Mantuan villa, that climax of associated crafts of decoration, which remains for us the symbol of the dream of art indulged by Raffaello in his Roman period.

These pupils of the Urbinate claimed now, on their master's death, and claimed with good reason, the right to carry on his great work in the Borgian apartments of the Vatican. The Sala de' Pontefici, or the Hall of Constantine, as it is sometimes called, remained to be painted. They possessed designs bequeathed by Raffaello for its decoration, and Leo, very rightly, decided to leave it in their hands.

Sebastiano del Piombo, however, made a vigorous effort to obtain the work for himself. His Raising of Lazarus, executed in avowed competition with the Transfiguration, had brought him into the first rank of Roman painters. It was seen what the man, with Michelangelo to back him up, could do. We cannot properly appreciate this picture in its present state. The glory of the colouring has passed away; and it was precisely here that Sebastiano may have surpassed Raffaello, as he was certainly superior to the school. Sebastiano wrote letter after letter to Michelangelo in Florence. He first mentions Raffaello's death, "whom may God forgive;" then says that the *"garzoni"* of the Urbinate are beginning to paint in oil upon the walls of the Sala de' Pontefici. "I pray you to remember me, and to recommend me to the Cardinal, and if I am the man to undertake the job, I should like you to set me to work at it; for I shall not disgrace you, as indeed I think I have not done already. I took my picture (the Lazarus) once more to the Vatican, and placed it beside Raffaello's (the Transfiguration), and I came without shame out of the comparison." In answer, apparently, to this first letter on the subject, Michelangelo wrote a humorous recommendation of his friend and gossip to the Cardinal Bernardo Dovizi da Bibbiena. It runs thus: "I beg your most reverend Lordship, not as a friend or servant, for I am not worthy to be either, but as a low fellow, poor and brainless, that you will cause Sebastian, the Venetian painter, now that Rafael is dead, to have some share in the works at the Palace. If it should seem to your Lordship that kind offices are thrown away upon a man like me, I might suggest that on some rare occasions a certain sweetness may be found in being kind even to fools, as onions taste well, for a change of food, to one who is tired of capons. You oblige men of mark every day. I beg your Lordship to try what obliging me is like. The obligation will be a very great one, and Sebastian is a worthy man. If, then, your kind offers are thrown away on me, they will not be so on Sebastian, for I am certain he will prove a credit to your Lordship."

In his following missives Sebastiano flatters Michelangelo upon the excellent effect produced by the letter. "The Cardinal informed me that the Pope had given the Hall of the Pontiffs to Raffaello's 'prentices, and they have begun with a figure in oils upon the wall, a marvellous production which eclipses all the rooms painted by their master, and proves that when it is finished, this hall will beat the record, and be the finest thing done in painting since the ancients. Then he asked if I had read your letter. I said, No. He laughed loudly, as though at a good joke, and I quitted him with compliments. Bandinelli, who is copying the Laocoon, tells me that the Cardinal showed him your letter, and also showed it to the Pope; in fact, nothing is talked about at the Vatican except your letter, and it makes everybody laugh." He adds that he does not think the hall ought to be committed to young men. Having discovered what sort of things they meant to paint there, battle-pieces and vast compositions, he judges the scheme beyond their scope. Michelangelo alone is equal to the task. Meanwhile, Leo, wishing to compromise matters, offered Sebastiano the great hall in the lower apartments of the Borgias, where Alexander VI. used to live, and where Pinturicchio painted—rooms shut up in pious horror by Julius when he came to occupy the palace of his hated and abominable predecessor. Sebastiano's reliance upon Michelangelo, and his calculation that the way to get possession of the coveted commission would depend on the latter's consenting to supply him with designs, emerge in the following passage: "The Cardinal told me that he was ordered by the Pope to offer me the lower hall. I replied that I could accept nothing without your permission, or until your answer came, which is not to hand at the date of writing. I added that, unless I were engaged to Michelangelo, even if the Pope commanded me to paint that hall, I would not do so, because I do not think myself inferior to

Raffaello's 'prentices, especially after the Pope, with his
own mouth, had offered me half of the upper hall; and anyhow, I do not regard it as creditable to myself to paint the
cellars, and they to have the gilded chambers. I said they
had better be allowed to go on painting. He answered that
the Pope had only done this to avoid rivalries. The men possessed designs ready for that hall, and I ought to remember
that the lower one was also a hall of the Pontiffs. My reply
was that I would have nothing to do with it; so that now
they are laughing at me, and I am so worried that I am
well-nigh mad." Later on he adds: "It has been my object, through you and your authority, to execute vengeance
for myself and you too, letting malignant fellows know
that there are other demigods alive beside Raffael da Urbino
and his 'prentices." The vacillation of Leo in this business,
and his desire to make things pleasant, are characteristic of
the man, who acted just in the same way while negotiating
with princes.

IX

When Michelangelo complained that he was "rovinato
per detta opera di San Lorenzo," he probably did not mean
that he was ruined in purse, but in health and energy. For
some while after Leo gave him his liberty, he seems to have
remained comparatively inactive. During this period the sacristy at S. Lorenzo and the Medicean tombs were probably in contemplation. Giovanni Cambi says that they were
begun at the end of March 1520. But we first hear something definite about them in a *Ricordo* which extends from
April 9 to August 19, 1521. Michelangelo says that on the
former of these dates he received money from the Cardinal
de' Medici for a journey to Carrara, whither he went and
stayed about three weeks, ordering marbles for "the tombs
which are to be placed in the new sacristy at S. Lorenzo.
And there I made out drawings to scale, and measured
models in clay for the said tombs." He left his assistant

Scipione of Settignano at Carrara as overseer of the work, and returned to Florence. On the 20th of July following he went again to Carrara, and stayed nine days. On the 16th of August the contractors for the blocks, all of which were excavated from the old Roman quarry of Polvaccio, came to Florence, and were paid for on account. Scipione returned on the 19th of August. It may be added that the name of Stefano, the miniaturist, who acted as Michelangelo's factotum through several years, is mentioned for the first time in this minute and interesting record.

That the commission for the sacristy came from the Cardinal Giulio, and not from the Pope, appears in the document I have just cited. The fact is confirmed by a letter written to Fattucci in 1523: "About two years have elapsed since I returned from Carrara, whither I had gone to purchase marbles for the tombs of the Cardinal." The letter is curious in several respects, because it shows how changeable through many months Giulio remained about the scheme; at one time bidding Michelangelo prepare plans and models, at another refusing to listen to any proposals; then warming up again, and saying that, if he lived long enough, he meant to erect the façade as well. The final issue of the affair was, that after Giulio became Pope Clement VII., the sacristy went forward, and Michelangelo had to put the sepulchre of Julius aside. During the pontificate of Adrian, we must believe that he worked upon his statues for that monument, since a Cardinal was hardly powerful enough to command his services; but when the Cardinal became Pope, and threatened to bring an action against him for moneys received, the case was altered. The letter to Fattucci, when carefully studied, leads to these conclusions.

Very little is known to us regarding his private life in the year 1521. We only possess one letter, relating to the purchase of a house. In October he stood godfather to the infant son of Niccolò Soderini, nephew of his old patron, the Gonfalonier.

This barren period is marked by only one considerable event—that is, the termination of the Cristo Risorto, or Christ Triumphant, which had been ordered by Metello Varj de' Porcari in 1514. The statue seems to have been rough-hewn at the quarries, packed up, and sent to Pisa on its way to Florence as early as December 1518, but it was not until March 1521 that Michelangelo began to occupy himself about it seriously. He then despatched Pietro Urbano to Rome with orders to complete it there, and to arrange with the purchaser for placing it upon a pedestal. Sebastiano's letters contain some references to this work, which enable us to understand how wrong it would be to accept it as a representative piece of Buonarroti's own handicraft. On the 9th of November 1520 he writes that his gossip, Giovanni da Reggio, "goes about saying that you did not execute the figure, but that it is the work of Pietro Urbano. Take good care that it should be seen to be from your hand, so that poltroons and babblers may burst." On the 6th of September 1521 he returns to the subject. Urbano was at this time resident in Rome, and behaving himself so badly, in Sebastiano's opinion, that he feels bound to make a severe report. "In the first place, you sent him to Rome with the statue to finish and erect it. What he did and left undone you know already. But I must inform you that he has spoiled the marble wherever he touched it. In particular, he shortened the right foot and cut the toes off; the hands too, especially the right hand, which holds the cross, have been mutilated in the fingers. Frizzi says they seem to have been worked by a biscuit-maker, not wrought in marble, but kneaded by some one used to dough. I am no judge, not being familiar with the method of stone-cutting; but I can tell you that the fingers look to me very stiff and dumpy. It is clear also that he has been peddling at the beard; and I believe my little boy would have done so with more sense, for it looks as though he had used a knife without a point to chisel the hair. This can easily be remedied, however. He has also spoiled one of the nostrils. A little more, and the whole nose would have been ruined, and only God could have restored it." Michelangelo apparently had already taken measures to transfer the Christ from Urbano's hands to those of the sculptor Federigo Frizzi. This irritated his former friend and workman. "Pietro shows a very ugly and malignant spirit after finding himself cast off by you. He does not seem to care for you or any one alive, but thinks he is a great master. He will soon find out his mistake, for the poor young man will never be able to make statues. He has forgotten all he knew of art, and the knees of your Christ are worth more than all Rome together." It was Sebastiano's wont to run babbling on this way. Once again he returns to Pietro Urbano. "I am informed that he has left Rome; he has not been seen for several days, has shunned the Court, and I certainly believe that he will come to a bad end. He gambles, wants all the women of the town, struts like a Ganymede in velvet shoes through Rome, and flings his cash about. Poor fellow! I am sorry for him since, after all, he is but young."

Such was the end of Pietro Urbano. Michelangelo was certainly unfortunate with his apprentices. One cannot help fancying he may have spoiled them by indulgence. Vasari, mentioning Pietro, calls him "a person of talent, but one who never took the pains to work."

Frizzi brought the Christ Triumphant into its present state, patching up what "the lither lad" from Pistoja had boggled. Buonarroti, who was sincerely attached to Varj, and felt his artistic reputation now at stake, offered to make a new statue. But the magnanimous Roman gentleman replied that he was entirely satisfied with the one he had received. He regarded and esteemed it "as a thing of gold," and, in refusing Michelangelo's offer, added that "this proved his noble soul and generosity, inasmuch as, when he had already made what could not be surpassed and was incomparable, he still wanted to serve his friend better." The

price originally stipulated was paid, and Varj added an autograph testimonial, strongly affirming his contentment with
the whole transaction.

These details prove that the Christ of the Minerva must
be regarded as a mutilated masterpiece. Michelangelo is
certainly responsible for the general conception, the pose,
and a large portion of the finished surface, details of which,
especially in the knees, so much admired by Sebastiano, and
in the robust arms, are magnificent. He designed the figure
wholly nude, so that the heavy bronze drapery which now
surrounds the loins, and bulges drooping from the left hip,
breaks the intended harmony of lines. Yet, could this
brawny man have ever suggested any distinctly religious
idea? Christ, victor over Death and Hell, did not triumph
by ponderosity and sinews. The spiritual nature of his conquest, the ideality of a divine soul disencumbered from the
flesh, to which it once had stooped in love for sinful man,
ought certainly to have been emphasised, if anywhere
through art, in the statue of a Risen Christ. Substitute a
scaling-ladder for the cross, and here we have a fine life-
guardsman, stripped and posing for some classic battle-
piece. We cannot quarrel with Michelangelo about the face
and head. Those vulgarly handsome features, that beard,
pomaded and curled by a barber's 'prentice, betray no signs
of his inspiration. Only in the arrangement of the hair,
hyacinthine locks descending to the shoulders, do we recognise the touch of the divine sculptor.

The Christ became very famous. Francis I. had it cast
and sent to Paris, to be repeated in bronze. What is more
strange, it has long been the object of a religious cult. The
right foot, so mangled by poor Pietro, wears a fine brass
shoe, in order to prevent its being kissed away. This almost
makes one think of Goethe's hexameter: "Wunderthätige
Bilder sind meist nur schlechte Gemälde." Still it must be
remembered that excellent critics have found the whole
work admirable. Gsell-Fels says: "It is his second Moses;

in movement and physique one of the greatest masterpieces; as a Christ-ideal, the heroic conception of a humanist." That last observation is just. We may remember that Vida was composing his *Christiad* while Frizzi was curling the beard of the Cristo Risorto. Vida always speaks of Jesus as *Heros*, and of God the Father as *Superum Pater Nimbipotens* or *Regnator Olympi*.

CHAPTER VIII

LEO X. expired upon the 1st day of December 1521. The vacillating game he played in European politics had just been crowned with momentary success. Some folk believed that the Pope died of joy after hearing that his Imperial allies had entered the town of Milan; others thought that he succumbed to poison. We do not know what caused his death. But the unsoundness of his constitution, overtaxed by dissipation and generous living, in the midst of public cares for which the man had hardly nerve enough, may suffice to account for a decease certainly sudden and premature. Michelangelo, born in the same year, was destined to survive him through more than eight lustres of the life of man.

Leo was a personality whom it is impossible to praise without reserve. The Pope at that time in Italy had to perform three separate functions. His first duty was to the Church. Leo left the See of Rome worse off than he found it: financially bankrupt, compromised by vague schemes set on foot for the aggrandisement of his family, discredited by many shameless means for raising money upon spiritual securities. His second duty was to Italy. Leo left the peninsula so involved in a mesh of meaningless entanglements, diplomatic and aimless wars, that anarchy and violence proved to be the only exit from the situation. His third duty was to that higher culture which Italy dispensed to Europe, and of which the Papacy had made itself the leading propagator. Here Leo failed almost as conspicuously as in all else he attempted. He debased the standard of art and literature by his ill-placed liberalities, seeking quick returns for careless expenditure, not selecting the finest spirits of his age for timely patronage, diffusing no lofty enthusiasm, but breeding round him mushrooms of mediocrity.

Nothing casts stronger light upon the low tone of Roman society created by Leo than the outburst of frenzy and execration which exploded when a Fleming was elected as his successor. Adrian Florent, belonging to a family surnamed Dedel, emerged from the scrutiny of the Conclave into the pontifical chair. He had been the tutor of Charles V., and this may suffice to account for his nomination. Cynical wits ascribed that circumstance to the direct and unexpected action of the Holy Ghost. He was the one foreigner who occupied the seat of S. Peter after the period when the metropolis of Western Christendom became an Italian principality. Adrian, by his virtues and his failings, proved that modern Rome, in her social corruption and religious indifference, demanded an Italian Pontiff. Single-minded and simple, raised unexpectedly by circumstances into his supreme position, he shut his eyes absolutely to art and culture, abandoned diplomacy, and determined to act only as the chief of the Catholic Church. In ecclesiastical matters Adrian was undoubtedly a worthy man. He returned to the original conception of his duty as the Primate of Occidental Christendom; and what might have happened had he lived to impress his spirit upon Rome, remains beyond the reach of calculation. Dare we conjecture that the sack of 1527 would have been averted?

Adrian reigned only a year and eight months. He had no time to do anything of permanent value, and was hardly powerful enough to do it, even if time and opportunity had been afforded. In the thunderstorm gathering over Rome and the Papacy, he represents that momentary lull during which men hold their breath and murmur. All the place-seekers, parasites, flatterers, second-rate artificers, folk of facile talents, whom Leo gathered round him, vented their rage against a Pope who lived sparsely, shut up the Belvedere, called statues "idols of the Pagans," and spent no farthing upon twangling lutes and frescoed chambers. Truly Adrian is one of the most grotesque and significant figures upon the page of modern history. His personal worth, his inadequacy to the needs of the age, and his incompetence to control the tempest loosed by Della Roveres, Borgias, and Medici around him, give the man a tragic irony.

After his death, upon the 23rd of September 1523, the Cardinal Giulio de' Medici was made Pope. He assumed the title of Clement VII. upon the 9th of November. The wits who saluted Adrian's doctor with the title of "Saviour of the Fatherland," now rejoiced at the election of an Italian and a Medici. The golden years of Leo's reign would certainly return, they thought; having no foreknowledge of the tragedy which was so soon to be enacted, first at Rome, and afterwards at Florence, Michelangelo wrote to his friend Topolino at Carrara: "You will have heard that Medici is made Pope; all the world seems to me to be delighted, and I think that here at Florence great things will soon be set on foot in our art. Therefore, serve well and faithfully."

II

Our records are very scanty, both as regards personal details and art-work, for the life of Michelangelo during the pontificate of Adrian VI. The high esteem in which he was held throughout Italy is proved by three incidents which may shortly be related. In 1522, the Board of Works for the cathedral church of S. Petronio at Bologna decided to complete the façade. Various architects sent in designs; among them Peruzzi competed with one in the Gothic style, and another in that of the Classical revival. Great differences of opinion arose in the city as to the merits of the rival plans, and the Board in July invited Michelangelo, through their secretary, to come and act as umpire. They promised to reward him magnificently. It does not appear that Michelangelo accepted the offer. In 1523, Cardinal Grimani, who was a famous collector of art-objects, wrote begging for some specimen of his craft. Grimani left it open to him "to choose material and subject; painting, bronze, or marble, according to his fancy." Michelangelo must have promised to fulfill the commission, for we have a letter from Grimani thanking him effusively. He offers to pay fifty ducats at the commencement of the work, and what Michelangelo thinks fit to demand at its conclusion: "for such is the excellence of your ability, that we shall take no thought of money-value." Grimani was Patriarch of Aquileja. In the same year, 1523, the Genoese entered into negotiations for a colossal statue of Andrea Doria, which they desired to obtain from the hand of Michelangelo. Its execution must have been seriously contemplated, for the Senate of Genoa banked 300 ducats for the purpose. We regret that Michelangelo could not carry out a work so congenial to his talent as this ideal portrait of the mighty Signor Capitano would have been; but we may console ourselves by reflecting that even his energies were not equal to all tasks imposed upon him. The real matter for lamentation is that they suffered so much waste in the service of vacillating Popes.

To the year 1523 belongs, in all probability, the last extant letter which Michelangelo wrote to his father. Lodovico was dissatisfied with a contract which had been drawn up on the 16th of June in that year, and by which a certain sum of money, belonging to the dowry of his late wife, was settled in reversion upon his eldest son. Michelangelo explains the tenor of the deed, and then breaks forth into the following bitter and ironical invective: "If my life is a nuisance to you, you have found the means of protecting yourself, and will inherit the key of that treasure which you say that I possess. And you will be acting rightly; for all Florence knows how mighty rich you were, and how I always robbed you, and deserve to be chastised. Highly will men think of you for this. Cry out and tell folk all you choose about me, but do not write again, for you prevent my working. What I have now to do is to make good all you have had from me during the past five-and-twenty years. I would rather not tell you this, but I cannot help it. Take care, and be on your guard against those whom it concerns you. A man dies but once, and does not come back again to patch up things ill done. You have put off till the death to do this. May God assist you!"

In another draft of this letter Lodovico is accused of going about the town complaining that he was once a rich man, and that Michelangelo had robbed him. Still, we must not take this for proved; one of the great artist's main defects was an irritable suspiciousness, which caused him often to exaggerate slights and to fancy insults. He may have attached too much weight to the grumblings of an old man, whom at the bottom of his heart he loved dearly.

III

Clement, immediately after his election, resolved on setting Michelangelo at work in earnest on the Sacristy. At the very beginning of January he also projected the building of the Laurentian Library, and wrote, through his Roman agent, Giovanni Francesco Fattucci, requesting to have two plans furnished, one in the Greek, the other in the Latin style. Michelangelo replied as follows: "I gather from your last that his Holiness our Lord wishes that I should furnish the design for the library. I have received no information, and do not know where it is to be erected. It is true that Stefano talked to me about the scheme, but I paid no heed. When he returns from Carrara I will inquire, and will do all that is in my power, *albeit architecture is not my profession.*" There is something pathetic in this reiterated assertion that his real art was sculpture. At the same time Clement wished to provide for him for life. He first proposed that Buonarroti should promise not to marry, and should enter into minor orders. This would have enabled him to enjoy some ecclesiastical benefice, but it would also have handed him over firmly bound to the service of the Pope. Circumstances already hampered him enough, and Michelangelo, who chose to remain his own master, refused. As Berni wrote: "Voleva far da se, non comandato." As an alternative, a pension was suggested. It appears that he only asked for fifteen ducats a month, and that his friend Pietro Gondi had proposed twenty-five ducats. Fattucci, on the 13th of January 1524, rebuked him in affectionate terms for his want of pluck, informing him that "Jacopo Salviati has given orders that Spina should be instructed to pay you a monthly provision of fifty ducats." Moreover, all the disbursements made for the work at S. Lorenzo were to be provided by the same agent in Florence, and to pass through Michelangelo's hands. A house was assigned him, free of rent, at S. Lorenzo, in order that he might be near his work. Henceforth he was in almost weekly correspondence with Giovanni Spina on affairs of business, sending in accounts and drawing money by means of his then trusted servant, Stefano, the miniaturist.

That Stefano did not always behave himself according to his master's wishes appears from the following characteristic letter addressed by Michelangelo to his friend Pietro Gondi: "The poor man, who is ungrateful, has a nature of this sort, that if you help him in his needs, he says that what you gave him came out of superfluities; if you put him in the way of doing work for his own good, he says you were obliged, and set him to do it because you were incapable; and all the benefits which he received he ascribes to the necessities of the benefactor. But when everybody can see that you acted out of pure benevolence, the ingrate waits until you make some public mistake, which gives him the opportunity of maligning his benefactor and winning credence, in order to free himself from the obligation under which he lies. This has invariably happened in my case. No one ever entered into relations with me—I speak of workmen—to whom I did not do good with all my heart. Afterwards, some trick of temper, or some madness, which they say is in my nature, which hurts nobody except myself, gives them an excuse for speaking evil of me and calumniating my character. Such is the reward of all honest men."

These general remarks, he adds, apply to Stefano, whom he placed in a position of trust and responsibility, in order to assist him. "What I do is done for his good, because I have undertaken to benefit the man, and cannot abandon him; but let him not imagine or say that I am doing it because of my necessities, for, God be praised, I do not stand in need of men." He then begs Gondi to discover what Stefano's real mind is. This is a matter of great importance to him for several reasons, and especially for this: "If I omitted to justify myself, and were to put another in his place, I should be published among the Piagnoni for the biggest traitor who ever lived, even though I were in the right."

We conclude, then, that Michelangelo thought of dismissing Stefano, but feared lest he should get into trouble with the powerful political party, followers of Savonarola, who bore the name of Piagnoni at Florence. Gondi must have patched the quarrel up, for we still find Stefano's name in the *Ricordi* down to April 4, 1524. Shortly after that date, Antonio Mini seems to have taken his place as Michelangelo's right-hand man of business. These details are not so insignificant as they appear. They enable us to infer that the Sacristy of S. Lorenzo may have been walled and roofed in before the end of April 1524; for, in an undated letter to Pope Clement, Michelangelo says that

Stefano has finished the lantern, and that it is universally admired. With regard to this lantern, folk told him that he would make it better than Brunelleschi's. "Different perhaps, but better, no!" he answered.

The letter to Clement just quoted is interesting in several respects. The boldness of the beginning makes one comprehend how Michelangelo was terrible even to Popes:—

"Most Blessed Father,—Inasmuch as intermediates are often the cause of grave misunderstandings, I have summoned up courage to write without their aid to your Holiness about the tombs at S. Lorenzo. I repeat, I know not which is preferable, the evil that does good, or the good that hurts. I am certain, mad and wicked as I may be, that if I had been allowed to go on as I had begun, all the marbles needed for the work would have been in Florence to-day, and properly blocked out, with less cost than has been expended on them up to this date; and they would have been superb, as are the others I have brought here."

After this he entreats Clement to give him full authority in carrying out the work, and not to put superiors over him. Michelangelo, we know, was extremely impatient of control and interference; and we shall see, within a short time, how excessively the watching and spying of busybodies worried and disturbed his spirits.

But these were not his only sources of annoyance. The heirs of Pope Julius, perceiving that Michelangelo's time and energy were wholly absorbed at S. Lorenzo, began to threaten him with a lawsuit. Clement, wanting apparently to mediate between the litigants, ordered Fattucci to obtain a report from the sculptor, with a full account of how matters stood. This evoked the long and interesting document which has been so often cited. There is no doubt whatever that Michelangelo acutely felt the justice of the Duke of Urbino's grievances against him. He was broken-hearted at seeming to be wanting in his sense of honour and duty. People, he says, accused him of putting the money which had been paid for the tomb out at usury, "living meanwhile at Florence and amusing himself." It also hurt him deeply to be distracted from the cherished project of his early manhood in order to superintend works for which he had no enthusiasm, and which lay outside his sphere of operation.

It may, indeed, be said that during these years Michelangelo lived in a perpetual state of uneasiness and anxiety about the tomb of Julius. As far back as 1518 the Cardinal Leonardo Grosso, Bishop of Agen, and one of Julius's executors, found it necessary to hearten him with frequent letters of encouragement. In one of these, after commending his zeal in extracting marbles and carrying on the monument, the Cardinal proceeds: "Be then of good courage, and do not yield to any perturbations of the spirit, for we put more faith in your smallest word than if all the world should say the contrary. We know your loyalty, and believe you to be wholly devoted to our person; and if there shall be need of aught which we can supply, we are willing, as we have told you on other occasions, to do so; rest then in all security of mind, because we love you from the heart, and desire to do all that may be agreeable to you." This good friend was dead at the time we have now reached, and the violent Duke Francesco Maria della Rovere acted as the principal heir of Pope Julius.

In a passion of disgust he refused to draw his pension, and abandoned the house at S. Lorenzo. This must have happened in March 1524, for his friend Leonardo writes to him from Rome upon the 24th: "I am also told that you have declined your pension, which seems to me mere madness, and that you have thrown the house up, and do not work. Friend and gossip, let me tell you that you have plenty of enemies, who speak their worst; also that the Pope and Pucci and Jacopo Salviati are your friends, and have plighted their troth to you. It is unworthy of you to break your word to them, especially in an affair of honour. Leave the matter of the tomb to those who wish you well, and who are able to set you free without the least encumbrance, and take care you do not come short in the Pope's work. Die first. And take the pension, for they give it with a willing heart." How long he remained in contumacy is not quite certain; apparently until the 29th of August. We have a letter written on that day to Giovanni Spina: "After I left you yesterday, I went back thinking over my affairs; and, seeing that the Pope has set his heart on S. Lorenzo, and how he urgently requires my service, and has appointed me a good provision in order that I may serve him with more convenience and speed; seeing also that not to accept it keeps me back, and that I have no good excuse for not serving his Holiness; I have changed my mind, and whereas I hitherto refused, I now demand it (*i.e.*, the salary), considering this far wiser, and for more reasons than I care to write; and, more especially, I mean to return to the house you took for me at S. Lorenzo, and settle down there like an honest man: inasmuch as it sets gossip going, and does me great damage not to go back there." From a *Ricordo* dated October 19, 1524, we learn in fact that he then drew his full pay for eight months.

IV

Since Michelangelo was now engaged upon the Medicean tombs at S. Lorenzo, it will be well to give some account of the several plans he made before deciding on the final scheme, which he partially executed. We may assume, I think, that the sacristy, as regards its general form and dimensions, faithfully represents the first plan approved by Clement. This follows from the rapidity and regularity with which the structure was completed. But then came the question of filling it with sarcophagi and statues. As early as November 28, 1520, Giulio de' Medici, at that time Cardinal, wrote from the Villa Magliana to Buonarroti, addressing him thus: "*Spectabilis vir, amice noster charissime.*" He says that he is pleased with the design for the chapel, and with the notion of placing the four tombs in the middle. Then he proceeds to make some sensible remarks upon the difficulty of getting these huge masses of statuary into the space provided for them. Michelangelo, as Heath Wilson has pointed out, very slowly acquired the sense of proportion on which technical architecture depends. His early sketches only show a feeling for mass and picturesque effect, and a strong inclination to subordinate the building to sculpture.

It may be questioned who were the four Medici for whom these tombs were intended. Cambi, in a passage quoted above, writing at the end of March 1520 (?), says that two were raised for Giuliano, Duke of Nemours, and Lorenzo, Duke of Urbino, and that the Cardinal meant one to be for himself. The fourth he does not speak about. It has been conjectured that Lorenzo the Magnificent and his brother Giuliano, fathers respectively of Leo and of Clement, were to occupy two of the sarcophagi; and also, with greater probability, that the two Popes, Leo and Clement, were associated with the Dukes.

Before 1524 the scheme expanded, and settled into a more definite shape. The sarcophagi were to support statue-portraits of the Dukes and Popes, with Lorenzo the Magnificent and his brother Giuliano. At their base, upon the ground, were to repose six rivers, two for each tomb, showing that each sepulchre would have held two figures. The rivers were perhaps Arno, Tiber, Metauro, Po, Taro, and Ticino. This we gather from a letter written to Michelangelo on the 23rd of May in that year. Michelangelo made designs to meet this plan, but whether the tombs were still detached from the wall does not appear. Standing inside the sacristy, it seems impossible that six statue-portraits and six river-gods on anything like a grand scale could have been crowded into the space, especially when we remember that there was to be an altar, with other objects described as ornaments—"gli altri ornamenti." Probably the Madonna and Child, with SS. Cosimo and Damiano, now extant in the chapel, formed an integral part of the successive schemes.

One thing is certain, that the notion of placing the tombs in the middle of the sacristy was soon abandoned. All the marble panelling, pilasters, niches, and so forth, which at present clothe the walls and dominate the architectural effect, are clearly planned for mural monuments. A rude sketch preserved in the Uffizi throws some light upon the intermediate stages of the scheme. It is incomplete, and was not finally adopted; but we see in it one of the four sides of the chapel, divided vertically above into three compartments, the middle being occupied by a Madonna, the two at the sides filled in with bas-reliefs. At the base, on sarcophagi or *cassoni*, recline two nude male figures. The space between these and the upper compartments seems to have been reserved for allegorical figures, since a colossal naked boy, ludicrously out of scale with the architecture and the recumbent figures, has been hastily sketched in. In architectural proportion and sculpturesque conception this design is very poor. It has the merit, however, of indicating a moment in the evolution of the project when the mural scheme had been adopted. The decorative details which surmount the composition confirm the feeling every one must have, that, in their present state, the architecture of the Medicean monuments remains imperfect.

In this process of endeavouring to trace the development of Michelangelo's ideas for the sacristy, seven original drawings at the British Museum are of the greatest importance. They may be divided into three groups. One sketch seems to belong to the period when the tombs were meant to be placed in the centre of the chapel. It shows a single facet of the monument, with two sarcophagi placed side by side and seated figures at the angles. Five are variations upon the mural scheme, which was eventually adopted. They differ considerably in details, proving what trouble the designer took to combine a large number of figures in a single plan. He clearly intended at some time to range the Medicean statues in pairs, and studied several types of curve for their sepulchral urns. The feature common to all of them is a niche, of door or window shape, with a powerfully indented architrave. Reminiscences of the design for the tomb of Julius are not infrequent; and it may be remarked, as throwing a side-light upon that irrecoverable project of his earlier manhood, that the figures posed upon the various spaces of architecture differ in their scale. Two belonging to this series are of especial interest, since we learn from them how he thought of introducing the rivers at the basement of the composition. It seems that he hesitated long about the employment of circular spaces in the framework of the marble panelling. These were finally rejected. One of the finest and most comprehensive of the drawings I am now describing contains a rough draft of a curved sarcophagus, with an allegorical figure reclining upon it, indicating the first conception of the Dawn. Another, blurred and indistinct, with clumsy architectural environment, exhibits two of these allegories, arranged much as we now see them at S. Lorenzo. A river-god, recumbent beneath the feet of a female statue, carries the eye down to the ground, and enables us to comprehend how these subordinate figures were wrought into the complex harmony of flowing lines he had imagined. The seventh study differs in conception from the rest; it stands alone. There are four handlings of what begins like a huge portal, and is gradually elaborated into an architectural scheme containing three great niches for statuary. It is powerful and simple in design, governed by semicircular arches—a feature which is absent from the rest.

All these drawings are indubitably by the hand of Michelangelo, and must be reckoned among his first free efforts to construct a working plan. The Albertina Collection at Vienna yields us an elaborate design for the sacristy, which appears to have been worked up from some of the rougher sketches. It is executed in pen, shaded with bistre, and belongs to what I have ventured to describe as office work. It may have been prepared for the inspection of Leo and the Cardinal. Here we have the sarcophagi in pairs, recumbent figures stretched upon a shallow curve inverted, colossal orders of a bastard Ionic type, a great central niche framing a seated Madonna, two male figures in side niches, suggestive of Giuliano and Lorenzo as they were at last conceived, four allegorical statues, and, to crown the whole structure, candelabra of a peculiar shape, with a central round, supported by two naked genii. It is difficult, as I have before observed, to be sure how much of the drawings executed in this way can be ascribed with safety to Michelangelo himself. They are carefully outlined, with the precision of a working architect; but the sculptural details bear the aspect of what may be termed a generic Florentine style of draughtsmanship.

Two important letters from Michelangelo to Fattucci, written in October 1525 and April 1526, show that he had then abandoned the original scheme, and adopted one which was all but carried into effect. "I am working as hard as I can, and in fifteen days I shall begin the other captain. Afterwards the only important things left will be the four rivers. The four statues on the sarcophagi, the four figures on the ground which are the rivers, the two captains, and Our Lady, who is to be placed upon the tomb at the head of the chapel; these are what I mean to do with my own hand. Of these I have begun six; and I have good hope of finishing them in due time, and carrying the others forward in part, which do not signify so much." The six he had begun are clearly the Dukes and their attendant figures of Day, Night, Dawn, Evening. The Madonna, one of his noblest works, came within a short distance of completion. SS. Cosimo and Damiano passed into the hands of Montelupo and Montorsoli. Of the four rivers we have only fragments in the shape of some exquisite little models. Where they could have been conveniently placed is difficult to imagine; possibly they were abandoned from a feeling that the chapel would be overcrowded.

v

According to the plan adopted in this book, I shall postpone such observations as I have to make upon the Medicean monuments until the date when Michelangelo laid down his chisel, and shall now proceed with the events of his life during the years 1525 and 1526.

He continued to be greatly troubled about the tomb of Julius II. The lawsuit instituted by the Duke of Urbino hung over his head; and though he felt sure of the Pope's powerful support, it was extremely important, both for his character and comfort, that affairs should be placed upon a satisfactory basis. Fattucci in Rome acted not only as Clement's agent in business connected with S. Lorenzo; he also was intrusted with negotiations for the settlement of the Duke's claims. The correspondence which passed between them forms, therefore, our best source of information for this period. On Christmas Eve in 1524 Michelangelo writes from Florence to his friend, begging him not to postpone a journey he had in view, if the only business which detained him was the trouble about the tomb. A pleasant air of manly affection breathes through this document, showing Michelangelo to have been unselfish in a matter which weighed heavily and daily on his spirits. How greatly he was affected can be inferred from a letter written to Giovanni Spina on the 19th of April 1525. While reading this, it must be remembered that the Duke laid his action for the recovery of a considerable balance, which he alleged to be due to him upon disbursements made for the monument. Michelangelo, on the contrary, asserted that he was out of pocket, as we gather from the lengthy report he forwarded in 1524 to Fattucci. The difficulty in the accounts seems to have arisen from the fact that payments for the Sistine Chapel and the tomb had been mixed up. The letter to Spina runs as follows: "There is no reason for sending a power of attorney about the tomb of Pope Julius, because I do not want to plead. They cannot bring a suit if I admit that I am in the wrong; so I assume that I have sued and lost, and have to pay; and this I am disposed to do, if I am able. Therefore, if the Pope will help me in the matter—and this would be the greatest satisfaction to me, seeing I am too old and ill to finish the work—he might, as intermediary, express his pleasure that I should repay what I have received for its performance, so as to release me from this burden, and to enable the relatives of Pope Julius to carry out the undertaking by any master whom they may choose to employ. In this way his Holiness could be of very great assistance to me. Of course I desire to reimburse as little as possible, always consistently with justice. His Holiness might employ some of my arguments, as, for instance, the time spent for the Pope at Bologna, and other times wasted without any compensation, according to the statements I have made in full to Ser Giovan Francesco (Fattucci). Directly the terms of restitution have been settled, I will engage my property, sell, and put myself in a position to repay the money. I shall then be able to think of the Pope's orders and to work; as it is, I can hardly be said to live, far less to work. There is no other way of putting an end to the affair more safe for myself, nor more agreeable, nor more certain to ease my mind. It can be done amicably without a lawsuit. I pray to God that the Pope may be willing to accept the mediation, for I cannot see that any one else is fit to do it."

Giorgio Vasari says that he came in the year 1525 for a short time as pupil to Michelangelo. In his own biography he gives the date, more correctly, 1524. At any rate, the period of Vasari's brief apprenticeship was closed by a journey which the master made to Rome, and Buonarroti placed the lad in Andrea del Sarto's workshop. "He left for Rome in haste. Francesco Maria, Duke of Urbino, was again molesting him, asserting that he had received 16,000 ducats to complete the tomb, while he stayed idling at Florence for his own amusement. He threatened that, if he did not attend to the work, he would make him suffer. So, when he arrived there, Pope Clement, who wanted to command his services, advised him to reckon with the Duke's agents, believing that, for what he had already done, he was rather creditor than debtor. The matter remained thus." We do not know when this journey to Rome took place. From a hint in the letter of December 24, 1524, to Fattucci, where Michelangelo observes that only he in person would be able to arrange matters, it is possible that we may refer it to the beginning of 1525. Probably he was able to convince, not only the Pope, but also the Duke's agents that he had acted with scrupulous honesty, and that his neglect of the tomb was due to circumstances over which he had no control, and which he regretted as acutely as anybody. There is no shadow of doubt that this was really the case. Every word written by Michelangelo upon the subject shows that he was heart-broken at having to abandon the long-cherished project.

Some sort of arrangement must have been arrived at. Clement took the matter into his own hands, and during the summer of 1525 amicable negotiations were in progress. On the 4th of September Michelangelo writes again to Fattucci, saying that he is quite willing to complete the tomb upon the same plan as that of the Pope Pius (now in the Church of S. Andrea della Valle)—that is, to adopt a mural system instead of the vast detached monument. This would take less time. He again urges his friend not to stay at Rome for the sake of these affairs. He hears that the plague is breaking out there. "And I would rather have you alive than my business settled. If I die before the Pope, I shall not have to settle any troublesome affairs. If I live, I am sure the Pope will settle them, if not now, at some other time. So come

back. I was with your mother yesterday, and advised her, in
the presence of Granacci and John the turner, to send for
you home."

While in Rome Michelangelo conferred with Clement
about the sacristy and library at S. Lorenzo. For a year after
his return to Florence he worked steadily at the Medicean
monuments, but not without severe annoyances, as appears
from the following to Fattucci: "The four statues I have
in hand are not yet finished, and much has still to be done
upon them. The four rivers are not begun, because the
marble is wanting, and yet it is here. I do not think it oppor-
tune to tell you why. With regard to the affairs of Julius,
I am well disposed to make the tomb like that of Pius in S.
Peter's, and will do so little by little, now one piece and
now another, and will pay for it out of my own pocket, if I
keep my pension and my house, as you promised me. I mean,
of course, the house at Rome, and the marbles and other
things I have there. So that, in fine, I should not have to
restore to the heirs of Julius, in order to be quit of the contract, anything which I have hitherto received; the tomb
itself, completed after the pattern of that of Pius, sufficing
for my full discharge. Moreover, I undertake to perform
the work within a reasonable time, and to finish the statues
with my own hand." He then turns to his present troubles
at Florence. The pension was in arrears, and busybodies annoyed him with interferences of all sorts. "If my pension
were paid, as was arranged, I would never stop working for
Pope Clement with all the strength I have, small though
that be, since I am old. At the same time I must not be
slighted and affronted as I am now, for such treatment
weighs greatly on my spirits. The petty spites I speak of
have prevented me from doing what I want to do these
many months; one cannot work at one thing with the hands,
another with the brain, especially in marble. 'Tis said here
that these annoyances are meant to spur me on; but I maintain that those are scurvy spurs which make a good steed jib.

I have not touched my pension during the past year, and struggle with poverty. I am left in solitude to bear my troubles, and have so many that they occupy me more than does my art; I cannot keep a man to manage my house through lack of means."

Michelangelo's dejection caused serious anxiety to his friends. Jacopo Salviati, writing on the 30th October from Rome, endeavoured to restore his courage. "I am greatly distressed to hear of the fancies you have got into your head. What hurts me most is that they should prevent your working, for that rejoices your ill-wishers, and confirms them in what they have always gone on preaching about your habits." He proceeds to tell him how absurd it is to suppose that Baccio Bandinelli is preferred before him. "I cannot perceive how Baccio could in any way whatever be compared to you, or his work be set on the same level as your own." The letter winds up with exhortations to work. "Brush these cobwebs of melancholy away; have confidence in his Holiness; do not give occasion to your enemies to blaspheme, and be sure that your pension will be paid; I pledge my word for it." Buonarroti, it is clear, wasted his time, not through indolence, but through allowing the gloom of a suspicious and downcast temperament—what the Italians call *accidia* —to settle on his spirits.

Skipping a year, we find that these troublesome negotiations about the tomb were still pending. He still hung suspended between the devil and the deep sea, the importunate Duke of Urbino and the vacillating Pope. Spina, it seems, had been writing with too much heat to Rome, probably urging Clement to bring the difficulties about the tomb to a conclusion. Michelangelo takes the correspondence up again with Fattucci on November 6, 1526. What he says at the beginning of the letter is significant. He knows that the political difficulties in which Clement had become involved were sufficient to distract his mind, as Julius once said, from any interest in "stones small or big." Well, the letter starts thus: "I know that Spina wrote in these days past to Rome very hotly about my affairs with regard to the tomb of Julius. If he blundered, seeing the times in which we live, I am to blame, for I prayed him urgently to write. It is possible that the trouble of my soul made me say more than I ought. Information reached me lately about the affair which alarmed me greatly. It seems that the relatives of Julius are very ill-disposed towards me. And not without reason.—The suit is going on, and they are demanding capital and interest to such an amount that a hundred of my sort could not meet the claims. This has thrown me into terrible agitation, and makes me reflect where I should be if the Pope failed me. I could not live a moment. It is that which made me send the letter alluded to above. Now, I do not want anything but what the Pope thinks right. I know that he does not desire my ruin and my disgrace."

He proceeds to notice that the building work at S. Lorenzo is being carried forward very slowly, and money spent upon it with increasing parsimony. Still he has his pension and his house; and these imply no small disbursements. He cannot make out what the Pope's real wishes are. If he did but know Clement's mind, he would sacrifice everything to please him. "Only if I could obtain permission to begin something either here or in Rome, for the tomb of Julius, I should be extremely glad; for, indeed, I desire to free myself from that obligation more than to live." The letter closes on a note of sadness: "If I am unable to write what you will understand, do not be surprised, for I have lost my wits entirely."

After this we hear nothing more about the tomb in Michelangelo's correspondence till the year 1531. During the intervening years Italy was convulsed by the sack of Rome, the siege of Florence, and the French campaigns in Lombardy and Naples. Matters only began to mend when Charles V. met Clement at Bologna in 1530, and established the affairs of the peninsula upon a basis which proved durable. That fatal lustre (1526-1530) divided the Italy of the Renaissance from the Italy of modern times with the abruptness of an Alpine watershed. Yet Michelangelo, aged fifty-one in 1526, was destined to live on another thirty-eight years, and, after the death of Clement, to witness the election of five successive Popes. The span of his life was not only extraordinary in its length, but also in the events it comprehended. Born in the mediæval pontificate of Sixtus IV., brought up in the golden days of Lorenzo de' Medici, he survived the Franco-Spanish struggle for supremacy, watched the progress of the Reformation, and only died when a new Church and a new Papacy had been established by the Tridentine Council amid states sinking into the repose of decrepitude.

VI

We must return from this digression and resume the events of Michelangelo's life in 1525.

The first letter to Sebastiano del Piombo is referred to April of that year. He says that a picture, probably the portrait of Anton Francesco degli Albizzi, is eagerly expected at Florence. When it arrived in May, he wrote again under the influence of generous admiration for his friend's performance: "Last evening our friend the Captain Cuio and certain other gentlemen were so kind as to invite me to sup with them. This gave me exceeding great pleasure, since it drew me forth a little from my melancholy, or shall we call it my mad mood. Not only did I enjoy the supper, which was most agreeable, but far more the conversation. Among the topics discussed, what gave me most delight was to hear your name mentioned by the Captain; nor was this all, for he still added to my pleasure, nay, to a superlative degree, by saying that, in the art of painting he held you to be sole and without peer in the whole world, and that so you were esteemed at Rome. I could not have been better pleased. You see that my judgment is confirmed; and so you must not deny that you are peerless, when I write it, since I have a crowd of witnesses to my opinion. There is a picture too of yours here, God be praised, which wins credence for me with every one who has eyes."

Correspondence was carried on during this year regarding the library at S. Lorenzo; and though I do not mean to treat at length about that building in this chapter, I cannot omit an autograph postscript added by Clement to one of his secretary's missives: "Thou knowest that Popes have no long lives; and we cannot yearn more than we do to behold the chapel with the tombs of our kinsmen, or at any rate to hear that it is finished. Likewise, as regards the library. Wherefore we recommend both to thy diligence. Meantime we will betake us (as thou saidst erewhile) to a wholesome patience, praying God that He may put it into thy heart to push the whole forward together. Fear not that either work to do or rewards shall fail thee while we live. Farewell, with the blessing of God and ours.—JULIUS."*

Michelangelo began the library in 1526, as appears from his *Ricordi*. Still the work went on slowly, not through his negligence, but, as we have seen, from the Pope's preoccupation with graver matters. He had a great many workmen in his service at this period, and employed celebrated masters in their crafts, as Tasso and Carota for wood-carving, Battista del Cinque and Ciapino for carpentry, upon the various fittings of the library. All these details he is said to have designed; and it is certain that he was considered responsible for their solidity and handsome appearance. Sebastiano, for instance, wrote to him about the benches: "Our Lord wishes that the whole work should be of carved walnut. He does not mind spending three florins more; for that is a trifle, if they are Cosimesque in style, I mean resemble the work done for the magnificent Cosimo." Michelangelo could not have been the solitary worker of legend and tradition. The nature of his present occupations rendered this

* Julius was the Pope's baptismal name.—ED.

impossible. For the completion of his achitectural works he needed a band of able coadjutors. Thus in 1526 Giovanni da Udine came from Rome to decorate the vault of the sacristy with frescoed arabesques. His work was nearly terminated in 1533, when some question arose about painting the inside of the lantern. Sebastiano, apparently in good faith, made the following burlesque suggestion: "For myself, I think that the Ganymede would go there very well; one could put an aureole about him, and turn him into a S. John of the Apocalypse when he is being caught up into the heavens." The whole of one side of the Italian Renaissance, its so-called neo-paganism, is contained in this remark.

While still occupied with thoughts about S. Lorenzo, Clement ordered Michelangelo to make a receptacle for the precious vessels and reliques collected by Lorenzo the Magnificent. It was first intended to place this chest, in the form of a ciborium, above the high altar, and to sustain it on four columns. Eventually, the Pope resolved that it should be a sacrarium, or cabinet for holy things, and that this should stand above the middle entrance door to the church. The chest was finished, and its contents remained there until the reign of the Grand Duke Pietro Leopoldo, when they were removed to the chapel next the old sacristy.

Another very singular idea occurred to his Holiness in the autumn of 1525. He made Fattucci write that he wished to erect a colossal statue on the piazza of S. Lorenzo, opposite the Stufa Palace. The giant was to surmount the roof of the Medicean Palace, with its face turned in that direction and its back to the house of Luigi della Stufa. Being so huge, it would have to be composed of separate pieces fitted together. Michelangelo speedily knocked this absurd plan on the head in a letter which gives a good conception of his dry and somewhat ponderous humour.

"About the Colossus of forty cubits, which you tell me is to go or to be placed at the corner of the loggia in the Medicean garden, opposite the corner of Messer Luigi della Stufa,

I have meditated not a little, as you bade me. In my opinion that is not the proper place for it, since it would take up too much room on the roadway. I should prefer to put it at the other, where the barber's shop is. This would be far better in my judgment, since it has the square in front, and would not encumber the street. There might be some difficulty about pulling down the shop, because of the rent. So it has occurred to me that the statue might be carved in a sitting position; the Colossus would be so lofty that if we made it hollow inside, as indeed is the proper method for a thing which has to be put together from pieces, the shop might be enclosed within it, and the rent be saved. And inasmuch as the shop has a chimney in its present state, I thought of placing a cornucopia in the statue's hand, hollowed out for the smoke to pass through. The head too would be hollow, like all the other members of the figure. This might be turned to a useful purpose, according to the suggestion made me by a huckster on the square, who is my good friend. He privily confided to me that it would make an excellent dovecote. Then another fancy came into my head, which is still better, though the statue would have to be considerably heightened. That, however, is quite feasible, since towers are built up of blocks; and then the head might serve as bell-tower to San Lorenzo, which is much in need of one. Setting up the bells inside, and the sound booming through the mouth, it would seem as though the Colossus were crying mercy, and mostly upon feast-days, when peals are rung most often and with bigger bells."

Nothing more is heard of this fantastic project; whence we may conclude that the irony of Michelangelo's epistle drove it out of the Pope's head.

CHAPTER IX

I

It lies outside the scope of this work to describe the series of events which led up to the sack of Rome in 1527. Clement, by his tortuous policy, and by the avarice of his administration, had alienated every friend and exasperated all his foes. The Eternal City was in a state of chronic discontent and anarchy. The Colonna princes drove the Pope to take refuge in the Castle of S. Angelo; and when the Lutheran rabble raised by Frundsberg poured into Lombardy, the Duke of Ferrara assisted them to cross the Po, and the Duke of Urbino made no effort to bar the passes of the Apennines. Losing one leader after the other, these ruffians, calling themselves an Imperial army, but being in reality the scum and offscourings of all nations, without any aim but plunder and ignorant of policy, reached Rome upon the 6th of May. They took the city by assault, and for nine months Clement, leaning from the battlements of Hadrian's Mausoleum, watched smoke ascend from desolated palaces and desecrated temples, heard the wailing of women and the groans of tortured men, mingling with the ribald jests of German drunkards and the curses of Castilian bandits. Roaming those galleries and gazing from those windows, he is said to have exclaimed in the words of Job: "Why died I not from the womb? why did I not give up the ghost when I came out of the belly?"

The immediate effect of this disaster was that the Medici lost their hold on Florence. The Cardinal of Cortona, with the young princes Ippolito and Alessandro de' Medici, fled from the city on the 17th of May, and a popular government was set up under the presidency of Niccolò Capponi.

During this year and the next, Michelangelo was at Florence; but we know very little respecting the incidents of his life. A *Ricordo* bearing the date April 29 shows the disturbed state of the town. "I record how, some days ago, Piero di Filippo Gondi asked for permission to enter the new sacristy at S. Lorenzo, in order to hide there certain goods belonging to his family, by reason of the perils in which we are now. To-day, upon the 29th of April 1527, he has begun to carry in some bundles, which he says are linen of his sisters; and I, not wishing to witness what he does or to know where he hides the gear away, have given him the key of the sacristy this evening."

There are only two letters belonging to the year 1527. Both refer to a small office which had been awarded to Michelangelo with the right to dispose of the patronage. He offered it to his favourite brother, Buonarroto, who does not seem to have thought it worth accepting.

The documents for 1528 are almost as meagre. We do not possess a single letter, and the most important *Ricordi* relate to Buonarroto's death and the administration of his property. He died of the plague upon the 2nd of July, to the very sincere sorrow of his brother. It is said that Michelangelo held him in his arms while he was dying, without counting the risk to his own life. Among the minutes of disbursements made for Buonarroto's widow and children after his burial, we find that their clothes had been destroyed because of the infection. All the cares of the family now fell on Michelangelo's shoulders. He placed his niece Francesca in a convent till the time that she should marry, repaid her dowry to the widow Bartolommea, and provided for the expenses of his nephew Lionardo.

For the rest, there is little to relate which has any bearing on the way in which he passed his time before the siege of Florence began. One glimpse, however, is afforded of his daily life and conversation by Benvenuto Cellini, who had settled in Florence after the sack of Rome, and was working in a shop he opened at the Mercato Nuovo. The episode is sufficiently interesting to be quoted. A Sienese gentleman had commissioned Cellini to make him a golden medal, to be worn in the hat. "The subject was to be Hercules wrenching the lion's mouth. While I was working at this piece, Michel Agnolo Buonarroti came oftentimes to see it. I had spent infinite pains upon the design, so that the attitude of the figure and the fierce passion of the beast were executed in quite a different style from that of any craftsman who had hitherto attempted such groups. This, together with the fact that the special branch of art was totally unknown to Michel Agnolo, made the divine master give such praises to my work that I felt incredibly inspired for further effort.

"Just then I met with Federigo Ginori, a young man of very lofty spirit. He had lived some years in Naples and being endowed with great charms of person and presence, had been the lover of a Neapolitan princess. He wanted to have a medal made with Atlas bearing the world upon his shoulders, and applied to Michel Agnolo for a design. Michel Agnolo made this answer: 'Go and find out a young goldsmith named Benvenuto; he will serve you admirably, and certainly he does not stand in need of sketches by me. However, to prevent your thinking that I want to save myself the trouble of so slight a matter, I will gladly sketch you something; but meanwhile speak to Benvenuto, and let him also make a model; he can then execute the better of the two designs.' Federigo Ginori came to me and told me what he wanted, adding thereto how Michel Agnolo had praised me, and how he had suggested I should make a waxen model while he undertook to supply a sketch. The words of that great man so heartened me, that I set myself to work at once with eagerness upon the model; and when I had finished it, a painter who was intimate with Michel Agnolo, called Giuliano Bugiardini, brought me the drawing of Atlas. On the same occasion I showed Giuliano my little model in wax, which was very different from Michel Agnolo's drawing; and Federigo, in concert with Bugiardini, agreed that I should work upon my model. So I took it in hand, and when Michel Agnolo saw it, he praised me to the skies."

The courtesy shown by Michelangelo on this occasion to Cellini may be illustrated by an inedited letter addressed to him from Vicenza. The writer was Valerio Belli, who describes himself as a cornelian-cutter. He reminds the sculptor of a promise once made to him in Florence of a design for an engraved gem. A remarkably fine stone has just come into his hands, and he should much like to begin to work upon it. These proofs of Buonarroti's liberality to brother artists are not unimportant, since he was unjustly accused during his lifetime of stinginess and churlishness.

II

At the end of the year 1528 it became clear to the Florentines that they would have to reckon with Clement VII. As early as August 18, 1527, France and England leagued together, and brought pressure upon Charles V., in whose name Rome had been sacked. Negotiations were proceeding, which eventually ended in the peace of Barcelona (June 20, 1529), whereby the Emperor engaged to sacrifice the Republic to the Pope's vengeance. It was expected that the remnant of the Prince of Orange's army would be marched up to besiege the town. Under the anxiety caused by these events, the citizens raised a strong body of militia, enlisted Malatesta Baglioni and Stefano Colonna as generals, and began to take measures for strengthening the defences. What may be called the War Office of the Florentine Republic bore the title of Dieci della Guerra, or the Ten. It was their duty to watch over and provide for all the interests of the commonwealth in military matters, and now at this juncture serious measures had to be taken for putting the city in a state of defence. Already in the year 1527, after the expulsion of the Medici, a subordinate board had been created, to whom very considerable executive and administrative faculties were delegated. This board, called the Nove della Milizia, or the Nine, were empowered to enrol all the burghers under arms, and to take charge of the walls, towers, bastions, and other fortifications. It was also within their competence to cause the destruction of buildings, and to compensate the evicted proprietors at a valuation which they fixed themselves. In the spring of 1529 the War Office decided to gain the services of Michelangelo, not only because he was the most eminent architect of his age in Florence, but also because the Buonarroti family had always been adherents of the Medicean party, and the Ten judged that his appointment to a place on the Nove di Milizia would be popular with the democracy. The patent conferring this office upon him, together with full authority over the work of fortification, was issued on the 6th of April. Its terms were highly complimentary. "Considering the genius and practical attainments of Michelangelo di Lodovico Buonarroti, our citizen, and knowing how excellent he is in architecture, beside his other most singular talents in the liberal arts, by virtue whereof the common consent of men regards him as unsurpassed by any masters of our times; and, moreover, being assured that in love and affection toward the country he is the equal of any other good and loyal burgher; bearing in mind, too, the labour he has undergone and the diligence he has displayed, gratis and of his free will, in the said work (of fortification) up to this day; and wishing to employ his industry and energies to the like effect in future; we, of our motion and initiative, do appoint him to be governor and procurator-general over the construction and fortification of the city walls, as well as every other sort of defensive operation and munition for the town of Florence, for one year certain, beginning with the present date; adding thereto full authority over all persons in respect to the said work of reparation or pertaining to it." From this preamble it appears that Michelangelo had been already engaged in volunteer service connected with the defence of Florence. A stipend of one golden florin per diem was fixed by the same deed; and upon the 22nd of April following a payment of thirty florins was decreed, for one month's salary, dating from the 6th of April.

If the Government thought to gain popular sympathy by Michelangelo's appointment, they made the mistake of alienating the aristocracy. It was the weakness of Florence at this momentous crisis in her fate, to be divided into parties, political, religious, social; whose internal jealousies deprived her of the strength which comes alone from unity. When Giambattista Busini wrote that interesting series of letters to Benedetto Varchi from which the latter drew important materials for his annals of the siege, he noted this fact. "Envy must always be reckoned as of some account in republics, especially when the nobles form a considerable element, as in ours: for they were angry, among other matters, to see a Carducci made Gonfalonier, Michelangelo a member of the Nine, a Cei or a Giugni elected to the Ten."

Michelangelo had scarcely been chosen to control the general scheme for fortifying Florence, when the Signory began to consider the advisability of strengthening the citadels of Pisa and Livorno, and erecting lines along the Arno. Their commissary at Pisa wrote urging the necessity of Buonarroti's presence on the spot. In addition to other pressing needs, the Arno, when in flood, threatened the ancient fortress of the city. Accordingly we find that Michelangelo went to Pisa on the 5th of June, and that he stayed there over the 13th, returning to Florence perhaps upon the 17th of the month. The commissary, who spent several days in conferring with him and in visiting the banks of the Arno, was perturbed in mind because Michelangelo refused to exchange the inn where he alighted for an apartment in the official residence. This is very characteristic of the artist. We shall soon find him, at Ferrara, refusing to quit his hostelry for the Duke's palace, and, at Venice, hiring a remote lodging on the Giudecca in order to avoid the hospitality of S. Mark.

An important part of Michelangelo's plan for the fortification of Florence was to erect bastions covering the hill of S. Miniato. Any one who stands upon the ruined tower of the church there will see at a glance that S. Miniato is the key to the position for a beleaguering force; and "if the enemy once obtained possession of the hill, he would become immediately master of the town." It must, I think, have been at this spot that Buonarroti was working before he received the appointment of controller-general of the works. Yet he found some difficulty in persuading the rulers of the state that his plan was the right one. Busini, using information supplied by Michelangelo himself at Rome in 1549, speaks as follows: "Whatever the reason may have been, Niccolò Capponi, while he was Gonfalonier, would not allow the hill of S. Miniato to be fortified, and Michelangelo, who is a man of absolute veracity, tells me that he had great trouble in convincing the other members of the Government, but that he could never convince Niccolò. However, he began the work, in the way you know, with those fascines of tow. But Niccolò made him abandon it, and sent him to another post; and when he was elected to the Nine, they despatched him twice or thrice outside the city. Each time, on his return, he found the hill neglected, whereupon he complained, feeling this a blot upon his reputation and an insult to his magistracy. Eventually, the works went on, until, when the besieging army arrived, they were tenable."

Michelangelo had hitherto acquired no practical acquaintance with the art of fortification. That the system of defence by bastions was an Italian invention (although Albert Dürer first reduced it to written theory in his book of 1527, suggesting improvements which led up to Vauban's method) is a fact acknowledged by military historians. But it does not appear that Michelangelo did more than carry out defensive operations in the manner familiar to his predecessors. Indeed, we shall see that some critics found reason to blame him for want of science in the construction of his outworks. When, therefore, a difference arose between the controller-general of defences and the Gonfalonier upon this question of strengthening S. Miniato, it was natural that the War Office should have thought it prudent to send their chief officer to the greatest authority upon fortification then alive in Italy. This was the Duke of Ferrara. Busini must serve as our text in the first instance upon this point. "Michelangelo says that, when neither Niccolò Capponi nor Baldassare Carducci would agree to the outworks at S. Miniato, he convinced all the leading men except Niccolò of their necessity, showing that Florence could not hold out a single day without them. Accordingly he began to throw up bastions with fascines of tow; but the result was far from perfect, as he himself confessed. Upon this, the Ten resolved to send him to Ferrara to inspect that renowned work of defence. Thither accordingly he went; nevertheless, he believes that Niccolò did this in order to get him out of the way, and to prevent the construction of the bastion. In proof thereof he adduces the fact that, upon his return, he found the whole work interrupted."

Furnished with letters to the Duke, and with special missives from the Signory and the Ten to their envoy, Galeotto Giugni, Michelangelo left Florence for Ferrara after the 28th of July, and reached it on the 2nd of August. He refused, as Giugni writes with some regret, to abandon his inn, but was personally conducted with great honour by the Duke all round the walls and fortresses of Ferrara. On what day he quitted that city, and whither he went immediately after his departure, is uncertain. The Ten wrote to Giugni on the 8th of August, saying that his presence was urgently required at Florence, since the work of fortification was going on apace, "a multitude of men being employed, and no respect being paid to feast-days and holidays." It would also seem that, toward the close of the month, he was expected at Arezzo, in order to survey and make suggestions on the defences of the city.

These points are not insignificant, since we possess a *Ricordo* by Michelangelo, written upon an unfinished letter bearing the date "Venice, September 10," which has been taken to imply that he had been resident in Venice fourteen days—that is, from the 28th of August. None of his contemporaries or biographers mention a visit to Venice at the end of August 1529. It has, therefore, been conjectured that he went there after leaving Ferrara, but that his mission was one of a very secret nature. This seems inconsistent with the impatient desire expressed by the War Office for his return to Florence after the 8th of August. Allowing for exchange of letters and rate of travelling, Michelangelo could not have reached home much before the 15th. It is also inconsistent with the fact that he was expected in Arezzo at the beginning of September. I shall have to return later on to the *Ricordo* in question, which has an important bearing on the next and most dramatic episode in his biography.

III

Michelangelo must certainly have been at Florence soon after the middle of September. One of those strange panics to which he was constitutionally subject, and which impelled him to act upon a suddenly aroused instinct, came now to interrupt his work at S. Miniato, and sent him forth into outlawry. It was upon the 21st of September that he fled from Florence, under circumstances which have given considerable difficulty to his biographers. I am obliged to disentangle the motives and to set forth the details of this escapade, so far as it is possible for criticism to connect them into a coherent narrative. With this object in view, I will begin by translating what Condivi says upon the subject.

"Michelangelo's sagacity with regard to the importance of S. Miniato guaranteed the safety of the town, and proved a source of great damage to the enemy. Although he had taken care to secure the position, he still remained at his post there, in case of accidents; and after passing some six months, rumours began to circulate among the soldiers about expected treason. Buonarroti, then, noticing these reports, and being also warned by certain officers who were his friends, approached the Signory, and laid before them what he had heard and seen. He explained the danger hanging over the city, and told them there was still time to provide against it, if they would. Instead of receiving thanks for this service, he was abused, and rebuked as being timorous and too suspicious. The man who made him this answer would have done better had he opened his ears to good advice; for when the Medici returned he was beheaded, whereas he might have kept himself alive. When Michelangelo perceived how little his words were worth, and in what certain peril the city stood, he caused one of the gates to be opened, by the authority which he possessed, and went forth with two of his comrades, and took the road for Venice."

As usual with Condivi, this paragraph gives a general and yet substantially accurate account of what really took place. The decisive document, however, which throws light upon Michelangelo's mind in the transaction, is a letter written by him from Venice to his friend Battista della Palla on the 25th of September. Palla, who was an agent for Francis I. in works of Italian art, antiques, and bric-à-brac, had long purposed a journey into France; and Michelangelo, considering the miserable state of Italian politics, agreed to join him. These explanations will suffice to make the import of Michelangelo's letter clear.

"Battista, dearest friend, I left Florence, as I think you know, meaning to go to France. When I reached Venice, I inquired about the road, and they told me I should have to pass through German territory, and that the journey is both perilous and difficult. Therefore I thought it well to ask you, at your pleasure, whether you are still inclined to go, and to beg you; and so I entreat you, let me know, and say where you want me to wait for you, and we will travel together. I left home without speaking to any of my friends, and in great confusion. You know that I wanted in any case to go to France, and often asked for leave, but did not get it. Nevertheless I was quite resolved, and without any sort of fear, to see the end of the war out first. But on Tuesday morning, September 21, a certain person came out by the gate at S. Niccolò, where I was attending to the bastions, and whispered in my ear that, if I meant to save my life, I must not stay at Florence. He accompanied me home, dined there, brought me horses, and never left my side till he got me outside the city, declaring that this was my salvation. Whether God or the devil was the man, I do not know.

"Pray answer the questions in this letter as soon as possible, because I am burning with impatience to set out. If you have changed your mind, and do not care to go, still let me know, so that I may provide as best I can for my own journey."

What appears manifest from this document is that Michelangelo was decoyed away from Florence by some one, who, acting on his sensitive nervous temperament, persuaded him that his life was in danger. Who the man was we do not know, but he must have been a person delegated by those who had a direct interest in removing Buonarroti from the place. If the controller-general of the defences already scented treason in the air, and was communicating his suspicions to the Signory, Malatesta Baglioni, the arch-traitor, who afterwards delivered Florence over for a price to Clement, could not but have wished to frighten him away.

From another of Michelangelo's letters we learn that he carried 3000 ducats in specie with him on the journey. It is unlikely that he could have disposed so much cash upon his person. He must have had companions.

Talking with Michelangelo in 1549—that is, twenty years after the event—Busini heard from his lips this account of the flight. "I asked Michelangelo what was the reason of his departure from Florence. He spoke as follows: 'I was one of the Nine when the Florentine troops mustered within our lines under Malatesta Baglioni and Mario Orsini and the other generals: whereupon the Ten distributed the men along the walls and bastions, assigning to each captain his own post, with victuals and provisions; and among the rest, they gave eight pieces of artillery to Malatesta for the defence of part of the bastions at S. Miniato. He did not, however, mount these guns within the bastions, but below them, and set no guard.' Michelangelo, as architect and magistrate, having to inspect the lines at S. Miniato, asked Mario Orsini how it was that Malatesta treated his artillery so carelessly. The latter answered: 'You must know that the men of his house are all traitors, and in time he too will betray this town.' These words inspired him with such terror that he was obliged to fly, impelled by dread lest the city should come to misfortune, and he together with it. Having thus resolved, he found Rinaldo Corsini, to whom he communicated his thought, and Corsini replied lightly: 'I will go with you.' So they mounted horse with a sum of money, and road to the Gate of Justice, where the guards would not let them pass. While waiting there, some one sung out: 'Let him by, for he is of the Nine, and it is Michelangelo.' So they went forth, three on horseback, he, Rinaldo, and that man of his who never left him. They came to Castelnuovo (in the Garfagnana), and heard that Tommaso Soderini and Niccolò Capponi were staying there. Michelangelo refused to go and see them, but Rinaldo went, and when he came back to Florence, as I shall relate, he reported how Niccolò had said to him: 'O Rinaldo, I dreamed to-night that Lorenzo Zampalochi had been made Gonfalonier;' alluding to Lorenzo Giacomini, who had a swollen leg, and had been his adversary in the Ten. Well, they took the road for Venice; but when they came to Polesella, Rinaldo proposed to push on to Ferrara and have an interview with Galeotto Giugni. This he did, and Michelangelo awaited him, for so he promised. Messer Galeotto, who was spirited and sound of heart, wrought so with Rinaldo that he persuaded him to turn back to Florence. But Michelangelo pursued his journey to Venice, where he took a house, intending in due season to travel into France."

Varchi follows this report pretty closely, except that he represents Rinaldo Corsini as having strongly urged him to take flight, "affirming that the city in a few hours, not to say days, would be in the hands of the Medici." Varchi adds that Antonio Mini rode in company with Michelangelo, and, according to his account of the matter, the three men came together to Ferrara. There the Duke offered hospitality to Michelangelo, who refused to exchange his inn for the palace, but laid all the cash he carried with him at the disposition of his Excellency.

Segni, alluding briefly to this flight of Michelangelo from Florence, says that he arrived at Castelnuovo with Rinaldo Corsini, and that what they communicated to Niccolò Capponi concerning the treachery of Malatesta and the state of the city, so affected the ex-Gonfalonier that he died of a fever after seven days. Nardi, an excellent authority on all that concerns Florence during the siege, confirms the account that Michelangelo left his post together with Corsini under a panic; "by common agreement, or through fear of war, as man's fragility is often wont to do." Vasari, who in his account of this episode seems to have had Varchi's narrative under his eyes, adds a trifle of information, to the effect that Michelangelo was accompanied upon his flight, not only by Antonio Mini, but also by his old friend Piloto. It may be worth adding that while reading in the Archivio Buonarroti, I discovered two letters from a friend named Piero Paesano addressed to Michelangelo on January 1, 1530, and April 21, 1532, both of which speak of his having "fled from Florence." The earlier plainly says: "I heard from Santi Quattro (the Cardinal, probably) that you have left Florence in order to escape from the annoyance and also from the evil fortune of the war in which the country is engaged." These letters, which have not been edited, and the first of which is important, since it was sent to Michelangelo in Florence, help to prove that Michelangelo's friends believed he had run away from Florence.

It was necessary to enter into these particulars, partly in order that the reader may form his own judgment of the motives which prompted Michelangelo to desert his official post at Florence, and partly because we have now to consider the *Ricordo* above mentioned, with the puzzling date, September 10. This document is a note of expenses incurred during a residence of fourteen days at Venice. It runs as follows:—

"Honoured Sir. In Venice, this tenth day of September . . . . . Ten ducats to Rinaldo Corsini. Five ducats to Messer Loredan for the rent of the house. Seventeen lire for the stockings of Antonio (Mini, perhaps). For two stools, a table to eat on, and a coffer, half a ducat. Eight soldi for straw. Forty soldi for the hire of the bed. Ten lire to the man (*fante*) who came from Florence. Three ducats to Bondino for the journey to Venice with boats. Twenty soldi to Piloto for a pair of shoes. Fourteen days' board in Venice, twenty lire."

It has been argued from the date of the unfinished letter below which these items are jotted down, that Michelangelo must have been in Venice early in September, before his flight from Florence at the end of that month. But whatever weight we may attach to this single date, there is no corroborative proof that he travelled twice to Venice, and everything in the *Ricordo* indicates that it refers to the period of his flight from Florence. The sum paid to Corsini comes first, because it must have been disbursed when that man broke the journey at Ferrara. Antonio Mini and Piloto are both mentioned: a house has been engaged, and furnished with Michelangelo's usual frugality, as though he contemplated a residence of some duration. All this confirms Busini, Varchi, Segni, Nardi, and Vasari in the general outlines of their reports. I am of opinion that, unassisted by further evidence, the *Ricordo*, in spite of its date, will not bear out Gotti's view that Michelangelo sought Venice on a privy mission at the end of August 1529. He was not likely to have been employed as ambassador extraordinary; the Signory required his services at home; and after Ferrara, Venice had little of importance to show the controller-general of defences in the way of earthworks and bastions.

IV

Varchi says that Michelangelo, when he reached Venice, "wishing to avoid visits and ceremonies, of which he was the greatest enemy, and in order to live alone, according to his custom, far away from company, retired quietly to the Giudecca; but the Signory, unable to ignore the advent of so eminent a man, sent two of their first noblemen to visit him in the name of the Republic, and to offer kindly all things which either he or any persons of his train might stand in need of. This public compliment set forth the greatness of his fame as artist, and showed in what esteem the arts are held by their magnificent and most illustrious lordships." Vasari adds that the Doge, whom he calls Gritti, gave him commission to design a bridge for the Rialto, marvellous alike in its construction and its ornament.

Meanwhile the Signory of Florence issued a decree of outlawry against thirteen citizens who had quitted the territory without leave. It was promulgated on the 30th of September, and threatened them with extreme penalties if they failed to appear before the 8th of October. On the 7th of October a second decree was published, confiscating the property of numerous exiles. But this document does not contain the name of Michelangelo; and by a third decree, dated November 16, it appears that the Government were satisfied with depriving him of his office and stopping his pay. We gather indeed, from what Condivi and Varchi relate, that they displayed great eagerness to get him back, and corresponded to this intent with their envoy at Ferrara. Michelangelo's flight from Florence seemed a matter of sufficient importance to be included in the despatches of the French ambassador resident at Venice. Lazare de Baïf, knowing his master's desire to engage the services of the great sculptor, and being probably informed of Buonarroti's own wish to retire to France, wrote several letters in the month of October, telling Francis that Michelangelo might be easily persuaded to join his court. We do not know, however, whether the King acted on this hint.

His friends at home took the precaution of securing his effects, fearing that a decree for their confiscation might be issued. We possess a schedule of wine, wheat, and furniture found in his house, and handed over by the servant Caterina to his old friend Francesco Granacci for safe keeping. They also did their best to persuade Michelangelo that he ought to take measures for returning under a safe-conduct. Galeotto Giugni wrote upon this subject to the War Office, under date October 13, from Ferrara. He says that Michelangelo has begged him to intercede in his favour, and that he is willing to return and lay himself at the feet of their lordships. In answer to this despatch, news was sent to Giugni on the 20th that the Signory had signed a safe-conduct for Buonarroti. On the 22nd Granacci paid Sebastiano di Francesco, a stone-cutter, to whom Michelangelo was much attached, money for his journey to Venice. It appears that this man set out upon the 23rd, carrying letters from Giovan Battista della Palla, who had now renounced all intention of retiring to France, and was enthusiastically engaged in the defence of Florence. On the return of the Medici, Palla was imprisoned in the castle of Pisa, and paid the penalty of his patriotism by death. A second letter which he wrote to Michelangelo on this occasion deserves to be translated, since it proves the high spirit with which the citizens of Florence were now awaiting the approach of the Prince of Orange and his veteran army. "Yesterday I sent you a letter, together with ten from other friends, and the safe-conduct granted by the Signory for the whole month of November, and though I feel sure that it will reach you safely, I take the precaution of enclosing a copy under this cover. I need hardly repeat what I wrote at great length in my last, nor shall I have recourse to friends for the same purpose. They all of them, I know, with one voice, without the least disagreement or hesitation, have exhorted you, immediately upon the receipt of their letters and the safe-conduct, to return home, in order to preserve your life, your country, your friends, your honour, and your property, and also to enjoy those times so earnestly desired and hoped for by you. If any one had foretold that I could listen without the least affright to news of an invading army marching on our walls, this would have seemed to me impossible. And yet I now assure you that I am not only quite fearless, but also full of confidence in a glorious victory. For many days past my soul has been filled with such gladness, that if God, either for our sins or for some other reason, according to the mysteries of His just judgment, does not permit that army to be broken in our hands, my sorrow will be the same as when one loses, not a good thing hoped for, but one gained and captured. To such an extent am I convinced in my fixed imagination of our success, and have put it to my capital account. I already foresee our militia system, established on a permanent basis, and combined with that of the territory, carrying our city to the skies. I contemplate a fortification of Florence, not temporary, as it now is, but with walls and bastions to be built hereafter. The principal and most difficult step has been already taken; the whole space round the town swept clean, without regard for churches or for monasteries, in accordance with the public need. I contemplate in these our fellow-citizens a noble spirit of disdain for all their losses and the bygone luxuries of villa-life; an admirable unity and fervour for the preservation of liberty; fear of God alone; confidence in Him and in the justice of our cause; innumerable other good things, certain to bring again the age of gold, and which I hope sincerely you will enjoy in company with all of us who are your friends. For all these reasons, I most earnestly entreat you, from the depth of my heart, to come at once and travel through Lucca, where I will meet you, and attend you with due form and ceremony until here: such is my intense desire that our country should not lose you, nor you her. If, after your arrival at Lucca, you should by some accident fail to find me, and you should not care to come to Florence without my company, write a word, I beg. I will set out at once, for I feel sure that I shall get permission. . . . God, by His goodness, keep you in good health, and bring you back to us safe and happy."

Michelangelo set forth upon his journey soon after the receipt of this letter. He was in Ferrara on the 9th of November, as appears from a despatch written by Galeotto Giugni, recommending him to the Government of Florence. Letters patent under the seal of the Duke secured him free passage through the city of Modena and the province of Garfagnana. In spite of these accommodations, he seems to have met with difficulties on the way, owing to the disturbed state of the country. His friend Giovan Battista Palla was waiting for him at Lucca, without information of his movements, up to the 18th of the month. He had left Florence on the 11th, and spent the week at Pisa and Lucca, expecting news in vain. Then, "with one foot in the stirrup," as he says, "the license granted by the Signory" having expired, he sends another missive to Venice, urging Michelangelo not to delay a day longer. "As I cannot persuade myself that you do not intend to come, I urgently request you to reflect, if you have not already started, that the property of those who incurred outlawry with you is being sold, and if you do not arrive within the term conceded by your safe-conduct—that is, during this month—the same will happen to yourself, without the possibility of any mitigation. If you do come, as I still hope and firmly believe, speak with my honoured friend Messer Filippo Calandrini here, to whom I have given directions for your attendance from this town without trouble to yourself. God keep you safe from harm, and grant we see you shortly in our country, by His aid, victorious."

With this letter, Palla, who was certainly a good friend to the wayward artist, and an amiable man to boot, disappears out of this history. At some time about the 20th of November, Michelangelo returned to Florence. We do not know how he finished the journey, and how he was received; but the sentence of outlawry was cummuted, on the 23rd, into exclusion from the Grand Council for three years. He set to work immediately at S. Miniato, strengthening the bastions, and turning the church-tower into a station for sharpshooters. Florence by this time had lost all her territory except a few strong places, Pisa, Livorno, Arezzo, Empoli, Volterra. The Emperor Charles V. signed her liberties away to Clement by the peace of Barcelona (June 20, 1529), and the Republic was now destined to be the appanage of his illegitimate daughter in marriage with the bastard Alessandro de' Medici. It only remained for the army of the Prince of Orange to reduce the city. When Michelangelo arrived, the Imperial troops were leaguered on the heights above the town. The inevitable end of the unequal struggle could be plainly foreseen by those who had not Palla's enthusiasm to sustain their faith. In spite of Ferrucci's genius and spirit, in spite of the good-will of the citizens, Florence was bound to fall. While admitting that Michelangelo abandoned his post in a moment of panic, we must do him the justice of remembering that he resumed it when all his darkest prognostications were being slowly but surely realised. The worst was that his old enemy, Malatesta Baglioni, had now opened a regular system of intrigue with Clement and the Prince of Orange, terminating in the treasonable cession of the city. It was not until August 1530 that Florence finally capitulated. Still the months which intervened between that date and Michelangelo's return from Venice were but a dying close, a slow agony interrupted by spasms of ineffectual heroism.

In describing the works at S. Miniato, Condivi lays great stress upon Michelangelo's plan for arming the bell-tower. "The incessant cannonade of the enemy had broken it in many places, and there was a serious risk that it might come crashing down, to the great injury of the troops within the bastion. He caused a large number of mattresses well stuffed with wool to be brought, and lowered these by night from the summit of the tower down to its foundations, protecting those parts which were exposed to fire. Inasmuch as the cornice projected, the mattresses hung free in the air, at the distance of six cubits from the wall; so that when the missiles of the enemy arrived, they did little or no damage, partly owing to the distance they had travelled, and partly to the resistance offered by this swinging, yielding panoply." An anonymous writer, quoted by Milanesi, gives a fairly intelligible account of the system adopted by Michelangelo. "The outer walls of the bastion were composed of unbaked bricks, the clay of which was mingled with chopped tow. Its thickness he filled in with earth; and," adds this critic, "of all the buildings which remained, this alone survived the siege." It was objected that, in designing these bastions, he multiplied the flanking lines and embrasures beyond what was either necessary or safe. But, observes the anonymous writer, all that his duty as architect demanded was that he should lay down a plan consistent with the nature of the ground, leaving details to practical engineers and military men. "If, then, he committed any errors in these matters, it was not so much his fault as that of the Government, who did not provide him with experienced coadjutors. But how can mere merchants understand the art of war, which needs as much science as any other of the arts, nay more, inasmuch as it is obviously more noble and more perilous?" The confidence now reposed in him is further demonstrated by a license granted on the 22nd of February 1530, empowering him to ascend the cupola of the Duomo on one special occasion with two companions, in order to obtain a general survey of the environs of Florence.

Michelangelo, in the midst of these serious duties, could not have had much time to bestow upon his art. Still there is no reason to doubt Vasari's emphatic statement that he went on working secretly at the Medicean monuments. To have done so openly while the city was in conflict to the death with Clement, would have been dangerous; and yet every one who understands the artist's temperament must feel that a man like Buonarroti was likely to seek rest and distraction from painful anxieties in the tranquillising labour of the chisel. It is also certain that, during the last months of the siege, he found leisure to paint a picture of Leda for the Duke of Ferrara, which will be mentioned in its proper place.

Florence surrendered in the month of August 1530. The terms were drawn up by Don Ferrante Gonzaga, who commanded the Imperial forces after the death of Filiberto, Prince of Orange, in concert with the Pope's commissary-general, Baccio Valori. Malatesta Baglioni, albeit he went about muttering that Florence "was no stable for mules" (alluding to the fact that all the Medici were bastards), approved of the articles, and showed by his conduct that he had long been plotting treason. The act of capitulation was completed on the 12th, and accepted unwillingly by the Signory. Valori, supported by Baglioni's military force, reigned supreme in the city, and prepared to reinstate the exiled family of princes. It said that Marco Dandolo of Venice, when news reached the Pregadi of the fall of Florence, exclaimed aloud: "Baglioni has put upon his head the cap of the biggest traitor upon record."

V

The city was saved from wreckage by a lucky quarrel between the Italian and Spanish troops in the Imperial camp. But no sooner was Clement aware that Florence lay at his mercy, than he disregarded the articles of capitulation, and began to act as an autocratic despot. Before confiding the government to his kinsmen, the Cardinal Ippolito and Alessandro Duke of Penna, he made Valori institute a series of criminal prosecutions against the patriots. Battista della Palla and Raffaello Girolami were sent to prison and poisoned. Five citizens were tortured and decapitated in one day of October. Those who had managed to escape from Florence were sentenced to exile, outlawry, and confiscation of goods by hundreds. Charles V. had finally to interfere and put a stop to the fury of the Pope's revenges. How cruel and exasperated the mind of Clement was, may be gathered from his treatment of Fra Benedetto da Foiano, who sustained the spirit of the burghers by his fiery preaching during the privations of the siege. Foiano fell into the clutches of Malatesta Baglioni, who immediately sent him down to Rome. By the Pope's orders the wretched friar was flung into the worst dungeon in the Castle of S. Angelo, and there slowly starved to death by gradual diminution of his daily dole of bread and water. Readers of Benvenuto Cellini's Memoirs will remember the horror with which he speaks of this dungeon and of its dreadful reminiscences, when it fell to his lot to be imprisoned there.

Such being the mood of Clement, it is not wonderful that Michelangelo should have trembled for his own life and liberty. As Varchi says, "He had been a member of the Nine, had fortified the hill and armed the bell-tower of S. Miniato. What was more annoying, he was accused, though falsely, of proposing to raze the palace of the Medici, where in his boyhood Lorenzo and Piero de' Medici had shown him honour as a guest at their own tables, and to name the space on which it stood the Place of Mules." For this reason he hid himself, as Condivi and Varchi assert, in the house of a trusty friend. The Senator Filippo Buonarroti, who diligently collected traditions about his illustrious ancestor, believed that his real place of retreat was the bell-tower of S. Nicolò, beyond the Arno. "When Clement's fury abated," says Condivi, "he wrote to Florence ordering that search should be made for Michelangelo, and adding that when he was found, if he agreed to go on working at the Medicean monuments, he should be left at liberty and treated with due courtesy. On hearing news of this, Michelangelo came forth from his hiding-place, and resumed the statues in the sacristy of S. Lorenzo, moved thereto more by fear of the Pope than by love for the Medici." From correspondence carried on between Rome and Florence during November and December, we learn that his former pension of fifty crowns a month was renewed, and that Giovan Battista Figiovanni, a Prior of S. Lorenzo, was appointed the Pope's agent and paymaster.

An incident of some interest in the art-history of Florence is connected with this return of the Medici, and probably also with Clement's desire to concentrate Michelangelo's energies upon the sacristy. So far back as May 10, 1508, Piero Soderini wrote to the Marquis of Massa-Carrara, begging him to retain a large block of marble until Michelangelo could come in person and superintend its rough-hewing for a colossal statue to be placed on the Piazza. After the death of Leo, the stone was assigned to Baccio Bandinelli; but Michelangelo, being in favour with the Government at the time of the expulsion of the Medici, obtained the grant of it. His first intention, in which Bandinelli followed him, was to execute a Hercules trampling upon Cacus, which should stand as pendant to his own David.

By a deliberation of the Signory, under date August 22, 1528, we are informed that the marble had been brought to Florence about three years earlier, and that Michelangelo now received instructions, couched in the highest terms of compliment, to proceed with a group of two figures until its accomplishment. If Vasari can be trusted, Michelangelo made numerous designs and models for the Cacus, but afterwards changed his mind, and thought that he would extract from the block a Samson triumphing over two prostrate Philistines. The evidence for this change of plan is not absolutely conclusive. The deliberation of August 22, 1528, indeed left it open to his discretion whether he should execute a Hercules and Cacus, or any other group of two figures; and the English nation at South Kensington possesses one of his noble little wax models for a Hercules. We may perhaps, therefore, assume that while Bandinelli adhered to the Hercules and Cacus, Michelangelo finally decided on a Samson. At any rate, the block was restored in 1530 to Bandinelli, who produced the misbegotten group which still deforms the Florentine Piazza.

Michelangelo had some reason to be jealous of Bandinelli, who exercised considerable influence at the Medicean court, and was an unscrupulous enemy both in word and deed. A man more widely and worse hated than Bandinelli never lived. If any piece of mischief happened which could be fixed upon him with the least plausibility, he bore the blame. Accordingly, when Buonarroti's workshop happened to be broken open, people said that Bandinelli was the culprit. Antonio Mini left the following record of the event: "Three months before the siege, Michelangelo's studio in Via Mozza was burst into with chisels; about fifty drawings of figures were stolen, and among them the designs for the Medicean tombs, with others of great value; also four models in wax and clay. The young men who did it left by accident a chisel marked with the letter M., which led to their discovery. When they knew they were detected, they made off or hid themselves, and sent to say they would return the stolen articles, and begged for pardon." Now the chisel branded with an M. was traced to Michelangelo, the father of Baccio Bandinelli, and no one doubted that he was the burglar.

The history of Michelangelo's Leda, which now survives only in doubtful reproductions, may be introduced by a passage from Condivi's account of his master's visit to Ferrara in 1529. "The Duke received him with great demonstrations of joy, no less by reason of his eminent fame than because Don Ercole, his son, was Captain of the Signory of Florence. Riding forth with him in person, there was nothing appertaining to the business of his mission which the Duke did not bring beneath his notice, whether fortifications or artillery. Beside this, he opened his own private treasure-room, displaying all its contents, and particularly some pictures and portraits of his ancestors, executed by masters in their time excellent. When the hour approached for Michelangelo's departure, the Duke jestingly said to him: 'You are my prisoner now. If you want me to let you go free, I require that you shall promise to make me something with your own hand, according to your will and fancy, be it sculpture or painting.' Michelangelo agreed; and when he arrived at Florence, albeit he was overwhelmed with work for the defences, he began a large piece for a saloon, representing the congress of the swan with Leda. The breaking of the egg was also introduced, from which sprang Castor and Pollux, according to the ancient fable. The Duke heard of this; and on the return of the Medici, he feared that he might lose so great a treasure in the popular disturbance which ensued. Accordingly he despatched one of his gentlemen, who found Michelangelo at home, and viewed the picture. After inspecting it, the man exclaimed: 'Oh! this is a mere trifle.' Michelangelo inquired what his own art was, being aware that men can only form a proper judgment in the arts they exercise. The other sneered and

answered: 'I am a merchant.' Perhaps he felt affronted at
the question, and at not being recognised in his quality of
nobleman; he may also have meant to depreciate the industry of the Florentines, who for the most part are occupied
with trade, as though to say: 'You ask me what my art is?
Is it possible you think a man like me could be a trader?'
Michelangelo, perceiving his drift, growled out: 'You are
doing bad business for your lord! Take yourself away!'
Having thus dismissed the ducal messenger, he made a present of the picture, after a short while, to one of his serving-
men, who, having two sisters to marry, begged for assistance.
It was sent to France, and there bought by King Francis,
where it still exists."

As a matter of fact, we know now that Antonio Mini,
for a long time Michelangelo's man of all work, became
part owner of this Leda, and took it with him to France. A
certain Francesco Tedaldi acquired pecuniary interest in the
picture, of which one Benedetto Bene made a copy at Lyons
in 1532. The original and the copy were carried by Mini to
Paris in 1533, and deposited in the house of Giuliano Buo-
naccorsi, whence they were transferred in some obscure way
to the custody of Luigi Alamanni, and finally passed into the
possession of the King. Meanwhile, Antonio Mini died, and
Tedaldi wrote a record of his losses and a confused account
of money matters and broker business, which he sent to
Michelangelo in 1540. The Leda remained at Fontaine-
bleau till the reign of Louis XIII., when M. Desnoyers,
Minister of State, ordered the picture to be destroyed because of its indecency. Pierre Mariette says that this order
was not carried into effect; for the canvas, in a sadly mutilated state, reappeared some seven or eight years before his
date of writing, and was seen by him. In spite of injuries, he
could trace the hand of a great master; "and I confess that
nothing I had seen from the brush of Michelangelo showed
better painting." He adds that it was restored by a second-
rate artist and sent to England. What became of Mini's

copy is uncertain. We possess a painting in the Dresden Gallery, a Cartoon in the collection of the Royal Academy of England, and a large oil picture, much injured, in the vaults of the National Gallery. In addition to these works, there is a small marble statue in the Museo Nazionale at Florence. All of them represent Michelangelo's design. If mere indecency could justify Desnoyers in his attempt to destroy a masterpiece, this picture deserved its fate. It represented the act of coition between a swan and a woman; and though we cannot hold Michelangelo responsible for the repulsive expression on the face of Leda, which relegates the marble of the Bargello to a place among pornographic works of art, there is no reason to suppose that the general scheme of his conception was abandoned in the copies made of it.

Michelangelo, being a true artist, anxious only for the presentation of his subject, seems to have remained indifferent to its moral quality. Whether it was a crucifixion, or a congress of the swan with Leda, or a rape of Ganymede, or the murder of Holofernes in his tent, or the birth of Eve, he sought to seize the central point in the situation, and to accentuate its significance by the inexhaustible means at his command for giving plastic form to an idea. Those, however, who have paid attention to his work will discover that he always found emotional quality corresponding to the nature of the subject. His ways of handling religious and mythological motives differ in sentiment, and both are distinguished from his treatment of dramatic episodes. The man's mind made itself a mirror to reflect the vision gloating over it; he cared not what that vision was, so long as he could render it in lines of plastic harmony, and express the utmost of the feeling which the theme contained.

Among the many statues left unfinished by Michelangelo is one belonging to this period of his life. "In order to ingratiate himself with Baccio Valori," says Vasari, "he began a statue of three cubits in marble. It was an Apollo drawing a shaft from his quiver. This he nearly finished. It stands now in the chamber of the Prince of Florence; a thing of rarest beauty, though not quite completed." This noble piece of sculpture illustrates the certainty and freedom of the master's hand. Though the last touches of the chisel are lacking, every limb palpitates and undulates with life. The marble seems to be growing into flesh beneath the hatched lines left upon its surface. The pose of the young god, full of strength and sinewy, is no less admirable for audacity than for ease and freedom. Whether Vasari was right in his explanation of the action of this figure may be considered more than doubtful. Were we not accustomed to call it an Apollo, we should rather be inclined to class it with the Slaves of the Louvre, to whom in feeling and design it bears a remarkable resemblance. Indeed, it might be conjectured with some probability that, despairing of bringing his great design for the tomb of Julius to a conclusion, he utilised one of the projected captives for his present to the all-powerful vizier of the Medicean tyrants. It ought, in conclusion, to be added, that there was nothing servile in Michelangelo's desire to make Valori his friend. He had accepted the political situation; and we have good reason, from letters written at a later date by Valori from Rome, to believe that this man took a sincere interest in the great artist. Moreover, Varchi, who is singularly severe in his judgment on the agents of the Medici, expressly states that Baccio Valori was "less cruel than the other Palleschi, doing many and notable services to some persons out of kindly feeling, and to others for money (since he had little and spent much); and this he was well able to perform, seeing he was then the lord of Florence, and the first citizens of the land paid court to him and swelled his train."

VI

During the siege Lodovico Buonarroti passed his time at Pisa. His little grandson, Lionardo, the sole male heir of the family, was with him. Born September 25, 1519, the boy was now exactly eleven years old, and by his father's death in 1528 he had been two years an orphan. Lionardo was ailing, and the old man wearied to return. His two sons, Gismondo and Giansimone, had promised to fetch him home when the country should be safe for travelling. But they delayed; and at last, upon the 30th of September, Lodovico wrote as follows to Michelangelo: "Some time since I directed a letter to Gismondo, from whom you have probably learned that I am staying here, and, indeed, too long; for the flight of Buonarroto's pure soul to heaven, and my own need and earnest desire to come home, and Nardo's state of health, all makes me restless. The boy has been for some days out of health and pining, and I am anxious about him." It is probable that some means were found for escorting them both safely to Settignano. We hear no more about Lodovico till the period of his death, the date of which has not been ascertained with certainty.

From the autumn of 1530 on to the end of 1533 Michelangelo worked at the Medicean monuments. His letters are singularly scanty during all this period, but we possess sufficient information from other sources to enable us to reconstruct a portion of his life. What may be called the chronic malady of his existence, that never-ending worry with the tomb of Julius, assumed an acute form again in the spring of 1531. The correspondence with Sebastiano del Piombo, which had been interrupted since 1525, now becomes plentiful, and enables us to follow some of the steps which led to the new and solemn contract of May 1532.

It is possible that Michelangelo thought he ought to go to Rome in the beginning of the year. If we are right in ascribing a letter written by Benvenuto della Volpaia from Rome upon the 18th of January to the year 1531, and not to 1532, he must have already decided on this step. The document is curious in several respects. "Yours of the 13th informs me that you want a room. I shall be delighted if I can be of service to you in this matter; indeed, it is nothing in respect to what I should like to do for you. I can offer you a chamber or two without the least inconvenience; and you could not confer on me a greater pleasure than by taking up your abode with me in either of the two places which I will now describe. His Holiness has placed me in the Belvedere, and made me guardian there. To-morrow my things will be carried thither, for a permanent establishment; and I can place at your disposal a room with a bed and everything you want. You can even enter by the gate outside the city, which opens into the spiral staircase, and reach your apartment and mine without passing through Rome. From here I can let you into the palace, for I keep a key at your service; and what is better, the Pope comes every day to visit us. If you decide on the Belvedere, you must let me know the day of your departure, and about when you will arrive. In that case I will take up my post at the spiral staircase of Bramante, where you will be able to see me. If you wish, nobody but my brother and Mona Lisabetta and I shall know that you are here, and you shall do just as you please; and, in short, I beg you earnestly to choose this plan. Otherwise, come to the Borgo Nuovo, to the houses which Volterra built, the fifth house toward S. Angelo. I have rented it to live there, and my brother Fruosino is also going to live and keep shop in it. There you will have a room or two, if you like, at your disposal. Please yourself, and give the letter to Tommaso di Stefano Miniatore, who will address it to Messer Lorenzo de' Medici, and I shall have it quickly."

Nothing came of these proposals. But that Michelangelo did not abandon the idea of going to Rome appears from a letter of Sebastiano's written on the 24th of February. It was the first which passed between the friends since the terrible events of 1527 and 1530. For once, the jollity of the epicurean friar has deserted him. He writes as though those awful months of the sack of Rome were still present to his memory. "After all those trials, hardships, and perils, God Almighty has left us alive and in health, by His mercy and piteous kindness. A thing, in sooth, miraculous, when I reflect upon it; wherefore His Majesty be ever held in gratitude. . . . Now, gossip mine, since we have passed through fire and water, and have experienced things we never dreamed of, let us thank God for all; and the little remnant left to us of life, may we at least employ it in such peace as can be had. For of a truth, what fortune does or does not do is of slight importance, seeing how scurvy and how dolorous she is. I am brought to this, that if the universe should crumble round me, I should not care, but laugh at all. Menighella will inform you what my life is, how I am. I do not yet seem to myself to be the same Bastiano I was before the Sack. I cannot yet get back into my former frame of mind." In a postscript to this letter, eloquent by its very naïveté, Sebastiano says that he sees no reason for Michelangelo's coming to Rome, except it be to look after his house, which is going to ruin, and the workshop tumbling to pieces.

In another letter, of April 29, Sebastiano repeats that there is no need for Michelangelo to come to Rome, if it be only to put himself right with the Pope. Clement is sincerely his friend, and has forgiven the part he played during the siege of Florence. He then informs his gossip that, having been lately at Pesaro, he met the painter Girolamo Genga, who promised to be serviceable in the matter of the tomb of Julius. The Duke of Urbino, according to this man's account, was very eager to see it finished. "I replied that the work was going forward, but that 8000 ducats were needed for its completion, and we did not know where to get this money. He said that the Duke would provide, but his Lordship was afraid of losing both the ducats and the work, and was inclined to be angry. After a good deal of talking, he asked whether it would not be possible to execute the tomb upon a reduced scale, so as to satisfy both parties. I answered that you ought to be consulted." We have reason to infer from this that the plan which was finally adopted, of making a mural monument with only a few figures from the hand of

Michelangelo, had already been suggested. In his next letter, Sebastiano communicates the fact that he has been appointed to the office of Piombatore; "and if you could see me in my quality of friar, I am sure you would laugh. I am the finest friar loon in Rome." The Duke of Urbino's agent, Hieronimo Staccoli, now appears for the first time upon the stage. It was through his negotiations that the former contracts for the tomb of Julius were finally annulled and a new design adopted. Michelangelo offered, with the view of terminating all disputes, to complete the monument on a reduced scale at his own cost, and furthermore to disburse the sum of 2000 ducats in discharge of any claims the Della Rovere might have against him. This seemed too liberal, and when Clement was informed of the project, he promised to make better terms. Indeed, during the course of these negotiations the Pope displayed the greatest interest in Michelangelo's affairs. Staccoli, on the Duke's part, raised objections; and Sebastiano had to remind him that, unless some concessions were made, the scheme of the tomb might fall through: "for it does not rain Michelangelos, and men could hardly be found to preserve the work, far less to finish it." In course of time the Duke's ambassador at Rome, Giovan Maria della Porta, intervened, and throughout the whole business Clement was consulted upon every detail.

Sebastiano kept up his correspondence through the summer of 1531. Meanwhile the suspense and anxiety were telling seriously on Michelangelo's health. Already in June news must have reached Rome that his health was breaking down; for Clement sent word recommending him to work less, and to relax his spirits by exercise. Toward the autumn he became alarmingly ill. We have a letter from Paolo Mini, the uncle of his servant Antonio, written to Baccio Valori on the 29th of September. After describing the beauty of two statues for the Medicean tombs, Mini says he fears that "Michelangelo will not live long, unless some measures are taken for his benefit. He works very hard, eats little and poorly, and sleeps less. In fact, he is afflicted with two kinds of disorder, the one in his head, the other in his heart. Neither is incurable, since he has a robust constitution; but for the good of his head, he ought to be restrained by our Lord the Pope from working through the winter in the sacristy, the air of which is bad for him; and for his heart, the best remedy would be if his Holiness could accommodate matters with the Duke of Urbino." In a second letter, of October 8, Mini insists again upon the necessity of freeing Michelangelo's mind from his anxieties. The upshot was that Clement, on the 21st of November, addressed a brief to his sculptor, whereby Buonarroti was ordered, under pain of excommunication, to lay aside all work except what was strictly necessary for the Medicean monuments, and to take better care of his health. On the 26th of the same month Benvenuto della Volpaia wrote, repeating what the Pope had written in his brief, and adding that his Holiness desired him to select some workshop more convenient for his health than the cold and cheerless sacristy.

In spite of Clement's orders that Michelangelo should confine himself strictly to working on the Medicean monuments, he continued to be solicited with various commissions. Thus the Cardinal Cybo wrote in December begging him to furnish a design for a tomb which he intended to erect. Whether Michelangelo consented is not known.

Early in December Sebastiano resumed his communications on the subject of the tomb of Julius, saying that Michelangelo must not expect to satisfy the Duke without executing the work, in part at least, himself. "There is no one but yourself that harms you: I mean, your eminent fame and the greatness of your works. I do not say this to flatter you. Therefore, I am of opinion that, without some shadow of yourself, we shall never induce those parties to do what we want. It seems to me that you might easily make designs and models, and afterwards assign the completion to any master whom you choose. But the shadow of yourself there must be. If you take the matter in this way, it will be a trifle; you will do nothing, and seem to do all; but remember that the work must be carried out under your shadow."

A series of despatches, forwarded between December 4, 1531, and April 29, 1532, by Giovan Maria della Porta to the Duke of Urbino, confirm the particulars furnished by the letters which Sebastiano still continued to write from Rome. At the end of 1531 Michelangelo expressed his anxiety to visit Rome, now that the negotiations with the Duke were nearly complete. Sebastiano, hearing this, replies: "You will effect more in half an hour than I can do in a whole year. I believe that you will arrange everything after two words with his Holiness; for our Lord is anxious to meet your wishes." He wanted to be present at the drawing up and signing of the contract. Clement, however, although he told Sebastiano that he should be glad to see him, hesitated to send the necessary permission, and it was not until the month of April 1532 that he set out. About the 6th, as appears from the indorsement of a letter received in his absence, he must have reached Rome. The new contract was not ready for signature before the 29th, and on that date Michelangelo left for Florence, having, as he says, been sent off by the Pope in a hurry on the very day appointed for its execution. In his absence it was duly signed and witnessed before Clement; the Cardinals Gonzaga and da Monte and the Lady Felice della Rovere attesting, while Giovan Maria della Porta and Girolamo Staccoli acted for the Duke of Urbino. When Michelangelo returned and saw the instrument, he found that several clauses prejudicial to his interests had been inserted by the notary. "I discovered more than 1000 ducats charged unjustly to my debit, also the house in which I live, and certain other hooks and crooks to ruin me. The Pope would certainly not have tolerated this knavery, as Fra Sebastiano can bear witness, since he wished me to complain to Clement and have the notary hanged. I swear I never received the moneys which Giovan Maria della Porta wrote against me, and caused to be engrossed upon the contract."

It is difficult to understand why Michelangelo should not have immediately taken measures to rectify these errors. He seems to have been well aware that he was bound to refund 2000 ducats, since the only letter from his pen belonging to the year 1532 is one dated May, and addressed to Andrea Quarantesi in Pisa. In this document he consults Quarantesi about the possibility of raising that sum, with 1000 ducats in addition. "It was in my mind, in order that I might not be left naked, to sell houses and possessions, and to let the lira go for ten soldi." As the contract was never carried out, the fraudulent passages inserted in the deed did not prove of practical importance. Della Porta, on his part, wrote in high spirits to his master: "Yesterday we executed the new contract with Michelangelo, for the ratification of which by your Lordship we have fixed a limit of two months. It is of a nature to satisfy all Rome, and reflects great credit on your Lordship for the trouble you have taken in concluding it. Michelangelo, who shows a very proper respect for your Lordship, has promised to make and send you a design. Among other items, I have bound him to furnish six statues by his own hand, which will be a world in themselves, because they are sure to be incomparable. The rest he may have finished by some sculptor at his own choice, provided the work is done under his direction. The Pope allows him to come twice a year to Rome, for periods of two months each, in order to push the work forward. And he is to execute the whole at his own costs." He proceeds to say, that since the tomb cannot be put up in S. Peter's, S. Pietro in Vincoli has been selected as the most suitable church. It appears that the Duke's ratification was sent upon the 5th of June and placed in the hands of Clement, so that Michelangelo probably did not see it for some months. Della Porta, writing to the Duke again upon the 19th of June, says that Clement promised to allow Michelangelo to come to Rome in the winter, and to reside there working at the tomb. But we have no direct information concerning his doings after the return to Florence at the end of April 1532.

It will be worth while to introduce Condivi's account of these transactions relating to the tomb of Julius, since it throws some light upon the sculptor's private feelings and motives, as well as upon the falsification of the contract as finally engrossed.

"When Michelangelo had been called to Rome by Pope Clement, he began to be harassed by the agents of the Duke of Urbino about the sepulchre of Julius. Clement, who wished to employ him in Florence, did all he could to set him free, and gave him for his attorney in this matter Messer Tommaso da Prato, who was afterwards datary. Michelangelo, however, knowing the devil disposition of Duke Alessandro toward him, and being in great dread on this account, also because he bore love and reverence to the memory of Pope Julius and to the illustrious house of Della Rovere, strained every nerve to remain in Rome and busy himself about the tomb. What made him more anxious was that every one accused him of having received from Pope Julius at least 16,000 crowns, and of having spent them on himself without fulfilling his engagements. Being a man sensitive about his reputation, he could not bear the dishonour of such reports, and wanted the whole matter to be cleared up; nor, although he was now old, did he shrink from the very onerous task of completing what he had begun so long ago. Consequently they came to strife together, and his antagonists were unable to prove payments to anything like the amount which had first been noised abroad; indeed, on the contrary, more than two thirds of the whole sum first stipulated by the two Cardinals was wanting. Clement then thinking he had found an excellent opportunity for setting him at liberty and making use of his whole energies, called Michelangelo to him, and said: 'Come, now, confess that you want to make this tomb, but wish to know who will pay you the balance.' Michelangelo, knowing well that the Pope was anxious to employ him on his own work, answered: 'Supposing some one is found to pay me.' To which Pope Clement: 'You are a great fool if you let yourself believe that any one will come forward to offer you a farthing.' Accordingly, his attorney, Messer Tommaso, and the agents of the Duke, after some negotiations, came to an agreement that a tomb should at least be made for the amount he had received. Michelangelo, thinking the matter had arrived at a good conclusion, consented with alacrity. He was much influenced by the elder Cardinal di Monte, who owed his advancement to Julius II., and was uncle of Julius III., our present Pope by grace of God. The arrangement was as follows: That he should make a tomb of one façade only; should utilise those marbles which he had already blocked out for the quadrangular monument, adapting them as well as circumstances allowed; and finally, that he should be bound to furnish six statues by his own hand. In spite of this arrangement, Pope Clement was allowed to employ Michelangelo in Florence or where he liked during four months of the year, that being required by his Holiness for his undertakings at S. Lorenzo. Such then was the contract made between the Duke and Michelangelo. But here it has to be observed, that after all accounts had been made up, Michelangelo secretly agreed with the agents of his Excellency that it should be reported that he had received some thousands of crowns above what had been paid to him; the object being to make his obligation to the Duke of Urbino seem more considerable, and to discourage Pope Clement from sending him to Florence, whither he was extremely unwilling to go. This acknowledgment was not only bruited about in words, but, without his knowledge or consent, was also inserted into the deed; not when this was drawn up, but when it was engrossed; a falsification which caused Michelangelo the utmost vexation. The ambassador, however, persuaded him that this would do him no real harm: it did not signify, he said, whether the contract specified a thousand or twenty thousand crowns, seeing they were agreed that the tomb should be reduced to suit the sums actually received; adding, that nobody was concerned in the matter except himself, and that Michelangelo might feel safe with him on account of the understanding between them. Upon this Michelangelo grew easy in his mind, partly because he thought he might have confidence, and partly because he wished the Pope to receive the impression I have described above. In this way the thing was settled for the time, but it did not end there; for when he had worked his four months in Florence and came back to Rome, the Pope set him to other tasks, and ordered him to paint the wall above the altar in the Sistine Chapel. He was a man of excellent judgment in such matters, and had meditated many different subjects for this fresco. At last he fixed upon the Last Judgment, considering that the variety and greatness of the theme would enable the illustrious artist to exhibit his powers in their full extent. Michelangelo, remembering the obligation he was under to the Duke of Urbino, did all he could to evade this new engagement; but when this proved impossible, he began to procrastinate, and, pretending to be fully occupied with the cartoons for his huge picture, he worked in secret at the statues intended for the monument."

VII

Michelangelo's position at Florence was insecure and painful, owing to the undisguised animosity of the Duke Alessandro. This man ruled like a tyrant of the worst sort, scandalising good citizens by his brutal immoralities, and terrorising them by his cruelties. "He remained," says Condivi, "in continual alarm; because the Duke, a young man, as is known to every one, of ferocious and revengeful temper, hated him exceedingly. There is no doubt that, but for the Pope's protection, he would have been removed from this world. What added to Alessandro's enmity was that when he was planning the fortress which he afterwards erected, he sent Messer Vitelli for Michelangelo, ordering him to ride with them, and to select a proper position for the building. Michelangelo refused, saying that he had received no commission from the Pope. The Duke waxed very wroth; and so, through this new grievance added to old grudges and the notorious nature of the Duke, Michelangelo not unreasonably lived in fear. It was certainly by God's aid that he happened to be away from Florence when Clement died." Michelangelo was bound under solemn obligations to execute no work but what the Pope ordered for himself or permitted by the contract with the heirs of Julius. Therefore he acted in accordance with duty when he refused to advise the tyrant in this scheme for keeping the city under permanent subjection. The man who had fortified Florence against the troops of Clement could not assist another bastard Medici to build a strong place for her ruin. It may be to this period of his life that we owe the following madigral, written upon the loss of Florentine liberty and the bad conscience of the despot :—

> Lady, for joy of lovers numberless
>   Thou wast created fair as angels are.
>   Sure God hath fallen asleep in heaven afar
> When one man calls the bliss of many his!
>   Give back to streaming eyes
>   The daylight of thy face, that seems to shun
> Those who must live defrauded of their bliss!
>
> Vex not your pure desire with tears and sighs:
>   For he who robs you of my light hath none.
>   Dwelling in fear, sin hath no happiness;
> Since, amid those who love, their joy is less,
>   Whose great desire great plenty still curtails,
>   Than theirs who, poor, have hope that never fails.

During the siege Michelangelo had been forced to lend the Signory a sum of about 1500 ducats. In the summer of 1533 he corresponded with Sebastiano about means for recovering this loan. On the 16th of August Sebastiano writes that he has referred the matter to the Pope. "I repeat, what I have already written, that I presented your memorial to his Holiness. It was about eight in the evening, and the Florentine ambassador was present. The Pope then ordered the ambassador to write immediately to the Duke; and this he did with such vehemence and passion as I do not think he has displayed on four other occasions concerning the affairs of Florence. His rage and fury were tremendous, and the words he used to the ambassador would stupefy you, could you hear them. Indeed, they are not fit to be written down, and I must reserve them for *viva voce*. I burn to have half an hour's conversation with you, for now I know our good and holy master to the ground. Enough, I think you must have already seen something of the sort. In brief, he has resolved that you are to be repaid the 400 ducats of the guardianship and the 500 ducats lent to the old Government." It may be readily imagined that this restitution of a debt incurred by Florence when she was fighting for her liberties, to which act of justice her victorious tyrant was compelled by his Papal kinsman, did not soften Alessandro's bad feeling for the creditor.

Several of Sebastiano's letters during the summer and autumn of 1533 refer to an edition of some madrigals by Michelangelo, which had been set to music by Bartolommeo Tromboncino, Giacomo Archadelt, and Costanzo Festa. We have every reason to suppose that the period we have now reached was the richest in poetical compositions. It was also in 1532 or 1533 that he formed the most passionate attachment of which we have any knowledge in his life; for he became acquainted about this time with Tommaso Cavalieri. A few years later he was destined to meet with Vittoria

Colonna. The details of these two celebrated friendships will be discussed in another chapter.

Clement VII. journeyed from Rome in September, intending to take ship at Leghorn for Nice and afterwards Marseilles, where his young cousin, Caterina de' Medici, was married to the Dauphin. He had to pass through S. Miniato al Tedesco, and thither Michelangelo went to wait upon him on the 22nd. This was the last, and not the least imposing, public act of the old Pope, who, six years after his imprisonment and outrage in the Castle of S. Angelo, was now wedding a daughter of his plebeian family to the heir of the French crown. What passed between Michelangelo and his master on this occasion is not certain.

The years 1532-1534 form a period of considerable chronological perplexity in Michelangelo's life. This is in great measure due to the fact that he was now residing regularly part of the year in Rome and part in Florence. We have good reason to believe that he went to Rome in September 1532, and stayed there through the winter. It is probable that he then formed the friendship with Cavalieri, which played so important a part in his personal history. A brisk correspondence carried on between him and his two friends, Bartolommeo Angelini and Sebastiano del Piombo, shows that he resided at Florence during the summer and early autumn of 1533. From a letter addressed to Figiovanni on the 15th of October, we learn that he was then impatient to leave Florence for Rome. But a *Ricordo*, bearing date October 29, 1533, renders it almost certain that he had not then started. Angelini's letters, which had been so frequent, stop suddenly in that month. This renders it almost certain that Michelangelo must have soon returned to Rome. Strangely enough there are no letters or *Ricordi* in his handwriting which bear the date 1534. When we come to deal with this year, 1534, we learn from Michelangelo's own statement to Vasari that he was in Florence during the summer, and that he reached Rome two days before the death of Clement VII., *i.e.*, upon September 23. Condivi observes that it was lucky for him that the Pope did not die while he was still at Florence, else he would certainly have been exposed to great peril, and probably been murdered or imprisoned by Duke Alessandro.

Nevertheless, Michelangelo was again in Florence toward the close of 1534. An undated letter to a certain Febo (di Poggio) confirms this supposition. It may probably be referred to the month of December. In it he says that he means to leave Florence next day for Pisa and Rome, and that he shall never return. Febo's answer, addressed to Rome, is date January 14, 1534, which, according to Florentine reckoning, means 1535.

We may take it, then, as sufficiently well ascertained that Michelangelo departed from Florence before the end of 1534, and that he never returned during the remainder of his life. There is left, however, another point of importance referring to this period, which cannot be satisfactorily cleared up. We do not know the exact date of his father, Lodovico's, death. It must have happened either in 1533 or in 1534. In spite of careful researches, no record of the event has yet been discovered, either at Settignano or in the public offices of Florence. The documents of the Buonarroti family yield no direct information on the subject. We learn, however, from the Libri delle Età, preserved at the Archivio di Stato, that Lodovico di Lionardo di Buonarrota Simoni was born upon the 11th of June 1444. Now Michelangelo, in his poem on Lodovico's death, says very decidedly that his father was ninety when he breathed his last. If we take this literally, it must be inferred that he died after the middle of June 1534. There are many reasons for supposing that Michelangelo was in Florence when this happened. The chief of these is that no correspondence passed between the Buonarroti brothers on the occasion, while Michelangelo's minutes regarding the expenses of his father's burial seem to indicate that he was personally responsible for their disbursement. I may finally remark that the schedule of property belonging to Michelangelo, recorded under the year 1534 in the archives of the Decima at Florence, makes no reference at all to Lodovico. We conclude from it that, at the time of its redaction, Michelangelo must have succeeded to his father's estate.

The death of Lodovico and Buonarroto, happening within a space of little more than five years, profoundly affected Michelangelo's mind, and left an indelible mark of sadness on his life. One of his best poems, a *capitolo*, or piece of verse in *terza rima* stanzas, was written on the occasion of his father's decease. In it he says that Lodovico had reached the age of ninety. If this statement be literally accurate, the old man must have died in 1534, since he was born upon the 11th of June 1444. But up to the present time, as I have observed above, the exact date of his death has not been discovered. One passage of singular and solemn beauty may be translated from the original:—

> Thou'rt dead of dying, and art made divine,
>   Nor fearest now to change or life or will;
>   Scarce without envy can I call this thine.
> Fortune and time beyond your temple-sill
>   Dare not advance, by whom is dealt for us
>   A doubtful gladness, and too certain ill.
> Cloud is there none to dim you glorious:
>   The hours distinct compel you not to fade:
>   Nor chance nor fate o'er you are tyrannous.
> Your splendour with the night sinks not in shade,
>   Nor grows with day, howe'er that sun ride high
>   Which on our mortal hearts life's heat hath rayed.
> Thus from thy dying I now learn to die,
>   Dear father mine! In thought I see thy place,
>   Where earth but rarely lets men climb the sky.

Not, as some deem, is death the worst disgrace
For one whose last day brings him to the first,
The next eternal throne to God's by grace.
There by God's grace I trust that thou art nursed,
And hope to find thee, if but my cold heart
High reason draw from earthly slime accursed.

CHAPTER X

I

THE collegiate church of S. Lorenzo at Florence had
long been associated with the Medicean family, who were
its most distinguished benefactors, Giovanni d'Averardo de'
Medici, together with the heads of six other Florentine
houses, caused it to be rebuilt at the beginning of the fifteenth century. He took upon himself the entire costs of
the sacristy and one chapel; it was also owing to his suggestion that Filippo Brunelleschi, in the year 1421, designed
the church and cloister as they now appear. When he died,
Giovanni was buried in its precincts, while his son Cosimo
de' Medici, the father of his country, continued these benevo-
lences, and bestowed a capital of 40,000 golden florins on
the Chapter. He too was buried in the church, a simple monument in the sacristy being erected to his memory. Lorenzo
the Magnificent followed in due course, and found his last
resting-place at S. Lorenzo.

We have seen in a previous chapter how and when Leo X.
conceived the idea of adding a chapel which should serve
as mausoleum for several members of the Medicean family
at S. Lorenzo, and how Clement determined to lodge the
famous Medicean library in a hall erected over the west side
of the cloister. Both of these undertakings, as well as the construction of a façade for the front of the church, were
assigned to Michelangelo. The ground plan of the monumental chapel corresponds to Brunelleschi's sacristy, and is

generally known as the Sagrestia Nuova. Internally Buonarroti altered its decorative panellings, and elevated the vaulting of the roof into a more ambitious cupola. This portion of the edifice was executed in the rough during his residence at Florence. The façade was never begun in earnest, and remains unfinished. The library was constructed according to his designs, and may be taken, on the whole, as a genuine specimen of his style in architecture.

The books which Clement lodged there were the priceless manuscripts brought together by Cosimo de' Medici in the first enthusiasm of the Revival, at that critical moment when the decay of the Eastern Empire transferred the wrecks of Greek literature from Constantinople to Italy. Cosimo built a room to hold them in the Convent of S. Marco, which Flavio Biondo styled the first library opened for the use of scholars. Lorenzo the Magnificent enriched the collection with treasures acquired during his lifetime, buying autographs wherever it was possible to find them, and causing copies to be made. In the year 1508 the friars of S. Marco sold this inestimable store of literary documents, in order to discharge the debts contracted by them during their ill-considered interference in the state affairs of the Republic. It was purchased for the sum of 2652 ducats by the Cardinal Giovanni de' Medici, a second son of Lorenzo the Magnificent, and afterwards Pope Leo X. He transferred them to his Roman villa, where the collection was still further enlarged by all the rarities which a prince passionate for literature and reckless in expenditure could there assemble. Leo's cousin and executor, Giulio de' Medici, Pope Clement VII., fulfilled his last wishes by transferring them to Florence, and providing the stately receptacle in which they still repose.

The task assigned to Michelangelo, when he planned the library, was not so simple as that of the new sacristy. Some correspondence took place before the west side of the cloister was finally decided on. What is awkward in the approach to the great staircase must be ascribed to the difficulty of fitting this building into the old edifice; and probably, if Michelangelo had carried out the whole work, a worthier entrance from the piazza into the loggia, and from the loggia into the vestibule, might have been devised.

II

Vasari, in a well-known passage of his Life of Michelangelo, reports the general opinion of his age regarding the novelties introduced by Buonarroti into Italian architecture. The art of building was in a state of transition. Indeed, it cannot be maintained that the Italians, after they abandoned the traditions of the Romanesque manner, advanced with certitude on any line of progress in this art. Their work, beautiful as it often is, ingenious as it almost always is, marked invariably by the individuality of the district and the builder, seems to be tentative, experimental. The principles of the Pointed Gothic style were never seized or understood by Italian architects. Even such cathedrals as those of Orvieto and Siena are splendid monuments of incapacity, when compared with the Romanesque churches of Pisa, S. Miniato, S. Zenone at Verona, the Cathedral of Parma. The return from Teutonic to Roman standards of taste, which marked the advent of humanism, introduced a hybrid manner. This, in its first commencement, was extremely charming. The buildings of Leo Battista Alberti, of Brunelleschi, and of Bramante are distinguished by an exquisite purity and grace combined with picturesqueness. No edifice in any style is more stately, and at the same time more musical in linear proportions, than the Church of S. Andrea at Mantua. The Cappella dei Pazzi and the Church of S. Spirito at Florence are gems of clear-cut and harmonious dignity. The courtyard of the Cancelleria at Rome, the Duomo at Todi, show with what supreme ability the great architect of Casteldurante blended sublimity with suavity, largeness and breadth with naïveté and delicately studied detail. But these first endeavours of the Romantic spirit to assimilate tne Classic mannerism—essays no less interesting than those of Boiardo in poetry, of Botticelli in painting, of Donatello and Omodei in sculpture—all of them alike, whether buildings, poems, paintings, or statues, displaying the genius of the Italic race, renascent, recalcitrant against the Gothic style, while still to some extent swayed by its influence (at one and the same time both Christian and chivalrous, Pagan and precociously cynical; yet charmingly fresh, unspoiled by dogma, uncontaminated by pedantry)—these first endeavours of the Romantic spirit to assimilate the Classic mannerism could not create a new style representative of the national life. They had the fault inherent in all hybrids, however fanciful and graceful. They were sterile and unprocreative. The warring elements, so deftly and beautifully blent in them, began at once to fall asunder. The San Galli attempted to follow classical precedent with stricter severity. Some buildings of their school may still be reckoned among the purest which remain to prove the sincerity of the Revival of Learning. The Sansovini exaggerated the naïveté of the earlier Renaissance manner, and pushed its picturesqueness over into florid luxuriance or decorative detail. Meanwhile, humanists and scholars worked slowly but steadily upon the text of Vitruvius, impressing the paramount importance of his theoretical writings upon practical builders. Neither students nor architects reflected that they could not understand Vitruvius; that, if they could understand him, it was by no means certain he was right; and that, if he was right for his own age, he would not be right for the sixteenth century after Christ. It was just at this moment, when Vitruvius began to dominate the Italian imagination, that Michelangelo was called upon to build. The genial adaptation of classical elements to modern sympathies and uses, which had been practised by Alberti, Brunelleschi, Bramante, yielded now to painful efforts after the appropriation of pedantic principles. Instead of working upon antique monuments with their senses and emotions, men approached them through the medium of scholastic erudition. Instead of seeing and feeling for themselves, they sought by dissection to confirm the written precepts of a defunct Roman writer. This diversion of a great art from its natural line of development supplies a striking instance of the fascination which authority exercises at certain periods of culture. Rather than trust their feeling for what was beautiful and useful, convenient and attractive, the Italians of the Renaissance surrendered themselves to learning. Led by the spirit of scholarship, they thought it their duty to master the text of Vitruvius, to verify his principles by the analysis of surviving antique edifices, and, having formed their own conception of his theory, to apply this, as well as they were able, to the requirements of contemporary life.

Two exits from the false situation existed: one was the picturesqueness of the Barocco style; the other was the specious vapid purity of the Palladian. Michelangelo, who was essentially the genius of this transition, can neither be ascribed to the Barocco architects, although he called them into being, nor yet can he be said to have arrived at the Palladian solution. He held both types within himself in embryo, arriving at a moment of profound and complicated difficulty for the practical architect; without technical education, but gifted with supreme genius, bringing the imperious instincts of a sublime creative amateur into every task appointed him. We need not wonder if a man of his calibre left the powerful impress of his personality upon an art in chaos, luring lesser craftsmen into the Barocco mannerism, while he provoked reaction in the stronger, who felt more scientifically what was needed to secure firm standing-ground. Bernini and the superb fountain of Trevi derive from Michelangelo on one side; Vignola's cold classic profiles and Palladio's resuscitation of old Rome in the Palazzo della Ragione at Vicenza emerge upon the other. It remained Buonarroti's greatest glory that, lessoned by experience and inspired for high creation by the vastness of the undertaking, he imagined a world's wonder in the cupola of S. Peter's.

III

Writing in the mid-stream of this architectural regurgitation, Vasari explains what contemporaries thought about Michelangelo's innovations. "He wished to build the new sacristy upon the same lines as the older one by Brunelleschi, but at the same time to clothe the edifice with a different style of decoration. Accordingly, he invented for the interior a composite adornment, of the newest and most varied manner which antique and modern masters joined together could have used. The novelty of his style consisted in those lovely cornices, capitals, basements, doors, niches, and sepulchres which transcended all that earlier builders, working by measurements, distribution of parts, and rule, had previously effected, following Vitruvius and the ancient relics. Such men were afraid to supplement tradition with original invention. The license he introduced gave great courage to those who studied his method, and emboldened them to follow on his path. Since that time, new freaks of fancy have been seen, resembling the style of arabesque and grotesque more than was consistent with tradition. For this emancipation of the art, all craftsmen owe him an infinite and everduring debt of gratitude, since he at one blow broke down the bands and chains which barred the path they trod in common."

If I am right in thus interpreting an unusually incoherent passage of Vasari's criticism, no words could express more clearly the advent of Barocco mannerism. But Vasari proceeds to explain his meaning with still greater precision. "Afterwards he made a plainer demonstration of his intention in the library of S. Lorenzo, by the splendid distribution of the windows, the arrangement of the upper chamber, and the marvellous entrance-hall into that enclosed building.

The grace and charm of art were never seen more perfectly displayed in the whole and in the parts of any edifice than here. I may refer in particular to the corbels, the recesses for statues, and the cornices. The staircase, too, deserves attention for its convenience, with the eccentric breakage of its flights of steps; the whole construction being so altered from the common usage of other architects as to excite astonishment in all who see it."

What emerges with distinctness from Vasari's account of Michelangelo's work at S. Lorenzo is that a practical Italian architect, who had been engaged on buildings of importance since this work was carried out, believed it to have infused freedom and new vigour into architecture. That freedom and new vigour we now know to have implied the Barocco style.

IV

In estimating Michelangelo's work at S. Lorenzo, we must not forget that at this period of his life he contemplated statuary, bronze bas-relief, and painting, as essential adjuncts to architecture. The scheme is, therefore, not so much constructive as decorative, and a great many of its most offensive qualities may be ascribed to the fact that the purposes for which it was designed have been omitted. We know that the façade of S. Lorenzo was intended to abound in bronze and marble carvings. Beside the Medicean tombs, the sacristy ought to have contained a vast amount of sculpture, and its dome was actually painted in fresco by Giovanni da Udine under Michelangelo's own eyes. It appears that his imagination still obeyed those leading principles which he applied in the rough sketch for the first sepulchre of Julius. The vestibule and staircase of the library cannot therefore be judged fairly now; for if they had been finished according to their maker's plan, the faults of their construction would have been compensated by multitudes of plastic shapes.

M. Charles Garnier, in *L'Œuvre et la Vie,* speaking with the authority of a practical architect, says: "Michelangelo was not, properly speaking, an architect. He made architecture, which is quite a different thing; and most often it was the architecture of a painter and sculptor, which points to colour, breadth, imagination, but also to insufficient studies and incomplete education. The thought may be great and strong, but the execution of it is always feeble and naïve. . . . He had not learned the language of the art. He has all the qualities of imagination, invention, will, which form a great composer; but he does not know the grammar, and can hardly write. . . . In seeking the great, he has too often found the tumid; seeking the original, he has fallen upon the strange, and also on bad taste."

There is much that is true in this critique, severe though it may seem to be. The fact is that Michelangelo aimed at picturesque effect in his buildings; not, as previous architects had done, by a lavish use of loosely decorative details, but by the piling up and massing together of otherwise dry orders, cornices, pilasters, windows, all of which, in his conception, were to serve as framework and pedestals for statuary. He also strove to secure originality and to stimulate astonishment by bizarre modulations of accepted classic forms, by breaking the lines of architraves, combining angularities with curves, adopting a violently accented rhythm and a tortured multiplicity of parts, wherever this was possible.

V

In this new style, so much belauded by Vasari, the superficial design is often rich and grandiose, making a strong pictorial appeal to the imagination. Meanwhile, the organic laws of structure have been sacrificed; and that chaste beauty which emerges from a perfectly harmonious distribution of parts, embellished by surface decoration only when the limbs and members of the building demand emphasis, may be sought for everywhere in vain. The substratum is a box, a barn, an inverted bottle; built up of rubble, brick, and concrete; clothed with learned details, which have been borrowed from the pseudo-science of the humanist. There is nothing here of divine Greek candour, of dominant Roman vigour, of Gothic vitality, of fanciful invention governed by a sincere sense of truth. Nothing remains of the shy graces, the melodious simplicities, the pure seeking after musical proportion, which marked the happier Italian effort of the early Renaissance, through Brunelleschi and Alberti, Bramante, Giuliano da Sangallo, and Peruzzi. Architecture in the highest sense of that word, has disappeared. A scenic scheme of panelling for empty walls has superseded the conscientious striving to construct a living and intelligible whole.

The fault inherent in Italian building after the close of the Lombard period, reaches its climax here. That fault was connected with the inability of the Italians to assimilate the true spirit of the Gothic style, while they attempted its imitation in practice. The fabrication of imposing and lovely façades at Orvieto, at Siena, at Cremona, and at Crema, glorious screens which masked the poverty of the edifice, and corresponded in no point to the organism of the structure, taught them to overrate mere surface-beauty. Their wonderful creativeness in all the arts which can be subordinated to architectural effect seduced them further. Nothing, for instance, taken by itself alone, can be more satisfactory than the façade of the Certosa at Pavia; but it is not, like the front of Chartres or Rheims or Amiens, a natural introduction to the inner sanctuary. At the end of the Gothic period architecture had thus come to be conceived as the art of covering shapeless structures with a wealth of arabesques in marble, fresco, bronze, mosaic.

The revival of learning and a renewed interest in the antique withdrew the Italians for a short period from this false position. With more or less of merit, successive builders, including those I have above mentioned, worked in a pure style: pure because it obeyed the laws of its own music, because it was intelligible and self-consistent, aiming at construction as the main end, subordinating decoration of richer luxuriance or of sterner severity to the prime purpose of the total scheme. But this style was too much the plaything of particular minds to create a permanent tradition. It varied in the several provinces of Italy, and mingled personal caprice with the effort to assume a classic garb. Meanwhile the study of Vitruvius advanced, and that pedantry which infected all the learned movements of the Renaissance struck deep and venomous roots into the art of building.

Michelangelo arrived at the moment I am attempting to indicate. He protested that architecture was not his trade. Over and over again he repeated this to his Medicean patrons; but they compelled him to build, and he applied himself with the predilections and prepossessions of a plastic artist to the task. The result was a retrogression from the point reached by his immediate predecessors to the vicious system followed by the pseudo-Gothic architects in Italy. That is to say, he treated the structure as an inert mass, to be made as substantial as possible, and then to be covered with details agreeable to the eye. At the beginning of his career he had a defective sense of the harmonic ratios upon which a really musical building may be constructed out of mere bricks and mortar—such, for example, as the Church of S. Giustina at Padua. He was overweighted with ill-assimilated erudition; and all the less desirable licenses of Brunelleschi's school, especially in the abuse of square recesses, he adopted without hesitation. It never seems to have occurred to him that doors which were intended for ingress and egress, windows which were meant to give light, and attics which had a value as the means of illumination from above, could not with any propriety be applied to the covering of blank dead spaces in the interiors of buildings.

The vestibule of the Laurentian Library illustrates his method of procedure. It is a rectangular box of about a cube

and two thirds, set length-way up. The outside of the building, left unfinished, exhibits a mere blank space of bricks.
The interior might be compared to a temple in the grotesque-
classic style turned outside in: colossal orders, meaningless
consoles, heavy windows, square recesses, numerous doors—
the windows, doors, and attics having no right to be there,
since they lead to nothing, lend view to nothing, clamour
for bronze and sculpture to explain their existence as niches
and receptacles for statuary. It is nevertheless indubitably
true that these incongruous and misplaced elements, crowded
together, leave a strong impression of picturesque force upon
the mind. From certain points and angles, the effect of the
whole, considered as a piece of deception and insincerity, is
magnificent. It would be even finer than it is, were not the
Florentine *pietra serena* of the stonework so repellent in its
ashen dulness, the plaster so white, and the false architectural system so painfully defrauded of the plastic forms for
which it was intended to subserve as setting.

We have here no masterpiece of sound constructive science, but a freak of inventive fancy using studied details
for the production of a pictorial effect. The details employed
to compose this curious illusion are painfully dry and sterile;
partly owing to the scholastic enthusiasm for Vitruvius,
partly to the decline of mediæval delight in naturalistic
decoration, but, what seems to me still more apparent,
through Michelangelo's own passionate preoccupation with
the human figure. He could not tolerate any type of art
which did not concede a predominant position to the form
of man. Accordingly, his work in architecture at this period
seems waiting for plastic illustration, demanding sculpture
and fresco for its illumination and justification.

It is easy, one would think, to make an appeal to the eye
by means of colossal orders, bold cornices, enormous consoles, deeply indented niches. How much more easy to construct a box, and then say, "Come, let us cover its inside
with an incongruous and inappropriate but imposing parade

of learning," than to lift some light and genial thing of beauty aloft into the air, as did the modest builder of the staircase to the hall at Christ Church, Oxford! The eye of the vulgar is entranced, the eye of the artist bewildered. That the imagination which inspired that decorative scheme was powerful, original, and noble, will not be denied; but this does not save us from the desolating conviction that the scheme itself is a specious and pretentious mask, devised to hide a hideous waste of bricks and mortar.

Michelangelo's imagination, displayed in this distressing piece of work, was indeed so masterful that, as Vasari says, a new delightful style in architecture seemed to be revealed by it. A new way of clothing surfaces, falsifying façades, and dealing picturesquely with the lifeless element of Vitruvian tradition had been demonstrated by the genius of one who was a mighty amateur in building. In other words, the *Barocco* manner had begun; the path was opened to prank, caprice, and license. It required the finer tact and taste of a Palladio to rectify the false line here initiated, and to bring the world back to a sense of seriousness in its effort to deal constructively and rationally with the pseudo-classic mannerism.

The qualities of wilfulness and amateurishness and seeking after picturesque effect, upon which I am now insisting, spoiled Michelangelo's work as architect, until he was forced by circumstance, and after long practical experience, to confront a problem of pure mathematical construction. In the cupola of S. Peter's he rose to the stern requirements of his task. There we find no evasion of the builder's duty by mere surface-decoration, no subordination of the edifice to plastic or pictorial uses. Such side-issues were excluded by the very nature of the theme. An immortal poem resulted, an aërial lyric of melodious curves and solemn harmonies, a thought combining grace and audacity translated into stone uplifted to the skies. After being cabined in the vestibule to the Laurentian Library, our soul escapes with gladness to those airy spaces of the dome, that great cloud on the verge of the Campagna, and feels thankful that we can take our leave of Michelangelo as architect elsewhere.

VI

While seeking to characterise what proved pernicious to contemporaries in Michelangelo's work as architect, I have been led to concentrate attention upon the Library at S. Lorenzo. This was logical; for, as we have seen, Vasari regarded that building as the supreme manifestation of his manner. Vasari never saw the cupola of S. Peter's in all its glory, and it may be doubted whether he was capable of learning much from it.

The sacristy demands separate consideration. It was an earlier work, produced under more favourable conditions of place and space, and is in every way a purer specimen of the master's style. As Vasari observed, the Laurentian Library indicated a large advance upon the sacristy in the development of Michelangelo's new manner.

At this point it may not unprofitably be remarked, that none of the problems offered for solution at S. Lorenzo were in the strictest sense of that word architectural. The façade presented a problem of pure panelling. The ground-plan of the sacristy was fixed in correspondence with Brunelleschi's; and here again the problem resolved itself chiefly into panelling. A builder of genius, working on the library, might indeed have displayed his science and his taste by some beautiful invention adapted to the awkward locality; as Baldassare Peruzzi, in the Palazzo Massimo at Rome, converted the defects of the site into graces by the exquisite turn he gave to the curved portion of the edifice. Still, when the scheme was settled, even the library bcame more a matter of panelling and internal fittings than of structural design. Nowhere at S. Lorenzo can we affirm that Michelangelo enjoyed the opportunity of showing what he could achieve in the production of a building independent in itself and planned throughout with a free hand. Had he been a born architect, he would probably have insisted upon constructing the Medicean mausoleum after his own conception instead of repeating Brunelleschi's ground-plan, and he would almost certainly have discovered a more genial solution for the difficulties of the library. But he protested firmly against being considered an architect by inclination or by education. Therefore he accepted the most obvious conditions of each task, and devoted himself to schemes of surface decoration.

The interior of the sacristy is planned with a noble sense of unity. For the purpose of illuminating a gallery of statues, the lighting may be praised without reserve; and there is no doubt whatever that Michelangelo intended every tabernacle to be filled with figures, and all the whitewashed spaces of the walls to be encrusted with bas-reliefs in stucco or painted in fresco. The recesses or niches, taking the form of windows, are graduated in three degrees of depth to suit three scales of sculptural importance. The sepulchres of the Dukes had to emerge into prominence; the statues subordinate to these main masses occupied shallower recesses; the shallowest of all, reserved for minor statuary, are adorned above with garlands, which suggest the flatness of the figures to be introduced. Architecturally speaking, the building is complete; but it sadly wants the plastic decoration for which it was designed, together with many finishing touches of importance. It is clear, for instance, that the square pedestals above the double pilasters flanking each of the two Dukes were meant to carry statuettes or candelabra, which would have connected the marble panelling with the cornices and stucchi and frescoed semicircles of the upper region. Our eyes are everywhere defrauded of the effect calculated by Michelangelo when he planned this chapel. Yet the total impression remains harmonious. Proportion has been observed in all the parts, especially in the relation of the larger to the smaller orders, and in the balance of the

doors and windows. Merely decorative carvings are used
with parsimony, and designed in a pure style, although they
exhibit originality of invention. The alternation of white
marble surfaces and mouldings with *pietra serena* pilasters,
cornices, and arches, defines the structural design, and gives
a grave but agreeable sense of variety. Finally, the recess
behind the altar adds lightness and space to what would
otherwise have been a box. What I have already observed
when speaking of the vestibule to the library must be repeated
here: the whole scheme is that of an exterior turned outside in, and its justification lies in the fact that it demanded
statuary and colour for its completion. Still the bold projecting cornices, the deeper and shallower niches resembling
windows, have the merit of securing broken lights and
shadows under the strong vertical illumination, all of which
are eminently picturesque.

No doubt remains now that tradition is accurate in identifying the helmeted Duke with Lorenzo de' Medici, and the
more graceful seated hero opposite with Giuliano. The recumbent figures on the void sepulchres beneath them are
with equal truth designated as Night and Day, Morning and
Evening. But Michelangelo condescended to no realistic
portraiture in the statues of the Dukes, and he also meant
undoubtedly to treat the phases of time which rule man's
daily life upon the planet as symbols for far-reaching
thoughts connected with our destiny. These monumental
figures are not men, not women, but vague and potent allegories of our mortal fate. They remain as he left them,
except that parts of Giuliano's statue, especially the hands,
seem to have been worked over by an assistant. The same
is true of the Madonna, which will ever be regarded, in
her imperfectly finished state, as one of the finest of his
sculptural conceptions. To Montelupo belongs the execution
of S. Damiano, and to Montorsoli that of S. Cosimo. Vasari
says that Tribolo was commissioned by Michelangelo to
carve statues of Earth weeping for the loss of Giuliano, and

Heaven rejoicing over his spirit. The death of Pope Clement, however, put a stop to these subordinate works, which, had they been accomplished, might perhaps have shown us how Buonarroti intended to fill the empty niches on each side of the Dukes.

When Michelangelo left Florence for good at the end of 1534, his statues had not been placed; but we have reason to think that the Dukes and the four allegorical figures were erected in his lifetime. There is something singular in the maladjustment of the recumbent men and women to the curves of the sarcophagi, and in the contrast between the roughness of their bases and the smooth polish of the chests they rest on. These discrepancies do not, however, offend the eye, and they may even have been deliberately adopted from a keen sense of what the Greeks called *asymmetreia* as an adjunct to effect. It is more difficult to understand what he proposed to do with the Madonna and her two attendant saints. Placed as they now are upon a simple ledge, they strike one as being too near the eye, and out of harmony with the architectural tone of the building. It is also noticeable that the saints are more than a head taller than the Dukes, while the Madonna overtops the saints by more than another head. We are here in a region of pure conjecture; and if I hazard an opinion, it is only thrown out as a possible solution of a now impenetrable problem. I think, then, that Michelangelo may have meant to pose these three figures where they are, facing the altar; to raise the Madonna upon a slightly projecting bracket above the level of SS. Damiano and Cosimo, and to paint the wall behind them with a fresco of the Crucifixion. That he had no intention of panelling that empty space with marble may be taken for granted, considering the high finish which has been given to every part of this description of work in the chapel. Treated as I have suggested, the statue of the Madonna, with the patron saints of the House of Medici, overshadowed by a picture of Christ's sacrifice, would have confronted the mystery of the Mass during every celebration at the altar. There are many designs for the Crucifixion, made by Michelangelo in later life, so lofty as almost to suggest a group of figures in the foreground, cutting the middle distance.

At the close of Michelangelo's life the sacristy was still unfinished. It contained the objects I have described—the marble panelling, the altar with its candelabra, the statues of the Dukes and their attendant figures, the Madonna and two Medicean patron saints—in fact, all that we find there now, with the addition of Giovanni da Udine's frescoes in the cupola, the relics of which have since been buried under cold Florentine whitewash.

All the views I have advanced in the foregoing paragraphs as to the point at which Michelangelo abandoned this chapel, and his probable designs for its completion, are in the last resort based upon an important document penned at the instance of the Duke of Florence by Vasari to Buonarroti, not long before the old man's death in Rome. This epistle has so weighty a bearing upon the matter in hand that I shall here translate it. Careful study of its fluent periods will convince an unprejudiced mind that the sacristy, as we now see it, is even less representative of its maker's design than it was when Vasari wrote. The frescoes of Giovanni da Udine are gone. It will also show that the original project involved a wealth of figurative decoration, statuary, painting, stucco, which never arrived at realisation.

VII

Vasari, writing in the spring of 1562, informs Michelangelo concerning the Academy of Design founded by Duke Cosimo de' Medici, and of the Duke's earnest desire that he should return to Florence in order that the sacristy at S. Lorenzo may be finished. "Your reasons for not coming are accepted as sufficient. He is therefore considering—forasmuch as the place is being used now for religious services by day and night, according to the intention of Pope Clement—he is considering, I say, a plan for erecting the statues which are missing in the niches above the sepulchres and the tabernacles above the doors. The Duke then wishes that all the eminent sculptors of this academy, in competition man with man, should each of them make one statue, and that the painters in like manner should exercise their art upon the chapel. Designs are to be prepared for the arches according to your own project, including works of painting and of stucco; the other ornaments and the pavement are to be provided; in short, he intends that the new academicians shall complete the whole imperfect scheme, in order that the world may see that, while so many men of genius still exist among us, the noblest work which was ever yet conceived on earth has not been left unfinished. He has commissioned me to write to you and unfold his views, begging you at the same time to favour him by communicating to himself or to me what your intentions were, or those of the late Pope Clement, with regard to the name and title of the chapel; moreover, to inform us what designs you made for the four tabernacles on each side of the Dukes Lorenzo and Giuliano; also what you projected for the eight statues above the doors and in the tabernacles of the corners; and, finally, what your idea was of the paintings to adorn the flat walls and the semicircular spaces of the chapel. He is particularly anxious that you should be assured of his determination to alter nothing you have already done or planned, but, on the contrary, to carry out the whole work according to your own conception. The academicians too are unanimous in their hearty desire to abide by this decision. I am furthermore instructed to tell you, that if you possess sketches, working cartoons, or drawings made for this purpose, the same would be of the greatest service in the execution of his project; and he promises to be a good and faithful administrator, so that honour may ensue. In case you do not feel inclined to do all this, through the burden of old

age or for any other reason, he begs you at least to communicate with some one who shall write upon the subject;
seeing that he would be greatly grieved, as indeed would the
whole of our academy, to have no ray of light from your
own mind, and possibly to add things to your masterpiece
which were not according to your designs and wishes. We
all of us look forward to being comforted by you, if not
with actual work, at least with words. His Excellency
founds this hope upon your former willingness to complete
the edifice by allotting statues to Tribolo, Montelupo, and
the Friar (Giovanni Angelo Montorsoli). The last named
of these masters is here, eagerly desirous to have the opportunity of doing you honour. So are Francesco Sangallo,
Giovanni Bologna, Benvenuto Cellini, Ammanato, Rossi
and Vincenzio Danti of Perugia, not to mention other
sculptors of note. The painters, headed by Bronzino, include
many talented young men, skilled in design, and colourists,
quite capable of establishing an honourable reputation. Of
myself I need not speak. You know well that in devotion,
attachment, love, and loyalty (and let me say this with
prejudice to no one) I surpass the rest of your admirers by
far. Therefore, I entreat you, of your goodness, to console
his Excellency, and all these men of parts, and our city, as
well as to show this particular favour to myself, who have
been selected by the Duke to write to you, under the impression that, being your familiar and loving friend, I might
obtain from you some assistance of sterling utility for the
undertaking. His Excellency is prepared to spend both substance and labour on the task, in order to honour you. Pray
then, albeit age is irksome, endeavour to aid him by unfold-
ing your views; for, in doing so, you will confer benefits
on countless persons, and will be the cause of raising all
these men of parts to higher excellence, each one of whom
has learned what he already knows in the sacristy, or rather
let me say our school."

This eloquent despatch informs us very clearly that the

walls of the sacristy, above the tall Corinthian order which encloses the part devoted to sculpture, were intended to be covered with stucco and fresco paintings, completing the polychromatic decoration begun by Giovanni da Udine in the cupola. Twelve statues had been designed for the niches in the marble panelling; and one word used by Vasari, *facciate*, leaves the impression that the blank walls round and opposite the altar were also to be adorned with pictures. We remain uncertain how Michelangelo originally meant to dispose of the colossal Madonna with SS. Damian and Cosimo.

Unhappily, nothing came of the Duke's project. Michelangelo was either unable or unwilling—probably unable—to furnish the necessary plans and drawings. In the eighth chapter of this book I have discussed the hesitations with regard to the interior of the sacristy which are revealed by some of his extant designs for it. We also know that he was not in the habit of preparing accurate working cartoons for the whole of a large scheme, but that he proceeded from point to point, trusting to slight sketches and personal supervision of the work. Thus, when Vasari wrote to him from Rome about the staircase of the library, he expressed a perfect readiness to help, but could only remember its construction in a kind of dream. We may safely assume, then, that he had not sufficient material to communicate; plans definite enough in general scope and detailed incident to give a true conception of his whole idea were lacking.

VIII

Passing to æsthetical considerations, I am forced to resume here what I published many years ago about the Sacristy of S. Lorenzo, as it now exists. Repeated visits to that shrine have only renewed former impressions, which will not bear to be reproduced in other language, and would lose some of their freshness by the stylistic effort. No other course remains then but to quote from my own writings, indorsing them with such weight as my signature may have acquired since they were first given to the world.

"The sacristy may be looked on either as the masterpiece of a sculptor who required fit setting for his statues, or of an architect who designed statues to enhance the structure he had planned. Both arts are used with equal ease, nor has the genius of Michelangelo dealt more masterfully with the human frame than with the forms of Roman architecture in this chapel. He seems to have paid no heed to classic precedent, and to have taken no pains to adapt the parts to the structural purpose of the building. It was enough for him to create a wholly novel framework for the modern miracle of sculpture it enshrines, attending to such rules of composition as determine light and shade, and seeking by the relief of mouldings and pilasters to enhance the terrible and massive forms that brood above the Medicean tombs. The result is a product of picturesque and plastic art as true to the Michelangelesque spirit as the Temple of the Wingless Victory to that of Pheidias. But where Michelangelo achieved a triumph of boldness, lesser natures were betrayed into bizarrerie; and this chapel of the Medici, in spite of its grandiose simplicity, proved a stumbling-block to subsequent architects by encouraging them to despise propriety and violate the laws of structure.

"We may assume then that the colossal statues of Giuliano and Lorenzo were studied with a view to their light and shadow as much as to their form; and this is a fact to be remembered by those who visit the chapel where Buonarroti laboured both as architect and sculptor. Of the two Medici, it is not fanciful to say that the Duke of Urbino is the most immovable of spectral shapes eternalised in marble; while the Duke of Nemours, more graceful and elegant, seems intended to present a contrast to this terrible thought-burdened form. The allegorical figures, stretched on segments of ellipses beneath the pedestals of the two Dukes, indicate phases of darkness and of light, of death and life. They are two women and two men; tradition names them Night and Day, Twilight and Dawning. Thus in the statues themselves and in their attendant genii we have a series of abstractions, symbolising the sleep and waking of existence, action and thought, the gloom of death, the lustre of life, and the intermediate states of sadness and of hope that form the borderland of both. Life is a dream between two slumbers; sleep is death's twin-brother; night is the shadow of death; death is the gate of life:—such is the mysterious mythology wrought by the sculptor of the modern world in marble. All these figures, by the intensity of their expression, the vagueness of their symbolism, force us to think and question. What, for example, occupies Lorenzo's brain? Bending forward, leaning his chin upon his wrist, placing the other hand upon his knee, on what does he for ever ponder?

"The sight, as Rogers said well, 'fascinates and is intolerable.' Michelangelo has shot the beaver of the helmet forward on his forehead, and bowed his head, so as to clothe the face in darkness. But behind the gloom there lurks no fleshless skull, as Rogers fancied. The whole frame of the powerful man is instinct with some imperious thought. Has he outlived his life and fallen upon everlasting contemplation? Is he brooding, injured and indignant, over his own doom and the extinction of his race? Is he condemned to witness in immortal immobility the woes of Italy he helped to cause? Or has the sculptor symbolised in him the burden of that personality we carry with us in this life, and bear for ever when we wake into another world? Beneath this incarnation of oppressive thought there lie, full length and naked, the figures of Dawn and Twilight, Morn and Evening. So at least they are commonly called, and these names are not inappropriate; for the breaking of the day and the approach of night are metaphors for many transient conditions of the soul. It is only as allegories in a large sense, comprehending both the physical and intellectual order, and capable of various interpretation, that any of these statues can be understood. Even the Dukes do not pretend to be portraits, and hence in part perhaps the uncertainty that has gathered round them. Very tranquil and noble is Twilight: a giant in repose, he meditates, leaning upon his elbow, looking down. But Dawn starts from her couch, as though some painful summons had reached her, sunk in dreamless sleep, and called her forth to suffer. Her waking to consciousness is like that of one who has been drowned, and who finds the return to life agony. Before her eyes, seen even through the mists of slumber, are the ruin and the shame of Italy. Opposite lies Night, so sorrowful, so utterly absorbed in darkness and the shade of death, that to shake off that everlasting lethargy seems impossible. Yet she is not dead. If we raise our voices, she too will stretch her limbs, and, like her sister, shudder into sensibility with sighs. Only we must not wake her; for he who fashioned her has told us that her sleep of stone is great good fortune. Both of these women are large and brawny, unlike the Fates of Pheidias, in their muscular maturity. The burden of Michelangelo's thought was too tremendous to be borne by virginal and graceful beings. He had to make women no less capable of suffering, no less world-wearied, than his country.

"Standing before these statues, we do not cry, How beautiful! We murmur, How terrible, how grand! Yet, after long gazing, we find them gifted with beauty beyond grace. In each of them there is a palpitating thought, torn from the artist's soul and crystallised in marble. It has been said that architecture is petrified music. In the Sacristy of S. Lorenzo we feel impelled to remember phrases of Beethoven. Each of these statues becomes for us a passion, fit for musical expression, but turned like Niobe to stone. They have the intellectual vagueness, the emotional certainty, that belong to the motives of a symphony. In their allegories, left without a key, sculpture has passed beyond her old domain of placid concrete form. The anguish of intolerable emotion, the quickening of the consciousness to a sense of suffering, the acceptance of the inevitable, the strife of the soul with destiny, the burden and the passion of mankind:—that is what they contain in their cold chisel-tortured marble. It is open to critics of the school of Lessing to object that here is the suicide of sculpture. It is easy to remark that those strained postures and writhen limbs may have perverted the taste of lesser craftsmen. Yet if Michelangelo was called to carve Medicean statues after the sack of Rome and the fall of Florence—if he was obliged in sober sadness to make sculpture a fit language for his sorrow-laden heart—how could he have wrought more truthfully than this? To imitate him without sharing his emotion or comprehending his thoughts, as the soulless artists of the decadence attempted, was without all doubt a grievous error. Surely also we may regret, not without reason, that in the evil days upon which he had fallen, the fair antique *Heiterkeit* and *Allgemeinheit* were beyond his reach."

That this regret is not wholly sentimental may be proved, I think, by an exchange of verses, which we owe to Vasari's literary sagacity. He tells us that when the statue of the Night was opened to the public view, it drew forth the following quatrain from an author unknown to himself by name:—

> *The Night thou seest here, posed gracefully*
> *In act of slumber, was by an Angel wrought*
> *Out of this stone; sleeping, with life she's fraught:*
> *Wake her, incredulous wight; she'll speak to thee.*

Michelangelo would have none of these academical conceits and compliments. He replied in four verses, which show well enough what thoughts were in his brain when he composed the nightmare-burdened, heavy-sleeping women:

> *Dear is my sleep, but more to be mere stone,*
> *So long as ruin and dishonour reign:*
> *To hear naught, to feel naught, is my great gain;*
> *Then wake me not; speak in an undertone.*

CHAPTER XI

I

AFTER the death of Clement VII., Michelangelo never returned to reside for any length of time at Florence. The rest of his life was spent in Rome, and he fell almost immediately under the kind but somewhat arbitrary patronage of Alessandro Farnese, who succeeded to the Papal chair in October 1534, with the title of Paul III.

One of the last acts of Clement's life had been to superintend the second contract with the heirs of Julius, by which Michelangelo undertook to finish the tomb upon a reduced scale within the space of three years. He was allowed to come to Rome and work there during four months annually. Paul, however, asserted his authority by upsetting these arrangements and virtually cancelling the contract.

"In the meanwhile," writes Condivi, "Pope Clement died, and Paul III. sent for him, and requested him to enter his service. Michelangelo saw at once that he would be interrupted in his work upon the Tomb of Julius. So he told Paul that he was not his own master, being bound to the Duke of Urbino until the monument was finished. The Pope grew angry, and exclaimed: 'It is thirty years that I have cherished this desire, and now that I am Pope, may I not indulge it? Where is the contract? I mean to tear it up.' Michelangelo, finding himself reduced to these straits, almost resolved to leave Rome and take refuge in the Genoese, at an abbey held by the Bishop of Aleria, who had been a creature of Julius, and was much attached to him. He hoped that the neighbourhood of the Carrara quarries, and the facility of transporting marbles by sea, would help him to complete his engagements. He also thought of settling at Urbino, which he had previously selected as a tranquil retreat, and where he expected to be well received for the sake of Pope Julius. Some months earlier, he even sent a man of his to buy a house and land there. Still he dreaded the greatness of the Pontiff, as indeed he had good cause to do; and for this reason he abandoned the idea of quitting Rome, hoping to pacify his Holiness with fair words.

"The Pope, however, stuck to his opinion; and one day he visited Michelangelo at his house, attended by eight or ten Cardinals. He first of all inspected the cartoon prepared in Clement's reign for the great work of the Sistine; then the statues for the tomb, and everything in detail. The most reverend Cardinal of Mantua, standing before the statue of Moses, cried out: 'That piece alone is sufficient to do honour to the monument of Julius.' Pope Paul, having gone through the whole workshop, renewed his request that Michelangelo should enter his servcie; and when the latter still resisted, he clinched the matter by saying: 'I will provide that the Duke of Urbino shall be satisfied with three statues from your hand, and the remaining three shall be assigned to some other sculptor.' Accordingly, he settled on the terms of a new contract with the agents of the Duke, which were confirmed by his Excellency, who did not care to displeasure the Pope. Michelangelo, albeit he was now relieved from the obligation of paying for the three statues, preferred to take this cost upon himself, and deposited 1580 ducats for the purpose. And so the Tragedy of the Tomb came at last to an end. This may now be seen at S. Pietro ad Vincula; and though, truth to tell, it is but a mutilated and botched-up remnant of Michelangelo's original design, the monument is still the finest to be found in Rome, and perhaps elsewhere in the world, if only for the three statues finished by the hand of the great master."

II

In this account, Condivi, has condensed the events of seven years. The third and last contract with the heirs of Julius was not ratified until the autumn of 1542, nor was the tomb erected much before the year 1550. We shall see that the tragedy still cost its hero many anxious days during this period.

Paul III., having obtained his object, issued a brief, whereby he appointed Michelangelo chief architect, sculptor, and painter at the Vatican. The instrument is dated September 1, 1535, and the terms with which it describes the master's eminence in the three arts are highly flattering. Allusion is directly made to the fresco of the Last Judgment, which may therefore have been begun about this date. Michelangelo was enrolled as member of the Pontifical household, with a permanent pension of 1200 golden crowns, to be raised in part on the revenues accruing from a ferry across the Po at Piacenza. He did not, however, obtain possession of this ferry until 1537, and the benefice proved so unremunerative that it was exchanged for a little post in the Chancery at Rimini.

When Michelangelo began to work again in the Sistine Chapel, the wall above the altar was adorned with three great sacred subjects by the hand of Pietro Perugino. In the central fresco of the Assumption Perugino introduced a portrait of Sixtus IV. kneeling in adoration before the ascending Madonna. The side panels were devoted to the Nativity and the finding of Moses. In what condition Michelangelo found these frescoes before the painting of the Last Judgment we do not know. Vasari says that he caused the wall to be rebuilt with well-baked carefully selected bricks, and sloped inwards so that the top projected half a cubit from the bottom. This was intended to secure the picture from dust. Vasari also relates that Sebastiano del Piombo, acting on his own responsibility, prepared this wall with a ground for oil-colours, hoping to be employed by Michelangelo, but that the latter had it removed, preferring the orthodox method of fresco-painting. The story, as it stands, is not very probable; yet we may perhaps conjecture that, before deciding on the system to be adopted for his great work, Buonarroti thought fit to make experiments in several surfaces. The painters of that period, as is proved by Sebastiano's practice, by Lionardo da Vinci's unfortunate innovations at Florence, and by the experiments of Raffaello's pupils in the hall of Constantine, not unfrequently invented methods for mural decoration which should afford the glow and richness of oil-colouring. Michelangelo may even have proposed at one time to intrust a large portion of his fresco to Sebastiano's executive skill, and afterwards have found the same difficulties in collaboration which reduced him to the necessity of painting the Sistine vault in solitude.

Be that as it may, when the doors of the chapel once closed behind the master, we hear nothing whatsoever about his doings till they opened again on Christmas Day in 1541. The reticence of Michelangelo regarding his own works is one of the most trying things about him. It is true indeed that his correspondence between 1534 and 1541 almost entirely fails; still, had it been abundant, we should probably have possessed but dry and laconic references to matters connected with the business of his art.

He must have been fully occupied on the Last Judgment during 1536 and 1537. Paul III. was still in correspondence with the Duke of Urbino, who showed himself not only willing to meet the Pope's wishes with regard to the Tomb of Julius, but also very well disposed toward the sculptor. In July 1537, Hieronimo Staccoli wrote to the Duke of Camerino about a silver salt-cellar which Michelangelo had designed at his request. This prince, Guidobaldo della Rovere, when he afterwards succeeded to the Duchy of Urbino, sent a really warm-hearted despatch to his "dearest Messer Michelangelo." He begins by saying that, though he still cherishes the strongest wish to see the monument of his uncle completed, he does not like to interrupt the fresco in the Sistine Chapel, upon which his Holiness has set his heart. He thoroughly trusts in Michelangelo's loyalty, and is assured that his desire to finish the tomb, for the honour of his former patron's memory, is keen and sincere. Therefore, he hopes that when the picture of the Last Judgment is terminated, the work will be resumed and carried to a prosperous conclusion. In the meantime, let Buonarroti attend to his health, and not put everything again to peril by overstraining his energies.

Signor Gotti quotes a Papal brief, issued on the 18th of September 1537, in which the history of the Tomb of Julius up to date is set forth, and Michelangelo's obligations toward the princes of Urbino are recited. It then proceeds to declare that Clement VII. ordered him to paint the great wall of the Sistine, and that Paul desires this work to be carried forward with all possible despatch. He therefore lets it be publicly known that Michelangelo has not failed to perform his engagements in the matter of the tomb through any fault or action of his own, but by the express command of his Holiness. Finally, he discharges him and his heirs from all liabilities, pecuniary or other, to which he may appear exposed by the unfulfilled contracts.

III

While thus engaged upon his fresco, Michelangelo received a letter, dated Venice, September 15, 1537, from that rogue of genius, Pietro Aretino. It opens in the strain of hyperbolical compliment and florid rhetoric which Aretino affected when he chose to flatter. The man, however, was an admirable stylist, the inventor of a new epistolary manner. Like a volcano, his mind blazed with wit, and buried sound sense beneath the scoriæ and ashes it belched forth. Gifted with a natural feeling for rhetorical contrast, he knew the effect of some simple and impressive sentence, placed like a gem of value in the midst of gimcrack conceits. Thus: "I should not venture to address you, had not my name, accepted by the ears of every prince in Europe, outworn much of its native indignity. And it is but meet that that I should approach you with this reverence; for the world has many kings, and one only Michelangelo.

Strange miracle, that Nature, who cannot place aught so high but that you explore it with your art, should be impotent to stamp upon her works that majesty which she contains within herself, the immense power of your style and your chisel! Wherefore, when we gaze on you, we regret no longer that we may not meet with Pheidias, Apelles, or Vitruvius, whose spirits were the shadow of your spirit." He piles the panegyric up to its climax, by adding it is fortunate for those great artists of antiquity that their masterpieces cannot be compared with Michelangelo's, since, "being arraigned before the tribunal of our eyes, we should perforce proclaim you unique as sculptor, unique as painter, and as architect unique." After the blare of this exordium, Aretino settles down to the real business of his letter, and communicates his own views regarding the Last Judgment, which he hears that the supreme master of all arts is engaged in depicting. "Who would not quake with terror while dipping his brush into the dreadful theme? I behold Antichrist in the midst of thronging multitudes, with an aspect such as only you could limn. I behold affright upon the forehead of the living; I see the signs of the extinction of the sun, the moon, the stars; I see the breath of life exhaling from the elements; I see Nature abandoned and apart, reduced to barrenness, crouching in her decrepitude; I see Time sapless and trembling, for his end has come, and he is seated on an arid throne; and while I hear the trumpets of the angels with their thunder shake the hearts of all, I see both Life and Death convulsed with horrible confusion, the one striving to resuscitate the dead, the other using all his might to slay the living; I see Hope and Despair guiding the squadrons of the good and the cohorts of the wicked; I see the theatre of clouds, blazing with rays that issue from the purest fires of heaven, upon which among his hosts Christ sits, ringed round with splendours and with terrors; I see the radiance of his face, coruscating flames of light both glad and awful, filling the blest with joy, the damned with fear intolerable. Then I behold the satellites of the abyss, who with horrid gestures, to the glory of the saints and martyrs, deride Cæsar and the Alexanders; for it is one thing to have trampled on the world, but more to have conquered self. I see Fame, with her crowns and palms trodden under foot, cast out among the wheels of her own chariots. And to conclude all, I see the dread sentence issue from the mouth of the Son of God. I see it in the form of two darts, the one of salvation, the other of damnation; and as they hustle down, I hear the fury of its onset shock the elemental frame of things, and, with the roar of thunderings and voices, smash the universal scheme to fragments. I see the vault of ether merged in gloom, illuminated only by the lights of Paradise and the furnaces of hell. My thoughts, excited by this vision of the day of Doom, whisper: 'If we quake in terror before the handiwork of Buonarroti, how shall we shake and shrink affrighted when He who shall judge passes sentence on our souls?' "

This descrpition of the Last Day, in which it is more than doubtful whether a man like Aretino had any sincere faith, possesses considerable literary interest. In the first place, it is curious as coming from one who lived on terms of closest intimacy with painters, and who certainly appreciated art; for this reason, that nothing less pictorial than the images evoked could be invented. Then, again, in the first half of the sixteenth century it anticipated the rhetoric of the *barocco* period——the eloquence of seventeenth-century divines, Dutch poets, Jesuit pulpiteers. Aretino's originality consisted in his precocious divination of a whole new age of taste and style, which was destined to supersede the purer graces of the Renaissance.

The letter ends with an assurance that if anything could persuade him to break a resolution he had formed, and to revisit Rome, it would be his great anxiety to view the Last Judgment of the Sistine Chapel with his own eyes.

Michelangelo sent an answer which may be cited as an example of his peculiar irony. Under the form of elaborate compliment it conceals the scorn he must have conceived for Aretino and his insolent advice. Yet he knew how dangerous the man could be, and felt obliged to humour him.

"Magnificent Messer Pietro, my lord and brother,— The receipt of your letter gave me both joy and sorrow. I rejoiced exceedingly, since it came from you, who are without peer in all the world for talent. Yet at the same time I grieved, inasmuch as, having finished a large part of the fresco, I cannot realise your conception, which is so complete, that if the Day of Judgment had come, and you had been present and seen it with your eyes, your words could not have described it better. Now, touching an answer to my letter, I reply that I not only desire it, but I entreat you to write one, seeing that kings and emperors esteem it the highest favour to be mentioned by your pen. Meanwhile, if I have anything that you would like, I offer it with all my heart. In conclusion, do not break your resolve of never revisiting Rome on account of the picture I am painting, for this would be too much."

Aretino's real object was to wheedle some priceless sketch or drawing out of the great master. This appears from a second letter written by him on the 20th of January 1538. "Does not my devotion deserve that I should receive from you, the prince of sculpture and of painting, one of those cartoons which you fling into the fire, to the end that during life I may enjoy it, and in death carry it with me to the tomb?" After all, we must give Aretino credit for genuine feelings of admiration toward illustrious artists like Titian, Sansovino, and Michelangelo. Writing many years after the date of these letters, when he has seen an engraving of the Last Judgment, he uses terms, extravagant indeed, but apparently sincere, about its grandeur of design. Then he repeats his request for a drawing. "Why will you not repay my devotion to your divine qualities by the gift of some scrap of a drawing, the least valuable in your eyes? I should certainly esteem two strokes of the chalk upon a piece of paper more than all the cups and chains which all the kings and princes gave me." It seems that Michelangelo continued to correspond with him, and that Benvenuto Cellini took part in their exchange of letters. But no drawings were sent; and in course of time the ruffian got the better of the virtuoso in Aretino's rapacious nature. Without ceasing to fawn and flatter Michelangelo, he sought occasion to damage his reputation. Thus we find him writing in January 1546 to the engraver Enea Vico, bestowing high praise upon a copper-plate which a certain Bazzacco had made from the Last Judgment, but criticising the picture as "licentious and likely to cause scandal with the Lutherans, by reason of its immodest exposure of the nakedness of persons of both sexes in heaven and hell." It is not clear what Aretino expected from Enea Vico. A reference to the Duke of Florence seems to indicate that he wished to arouse suspicions among great and influential persons regarding the religious and moral quality of Michelangelo's work.

This malevolent temper burst out at last in one of the most remarkable letters we possess of his. It was obviously intended to hurt and insult Michelangelo as much as lay within his power of innuendo and direct abuse. The invective offers so many points of interest with regard to both men, that I shall not hesitate to translate it here in full.

"Sir, when I inspected the complete sketch of the whole of your Last Judgment, I arrived at recognising the eminent graciousness of Raffaello in its agreeable beauty of invention.

"Meanwhile, as a baptized Christian, I blush before the license, so forbidden to man's intellect, which you have used in expressing ideas connected with the highest aims and final ends to which our faith aspires. So, then, that Michelangelo stupendous in his fame, that Michelangelo renowned for prudence, that Michelangelo whom all admire, has chosen to display to the whole world an impiety of irreligion only equalled by the perfection of his painting! Is it possible that you, who, since you are divine, do not condescend to consort with human beings, have done this in the greatest temple built to God, upon the highest altar raised to Christ, in the most sacred chapel upon earth, where the mighty hinges of the Church, the venerable priests of our religion, the Vicar of Christ, with solemn ceremonies and holy prayers, confess, contemplate, and adore his body, his blood, and his flesh?

"If it were not infamous to introduce the comparison, I would plume myself upon my virtue when I wrote *La Nanna*. I would demonstrate the superiority of my reserve to your indiscretion, seeing that I, while handling themes lascivious and immodest, use language comely and decorous, speak in terms beyond reproach and inoffensive to chaste ears. You, on the contrary, presenting so awful a subject, exhibit saints and angels, these without earthly decency, and those without celestial honours.

"The pagans, when they modelled a Diana, gave her clothes; when they made a naked Venus, hid the parts which are not shown with the hand of modesty. And here there comes a Christian, who, because he rates art higher than the faith, deems it a royal spectacle to portray martyrs and virgins in improper attitudes, to show men dragged down by their shame, before which things houses of ill-fame would shut the eyes in order not to see them. Your art would be at home in some voluptuous bagnio, certainly not in the highest chapel of the world. Less criminal were it if you were an infidel, than, being a believer, thus to sap the faith of others. Up to the present time the splendour of such audacious marvels hath not gone unpunished; for their very superexcellence is the death of your good name. Restore them to repute by turning the indecent parts of the damned to flames, and those of the blessed to sunbeams; or imitate the modesty of Florence, who hides your David's shame beneath some gilded leaves. And yet that statue is exposed upon a public square, not in a consecrated chapel.

"As I wish that God may pardon you, I do not write this out of any resentment for the things I begged of you. In truth, if you had sent me what you promised, you would only have been doing what you ought to have desired most eagerly to do in your own interest; for this act of courtesy would silence the envious tongues which say that only certain Gerards and Thomases dispose of them.

"Well, if the treasure bequeathed you by Pope Julius, in order that you might deposit his ashes in an urn of your own carving, was not enough to make you keep your plighted word, what can I expect from you? It is not your ingratitude, your avarice, great painter, but the grace and merit of the Supreme Shepherd, which decide his fame. God wills that Julius should live renowned for ever in a simple tomb, inurned in his own merits, and not in some proud monument dependent on your genius. Meantime, your failure to discharge your obligations is reckoned to you as an act of thieving.

"Our souls need the tranquil emotions of piety more than the lively impressions of plastic art. May God, then, inspire his Holiness Paul with the same thoughts as he instilled into Gregory of blessed memory, who rather chose to despoil Rome of the proud statues of the Pagan deities than to let their magnificence deprive the humbler images of the saints of the devotion of the people.

"Lastly, when you set about composing your picture of the universe and hell and heaven, if you had steeped your heart with those suggestions of glory, of honour, and of terror proper to the theme which I sketched out and offered to you in the letter I wrote you and the whole world reads, I venture to assert that not only would nature and all kind influences cease to regret the illustrious talents they endowed you with, and which to-day render you, by virtue of your art, an image of the marvellous: but Providence,

who sees all things, would herself continue to watch over
such a masterpiece, so long as order lasts in her government
of the hemispheres.

"Your servant,

"THE ARETINE.

"Now that I have blown off some of the rage I feel
against you for the cruelty you used to my devotion, and
have taught you to see that, while you may be divine, I am
not made of water, I bid you tear up this letter, for I have
done the like, and do not forget that I am one to whose
epistles kings and emperors reply.

"To the great MICHELANGELO BUONARROTI in Rome."

The malignancy of this letter is only equalled by its
stylistic ingenuity. Aretino used every means he could devise
to wound and irritate a sensitive nature. The allusion to
Raffaello, the comparison of his own pornographic dialogues
with the Last Judgment in the Sistine, the covert hint that
folk gossiped about Michelangelo's relations to young men,
his sneers at the great man's exclusiveness, his cruel insinuations with regard to the Tomb of Julius, his devout hope
that Paul will destroy the fresco, and the impudent eulogy
of his precious letter on the Last Day, were all nicely calculated to annoy. Whether the missive was duly received by
Buonarroti we do not know. Gaye asserts that it appears to
have been sent through the post. He discovered it in the
Archives of the Strozzi Palace.

The virtuous Pietro Aretino was not the only one to be
scandalised by the nudities of the Last Judgment; and indeed it must be allowed that when Michelangelo treated
such a subject in such a manner, he was pushing the principle of art for art's sake to its extremity. One of the most
popular stories told about this work shows that it early began to create a scandal. When it was three fourths finished,
Pope Paul went to see the fresco, attended by Messer

Biagio da Cesena, his Master of the Ceremonies. On being asked his opinion of the painting, Messer Biagio replied that he thought it highly improper to expose so many naked figures in a sacred picture, and that it was more fit for a place of debauchery than for the Pope's chapel. Michelangelo, nettled by this, drew the prelate's portrait to the life, and placed him in hell with horns on his head and a serpent twisted round his loins. Messer Biagio, finding himself in this plight, and being no doubt laughed at by his friends, complained to the Pope, who answered that he could do nothing to help him. "Had the painter sent you to Purgatory, I would have used my best efforts to get you released; but I exercise no influence in hell; *ubi nulla est redemptio.*" Before Michelangelo's death, his follower, Daniele da Volterra, was employed to provide draperies for the most obnoxious figures, and won thereby the name of *Il Braghettone,* or the breeches-maker. Paul IV. gave the painter this commission, having previously consulted Buonarroti on the subject. The latter is said to have replied to the Pope's messenger: "Tell his Holiness that this is a small matter, and can easily be set straight. Let him look to setting the world in order: to reform a picture costs no great trouble." Later on, during the Pontificate of Pio V., a master named Girolamo da Fano continued the process begun by Daniele da Volterra. As a necessary consequence of this tribute to modesty, the scheme of Michelangelo's colouring and the balance of his masses have been irretrievably damaged.

IV

Vasari says that not very long before the Last Judgment was finished, Michelangelo fell from the scaffolding, and seriously hurt his leg. The pain he suffered and his melancholy made him shut himself up at home, where he refused to be treated by a doctor. There was a Florentine physician in Rome, however, of capricious humour, who admired the arts, and felt a real affection for Buonarroti. This man contrived to creep into the house by some privy entrance, and roamed about it till he found the master. He then insisted upon remaining there on watch and guard until he had effected a complete cure. The name of this excellent friend, famous for his skill and science in those days, was Baccio Rontini.

After his recovery Michelangelo returned to work, and finished the Last Judgment in a few months. It was exposed to the public on Christmast Day in 1541.

Time, negligence, and outrage, the dust of centuries, the burned papers of successive conclaves, the smoke of altar-candles, the hammers and the hangings of upholsterers, the brush of the breeches-maker and restorer, have so dealt with the Last Judgment that it is almost impossible to do it justice now. What Michelangelo intended by his scheme of colour is entirely lost. Not only did Daniele da Volterra, an execrable colourist, dab vividly tinted patches upon the modulated harmonies of flesh-tones painted by the master; but the whole surface has sunk into a bluish fog, deepening to something like lamp-black around the altar. Nevertheless, in its composition the fresco may still be studied; and after due inspection, aided by photographic reproductions of each portion, we are not unable to understand the enthusiasm which so nobly and profoundly planned a work of art aroused among contemporaries.

It has sometimes been asserted that this enormous painting, the largest and most comprehensive in the world, is a tempest of contending forms, a hurly-burly of floating, falling, soaring, and descending figures. Nothing can be more opposed to the truth. Michelangelo was sixty-six years of age when he laid his brush down at the end of the gigantic task. He had long outlived the spontaneity of youthful ardour. His experience through half a century in the planning of monuments, the painting of the Sistine vault, the designing of façades and sacristies and libraries, had developed the architectonic sense which was always powerful in his conceptive faculty. Consequently, we are not surprised to find that, intricate and confused as the scheme may appear to an unpractised eye, it is in reality a design of mathematical severity, divided into four bands or planes of grouping. The wall, since it occupies one entire end of a long high building, is naturally less broad than lofty. The pictorial divisions are therefore horizontal in the main, though so combined and varied as to produce the effect of multiplied curves, balancing and antiphonally inverting their lines of sinuosity. The pendentive upon which the prophet Jonah sits, descends and breaks the surface at the top, leaving a semicircular compartment on each side of its corbel. Michelangelo filled these upper spaces with two groups of wrestling angels, the one bearing a huge cross, the other a column, in the air. The cross and whipping-post are the chief emblems of Christ's Passion. The crown of thorns is also there, the sponge, the ladder, and the nails. It is with no merciful intent that these signs of our Lord's suffering are thus exhibited. Demonic angels, tumbling on clouds like Leviathans, hurl them to and fro in brutal wrath above the crowd of souls, as though to demonstrate the justice of damnation. In spite of a God's pain and shameful death, mankind has gone on sinning. The Judge is what the crimes of the world and Italy have made him. Immediately below the corbel, and well detached from the squadrons of attendant saints, Christ rises from His throne. His face is turned in the direction of the damned, His right hand is lifted as though loaded with thunderbolts for their annihilation. He is a ponderous young athlete; rather say a mass of hypertrophied muscles, with the features of a vulgarised Apollo. The Virgin sits in a crouching attitude at His right side, slightly averting her head, as though in painful expectation of the coming sentence. The saints and martyrs who surround Christ and His Mother, while forming one of the chief planes in the composition, are arranged in four unequal groups of subtle and surprising intricacy. All bear the emblems of their cruel deaths, and shake them in the sight of Christ as though appealing to His judgment-seat. It has been charitably suggested that they intend to supplicate for mercy. I cannot, however, resist the impression that they are really demanding rigid justice. S. Bartholomew flourishes his flaying-knife and dripping skin with a glare of menace. S. Catherine struggles to raise her broken wheel. S. Sebastian frowns down on hell with a sheaf of arrows quivering in his stalwart arm. The saws, the carding-combs, the crosses, and the gridirons, all subserve the same purpose of reminding Christ that, if He does not damn the wicked, confessors will have died with Him in vain. It is singular that, while Michelangelo depicted so many attitudes of expectation, eagerness, anxiety, and astonishment in the blest, he has given to none of them the expression of gratitude, or love, or sympathy, or shrinking awe. Men and women, old and young alike, are human beings of Herculean build. Paradise, according to Buonarroti's conception, was not meant for what is graceful, lovely, original, and tender. The hosts of heaven are adult and over-developed gymnasts. Yet, while we record these impressions, it would be unfair to neglect the spiritual beauty of some souls embracing after long separation in the grave, with folding arms, and clasping hands, and clinging lips. While painting these, Michelangelo thought peradventure of his father and his brother.

The two planes which I have attempted to describe occupy the upper and the larger portion of the composition. The third in order is made up of three masses. In the middle floats a band of Titanic cherubs, blowing their long trumpets over earth and sea to wake the dead. Dramatically, nothing can be finer than the strained energy and superhuman force of these superb creatures. Their attitudes compel our imagination to hear the crashing thunders of the trump of doom. To the left of the spectator are souls ascending to be judged, some floating through vague ether, enwrapped with graveclothes, others assisted by descending saints and angels, who reach a hand, a rosary, to help the still gross spirit in its flight. To the right are the condemned, sinking downwards to their place of torment, spurned by seraphs, cuffed by angelic grooms, dragged by demons, hurling, howling, huddled in a mass of horror. It is just here, and still yet farther down, that Michelangelo put forth all his power as a master of expression. While the blessed display nothing which is truly proper to their state of holiness and everlasting peace, the damned appear in every realistic aspect of most stringent agony and terror. The colossal forms of flesh with which the multitudes of saved and damned are equally endowed, befit that extremity of physical and mental anguish more than they suit the serenity of bliss eternal. There is a wretch, twined round with fiends, gazing straight before him as he sinks; one half of his face is buried in his hand, the other fixed in a stony spasm of despair, foreshadowing perpetuity of hell. Nothing could express with sublimity of a higher order the sense of irremediable loss, eternal pain, a future endless without hope, than the rigid dignity of this not ignoble sinner's dread. Just below is the place to which the doomed are sinking. Michelangelo reverted to Dante for the symbolism chosen to portray hell. Charon, the demon, with eyes of burning coal, compels a crowd of spirits in his ferryboat. They land and are received by devils, who drag them before Minos, judge of the infernal regions. He towers at the extreme right end of the fresco, indicating that the nether regions yawn infinitely deep, beyond our ken; just as the angels above Christ suggest a region of light and glory, extending upward through illimitable space. The scene of judgment on which attention is concentrated forms but an episode in the universal, sempiternal scheme of things. Balancing hell, on the left hand of the spectator, is brute earth, the grave, the forming and the swallowing clay, out of which souls, not yet acquitted or condemned, emerge with difficulty, in varied forms of skeletons or corpses, slowly thawing into life eternal.

Vasari, in his description of the Last Judgment, seized upon what after all endures as the most salient aspect of this puzzling work, at once so fascinating and so repellent. "It is obvious," he says, "that the peerless painter did not aim at anything but the portrayal of the human body in perfect proportions and most varied attitudes, together with the passions and affections of the soul. That was enough for him, and here he has no equal. He wanted to exhibit the grand style: consummate draughtsmanship in the nude, mastery over all problems of design. He concentrated his power upon the human form, attending to that alone, and neglecting all subsidiary things, as charm of colour, capricious inventions, delicate devices and novelties of fancy." Vasari might have added that Michelangelo also neglected what ought to have been a main object of his art: convincing eloquence, the solemnity proper to his theme, spirituality of earthly grossness quit. As a collection of athletic nudes in all conceivable postures of rest and action, of foreshortening, of suggested movement, the Last Judgment remains a stupendous miracle. Nor has the aged master lost his cunning for the portrayal of divinely simple faces, superb limbs, masculine beauty, in the ideal persons of young men. The picture, when we dwell long enough upon its details, emerges into prominence, moreover, as indubitably awe-inspiring, terrifying, dreadful in its poignant expression of wrath, retaliation, thirst for vengeance, cruelty, and helpless horror. But the supreme point even of Doomsday, of the Dies Iræ, has not been seized. We do not hear the still small voice of pathos and of human hope which thrills through Thomas a Celano's hymn:—

> *Quærens me sedisti lassus,*
> *Redemisti crucem passus:*
> *Tantus labor non sit cassus.*

The note is one of sustained menace and terror, and the total scheme of congregated forms might be compared to a sense-deafening solo on a trombone. While saying this, we must remember that it was the constant impulse of Michelangelo to seize one moment only, and what he deemed the most decisive moment, in the theme he had to develop. Having selected the instant of time at which Christ, half risen from his Judgment-seat of cloud, raises an omnific hand to curse, the master caused each fibre of his complex composition to thrill with the tremendous passion of that coming sentence. The long series of designs for Crucifixions, Depositions from the Cross, and Pietàs which we possess, all of them belonging to a period of his life not much later than 1541, prove that his nature was quite as sensitive to pathos as to terror; only, it was not in him to attempt a combination of terror and pathos.

"He aimed at the portrayal of the human body. He wanted to exhibit the grand style." So says Vasari, and Vasari is partly right. But we must not fall into the paradox, so perversely maintained by Ruskin in his lecture on Tintoretto and Michelangelo, that the latter was a cold and heartless artist, caring chiefly for the display of technical skill and anatomical science. Partial and painful as we may find the meaning of the Last Judgment, that meaning has been only too powerfully and personally felt. The denunciations of the prophets, the woes of the Apocalypse, the invectives of Savonarola, the tragedies of Italian history, the sense of present and indwelling sin, storm through and through it. Technically, the masterpiece bears signs of fatigue and discontent, in spite of its extraordinary vigour of conception and execution. The man was old and tired, thwarted in his wishes and oppressed with troubles. His very science had become more formal, his types more arid and schematic, than they used to be. The thrilling life, the divine afflatus, of the Sistine vault have passed out of the Last Judgment. Wholly admirable, unrivalled, and unequalled by any other human work upon a similar scale as this fresco may be in its command over the varied resources of the human body, it does not strike our mind as the production of a master glorying in carnal pride and mental insolence, but rather as that of one discomfited and terrified, upon the point of losing heart.

Henri Beyle, jotting down his impressions in the Sistine Chapel, was reminded of the Grand Army's flight after the burning of Moscow. "When, in our disastrous retreat from Russia, it chanced that we were suddenly awakened in the middle of the dark night by an obstinate cannonading, which at each moment seemed to gain in nearness, then all the forces of a man's nature gathered close around his heart; he felt himself in the presence of fate, and having no attention left for things of vulgar interest, he made himself ready to dispute his life with destiny. The sight of Michelangelo's picture has brought back to my consciousness that almost forgotten sensation." This is a piece of just and sympathetic criticism, and upon its note I am fain to close.

V

It is probable that the fame of the Last Judgment spread rapidly abroad through Italy, and that many visits to Rome were made for the purpose of inspecting it. Complimentary sonnets must also have been addressed to the painter. I take it that Niccolò Martelli sent some poems on the subject from Florence, for Michelangelo replied upon the 20th of January 1542 in the following letter of singular modesty and urbane kindness:—

"I received from Messer Vincenzo Perini your letter with two sonnets and a madrigal. The letter and the sonnet addressed to me are so marvellously fine, that if a man should find in them anything to castigate, it would be impossible to castigate him as thoroughly as they are castigated. It is true they praise me so much, that had I Paradise in my bosom, less of praise would suffice. I perceive that you suppose me to be just what God wishes that I were. I am a poor man and of little merit, who plod along in the art which God gave me, to lengthen out my life as far as possible. Such as I am, I remain your servant and that of all the house of Martelli. I thank you for your letter and the poems, but not as much as duty bids, for I cannot soar to such heights of courtesy."

When the Last Judgment was finished, Michelangelo not unreasonably hoped that he might resume his work upon the Tomb of Julius. But this was not to be. Antonio da San Gallo had just completed the Chapel of the Holy Sacrament in the Vatican, which is known as the Cappella Paolina, and the Pope resolved that its frescoes should be painted by Buonarroti. The Duke of Urbino, yielding to his wishes, wrote to Michelangelo upon the 6th of March 1542, saying that he should be quite satisfied if the three statues by his hand, including the Moses, were assigned to the tomb, the execution of the rest being left to competent workmen under his direction.

In effect, we possess documents proving that the tomb was consigned to several masters during this year, 1542. The first is a contract dated February 27, whereby Raffaello da Montelupo undertakes to finish three statues, two of these being the Active Life and the Contemplative. The second is a contract dated May 16, in which Michelangelo assigns the architectural and ornamental portion of the monument conjointly to Giovanni de' Marchesi and Francesco d' Amadore, called Urbino, providing that differences which may arise between them shall be referred to Donato Giannotti. There is a third contract, under date June 1, about the same work intrusted to the same two craftsmen, prescribing details with more exactitude. It turned out that the apprehension of disagreement between the masters about the division of their labour was not unfounded, for Michelangelo wrote twice in July to his friend Luigi del Riccio, complaining bitterly of their dissensions, and saying that he has lost two months in these trifles. He adds that one of them is covetous, the other mad, and he fears their quarrel may end in wounds or murder. The matter disturbs his mind greatly, chiefly on account of Urbino, because he has brought him up, and also because of the time wasted over "their ignorance and bestial stupidity." The dispute was finally settled by the intervention of three master-masons (acting severally for Michelangelo, Urbino, and Giovanni), who valued the respective portions of the work.

I must interrupt this narrative of the tomb to explain who some of the persons just mentioned were, and how they came to be connected with Buonarroti. Donato Giannotti was the famous writer upon political and literary topics, who, after playing a conspicuous part in the revolution of Florence against the Medici, now lived in exile at Rome. His dialogues on Dante, and Francesco d'Olanda's account of the meetings at S. Silvestro, prove that he formed a member of that little circle which included Michelangelo and Vittoria Colonna. Luigi del Riccio was a Florentine merchant, settled in the banking-house of the Strozzi at Rome. For many years he acted as Michelangelo's man of business; but their friendship was close and warm in many other ways. They were drawn together by a common love of poetry, and by the charm of a rarely gifted youth called Cecchino dei Bracci. Urbino was the great sculptor's servant and man of all work, the last and best of that series, which included Stefano Miniatore, Pietro Urbino, Antonio Mini. Michelangelo made Urbino's fortune, mourned his death, and undertook the guardianship of his children, as will appear in due course. All through his life the great sculptor was dependent upon some trusted servant, to whom he became personally attached, and who did not always repay his kindness with gratitude. After Urbino's death, Ascanio Condivi filled a similar post, and to this circumstance we owe the most precious of our contemporary biographies.

Our most important document with regard to the Tomb of Julius is an elaborate petition addressed by Michelangelo to Paul III. upon the 20th of July. It begins by referring to the contract of April 18, 1532, and proceeds to state that the Pope's new commission for the Cappella Paolina has interfered once more with the fulfilment of the sculptor's engagements. Then it recites the terms suggested by the Duke of Urbino in his letter of March 6, 1542, according to which three of the statues of the tomb may be assigned to capable craftsmen, while the other three, including the Moses, will have to be finished by Michelangelo himself. Raffaello da Montelupo has already undertaken the Madonna and Child, a Prophet, and a Sibyl. Giovanni de' Marchese and Francesco da Urbino are at work upon the architecture. It remains for Michelangelo to furnish the Moses and two Captives, all three of which are nearly completed. The Captives, however, were designed for a much larger monument, and will not suit the present scheme. Accordingly, he has blocked out two other figures, representing the Active and Contemplative Life. But even these he is unable to finish, since the painting of the chapel absorbs his time and energy. He therefore prays the Pope to use his influence with the Duke of Urbino, so that he may be henceforward wholly and absolutely freed from all obligations in the matter of the tomb. The Moses he can deliver in a state of perfection, but he wishes to assign the Active and Contemplative Life to Raffaello or to any other sculptor who may be preferred by the Duke. Finally, he is prepared to deposit a sum of 1200 crowns for the total costs, and to guarantee that the work shall be efficiently executed in all its details.

It is curious that in this petition and elsewhere no mention is made of what might be considered the most important portion of the tomb—namely, the portrait statue of Julius.

The document was presented to Messer Piero Giovanni Aliotti, Bishop of Forlì, and keeper of the wardrobe to Pope Paul. Accordingly, the final contract regarding the tomb was drawn up and signed upon the 20th of August. I need not recapitulate its terms, for I have already printed a summary of them in a former chapter of this work. Suffice it to say that Michelangelo was at last released from all active responsibility with regard to the tomb, and that the vast design of his early manhood now dwindled down to the Moses. To Raffaello da Montelupo was left the completion of the remaining five statues.

This lamentable termination to the cherished scheme of his lifetime must have preyed upon Michelangelo's spirits. The letters in which he alludes to it, after the contract had been signed, breathe a spirit of more than usual fretfulness. Moreover, the Duke of Urbino now delayed to send his ratification, by which alone the deed could become valid. In October, writing to Del Riccio, Michelangelo complains that Messer Aliotti is urging him to begin painting in the chapel; but the plaster is not yet fit to work on. Meanwhile, although he has deposited 1400 crowns, "which would have kept him working for seven years, and would have enabled him to finish two tombs," the Duke's ratification does not come. "It is easy enough to see what that means without writing it in words! Enough; for the loyalty of thirty-six years, and for having given myself of my own free will to others, I deserve no better. Painting and sculpture, labour and good faith, have been my ruin, and I go continually from bad to worse. Better would it have been for me if I had set myself to making matches in my youth! I should not be in such distress of mind. . . . I will not remain under this burden, nor be vilified every day for a swindler by those who have robbed my life and honour. Only death or the Pope can extricate me." It appears that at this time the Duke of Urbino's agents were accusing him of having lent out moneys which he had received on account for the execution of the monument. Then follows, in the same month of October, that stormy letter to some prelate, which is one of the most weighty autobiographical documents from the hand of Michelangelo in our possession.

"Monsignore,—Your lordship sends to tell me that I

must begin to paint, and have no anxiety. I answer that one paints with the brain and not with the hands; and he who has not his brains at his command produces work that shames him. Therefore, until my business is settled, I can do nothing good. The ratification of the last contract does not come. On the strength of the other, made before Clement, I am daily stoned as though I had crucified Christ. . . . My whole youth and manhood have been lost, tied down to this tomb. . . . I see multitudes with incomes of 2000 or 3000 crowns lying in bed, while I with all my immense labour toil to grow poor. . . . I am not a thief and usurer, but a citizen of Florence, noble, the son of an honest man, and do not come from Cagli." (These and similar outbursts of indignant passion scattered up and down the epistle, show to what extent the sculptor's irritable nature had been exasperated by calumnious reports. As he openly declares, he is being driven mad by pin-pricks. Then follows the detailed history of his dealings with Julius, which, as I have already made copious use of it, may here be given in outline.) "In the first year of his pontificate, Julius commissioned me to make his tomb, and I stayed eight months at Carrara quarrying marbles and sending them to the Piazza of S. Peter's, where I had my lodgings behind S. Caterina. Afterwards the Pope decided not to build his tomb during his lifetime, and set me down to painting. Then he kept me two years at Bologna casting his statue in bronze, which has been destroyed. After that I returned to Rome and stayed with him until his death, always keeping my house open without post or pension, living on the money for the tomb, since I had no other income. After the death of Julius, Aginensis wanted me to go on with it, but on a larger scale. So I brought the marbles to the Macello dei Corvi, and got that part of the mural scheme finished which is now walled in at S. Pietro in Vincoli, and made the figures which I have at home still. Meanwhile, Leo, not wishing me to work at the tomb, pretended that he wanted to complete the façade of S. Lorenzo at Florence, and begged me of the Cardinal.

"To continue my history of the tomb of Julius, I say that when he changed his mind about building it in his life-time, some shiploads of marble came to the Ripa, which I had ordered a short while before from Carrara, and as I could not get money from the Pope to pay the freightage, I had to borrow 150 or 200 ducats from Baldassare Bal-ducci—that is, from the bank of Jacopo Gallo. At the same time workmen came from Florence, some of whom are still alive; and I furnished the house which Julius gave me behind S. Caterina with beds and other furniture for the men, and what was wanted for the work of the tomb. All this being done without money, I was greatly embarrassed. Accordingly, I urged the Pope with all my power to go for-ward with the business, and he had me turned away by a groom one morning when I came to speak upon the mat-ter." (Here intervenes the story of the flight to Florence, which has been worked up in the course of Chapter IV.) "Later on, while I was at Florence, Julius sent three briefs to the Signory. At last the latter sent for me and said: 'We do not want to go to war with Pope Julius because of you. You must return; and if you do so, we will write you letters of such authority that if he does you harm, he will be doing it to this Signory.' Accordingly, I took the letters, and went back to the Pope, and what followed would be long to tell!

"All the dissensions between Pope Julius and me arose from the envy of Bramante and Raffaello da Urbino; and this was the cause of my not finishing the tomb in his life-time. They wanted to ruin me. Raffaello had indeed good reason, for all he had of art, he had from me."

Twice again in October Michelangelo wrote to Luigi del Riccio about the ratification of his contract. "I cannot live, far less paint." "I am resolved to stop at home and finish the three figures, as I agreed to do. This would be better for me than to drag my limbs daily to the Vatican. Let him who likes get angry. If the Pope wants me to paint, he must send for the Duke's ambassador and procure the ratification."

What happened at this time about the tomb can be understood by help of a letter written to Salvestro da Montauto on the 3rd of February 1545. Michelangelo refers to the last contract, and says that the Duke of Urbino ratified the deed. Accordingly, five statues were assigned to Raffaello da Montelupo. "But while I was painting the new chapel for Pope Paul III., his Holiness, at my earnest prayer, allowed me a little time, during which I finished two of them, namely, the Active and Contemplative Life, with my own hand."

With all his good-will, however, Michelangelo did not wholly extricate himself from the anxieties of this miserable affair. As late as the year 1553, Annibale Caro wrote to Antonio Gallo entreating him to plead for the illustrious old man with the Duke of Urbino. "I assure you that the extreme distress caused him by being in disgrace with his Excellency is sufficient to bring his grey hairs to the grave before his time."

VI

The Tomb of Julius, as it now appears in the Church of S. Pietro in Vincoli in Rome, is a monument composed of two discordant parts, by inspecting which a sympathetic critic is enabled to read the dreary history of its production. As Condivi allows, it was a thing "rattoppata e rifatta," patched together and hashed up.

The lower half represents what eventually survived from the grandiose original design for one façade of that vast mount of marble which was to have been erected in the Tribune of St. Peter's. The socles, upon which captive Arts and Sciences were meant to stand, remain; but instead of statues, inverted consoles take their places, and lead lamely up to the heads and busts of terminal old men. The pilasters of these terms have been shortened. There are four of them, enclosing two narrow niches, where beautiful female figures, the Active Life and the Contemplative Life, still testify to the enduring warmth and vigour of the mighty sculptor's genius. As single statues duly worked into a symmetrical scheme, these figures would be admirable, since grace of line and symbolical contrast of attitude render both charming. In their present position they are reduced to comparative insignificance by heavy architectural surroundings. The space left free between the niches and the terms is assigned to the seated statue of Moses, which forms the main attraction of the monument, and of which, as a masterpiece of Michelangelo's best years, I shall have to speak later on.

The architectural plan and the surface decoration of this lower half are conceived in a style belonging to the earlier Italian Renaissance. Arabesques and masks and foliated patterns adorn the flat slabs. The recess of each niche is arched with a concave shell. The terminal busts are boldly modelled, and impose upon the eye. The whole is rich in detail, and, though somewhat arid in fanciful invention, it carries us back to the tradition of Florentine work by Mino da Fiesole and Desiderio da Settignano.

When we ascend to the upper portion, we seem to have passed, as indeed we do pass, into the region of the new manner created by Michelangelo at S. Lorenzo. The orders of the pilasters are immensely tall in proportion to the spaces they enclose. Two of these spaces, those on the left and right side, are filled in above with meaningless rectangular recesses, while seated statues occupy less than a whole half in altitude of the niches. The architectural design is nondescript, corresponding to no recognised style, unless it be a bastard Roman Doric. There is absolutely no decorative element except four shallow masks beneath the abaci of the pilasters. All is cold and broad and dry, contrasting strangely with the accumulated details of the lower portion. In the central niche, immediately above the Moses, stands a Madonna of fine sculptural quality, beneath a shallow arch, which repeats the shell-pattern. At her feet lies the extended figure of Pope Julius II., crowned with the tiara, raising himself in a half-recumbent attitude upon his right arm.

Of the statues in the upper portion, by far the finest in artistic merit is the Madonna. This dignified and gracious lady, holding the Divine Child in her arms, must be reckoned among Buonarroti's triumphs in dealing with the female form. There is more of softness and sweetness here than in the Madonna of the Medicean sacristy, while the infant playing with a captured bird is full of grace. Michelangelo left little in this group for the chisel of Montelupo to deform by alteration. The seated female, a Sibyl, on the left, bears equally the stamp of his design. Executed by himself, this would have been a masterpiece for grandeur of line and dignified repose. As it is, the style, while seeming to aim at breadth, remains frigid and formal. The so-called Prophet on the other side counts among the signal failures of Italian sculpture. It has neither beauty nor significance. Like a heavy Roman consul of the Decadence, the man sits there, lumpy and meaningless; we might take it for a statue-portrait erected by some provincial municipality to celebrate a local magnate; but of prophecy or inspiration there is nothing to detect in this inert figure. We wonder why he should be placed so near a Pope.

It is said that Michelangelo expressed dissatisfaction with Montelupo's execution of the two statues finally committed to his charge, and we know from documents that the man was ill when they were finished. Still we can hardly excuse the master himself for the cold and perfunctory performance of a task which had such animated and heroic beginnings. Competent judges, who have narrowly surveyed the monument, say that the stones are badly put together, and the workmanship is defective in important requirements of the sculptor-mason's craft. Those who defend Buonarroti must fall back upon the theory that weariness and disappointment made him at last indifferent to the fate of a design which had cost him so much anxiety, pecuniary difficulties, and frustrated expectations in past years. He let the Tomb of Julius, his first vast dream of art, be botched up out of dregs and relics by ignoble hands, because he was heart-sick and out of pocket.

As artist, Michelangelo might, one thinks, have avoided the glaring discord of styles between the upper and the lower portions of the tomb; but sensitiveness to harmony of manner lies not in the nature of men who rapidly evolve new forms of thought and feeling from some older phase. Probably he felt the width and the depth of that gulf which divided himself in 1505 from the same self in 1545, less than we do. Forty years in a creative nature introduce subtle changes, which react upon the spirit of the age, and provoke subsequent criticism to keen comments and comparisons. The individual and his contemporaries are not so well aware of these discrepancies as posterity.

The Moses, which Paul and his courtiers thought sufficient to commemorate a single Pope, stands as the eminent jewel of this defrauded tomb. We may not be attracted by it. We may even be repelled by the goat-like features, the enormous beard, the ponderous muscles, and the grotesque garments of the monstrous statue. In order to do it justice, let us bear in mind that the Moses now remains detached from a group of environing symbolic forms which Michelangelo designed. Instead of taking its place as one among eight corresponding and counterbalancing giants, it is isolated, thrust forward on the eye; whereas it was intended to be viewed from below in concert with a scheme of balanced figures, male and female, on the same colossal scale.

Condivi writes not amiss, in harmony with the gusto of his age, and records what a gentle spirit thought about the Moses then: "Worthy of all admiration is the statue of Moses, duke and captain of the Hebrews. He sits posed in the attitude of a thinker and a sage, holding beneath his right arm the tables of the law, and with the left hand giving support to his chin, like one who is tired and full of anxious cares. From the fingers of this hand escape long flowing lines of beard, which are very beautiful in their effect upon the eye. The face is full of vivid life and spiritual force, fit to inspire both love and terror, as perhaps the man in truth did. He bears, according to the customary wont of artists while portraying Moses, two horns upon the head, not far removed from the summit of the brows. He is robed and girt about the legs with hosen, the arms bare, and all the rest after the antique fashion. It is a marvellous work, and full of art: mostly in this, that underneath those subtleties of raiment one can perceive the naked form, the garments detracting nothing from the beauty of the body; as was the universal way of working with this master in all his clothed figures, whether painted or sculptured."

Except that Condivi dwelt too much upon the repose of this extraordinary statue, too little upon its vivacity and agitating unrest, his description serves our purpose as well as any other. He does not seem to have felt the turbulence and carnal insolence which break our sense of dignity and beauty now.

Michelangelo left the Moses incomplete in many details, after bringing the rest of the figure to a high state of polish. Tooth-marks of the chisel are observable upon the drapery, the back, both hands, part of the neck, the hair, and the salient horns. It seems to have been his habit, as Condivi and Cellini report, to send a finished statue forth with some sign-manual of roughness in the final touches. That gave his work the signature of the sharp tools he had employed upon it. And perhaps he loved the marble so well that he did not like to quit the good white stone without sparing a portion of its clinging strength and stubbornness, as symbol of the effort of his brain and hand to educe live thought from inert matter.

In the century after Michelangelo's death a sonnet was written by Giovanni Battista Felice Zappi upon this Moses. It is famous in Italian literature, and expresses adequately the ideas which occur to ordinary minds when they approach the Moses. For this reason I think that it is worthy of being introduced in a translation here:—

> *Who is the man who, carved in this huge stone,*
> *   Sits giant, all renownèd things of art*
> *   Transcending? he whose living lips, that start,*
> *   Speak eager words? I hear, and take their tone.*
> *He sure is Moses. That the chin hath shown*
> *   By its dense honour, the brows' beam bipart:*
> *   'Tis Moses, when he left the Mount, with part,*
> *   A great part, of God's glory round him thrown.*
> *Such was the prophet when those sounding vast*
> *   Waters he held suspense about him; such*
> *   When he the sea barred, made it gulph his foe.*
> *And you, his tribes, a vile calf did you cast?*
> *   Why not an idol worth like this so much?*
> *   To worship that had wrought you lesser woe.*

VII

Before quitting the Tomb of Julius, I must discuss the question of eight scattered statues, partly unfinished, which are supposed, on more or less good grounds, to have been designed for this monument. About two of them, the bound Captives in the Louvre, there is no doubt. Michelangelo mentions these in his petition to Pope Paul, saying that the change of scale implied by the last plan obliged him to abstain from using them. We also know their history. When the sculptor was ill at Rome in 1544, Luigi del Riccio nursed him in the palace of the Strozzi. Gratitude for this hospitality induced him to make a present of the statues to Ruberto degli Strozzi, who took them to France and offered them to the King. Francis gave them to the Constable de

Montmorenci; and he placed them in his country-house of Ecouen. In 1793 the Republic offered them for sale, when they were bought for the French nation by M. Lenoir.

One of these Captives deserves to be called the most fascinating creation of the master's genius. Together with the Adam, it may be taken as fixing his standard of masculine beauty. He is a young man, with head thrown back, as though in swoon or slumber; the left arm raised above the weight of massy curls, the right hand resting on his broad full bosom. There is a divine charm in the tranquil face, tired but not fatigued, sad but not melancholy, suggesting that the sleeping mind of the immortal youth is musing upon solemn dreams. Praxiteles might have so expressed the Genius of Eternal Repose; but no Greek sculptor would have given that huge girth to the thorax, or have exaggerated the mighty hand with such delight in sinewy force. These qualities, peculiar to Buonarroti's sense of form, do not detract from the languid pose and supple rhythm of the figure, which flows down, a sinuous line of beauty, through the slightly swelling flanks, along the finely moulded thighs, to loveliest feet emerging from the marble. It is impossible, while gazing on this statue, not to hear a strain of intellectual music. Indeed, like melody, it tells no story, awakes no desire, but fills the soul with something beyond thought or passion, subtler and more penetrating than words.

The companion figure has not equal grace. Athletically muscular, though adolescent, the body of this young man, whose hands are tied behind his back, is writhed into an attitude of vehement protest and rebellion. He raises his face with appealing pain to heaven. The head, which is only blocked out, overweighs the form, proving that Michelangelo, unlike the Greeks, did not observe a fixed canon of proportion for the human frame. This statue bears a strong resemblance in feeling and conception to the Apollo designed for Baccio Valori.

There are four rough-hewn male figures, eccentrically

wrought into the rock-work of a grotto in the Boboli Gardens, which have been assigned to the Tomb of Julius. This attribution involves considerable difficulties. In the first place, the scale is different, and the stride of one of them, at any rate, is too wide for the pedestals of that monument. Then their violent contortions and ponderous adult forms seem to be at variance with the spirit of the Captives. Mr. Heath Wilson may perhaps be right in his conjecture that Michelangelo began them for the sculptural decoration on the façade of S. Lorenzo. Their incompleteness baffles criticism; yet we feel instinctively that they were meant for the open air and for effect at a considerable distance. They remind us of Deucalion's men growing out of the stones he threw behind his back. We could not wish them to be finished, or to lose their wild attraction, as of primeval beings, the remnants of dim generations nearer than ourselves to elemental nature. No better specimens of Buonarroti's way of working in the marble could be chosen. Almost savage hatchings with the point blend into finer touches from the toothed chisel; and here and there the surface has been treated with innumerable smoothing lines that round it into skin and muscle. To a man who chiselled thus, marble must have yielded like softest freestone beneath his tools; and how recklessly he wrought is clear from the defective proportions of one old man's figure, whose leg below the knee is short beyond all excuse.

A group of two figures, sometimes called the Victory, now in the Bargello Palace, was catalogued without hesitation by Vasari among the statues for the tomb. A young hero, of gigantic strength and height, stands firmly poised upon one foot, while his other leg, bent at the knee, crushes the back of an old man doubled up beneath him. In the face of the vanquished warrior critics have found a resemblance to Michelangelo. The head of the victorious youth seems too small for his stature, and the features are almost brutally vacuous, though burning with an insolent and carnal beauty. The whole forcible figure expresses irresistible energy and superhuman litheness combined with massive strength. This group cannot be called pleasing, and its great height renders it almost inconceivable that it was meant to range upon one monument with the Captives of the Louvre. There are, however, so many puzzles and perplexities connected with that design in its several stages, that we dare affirm or deny nothing concerning it. M. Guillaume, taking it for granted that the Victory was intended for the tomb, makes the plausible suggestion that some of the peculiarities which render it in composition awkward, would have been justified by the addition of bronze wings. Mr. Heath Wilson, seeking after an allegory, is fain to believe that it represents Michelangelo's own state of subjection while employed upon the Serravezza quarries.

Last comes the so-called Adonis of the Bargello Palace, which not improbably was designed for one of the figures prostrate below the feet of a victorious Genius. It bears, indeed, much resemblance to a roughly indicated nude at the extreme right of the sketch for the tomb. Upon this supposition, Michelangelo must have left it in a very unfinished state, with an unshaped block beneath the raised right thigh. This block has now been converted into a boar. Extremely beautiful as the Adonis undoubtedly is, the strained, distorted attitude seems to require some explanation. That might have been given by the trampling form and robes of a Genius. Still it is difficult to comprehend why the left arm and hand, finished, I feel almost sure, by Michelangelo, should have been so carefully executed. The Genius, if draped, would have hidden nearly the whole of that part of the statue. The face of this Adonis displays exactly the same type as that of the so-called Victory and of Giuliano de' Medici. Here the type assumes singular loveliness.

CHAPTER XII

I

AFTER the death of Clement VII. Michelangelo never returned to reside at Florence. The rest of his life was spent in Rome. In the year 1534 he had reached the advanced age of fifty-nine, and it is possible that he first became acquainted with the noble lady Vittoria Colonna about 1538. Recent students of his poetry and friendships have suggested that their famous intimacy began earlier, during one of his not infrequent visits to Rome. But we have no proof of this. On the contrary, the only letters extant which he sent to her, two in number, belong to the year 1545. It is certain that anything like friendship between them grew up at some considerable time after his final settlement in Rome.

Vittoria was the daughter of Fabrizio Colonna, Grand Constable of Naples, by his marriage with Agnesina di Montefeltro, daughter of Federigo, Duke of Urbino. Blood more illustrious than hers could not be found in Italy. When she was four years old, her parents betrothed her to Ferrante Francesco d'Avalos, a boy of the same age, the only son of the Marchese di Pescara. In her nineteenth year the affianced couple were married at Ischia, the fief and residence of the house of D'Avalos. Ferrante had succeeded to his father's title early in boyhood, and was destined for a brilliant military career. On the young bride's side at least it was a love-match. She was tenderly attached to her handsome husband, ignorant of his infidelities, and blind to his fatal faults of character. Her happiness proved of short duration. In 1512 Pescara was wounded and made prisoner at the battle of Ravenna, and, though he returned to his wife for a short interval, duty called him again to the field of war in Lombardy in 1515. After this date Vittoria saw him but seldom. The last time they met was in October 1522. As general of the Imperial forces, Pescara spent the next years in perpetual military operations. Under his leadership the battle of Pavia was won in 1525, and King Francis became his master's prisoner. So far, nothing but honour, success, and glory waited on the youthful hero. But now the tide turned. Pescara, when he again settled down at Milan, began to plot with Girolamo Morone, Grand Chancellor of Francesco Sforza's duchy. Morone had conceived a plan for reinstating his former lord in Milan by the help of an Italian coalition. He offered Pescara the crown of Naples if he would turn against the Emperor. The Marquis seems at first to have lent a not unwilling ear to these proposals, but seeing reason to doubt the success of the scheme, he finally resolved to betray Morone to Charles V., and did this with cold-blooded ingenuity. A few months afterwards, on November 25, 1525, he died, branded as a traitor, accused of double treachery, both to his sovereign and his friend.

If suspicions of her husband's guilt crossed Vittoria's mind, as we have some reason to believe they did, these were not able to destroy her loyalty and love. Though left so young a widow and childless, she determined to consecrate her whole life to his memory and to religion. His nephew and heir, the Marchese del Vasto, became her adopted son. The Marchioness survived Pescara two-and-twenty years, which were spent partly in retirement at Ischia, partly in journeys, partly in convents at Orvieto and Viterbo, and finally in a semi-monastic seclusion at Rome. The time spared from pious exercises she devoted to study, the composition of poetry, correspondence with illustrious men of letters, and the society of learned persons. Her chief friends belonged to that group of earnest thinkers who felt the influences of the Reformation without ceasing to be loyal children of the Church. With Vittoria's name are inseparably connected those of Gasparo Contarini, Reginald Pole, Giovanni Morone, Jacopo Sadoleto, Marcantonio Flaminio, Pietro Carnesecchi, and Fra Bernardino Ochino. The last of these avowed his Lutheran principles, and was severely criticised by Vittoria Colonna for doing so. Carnesecchi was burned for heresy. Vittoria never adopted Protestantism, and died an orthodox Catholic. Yet her intimacy with men of liberal opinions exposed her to mistrust and censure in old age. The movement of the Counter-Reformation had begun, and any kind of speculative freedom aroused suspicion. This saintly princess was accordingly placed under the supervision of the Holy Office, and to be her friend was slightly dangerous. It is obvious that Vittoria's religion was of an evangelical type, inconsistent with the dogmas developed by the Tridentine Council; and it is probable that, like her friend Contarini, she advocated a widening rather than a narrowing of Western Christendom. To bring the Church back to purer morals and sincerity of faith was their aim. They yearned for a reformation and regeneration from within.

In all these matters, Michelangelo, the devout student of the Bible and the disciple of Savonarola, shared Vittoria's sentiments. His nature, profoundly and simply religious from the outset, assumed a tone of deeper piety and habitual devotion during the advance of years. Vittoria Colonna's influence at this period strengthened his Christian emotions, which remained untainted by asceticism or superstition. They were further united by another bond, which was their common interest in poetry. The Marchioness of Pescara was justly celebrated during her lifetime as one of the most natural writers of Italian verse. Her poems consist principally of sonnets consecrated to the memory of her husband, or composed on sacred and moral subjects. Penetrated by genuine feeling, and almost wholly free from literary affectation, they have that dignity and sweetness which belong to the spontaneous utterances of a noble heart. Whether she treats of love or of religion, we find the same simplicity and sincerity of style. There is nothing in her pious meditations that a Christian of any communion may not read with profit, as the heartfelt outpourings of a soul athirst for God and nourished on the study of the gospel.

Michelangelo preserved a large number of her sonnets, which he kept together in one volume. Writing to his nephew Lionardo in 1554, he says: "Messer Giovan Francesco (Fattucci) asked me about a month ago if I possessed any writings of the Marchioness. I have a little book bound in parchment, which she gave me some ten years ago. It has one hundred and three sonnets, not counting another forty she afterwards sent on paper from Viterbo. I had these bound into the same book, and at that time I used to lend them about to many persons, so that they are all of them now in print. In addition to these poems I have many letters which she wrote from Orvieto and Viterbo. These then are the writings I possess of the Marchioness." He composed several pieces, madrigals and sonnets, under the genial influence of this exchange of thoughts. It was a period at which his old love of versifying revived with singular activity. Other friends, like Tommaso Cavalieri, Luigi del Riccio, and afterwards Vasari, enticed his Muse to frequent utterance. Those he wrote for the Marchioness were distributed in manuscript among his private friends, and found their way into the first edition of his collected poems. But it is a mistake to suppose that she was the sole or even the chief source of his poetical inspiration.

We shall see that it was his custom to mark his feeling for particular friends by gifts of drawings as well as of poems. He did this notably in the case of both Vittoria Colonna and Tommaso dei Cavalieri. For the latter he designed subjects from Greek mythology; for the former, episodes in the Passion of our Lord. "At the request of this lady," says Condivi, "he made a naked Christ, at the moment when, taken from the cross, our Lord would have fallen like an abandoned corpse at the feet of his most holy Mother, if two angels did not support him in their arms. She sits below the cross with a face full of tears and sorrow, lifting both her widespread arms to heaven, while on the stem of the tree above is written this legend, 'Non vi si pensa quanto langue costa.' The cross is of the same kind as that which was carried in procession by the White Friars at the time of the plague of 1348, and afterwards deposited in the Church of S. Croce at Florence. He also made, for love of her, the design of a Jesus Christ upon the cross, not with the aspect of one dead, as is the common wont, but in a divine attitude, with face raised to the Father, seeming to exclaim, 'Eli! Eli!' In this drawing the body does not appear to fall, like an abandoned corpse, but as though in life to writhe and quiver with the agony it feels."

Of these two designs we have several more or less satisfactory mementoes. The Pietà was engraved by Giulio Bonasoni and Tudius Bononiensis (date 1546), exactly as Condivi describes it. The Crucifixion survives in a great number of pencil-drawings, together with one or two pictures painted by men like Venusti, and many early engravings of the drawings. One sketch in the Taylor Museum at Oxford is generally supposed to represent the original designed for Vittoria.

II

What remains of the correspondence between Michelangelo and the Marchioness opens with a letter referring to their interchange of sonnets and drawings. It is dated Rome, 1545. Vittoria had evidently sent him poems, and he wishes to make her a return in kind: "I desired, lady, before I accepted the things which your ladyship has often expressed the will to give me—I desired to produce something for you with my own hand, in order to be as little as possible unworthy of this kindness. I have now come to recognise that the grace of God is not to be bought, and that to keep it waiting is a grievous sin. Therefore I acknowledge my error, and willingly accept your favours. When I possess them, not indeed because I shall have them in my house, but for that I myself shall dwell in them, the place will seem to encircle me with Paradise. For which felicity I shall remain ever more obliged to your ladyship than I am already, if that is possible.

"The bearer of this letter will be Urbino, who lives in my service. Your ladyship may inform him when you would like me to come and see the head you promised to show me."

This letter is written under the autograph copy of a sonnet which must have been sent with it, since it expresses the same thought in its opening quatrain. My translation of the poem runs thus:

> Seeking at least to be not all unfit
>   For thy sublime and boundless courtesy,
>   My lowly thoughts at first were fain to try
>   What they could yield for grace so infinite.
> But now I know my unassisted wit
>   Is all too weak to make me soar so high,
>   For pardon, lady, for this fault I cry,
>   And wiser still I grow, remembering it.
> Yea, well I see what folly 'twere to think
>   That largess dropped from thee like dews from heaven
>   Could e'er be paid by work so frail as mine!
> To nothingness my art and talent sink;
>   He fails who from his mortal stores hath given
>   A thousandfold to match one gift divine.

Michelangelo's next letter refers to the design for the Crucified Christ, described by Condivi. It is pleasant to find that this was sent by the hand of Cavalieri: "Lady Marchioness,—Being myself in Rome, I thought it hardly fitting to give the Crucified Christ to Messer Tommaso, and to make him an intermediary between your ladyship and me, your servant; especially because it has been my earnest wish to perform more for you than for any one I ever knew upon the world. But absorbing occupations, which still engage me, have prevented my informing your ladyship of this. Moreover, knowing that you know that love needs no taskmaster, and that he who loves doth not sleep, I thought the less of using go-betweens. And though I seemed to have forgotten, I was doing what I did not talk about in order to effect a thing that was not looked for. My purpose has been spoiled: *He sins who faith like this so soon forgets.*"

A sonnet which may or may not have been written at this time, but seems certainly intended for the Marchioness, shall here be given as a pendant to the letter:—

> *Blest spirit, who with loving tenderness*
> *Quickenest my heart, so old and near to die,*
> *Who 'mid thy joys on me dost bend an eye,*
> *Though many nobler men around thee press!*
> *As thou wert erewhile wont my sight to bless,*
> *So to console my mind thou now dost fly;*
> *Hope therefore stills the pangs of memory,*
> *Which, coupled with desire, my soul distress.*
> *So finding in thee grace to plead for me—*
> *Thy thoughts for me sunk in so sad a case—*
> *He who now writes returns thee thanks for these.*
> *Lo! it were foul and monstrous usury*
> *To send thee ugliest paintings in the place*
> *Of thy fair spirit's living phantasies.*

Unfortunately we possess no other document in prose addressed immediately to Vittoria. But four of her letters to him exist, and from these I will select some specimens reflecting light upon the nature of the famous intimacy. The Marchioness writes always in the tone and style of a great princess, adding that peculiar note of religious affectionateness which the French call "*onction*," and marking her strong admiration of the illustrious artist. The letters are not dated; but this matters little, since they only turn on literary courtesies exchanged, drawings presented, and pious interests in common.

"Unique Master Michelangelo, and my most singular friend,—I have received your letter, and examined the crucifix, which truly hath crucified in my memory every other picture I ever saw. Nowhere could one find another figure of our Lord so well executed, so living, and so exquisitely finished. Certes, I cannot express in words how subtly and marvellously it is designed. Wherefore I am resolved to take the work as coming from no other hand but yours, and accordingly I beg you to assure me whether this is really yours or another's. Excuse the question. If it is yours, I must possess it under any conditions. In case it is not yours, and you want to have it carried out by your assistant, we will talk the matter over first. I know how extremely difficult it would be to copy it, and therefore I would rather let him finish something else than this. But if it be in fact yours, rest assured, and make the best of it, that it will never come again into your keeping. I have examined it minutely in full light and by the lens and mirror, and never saw anything more perfect.—Yours to command,

"THE MARCHIONESS OF PESCARA."

Like many grand ladies of the highest rank, even though they are poetesses, Vittoria Colonna did not always write grammatically or coherently. I am not therefore sure that I have seized the exact meaning of this diplomatical and flattering letter. It would appear, however, that Michelangelo had sent her the drawing for a crucifix, intimating that, if she liked it, he would intrust its execution to one of his workmen, perhaps Urbino. This, as we know, was a common practice adopted by him in old age, in order to avoid commissions which interfered with his main life-work at S. Peter's. The noble lady, fully aware that the sketch is an original, affects some doubt upon the subject, declines the intervention of a common craftsman, and declares her firm resolve to keep it, leaving an impression that she would gladly possess the crucifix if executed by the same hand which had supplied the masterly design.

Another letter refers to the drawing of a Christ upon the cross between two angels.

"Your works forcibly stimulate the judgment of all who look at them. My study of them made me speak of adding goodness to things perfect in themselves, and I have seen now that 'all is possible to him who believes.' I had the greatest faith in God that He would bestow upon you supernatural grace for the making of this Christ. When I came to examine it, I found it so marvellous that it surpasses all my expectations. Wherefore, emboldened by your miracles, I conceived a great desire for that which I now see marvellously accomplished: I mean that the design is in all parts perfect and consummate, and one could not desire more, nor could desire attain to demanding so much. I tell you that I am mighty pleased that the angel on the right hand is by far the fairer, since Michael will place you, Michelangelo, upon the right hand of our Lord at that last day. Meanwhile, I do not know how else to serve you than by making orisons to this sweet Christ, whom you have drawn so well and exquisitely, and praying you to hold me yours to command as yours in all and for all."

The admiration and the good-will of the great lady transpire in these somewhat incoherent and studied paragraphs. Their verbiage leaves much to be desired in the way of logic and simplicity. It is pleasanter perhaps to read a familiar note, sent probably by the hand of a servant to Buonarroti's house in Rome.

"I beg you to let me have the crucifix a short while in my keeping, even though it be unfinished. I want to show it to some gentlemen who have come from the Most Reverend the Cardinal of Mantua. If you are not working, will you not come to-day at your leisure and talk with me? —Yours to command,

"THE MARCHIONESS OF PESCARA."

It seems that Michelangelo's exchange of letters and poems became at last too urgent. We know it was his way (as in the case of Luigi del Riccio) to carry on an almost daily correspondence for some while, and then to drop it altogether when his mood changed. Vittoria, writing from Viterbo, gives him a gentle and humorous hint that he is taking up too much of her time:

"Magnificent Messer Michelangelo,—I did not reply earlier to your letter, because it was, as one might say, an answer to my last: for I thought that if you and I were to go on writing without intermission according to my obligation and your courtesy, I should have to neglect the Chapel of S. Catherine here, and be absent at the appointed hours for company with my sisterhood, while you would have to leave the Chapel of S. Paul, and be absent from morning through the day from your sweet usual colloquy with painted forms, the which with their natural accents do not speak to you less clearly than the living persons round me speak to me. Thus we should both of us fail in our duty, I to the brides, you to the vicar of Christ. For these reasons, inasmuch as I am well assured of our steadfast friendship and firm affection, bound by knots of Christian kindness, I do not think it necessary to obtain the proof of your good-will in letters by writing on my side, but rather to await with well-prepared mind some substantial occasion for serving you. Meanwhile I address my prayers to that Lord of whom you spoke to me with so fervent and humble a heart when I left Rome, that when I return thither I may find you with His image renewed and enlivened by true faith in your soul, in like measure as you have painted it with perfect art in my Samaritan. Believe me to remain always yours and your Urbino's."

This letter must have been written when Michelangelo was still working on the frescoes of the Cappella Paolina, and therefore before 1549. The check to his importunacy, given with genial tact by the Marchioness, might be taken, by those who believe their *liaison* to have had a touch of passion in it, as an argument in favour of that view. The great age which Buonarroti had now reached renders this, however, improbable; while the general tenor of their correspondence is that of admiration for a great artist on the lady's side, and of attraction to a noble nature on the man's side, cemented by religious sentiment and common interests in serious topics.

III

All students of Michelangelo's biography are well acquainted with the Dialogues on Painting, composed by the Portuguese miniature artist, Francis of Holland. Written in the quaint style of the sixteenth century, which curiously blent actual circumstance and fact with the author's speculation, these essays present a vivid picture of Buonarroti's conferences with Vittoria Colonna and her friends. The dialogues are divided into four parts, three of which profess to give a detailed account of three several Sunday conversations in the Convent of S. Silvestro on Monte Cavallo. After describing the objects which brought him to Rome, Francis says: "Above all, Michelangelo inspired me with such esteem, that when I met him in the palace of the Pope or on the streets, I could not make my mind up to leave him until the stars forced us to retire." Indeed, it would seem from his frank admissions in another place that the Portuguese painter had become a little too attentive to the famous old man, and that Buonarroti "did all he could to shun his company, seeing that when they once came together, they could not separate." It happened one Sunday that Francis paid a visit to his friend Lattanzio Tolomei, who had gone abroad, leaving a message that he would be found in the Church of S. Silvestro, where he was hoping to hear a lecture by Brother Ambrose of Siena on the Epistles of S. Paul, in company with the Marchioness. Accordingly he repaired to this place, and was graciously received by the noble lady. She courteously remarked that he would probably enjoy a conversation with Michelangelo more than a sermon from Brother Ambrose, and after an interval of compliments a servant was sent to find him. It chanced that Buonarroti was walking with the man whom Francis of Holland calls "his old friend and colour-grinder," Urbino, in the direction of the Thermæ. So the lackey, having the good chance to meet him, brought him at once to the convent. The Marchioness made him sit between her and Messer Tolomei, while Francis took up his position at a little distance. The conversation then began, but Vittoria Colonna had to use the tact for which she was celebrated before she could engage the wary old man on a serious treatment of his own art.

He opened his discourse by defending painters against the common charge of being "eccentric in their habits, difficult to deal with, and unbearable; whereas, on the contrary, they are really most humane." Common people do not consider, he remarked, that really zealous artists are bound to abstain from the idle trivialities and current compliments of society, not because they are haughty or intolerant by nature, but because their art imperiously claims the whole of their energies. "When such a man shall have the same leisure as you enjoy, then I see no objection to your putting him to death if he does not observe your rules of etiquette and ceremony. You only seek his company and praise him in order to obtain honour through him for yourselves, nor do you really mind what sort of man he is, so long as kings and emperors converse with him. I dare affirm that any artist who tries to satisfy the better vulgar rather than men of his own craft, one who has nothing singular, eccentric, or at least reputed to be so, in his person, will never become a superior talent. For my part, I am bound to confess that even his Holiness sometimes annoys and wearies me by begging for too much of my company. I am most anxious to serve him, but, when there is nothing important going forward, I think I can do so better by studying at home than by dancing attendance through a whole day on my legs in his reception-rooms. He allows me to tell him so; and I may add that the serious occupations of my life have won for me such liberty of action that, in talking to the Pope, I often forget where I am, and place my hat upon my head. He does not eat me up on that account, but treats me with indulgence, knowing that it is precisely at such times that I am working hard to serve him. As for solitary habits, the world is right in condemning a man who, out of pure affectation or ecentricity, shuts himself up alone, loses his friends, and sets society against him. Those, however, who act in this way naturally, because their profession obliges them to lead a recluse life, or because their character rebels against feigned politenesses and conventional usage, ought in common justice to be tolerated. What claim by right have you on him? Why should you force him to take part in those vain pastimes, which his love for a quiet life induces him to shun? Do you not know that there are sciences which demand the whole of a man, without leaving the least portion of his spirit free for your distractions?" This apology for his own life, couched in a vindication of the artistic temperament, breathes an accent of sincerity, and paints Michelangelo as he really was, with his somewhat haughty sense of personal dignity. What he says about his absence of mind in the presence of great princes might be illustrated by a remark attributed to Clement VII. "When Buonarroti comes to see me, I always take a seat and bid him to be seated, feeling sure that he will do so without leave or licénse."

The conversation passed by natural degrees to a consideration of the fine arts in general. In the course of this discussion, Michelangelo uttered several characteristic opinions, strongly maintaining the superiority of the Italian to the Flemish and German schools, and asserting his belief that, while all objects are worthy of imitation by the artist, the real touch stone of excellence lies in his power to represent the human form. His theory of the arts in their reciprocal relations and affinities throws interesting light upon the qualities of his own genius and his method in practice. "The science of design, or of line-drawing, if you like to use this term, is the source and very essence of painting, sculpture, architecture, and of every form of representation, as well too as of all the sciences. He who has made himself a master in this art possesses a great treasure. Sometimes, when I meditate upon these topics, it seems to me that I can discover but one art or science, which is design, and that all the works of the human brain and hand are either design itself or a branch of that art." This theme he develops at some length, showing how a complete mastery of drawing is necessary not only to the plastic arts of painting and sculpture, but also to the constructive and mechanical arts of architecture, fortification, gun-foundry, and so forth, applying the same principle to the minutest industries.

With regard to the personal endowments of the artist, he maintained that "a lofty style, grave and decorous, was essential to great work. Few artists understand this, and endeavour to appropriate these qualities. Consequently we find many members of the confraternity who are only artists in name. The world encourages this confusion of ideas, since few are capable of distinguishing between a fellow who has nothing but his colour-box and brushes to make him a painter, and the really gifted natures who appear only at wide intervals." He illustrates the position that noble qualities in the artist are indispensable to nobility in the work of art, by a digression on religious painting and sculpture. "In order to represent in some degree the adored image of our Lord, it is not enough that a master should be great and able. I maintain that he must also be a man of good conduct and morals, if possible a saint, in order that the Holy Ghost may rain down inspiration on his understanding. Ecclesiastical and secular princes ought, therefore, to permit only the most illustrious among the artists of their realm to paint the benign sweetness of our Saviour, the purity of our Lady, and the virtues of the saints. It often happens that ill-executed images distract the minds of worshippers and ruin their devotion, unless it be firm and fervent. Those, on the contrary, which are executed in the high style I have described, excite the soul to contemplation and to tears, even among the least devout, by inspiring reverence and fear through the majesty of their aspect." This doctrine is indubitably sound. To our minds, nevertheless, it rings a little hollow on the lips of the great master who modelled the Christ of the Minerva and painted the Christ and Madonna of the Last Judgment. Yet we must remember that, at the exact period when these dialogues took place, Buonarroti, under the influence of his friendship with Vittoria Colonna, was devoting his best energies to the devout expression of the Passion of our Lord. It is deeply to be regretted that, out of the numerous designs which remain to us from this endeavour, all of them breathing the purest piety, no monumental work except the Pietà at Florence emerged for perpetuity.

Many curious points, both of minute criticism and broad opinion, might still be gleaned from the dialogues set down by Francis of Holland. It must suffice here to resume what Michelangelo maintained about the artist's method. One of the interlocutors begged to be informed whether he thought that a master ought to aim at working slowly or quickly. "I will tell you plainly what I feel about this matter. It is both good and useful to be able to work with promptitude and address. We must regard it as a special gift from God to be able to do that in a few hours which other men can only perform in many days of labour. Consequently, artists who paint rapidly, without falling in quality below those who paint but slowly, deserve the highest commendation. Should this rapidity of execution, however, cause a man to transgress the limits of sound art, it would have been better to have proceeded with more tardiness and study. A good artist ought never to allow the impetuosity of his nature to overcome his sense of the main end of art, perfection. Therefore we cannot call slowness of execution a defect, nor yet the expenditure of much time and trouble, if this be employed with the view of attaining greater perfection. The one unpardonable fault is bad work. And here I would remind you of a thing essential to our art, which you will certainly not ignore, and to which I believe you attach the full importance it deserves. In every kind of plastic work we ought to strive with all our might at making what has cost time and labour look as though it had been produced with facility and swiftness. It sometimes happens, but rarely, that a portion of our work turns out excellent with little pains bestowed upon it. Most frequently, however, it is the expenditure of care and trouble which conceals our toil. Plutarch relates that a bad painter showed Apelles a picture, saying: 'This is from my hand; I have just made it in a moment.' The other replied: 'I should have recognised the fact without your telling me; and I marvel that you do not make a multitude of such things every day.' " Michelangelo is reported to have made a similar remark to Vasari when the latter took him to inspect some frescoes he had painted, observing that they had been dashed off quickly.

We must be grateful to Francis of Holland for this picture of the Sunday-morning interviews at S. Silvestro. The place was cool and tranquil. The great lady received her guests with urbanity, and led the conversation with high-bred courtesy and tact. Fra Ambrogio, having discoursed upon the spiritual doctrines of S. Paul's Epistles, was at liberty to turn an attentive ear to purely æsthetical speculations. The grave and elderly Lattanzio Tolomei added the weight of philosophy and literary culture to the dialogue. Michelangelo, expanding in the genial atmosphere, spoke frankly on the arts which he had mastered, not dictating *ex cathedra* rules, but maintaining a note of modesty and common-sense and deference to the opinion of others. Francis engaged on equal terms in the discussion. His veneration for Buonarroti, and the eagerness with which he noted all the great man's utterances, did not prevent him from delivering lectures at a somewhat superfluous length.

In short, we may fairly accept his account of these famous conferences as a truthful transcript from the refined and witty social gatherings of which Vittoria Colonna formed the centre.

IV

This friendship with Vittoria Colonna forms a very charming episode in the history of Michelangelo's career, and it was undoubtedly one of the consolations of his declining years. Yet too great stress has hitherto been laid on it by his biographers. Not content with exaggerating its importance in his life, they have misinterpreted its nature. The world seems unable to take interest in a man unless it can contrive to discover a love-affair in his career. The singular thing about Michelangelo is that, with the exception of Vittoria Colonna, no woman is known to have influenced his heart or head in any way. In his correspondence he never mentions women, unless they be aunts, cousins, grand-nieces, or servants. About his mother he is silent. We have no tradition regarding amours in youth or middle age; and only two words dropped by Condivi lead us to conjecture that he was not wholly insensible to the physical attractions of the female. Romancers and legend-makers have, therefore, forced Vittoria Colonna to play the rôle of Juliet in Michelangelo's life-drama. It has not occurred to these critics that there is something essentially disagreeable in the thought of an aged couple entertaining an amorous correspondence. I use these words deliberately, because poems which breathe obvious passion of no merely spiritual character have been assigned to the number he composed for Vittoria Colonna. This, as we shall see, is chiefly the fault of his first editor, who printed all the sonnets and madrigals as though they were addressed to one woman or another. It is also in part due to the impossibility of determining their exact date in the majority of instances. Verses, then, which were designed for several objects of his affection, male or female, have been indiscriminately referred to Vittoria Colonna, whereas we can only attribute a few poems with certainty to her series.

This mythus of Michelangelo's passion for the Marchioness of Pescara has blossomed and brought forth fruit abundantly from a single and pathetic passage in Condivi. "In particular, he greatly loved the Marchioness of Pescara, of whose divine spirit he was enamoured, being in return dearly beloved by her. He still preserves many of her letters, breathing honourable and most tender affection, and such as were wont to issue from a heart like hers. He also wrote to her a great number of sonnets, full of wit and sweet longing. She frequently removed from Viterbo and other places, whither she had gone for solace or to pass the summer, and came to Rome with the sole object of seeing Michelangelo. He for his part, loved her so, that I remember to have heard him say that he regretted nothing except that when he went to visit her upon the moment of her passage from this life, he did not kiss her forehead or her face, as he did kiss her hand. Her death was the cause that oftentimes he dwelt astonied, thinking of it, even as a man bereft of sense."

Michelangelo himself, writing immediately after Vittoria's death, speaks of her thus: "She felt the warmest affection for me, and I not less for her. Death has robbed me of a great friend." It is curious that he here uses the masculine gender: "un grande amico." He also composed two sonnets, which were in all probability inspired by the keen pain of this bereavement. To omit them here would be unjust to the memory of their friendship:—

When my rude hammer to the stubborn stone
  Gives human shape, now that, now this, at will,
  Following his hand who wields and guides it still,
  It moves upon another's feet alone:

But that which dwells in heaven, the world doth fill
  With beauty by pure motions of its own;
  And since tools fashion tools which else were none,
  Its life makes all that lives with living skill.
Now, for that every stroke excels the more
  The higher at the forge it doth ascend,
  Her soul that fashioned mine hath sought the skies;
Wherefore unfinished I must meet my end,
  If God, the great Artificer, denies
  That aid which was unique on earth before.

———

When she who was the source of all my sighs
  Fled from the world, herself, my straining sight,
  Nature, who gave us that unique delight,
  Was sunk in shame, and we had weeping eyes.
Yet shall not vauntful Death enjoy the prize,
  This sun of suns which then he veiled in night;
  For Love hath triumphed, lifting up her light
  On earth and 'mid the saints in Paradise.
What though remorseless and impiteous doom
  Deemed that the music of her deeds would die,
  And that her splendour would be sunk in gloom?
The poet's page exalts her to the sky
  With life more living in the lifeless tomb,
  And Death translates her soul to reign on high.

It will not, perhaps, be out of place here to offer English versions of three madrigals, one of which was certainly written for Vittoria Colonna in her lifetime, while another may have been composed after her death. I may introduce them by remarking that when Michelangelo adopted this form of lyric, looser than the sonnet, he was wont to indulge in even more extravagant conceits. The first proves that he regarded the Marchioness as his Egeria in the spiritual life, and that the gathering clouds of old age were making him reflect upon the final issues of man's soul:—

Now to the right, now to the left hand driven,
Wander my steps, seeking eternal weal.
Both vice and virtue make appeal
Unto my heart perplexed, which tires me still:—
Like one who sees not heaven,
But blunders on distraught o'er vale and hill.
I send you paper, beg you take a quill,
And with your sacred ink
Make love give light, and mercy truth impart;
So that my soul, delivered, purged of ill,
Shall not be drawn to error's brink,
Through life's brief remnant, by a blinded heart.
I ask of thee, that goddess art,
Lady, if up in heaven doth lower dwell
A contrite sin than virtue, lord o'er hell.

The second is interesting for the light it seems to throw upon Vittoria Colonna's influence. Michelangelo describes her as a woman through whose lips a man, or rather a god, speaks to him, causing a complete change in his moral nature, and luring him from previous emotions of which he now repents:—

A man within a woman, nay, a god,
Speaks through her spoken word:
I therefore, who have heard,
Must suffer change, and shall be mine no more.
She lured me from the paths I whilom trod.
Borne from my former state by her away,
I stand aloof, and mine own self deplore.
Above all vain desire
The beauty of her face doth lift my clay;
All lesser loveliness seems charnel mire.
O lady, who through fire
And water leadest souls to joys eterne,
Let me no more unto myself return.

The third illustrates in a singular manner that custom of sixteenth-century literature which Shakespeare followed in his sonnets, of weaving poetical images out of thoughts borrowed from law and business. It is also remarkable in this respect, that Michelangelo has here employed precisely the same conceit for Vittoria Colonna which he found serviceable when at an earlier date he wished to deplore the death of the Florentine, Cecchino dei Bracci. For both of them he says that Heaven bestowed upon the beloved object all its beauties, instead of scattering these broad-cast over the human race, which, had it done so, would have entailed the bankruptcy and death of all:—

> *So that high heaven should have not to distrain*
> *From several that vast beauty ne'er yet shown,*
> *To one exalted dame alone*
> *The total sum was lent in her pure self:—*
> *Heaven had made sorry gain,*
> *Recovering from the crowd its scattered pelf.*
> *Now in a puff of breath,*
> *Nay, in one second, God*
> *Hath ta'en her back through death,*
> *Back from the senseless folk and from our eyes.*
> *Yet earth's oblivious sod,*
> *Albeit her body dies,*
> *Will bury not her live words fair and holy.*
> *Ah, cruel mercy! Here thou showest solely*
> *How, had heaven lent us ugly what she took,*
> *And death the debt reclaimed, all men were broke.*

Without disputing the fact that a very sincere emotion underlay these verses, it must be submitted that, in the words of Samuel Johnson about "Lycidas," "he who thus grieves will excite no sympathy; he who thus praises will confer no honour." This conviction will be enforced when we reflect that the thought upon which the madrigal above translated has been woven (1547) had been already used for Cecchino

dei Bracci in 1544. It is clear that, in dealing with Michelangelo's poetical compositions, we have to accept a mass of
conventional utterances, penetrated with a few firmly
grasped Platonical ideas. It is only after long familiarity
with his work that a man may venture to distinguish between
the accents of the heart and the head-notes in the case of
so great a master using an art he practised mainly as an
amateur. I shall have to return to these considerations when
I discuss the value of his poetry taken as a whole.

The union of Michelangelo and Vittoria was beautiful
and noble, based upon the sympathy of ardent and high-
feeling natures. Nevertheless we must remember that when
Michelangelo lost his old servant Urbino, his letters and the
sonnet written upon that occasion express an even deeper
passion of grief.

Love is an all-embracing word, and may well be used to
describe this exalted attachment, as also to qualify the great
sculptor's affection for a faithful servant or for a charming
friend. We ought not, however, to distort the truth of
biography or to corrupt criticism, from a personal wish to
make more out of his feeling than fact and probability
warrant. This is what has been done by all who approached
the study of Michelangelo's life and writings. Of late years,
the determination to see Vittoria Colonna through every
line written by him which bears the impress of strong emotion, and to suppress other aspects of his sensibility, has been
so deliberate, that I am forced to embark upon a discussion
which might otherwise have not been brought so promi-
nently forward. For the understanding of his character, and
for a proper estimate of his poetry, it has become indispensable to do so.

V

Michelangelo's best friend in Rome was a young nobleman called Tommaso Cavalieri. Speaking of his numerous
allies and acquaintances, Vasari writes: "Immeasurably

more than all the rest, he loved Tommaso dei Cavalieri, a Roman gentleman, for whom, as he was young and devoted to the arts, Michelangelo made many stupendous drawings of superb heads in black and red chalk, wishing him to learn the method of design. Moreover, he drew for him a Ganymede carried up to heaven by Jove's eagle, a Tityos with the vulture feeding on his heart, the fall of Phaëton with the sun's chariot into the river Po, and a Bacchanal of children; all of them things of the rarest quality, and drawings the like of which were never seen. Michelangelo made a cartoon portrait of Messer Tommaso, life-size, which was the only portrait that he ever drew, since he detested to imitate the living person, unless it was one of incomparable beauty." Several of Michelangelo's sonnets are addressed to Tommaso Cavalieri. Benedetto Varchi, in his commentary, introduces two of them with these words: "The first I shall present is one addressed to M. Tommaso Cavalieri, a young Roman of very noble birth, in whom I recognised, while I was sojourning at Rome, not only incomparable physical beauty, but so much elegance of manners, such excellent intelligence, and such graceful behaviour, that he well deserved, and still deserves, to win the more love the better he is known." Then Varchi recites the sonnet:—

Why should I seek to ease intense desire
  With still more tears and windy words of grief,
  When heaven, or late or soon, sends no relief
  To souls whom love hath robed around with fire?
Why need my aching heart to death aspire,
  When all must die? Nay, death beyond belief
  Unto these eyes would be both sweet and brief,
  Since in my sum of woes all joys expire!
Therefore, because I cannot shun the blow
  I rather seek, say who must rule my breast,
  Gliding between her gladness and her woe?

If only chains and bands can make me blest,
No marvel if alone and bare I go,
An armèd KNIGHT'S *captive and slave confessed.*

"The other shall be what follows, written perhaps for the same person, and worthy, in my opinion, not only of the ripest sage, but also of a poet not unexercised in writing verse:—

With your fair eyes a charming light I see,
For which my own blind eyes would peer in vain;
Stayed by your feet, the burden I sustain
Which my lame feet find all too strong for me;
Wingless upon your pinions forth I fly;
Heavenward your spirit stirreth me to strain;
E'en as you will, I blush and blanch again,
Freeze in the sun, burn 'neath a frosty sky.
Your will includes and is the lord of mine;
Life to my thoughts within your heart is given;
My words begin to breathe upon your breath:
Like to the moon am I, that cannot shine
Alone; for, lo! our eyes see naught in heaven
Save what the living sun illumineth."

The frank and hearty feeling for a youth of singular distinction which is expressed in these sonnets, gave no offence to society during the period of the earlier Renaissance; but after the Tridentine Council social feeling altered upon this and similar topics. While morals remained what they had been, language and manners grew more nice and hypocritical. It happened thus that grievous wrong was done to the text of Michelangelo's poems, with the best intentions, by their first editor. Grotesque misconceptions, fostered by the same mistaken zeal, are still widely prevalent.

When Michelangelo the younger arranged his grand-uncle's poems for the press, he was perplexed by the first

of the sonnets quoted by Varchi. The last line, which runs
in the Italian thus—

Resto prigion d'un Cavalier armato,

has an obvious play of words upon Cavalieri's surname.
This he altered into

Resto prigion d'un cor di virtù armato.

The reason was that, if it stood unaltered, "the ignorance
of men would have occasion to murmur." "Varchi," he
adds, "did wrong in printing it according to the text."
"Remember well," he observes, "that this sonnet, as well as
the preceding number and some others, are concerned, as is
manifest, with a masculine love of the Platonic species."
Michelangelo the younger's anxiety for his granduncle's
memory induced him thus to corrupt the text of his poems.
The same anxiety has led their latest editor to explain away
the obvious sense of certain words. Signor Guasti approves
of the first editor's pious fraud, on the ground that morality
has higher claims than art; but he adds that the expedient
was not necessary: "for these sonnets do not refer to masculine love, nor yet do any others. In the first (xxxi.) the lady
is compared to an armed knight, because she carries the
weapons of her sex and beauty; and while I think on it, an
example occurs to my mind from Messer Cino in support
of the argument. As regards the second (lxii.), those who
read these pages of mine will possibly remember that
Michelangelo, writing of the dead Vittoria Colonna, called
her *amico*; and on reflection, this sounds better than *amica*,
in the place where it occurs. Moreover, there are not wanting in these poems instances of the term *signore*, or lord,
applied to the beloved lady; which is one of the many peri-
phrastical expressions used by the Romance poets to indicate
their mistress." It is true that Cino compares his lady in one
sonnet to a knight who has carried off the prize of beauty
in the lists of love and grace by her elegant dancing. But

he never calls a lady by the name of *cavaliere*. It is also indubitable that the Tuscans occasionally addressed the female or male object of their adoration under the title of *signore*, lord of my heart and soul. But such instances weigh nothing against the direct testimony of a contemporary like Varchi, into whose hands Michelangelo's poems came at the time of their composition, and who was well acquainted with the circumstances of their composition. There is, moreover, a fact of singular importance bearing on this question, to which Signor Guasti has not attached the value it deserves. In a letter belonging to the year 1549, Michelangelo thanks Luca Martini for a copy of Varchi's commentary on his sonnet, and begs him to express his affectionate regards and hearty thanks to that eminent scholar for the honour paid him. In a second letter addressed to G. F. Fattucci, under date October 1549, he conveys "the thanks of Messer Tomao de' Cavalieri to Varchi for a certain little book of his which has been printed, and in which he speaks very honourably of himself, and not less so of me." In neither of these letters does Michelangelo take exception to Varchi's interpretation of Sonnet xxxi. Indeed, the second proves that both he and Cavalieri were much pleased with it. Michelangelo even proceeds to inform Fattucci that Cavalieri "has given me a sonnet which I made for him in those same years, begging me to send it on as a proof and witness that he really is the man intended. This I will enclose in my present letter." Furthermore, we possess an insolent letter of Pietro Aretino, which makes us imagine that the "ignorance of the vulgar" had already begun to "murmur." After complaining bitterly that Michelangelo refused to send him any of his drawings, he goes on to remark that it would be better for the artist if he did so, "inasmuch as such an act of courtesy would quiet the insidious rumours which assert that only Gerards and Thomases can dispose of them." We have seen from Vasari that Michelangelo executed some famous designs for Tommaso Cavalieri. The same authority asserts that he presented "Gherardo Perini, a Florentine gentleman, and his very dear friend," with three splendid drawings in black chalk. Tommaso Cavalieri and Gherardo Perini, were, therefore, the "Gerards and Thomases" alluded to by Aretino.

Michelangelo the younger's and Cesare Guasti's method of defending Buonarroti from a malevolence which was only too well justified by the vicious manners of the time, seems to me so really injurious to his character, that I feel bound to carry this investigation further. First of all, we ought to bear in mind what Buonarroti admitted concerning his own temperament. "You must know that I am, of all men who were ever born, the most inclined to love persons. Whenever I behold some one who possesses any talent or displays any dexterity of mind, who can do or say something more appropriately than the rest of the world, I am compelled to fall in love with him; and then I give myself up to him so entirely that I am no longer my own property, but wholly his." He mentions this as a reason for not going to dine with Luigi del Riccio in company with Donato Giannotti and Antonio Petrejo. "If I were to do so, as all of you are adorned with talents and agreeable graces, each of you would take from me a portion of myself, and so would the dancer, and so would the lute-player, if men with distinguished gifts in those arts were present. Each person would filch away a part of me, and instead of being refreshed and restored to health and gladness, as you said, I should be utterly bewildered and distraught, in such wise that for many days to come I should not know in what world I was moving." This passage serves to explain the extreme sensitiveness of the great artist to personal charm, grace, accomplishments, and throws light upon the self-abandonment with which he sometimes yielded to the attractions of delightful people.

We possess a series of Michelangelo's letters addressed to or concerned with Tommaso Cavalieri, the tone of which is certainly extravagant. His biographer, Aurelio Gotti, moved by the same anxiety as Michelangelo the younger and Guasti, adopted the extraordinary theory that they were really directed to Vittoria Colonna, and were meant to be shown to her by the common friend of both, Cavalieri. "There is an epistle to this young man," he says, "so studied in its phrases, so devoid of all naturalness, that we cannot extract any rational sense from it without supposing that Cavalieri was himself a friend of the Marchioness, and that Michelangelo, while writing to him, intended rather to address his words to the Colonna." Of this letter, which bears the date of January 1, 1533, three drafts exist, proving the great pains taken by Michelangelo in its composition.

"Without due consideration, Messer Tomao, my very dear lord, I was moved to write to your lordship, not by way of answer to any letter received from you, but being myself the first to make advances, as though I felt bound to cross a little stream with dry feet, or a ford made manifest by paucity of water. But now that I have left the shore, instead of the trifling river I expected, the ocean with its towering waves appears before me, so that, if it were possible, in order to avoid drowning, I would gladly retrace my steps to the dry land whence I started. Still, as I am here, I will e'en make of my heart a rock, and proceed farther; and if I shall not display the art of sailing on the sea of your powerful genius, that genius itself will excuse me, nor will be disdainful of my inferiority in parts, nor desire from me that which I do not possess, inasmuch as he who is unique in all things can have peers in none. Therefore your lordship, the light of our century without paragon upon this world, is unable to be satisfied with the productions of other men, having no match or equal to yourself. And if, peradventure, something of mine, such as I hope and promise to perform, give pleasure to your mind, I shall esteem it more fortunate than excellent; and should I be ever sure of pleasing your lordship, as is said, in any particular, I will devote the present time and all my future to your service; indeed, it will grieve me much that I cannot regain the past, in order to devote a longer space to you than the future only will allow, seeing I am now too old. I have no more to say. Read the heart, and not the letter, because 'the pen toils after man's good-will in vain.'

"I have to make excuses for expressing in my first letter a marvellous astonishment at your rare genius; and thus I do so, having recognised the error I was in; for it is much the same to wonder at God's working miracles as to wonder at Rome producing divine men. Of this the universe confirms us in our faith."

It is clear that Michelangelo alludes in this letter to the designs which he is known to have made for Cavalieri, and the last paragraph has no point except as an elaborate compliment addressed to a Roman gentleman. It would be quite out of place if applied to Vittoria Colonna. Gotti finds the language strained and unnatural. We cannot deny that it differs greatly from the simple diction of the writer's ordinary correspondence. But Michelangelo did sometimes seek to heighten his style, when he felt that the occasion demanded a special effort; and then he had recourse to the laboured images in vogue at that period, employing them with something of the ceremonious cumbrousness displayed in his poetry. The letters to Pietro Aretino, Niccolò Martelli, Vittoria Colonna, Francis I., Luca Martini, and Giorgio Vasari might be quoted as examples.

As a postscript to this letter, in the two drafts which were finally rejected, the following enigmatical sentence is added:—

"It would be permissible to give the name of the things a man presents, to him who receives them; but proper sense of what is fitting prevents it being done in this letter."

Probably Michelangelo meant that he should have liked

to call Cavalieri his friend, since he had already given him friendship. The next letter, July 28, 1533, begins thus:—

"My dear Lord,—Had I not believed that I had made you certain of the very great, nay, measureless love I bear you, it would not have seemed strange to me nor have roused astonishment to observe the great uneasiness you show in your last letter, lest, through my not having written, I should have forgotten you. Still it is nothing new or marvellous when so many other things go counter, that this also should be topsy-turvy. For what your lordship says to me, I could say to yourself: nevertheless, you do this perhaps to try me, or to light a new and stronger flame, if that indeed were possible: but be it as it wills: I know well that, at this hour, I could as easily forget your name as the food by which I live; nay, it were easier to forget the food, which only nourishes my body miserably, than your name, which nourishes both body and soul, filling the one and the other with such sweetness that neither weariness nor fear of death is felt by me while memory preserves you to my mind. Think, if the eyes could also enjoy their portion, in what condition I should find myself."

This second letter has also been extremely laboured; for we have three other turns given in its drafts to the image of food and memory. That these two documents were really addressed to Cavalieri, without any thought of Vittoria Colonna, is proved by three letters sent to Michelangelo by the young man in question. One is dated August 2, 1533, another September 2, and the third bears no date. The two which I have mentioned first belong to the summer of 1533; the third seems to be the earliest. It was clearly written on some occasion when both men were in Rome together, and at the very beginning of their friendship. I will translate them in their order. The first undated letter was sent to Michelangelo in Rome, in answer to some writing of the illustrious sculptor which we do not possess:—

"I have received from you a letter, which is the more acceptable because it was so wholly unexpected. I say unexpected, because I hold myself unworthy of such condescension in a man of your eminence. With regard to what Pierantonio spoke to you in my praise, and those things of mine which you have seen, and which you say have aroused in you no small affection for me, I answer that they were insufficient to impel a man of such transcendent genius, without a second, not to speak of a peer, upon this earth, to address a youth who was born but yesterday, and therefore is as ignorant as it is possible to be. At the same time I cannot call you a liar. I rather think then, nay, am certain, that the love you bear me is due to this, that you being a man most excellent in art, nay, art itself, are forced to love those who follow it and love it, among whom am I; and in this, according to my capacity, I yield to few. I promise you truly that you shall receive from me for your kindness affection equal, and perhaps greater, in exchange; for I never loved a man more than I do you, nor desired a friendship more than I do yours. About this, though my judgment may fail in other things, it is unerring; and you shall see the proof, except only that fortune is adverse to me in that now, when I might enjoy you, I am far from well. I hope, however, if she does not begin to trouble me again, that within a few days I shall be cured, and shall come to pay you my respects in person. Meanwhile I shall spend at least two hours a day in studying two of your drawings, which Pierantonio brought me: the more I look at them, the more they delight me; and I shall soothe my complaint by cherishing the hope which Pierantonio gave me, of letting me see other things of yours. In order not to be troublesome, I will write no more. Only I beg you remember, on occasion, to make use of me; and recommend myself in perpetuity to you.—Your most affectionate servant.

"THOMAO CAVALIERE."

The next letters were addressed to Michelangelo in Florence:—

"Unique, my Lord,—I have received from you a letter, very acceptable, from which I gather that you are not a little saddened at my having written to you about forgetting. I answer that I did not write this for either of the following reasons: to wit, because you have not sent me anything, or in order to fan the flame of your affection. I only wrote to jest with you, as certainly I think I may do. Therefore, do not be saddened, for I am quite sure you will not be able to forget me. Regarding what you write to me about that young Nerli, he is much my friend, and having to leave Rome, he came to ask whether I needed anything from Florence. I said no, and he begged me to allow him to go in my name to pay you my respects, merely on account of his own desire to speak with you. I have nothing more to write, except that I beg you to return quickly. When you come you will deliver me from prison, because I wish to avoid bad companions; and having this desire, I cannot converse with any one but you. I recommend myself to you a thousand times.—Yours more than his own,

"THOMAO CAVALIERE.

"ROME, *August* 2, 1533."

It appears from the third letter, also sent to Florence, that during the course of the month Michelangelo had despatched some of the drawings he made expressly for his friend:—

"Unique, my Lord,—Some days ago I received a letter from you, which was very welcome, both because I learned from it that you were well, and also because I can now be sure that you will soon return. I was very sorry not to be able to answer at once. However, it consoles me to think that, when you know the cause, you will hold me excused. On the day your letter reached me, I was attacked with vomiting and such high fever that I was on the point of death; and certainly I should have died, if it (*i.e.*, the letter) had not somewhat revived me. Since then, thank God, I have been always well. Messer Bartolommeo (Angelini) has now brought me a sonnet sent by you, which has made me feel it my duty to write. Some three days since I received my Phaëthon, which is exceedingly well done. The Pope, the Cardinal de' Medici, and every one, have seen it; I do not know what made them want to do so. The Cardinal expressed a wish to inspect all your drawings, and they pleased him so much that he said he should like to have the Tityos and Ganymede done in crystal. I could not manage to prevent him from using the Tityos, and it is now being executed by Maestro Giovanni. Hard I struggled to save the Ganymede. The other day I went, as you requested, to Fra Sebastiano. He sends a thousand messages, but only to pray you to come back.—Your affectionate,

"THOMAO CAVALIERE.

"ROME, *September* 6."

All the drawings mentioned by Vasari as having been made for Cavalieri are alluded to here, except the Bacchanal of Children. Of the Phaëthon we have two splendid examples in existence, one at Windsor, the other in the collection of M. Emile Galichon. They differ considerably in details, but have the same almost mathematical exactitude of pyramidal composition. That belonging to M. Galichon must have been made in Rome, for it has this rough scrawl in Michelangelo's hand at the bottom, "Tomao, se questo scizzo non vi piace, ditelo a Urbino." He then promises to make another. Perhaps Cavalieri sent word back that he did not like something in the sketch—possibly the women writhing into trees—and that to this circumstance we owe the Windsor drawing, which is purer in style. There is a fine Tityos with the vulture at Windsor, so exquisitely finished and perfectly preserved that one can scarcely believe it passed through the hands of Maestro Giovanni. Windsor, too, possesses a very delicate Ganymede, which seems intended for an intaglio. The subject is repeated in an unfinished pen-design at the Uffizi, incorrectly attributed to Michelangelo, and is represented by several old engravings. The Infant Bacchanals again exist at Windsor, and fragmentary jottings upon the margin of other sketches intended for the same theme survive.

VI

A correspondence between Bartolommeo Angelini in Rome and Michelangelo in Florence during the summers of 1532 and 1533 throws some light upon the latter's movements, and also upon his friendship for Tommaso Cavalieri. The first letter of this series, written on the 21st of August 1532, shows that Michelangelo was then expected in Rome. "Fra Sebastiano says that you wish to dismount at your own house. Knowing then that there is nothing but the walls, I hunted up a small amount of furniture, which I have had sent thither, in order that you may be able to sleep and sit down and enjoy some other conveniences. For eating, you will be able to provide yourself to your own liking in the neighbourhood." From the next letter (September 18, 1532) it appears that Michelangelo was then in Rome. There ensues a gap in the correspondence, which is not resumed until July 12, 1533. It now appears that Buonarroti had recently left Rome at the close of another of his visits. Angelini immediately begins to speak of Tommaso Cavalieri. "I gave that soul you wot of to M. Tommao, who sends you his very best regards, and begs me to communicate any letters I may receive from you to him. Your house is watched continually every night, and I often go to visit it by day. The hens and master cock are in fine feather, and the cats complain greatly over your absence, albeit they have plenty to eat." Angelini never writes now without mentioning Cavalieri. Since this name does not occur in the correspondence before the date of July 12, 1533, it is possible that Michelangelo made the acquaintance during his residence at Rome in the preceding winter. His letters to Angelini must have conveyed frequent expressions of anxiety concerning Cavalieri's affection; for the replies invariably contain some reassuring words (July 26): "Yours makes me understand how great is the love you bear him; and in truth, so far as I have seen, he does not love you less than you love him." Again (August 11, 1533): "I gave your letter to M. Thomao, who sends you his kindest remembrances, and shows the very strongest desire for your return, saying that when he is with you, then he is really happy, because he possesses all that he wishes for upon this world. So then, it seems to me that, while you are fretting to return, he is burning with desire for you to do so. Why do you not begin in earnest to make plans for leaving Florence? It would give peace to yourself and all of us, if you were here. I have seen your soul, which is in good health and under good guardianship. The body waits for your arrival."

This mysterious reference to the soul, which Angelini gave, at Buonarroti's request, to young Cavalieri, and which he now describes as prospering, throws some light upon the passionate phrases of the following mutilated letter, addressed to Angelini by Michelangelo upon the 11th of October. The writer, alluding to Messer Tommao, says that, having given him his heart, he can hardly go on living in his absence: "And so, if I yearn day and night without intermission to be in Rome, it is only in order to return again to life, which I cannot enjoy without the soul." This conceit is carried on for some time, and the letter winds up with the following sentence: "My dear Bartolommeo, although you may think that I am joking with you, this is not the case. I am talking sober sense, for I have grown twenty years older and twenty pounds lighter since I have been here." This epistle, as we shall see in due course, was acknowledged. All Michelangelo's intimates in Rome became acquainted with the details of this friendship. Writing to

Sebastiano from Florence in this year, he says: "I beg you, if you see Messer T. Cavalieri, to recommend me to him infinitely; and when you write, tell me something about him to keep him in my memory; for if I were to lose him from my mind, I believe that I should fall down dead straightway." In Sebastiano's letters there is one allusion to Cavalieri, who had come to visit him in the company of Bartolommeo Angelini, when he was ill.

It is not necessary to follow all the references to Tommaso Cavalieri contained in Angelini's letters. They amount to little more than kind messages and warm wishes for Michelangelo's return. Soon, however, Michelangelo began to send poems, which Angelini acknowledges (September 6): "I have received the very welcome letter you wrote me, together with your graceful and beautiful sonnet, of which I kept a copy, and then sent it on to M. Thomao. He was delighted to possess it, being thereby assured that God has deigned to bestow upon him the friendship of a man endowed with so many noble gifts as you are." Again he writes (October 18): "Yours of the 12th is to hand, together with M. Thomao's letter and the most beautiful sonnets. I have kept copies, and sent them on to him for whom they were intended, because I know with what affection he regards all things that pertain to you. He promised to send an answer which shall be enclosed in this I now am writing. He is counting not the days merely, but the hours, till you return." In another letter, without date, Angelini says, "I gave your messages to M. Thomao, who replied that your presence would be dearer to him than your writing, and that if it seems to you a thousand years, to him it seems ten thousand, till you come. I received your gallant (galante) and beautiful sonnet; and though you said nothing about it, I saw at once for whom it was intended, and gave it to him. Like everything of yours, it delighted him. The tenor of the sonnet shows that love keeps you perpetually restless. I do not think this ought to be the effect of love, and so I send you one of my poor performances to prove the contrary opinion." We may perhaps assume that this sonnet was the famous No. xxxi., from the last line of which every one could perceive that Michelangelo meant it for Tommaso Cavalieri.

VII

It is significant that, while Michelangelo's affection for the young Roman was thus acquiring force, another friendship, which must have once been very dear to him, sprang up and then declined, but not apparently through his own fault or coldness. We hear of Febo di Poggio in the following autumn for the first and last time. Before proceeding to speak of him, I will wind up what has to be said about Tommaso Cavalieri. Not long after the date of the last letter quoted above, Michelangelo returned to Rome, and settled there for the rest of his life. He continued to the end of his days in close friendship with Cavalieri, who helped to nurse him during his last illness, who took charge of his effects after his death, and who carried on the architectural work he had begun at the Capitol.

Their friendship seems to have been uninterrupted by any disagreement, except on one occasion when Michelangelo gave way to his suspicious irritability, quite at the close of his long life. This drew forth from Cavalieri the following manly and touching letter:—

"Very magnificent, my Lord,—I have noticed during several days past that you have some grievance—what, I do not know—against me. Yesterday I became certain of it when I went to your house. As I cannot imagine the cause, I have thought it best to write this, in order that, if you like, you may inform me. I am more than positive that I never offended you. But you lend easy credence to those whom perhaps you ought least to trust; and some one has possibly told you some lie, for fear I should one day reveal the many knaveries done under your name, the which do you little honour; and if you desire to know about them, you shall. Only I cannot, nor, if I could, should I wish to force myself—but I tell you frankly that if you do not want me for a friend, you can do as you like, but you cannot compel me not to be a friend to you. I shall always try to do you service; and only yesterday I came to show you a letter written by the Duke of Florence, and to lighten your burdens, as I have ever done until now. Be sure you have no better friend than me; but on this I will not dwell. Still, if you think otherwise, I hope that in a short time you will explain matters; and I know that you know I have always been your friend without the least interest of my own. Now I will say no more, lest I should seem to be excusing myself for something which does not exist, and which I am utterly unable to imagine. I pray and conjure you, by the love you bear to God, that you tell me what you have against me, in order that I may disabuse you. Not having more to write, I remain your servant,

"THOMAO DE' CAVALIERI.

"From my house, *November* 15, 1561."

It is clear from this letter, and from the relations which subsisted between Michelangelo and Cavalieri up to the day of his death, that the latter was a gentleman of good repute and honour, whose affection did credit to his friend. I am unable to see that anything but an injury to both is done by explaining away the obvious meaning of the letters and the sonnets I have quoted. The supposition that Michelangelo intended the Cavalieri letters to reach Vittoria Colonna through that friend's hands does not, indeed, deserve the complete refutation which I have given it. I am glad, however, to be able to adduce the opinion of a caustic Florentine scholar upon this topic, which agrees with my own, and which was formed without access to the original documents which I have been enabled to make use of. Fanfani says: "I have searched, but in vain, for documentary proofs of the passion which Michelangelo is supposed to have felt for Vittoria Colonna, and which she returned with ardour according to the assertion of some critics. My own belief, concurring with that of better judges than myself, is that we have here to deal with one of the many baseless stories told about him. Omitting the difficulties presented by his advanced age, it is wholly contrary to all we know about the Marchioness, and not a little damaging to her reputation for austerity, to suppose that this admirable matron, who, after the death of her husband, gave herself up to God, and abjured the commerce of the world, should, later in life, have carried on an intrigue, as the saying is, upon the sly, particularly when a third person is imposed on our credulity, acting the part of go-between and cloak in the transaction, as certain biographers of the great artist, and certain commentators of his poetry, are pleased to assert, with how much common-sense and what seriousness I will not ask."

VIII

The history of Luigi del Riccio's affection for a lad of Florence called Cecchino dei Bracci, since this is interwoven with Michelangelo's own biography and the criticism of his poems, may be adduced in support of the argument I am developing. Cecchino was a youth of singular promise and personal charm. His relative, the Florentine merchant, Luigi del Riccio, one of Buonarroti's most intimate friends and advisers, became devotedly attached to the boy. Michelangelo, after his return to Rome in 1534, shared this friend Luigi's admiration for Cecchino; and the close intimacy into which the two elder men were drawn, at a somewhat later period of Buonarroti's life, seems to have been cemented by their common interest in poetry and their common feeling for a charming personality. We have a letter of uncertain date, in which Michelangelo tells Del Riccio that he has sent him a madrigal, begging him, if he thinks fit, to commit the verses "to the fire—that is, to what consumes me." Then he asks him to resolve a certain problem which has occurred to his mind during the night, "for while I was saluting *our idol* in a dream, it seemed to me that he laughed, and in the same instant threatened me; and not knowing which of these two moods I have to abide by, I beg you to find out from him; and on Sunday, when we meet again, you will inform me." Cecchino, who is probably alluded to in this letter, died at Rome on the 8th of January 1542, and was buried in the Church of Araceli. Luigi felt the blow acutely. Upon the 12th of January he wrote to his friend Donato Giannotti, then at Vicenza, in the following words:—

"Alas, my friend Donato! Our Cecchino is dead. All Rome weeps. Michelangelo is making for me the design of a decent sepulture in marble; and I pray you to write me the epitaph, and to send it to me with a consolatory letter, if time permits, for my grief has distraught me. Patience! I live with a thousand and a thousand deaths each hour. O God! How has Fortune changed her aspect!" Giannotti replied, enclosing three fine sonnets, the second of which, beginning—

> *Messer Luigi mio, di noi che fia*
> *Che sian restati senza il nostro sole?*

seems to have taken Michelangelo's fancy. Many good pens in Italy poured forth laments on this occasion. We have verses written by Giovanni Aldobrandini, Carlo Gondi, Fra Paolo del Rosso, and Anton Francesco Grazzini, called Il Lasca. Not the least touching is Luigi's own threnody, which starts upon this note:—

> *Idol mio, che la tua leggiadra spoglia*
> *Mi lasciasti anzi tempo.*

Michelangelo, seeking to indulge his own grief and to soothe that of his friend Luigi, composed no fewer than forty-two epigrams of four lines each, in which he celebrated the beauty and rare personal sweetness of Cecchino in laboured philosophical conceits. They rank but low among his poems, having too much of scholastic trifling and too little of the accent of strong feeling in them. Certainly these pieces did not deserve the pains which Michelangelo the younger bestowed, when he altered the text of a selection from them so as to adapt their Platonic compliments to some female. Far superior is a sonnet written to Del Riccio upon the death of the youth, showing how recent had been Michelangelo's acquaintance with Cecchino, and containing an unfulfilled promise to carve his portrait:—

> Scarce had I seen for the first time his eyes,
>   Which to your living eyes were life and light,
>   When, closed at last in death's injurious night,
>   He opened them on God in Paradise.
> I know it, and I weep—too late made wise:
>   Yet was the fault not mine; for death's fell spite
>   Robbed my desire of that supreme delight
>   Which in your better memory never dies.
> Therefore, Luigi, if the task be mine
>   To make unique Cecchino smile in stone
>   For ever, now that earth hath made him dim,
> If the beloved within the lover shine,
>   Since art without him cannot work alone,
>   You must I carve to tell the world of him.

The strange blending of artificial conceits with spontaneous feeling in these poetical effusions, the deep interest taken in a mere lad like Cecchino by so many eminent personages, and the frank publicity given to a friendship based apparently upon the beauty of its object, strike us now as almost unintelligible. Yet we have the history of Shakespeare's Sonnets, and the letters addressed by Languet to young Sidney, in evidence that fashion at the end of the sixteenth century differed widely from that which prevails at the close of the nineteenth.

IX

Some further light may here be thrown upon Michel-angelo's intimacy with young men by two fragments extracted independently from the Buonarroti Archives by Milanesi and Guasti. In the collection of the letters we find the following sorrowful epistle, written in December 1533, upon the eve of Michelangelo's departure from Florence. It is addressed to a certain Febo:—

"FEBO,—Albeit you bear the greatest hatred toward my person—I know not why—I scarcely believe, because of the love I cherish for you, but probably through the words of others, to which you ought to give no credence, having proved me—yet I cannot do otherwise than write to you this letter. I am leaving Florence to-morrow, and am going to Pescia to meet the Cardinal di Cesis and Messer Baldassare. I shall journey with them to Pisa, and thence to Rome, and I shall never return again to Florence. I wish you to understand that, so long as I live, wherever I may be, I shall always remain at your service with loyalty and love, in a measure unequalled by any other friend whom you may have upon this world.

"I pray God to open your eyes from some other quarter, in order that you may come to comprehend that he who desires your good more than his own welfare, is able to love, not to hate like an enemy."

Milanesi prints no more of the manuscript in his edition of the Letters. But Guasti, conscientiously collecting fragments of Michelangelo's verses, gives six lines, which he found at the foot of the epistle:—

Vo' sol del mie morir contento veggio:
  La terra piange, e 'l ciel per me si muove;
  E vo' men pietà stringe ov' io sto peggio.

O sol che scaldi il mondo in ogni dove,
O Febo, o luce eterna de' mortali,
Perchè a me sol ti scuri e non altrove?

———

Naught comforts you, I see, unless I die:
Earth weeps, the heavens for me are moved to woe;
You feel of grief the less, the more grieve I.
O sun that warms the world where'er you go,
O Febo, light eterne for mortal eyes!
Why dark to me alone, elsewhere not so?

These verses seem to have been written as part of a long Capitolo which Michelangelo himself, the elder, used indifferently in addressing Febo and his abstract "donna." Who Febo was, we do not know. But the sincere accent of the letter and the lyric cry of the rough lines leave us to imagine that he was some one for whom Michelangelo felt very tenderly in Florence.

Milanesi prints this letter to Febo with the following title, "*A Febo (di Poggio).*" This proves that he at any rate knew it had been answered by some one signing "Febo di Poggio." The autograph, in an illiterate hand and badly spelt, is preserved among the Buonarroti Archives, and bears date January 14, 1534. Febo excuses himself for not having been able to call on Michelangelo the night before he left Florence, and professes to have come the next day and found him already gone. He adds that he is in want of money, both to buy clothes and to go to see the games upon the Monte. He prays for a gratuity, and winds up: "Vostro da figliuolo (yours like a son), Febo di Poggio." I will add a full translation here:—

"Magnificent M. Michelangelo, to be honoured as a father,—I came back yesterday from Pisa, whither I had gone to see my father. Immediately upon my arrival, that friend of yours at the bank put a letter from you into my hands, which I received with the greatest pleasure, having

heard of your well-being. God be praised, I may say the
same about myself. Afterwards I learned what you say
about my being angry with you. You know well I could not
be angry with you, since I regard you in the place of a
father. Besides, your conduct toward me has not been of the
sort to cause in me any such effect. That evening when you
left Florence, in the morning I could not get away from
M. Vincenzo, though I had the greatest desire to speak with
you. Next morning I came to your house, and you were
already gone, and great was my disappointment at your leaving Florence without my seeing you.

"I am here in Florence; and when you left, you told me
that if I wanted anything, I might ask it of that friend of
yours; and now that M. Vincenzo is away, I am in want
of money, both to clothe myself, and also to go to the Monte,
to see those people fighting, for M. Vincenzo is there. Accordingly, I went to visit that friend at the bank, and he told
me that he had no commission whatsoever from you; but
that a messenger was starting to-night for Rome, and that
an answer could come back within five days. So then, if you
give him orders, he will not fail. I beseech you, then, to
provide and assist me with any sum you think fit, and do
not fail to answer.

"I will not write more, except that with all my heart
and power I recommend myself to you, praying God to keep
you from harm.—Yours in the place of a son,

"FEBO DI POGGIO.

"FLORENCE, *January* 4, 1534."

X

In all the compositions I have quoted as illustrative of
Michelangelo's relations with young men, there is a singular
humility which gives umbrage to his editors. The one epistle
to Gherardo Perini, cited above, contains the following
phrases: "I do not feel myself of force enough to correspond
to your kind letter;" "Your most faithful and poor friend."

Yet there was nothing extraordinary in Cavalieri, Cecchino, Febo, or Perini, except their singularity of youth and grace, good parts and beauty. The vulgar are offended when an illustrious man pays homage to these qualities, forgetful of Shakespeare's self-abasement before Mr. W. H. and of Languet's prostration at the feet of Sidney. In the case of Michelangelo, we may find a solution of this problem, I think, in one of his sonnets. He says, writing a poem belonging very probably to the series which inspires Michelangelo the younger with alarm:—

> *As one who will re-seek her home of light,*
> *Thy form immortal to this prison-house*
> *Descended, like an angel piteous,*
> *To heal all hearts and make the whole world bright.*
> *'Tis this that thralls my soul in love's delight,*
> *Not thy clear face of beauty glorious;*
> *For he who harbours virtue still will choose*
> *To love what neither years nor death can blight.*
> *So fares it ever with things high and rare*
> *Wrought in the sweat of nature; heaven above*
> *Showers on their birth the blessings of her prime:*
> *Nor hath God deigned to show Himself elsewhere*
> *More clearly than in human forms sublime,*
> *Which, since they image Him, alone I love.*

It was not, then, to this or that young man, to this or that woman, that Michelangelo paid homage, but to the eternal beauty revealed in the mortal image of divinity before his eyes. The attitude of the mind, the quality of passion, implied in these poems, and conveyed more clumsily through the prose of the letters, may be difficult to comprehend. But until we have arrived at seizing them we shall fail to understand the psychology of natures like Michelangelo. No language of admiration is too strong, no self-humiliation too complete, for a soul which has recognised deity made manifest in one of its main attributes, beauty. In the sight of a philosopher, a poet, and an artist, what are kings, popes, people of importance, compared with a really perfect piece of God's handiwork?

> *From thy fair face I learn, O my loved lord,*
> *That which no mortal tongue can rightly say;*
> *The soul imprisoned in her house of clay,*
> *Holpen by thee, to God hath often soared.*
> *And though the vulgar, vain, malignant horde*
> *Attribute what their grosser wills obey,*
> *Yet shall this fervent homage that I pay,*
> *This love, this faith, pure joys for us afford.*
> *Lo, all the lovely things we find on earth,*
> *Resemble for the soul that rightly sees*
> *That source of bliss divine which gave us birth:*
> *Nor have we first-fruits or remembrances*
> *Of heaven elsewhere. Thus, loving loyally,*
> *I rise to God, and make death sweet by thee.*

We know that, in some way or other, perhaps during those early years at Florence among the members of the Platonic Academy, Michelangelo absorbed the doctrines of the *Phædrus* and *Symposium*. His poems abound in references to the contrast between Uranian and Pandemic, celestial and vulgar, Eros. We have even one sonnet in which he distinctly states the Greek opinion that the love of women is unworthy of a soul bent upon high thoughts and virile actions. It reads like a verse transcript from the main argument of the *Symposium*:—

> *Love is not always harsh and deadly sin,*
> *When love for boundless beauty makes us pine;*
> *The heart, by love left soft and infantine,*
> *Will let the shafts of God's grace enter in.*
> *Love wings and wakes the soul, stirs her to win*
> *Her flight aloft, nor e'er to earth decline;*
> *'Tis the first step that leads her to the shrine*
> *Of Him who slakes the thirst that burns within.*

The love of that whereof I speak ascends:
Woman is different far; the love of her
But ill befits a heart manly and wise.
The one love soars, the other earthward tends;
The soul lights this, while that the senses stir;
And still lust's arrow at base quarry flies.

The same exalted Platonism finds obscure but impassioned expression in this fragment of a sonnet (No. lxxix.):—

For Love's fierce wound, and for the shafts that harm,
True medicine 'twould have been to pierce my heart;
But my soul's Lord owns only one strong charm,
Which makes life grow where grows life's mortal
    smart.
My Lord dealt death, when with his powerful arm
He bent Love's bow. Winged with that shaft, from
    Love
An angel flew, cried, "Love, nay Burn! Who dies,
Hath but Love's plumes whereby to soar above!
Lo, I am He who from thine earliest years
Toward heaven-born Beauty raised thy faltering eyes.
Beauty alone lifts live man to heaven's spheres."

Feeling like this, Michelangelo would have been justly indignant with officious relatives and critics, who turned his *amici* into *animi*, redirected his Cavalieri letters to the address of Vittoria Colonna, discovered Florence in Febo di Poggio, and ascribed all his emotional poems to some woman.

There is no doubt that both the actions and the writings of contemporaries justified a considerable amount of scepticism regarding the purity of Platonic affections. The words and lives of many illustrious persons gave colour to what Segni stated in his History of Florence, and what Savonarola found it necessary to urge upon the people from his pulpit.

But we have every reason to feel certain that, in a malicious age, surrounded by jealous rivals, with the fierce light of his transcendent glory beating round his throne, Buonarroti suffered from no scandalous reports, and maintained an untarnished character for sobriety of conduct and purity of morals.

The general opinion regarding him may be gathered from Scipione Ammirati's History (under the year 1564). This annalist records the fact that "Buonarotti having lived for ninety years, there was never found through all that length of time, and with all that liberty to sin, any one who could with right and justice impute to him a stain or any ugliness of manners."

How he appeared to one who lived and worked with him for a long period of intimacy, could not be better set forth than in the warm and ingenuous words of Condivi: "He has loved the beauty of the human body with particular devotion, as is natural with one who knows that beauty so completely; and has loved it in such wise that certain carnally minded men, who do not comprehend the love of beauty, except it be lascivious and indecorous, have been led thereby to think and to speak evil of him: just as though Alcibiades, that comeliest young man, had not been loved in all purity by Socrates, from whose side, when they reposed together, he was wont to say that he arose not otherwise than from the side of his own father. Oftentimes have I heard Michelangelo discoursing and expounding on the theme of love, and have afterwards gathered from those who were present upon these occasions that he spoke precisely as Plato wrote, and as we may read in Plato's works upon this subject. I, for myself, do not know what Plato says; but I know full well that, having so long and so intimately conversed with Michelangelo, I never once heard issue from that mouth words that were not of the truest honesty, and such as had virtue to extinguish in the heart of youth any disordered and uncurbed desire which might assail it. I am sure, too, that no vile thoughts were born in him, by this token, that he loved not only the beauty of human beings, but in general all fair things, as a beautiful horse, a beautiful dog, a beautiful piece of country, a beautiful plant, a beautiful mountain, a beautiful wood, and every site or thing in its kind fair and rare, admiring them with marvellous affection. This was his way; to choose what is beautiful from nature, as bees collect the honey from flowers, and use it for their purpose in their workings: which indeed was always the method of those masters who have acquired any fame in painting. That old Greek artist, when he wanted to depict a Venus, was not satisfied with the sight of one maiden only. On the contrary, he sought to study many; and culling from each the particular in which she was most perfect, to make use of these details in his Venus. Of a truth, he who imagines to arrive at any excellence without following this system (which is the source of a true theory in the arts), shoots very wide indeed of his mark."

Condivi perhaps exaggerated the influence of lovely nature, horses, dogs, flowers, hills, woods, &c., on Michelangelo's genius. His work, as we know, is singularly deficient in motives drawn from any province but human beauty; and his poems and letters contain hardly a trace of sympathy with the external world. Yet, in the main contention, Condivi told the truth. Michelangelo's poems and letters, and the whole series of his works in fresco and marble, suggest no single detail which is sensuous, seductive, enfeebling to the moral principles. Their tone may be passionate; it is indeed often red-hot with a passion like that of Lucretius and Beethoven; but the genius of the man transports the mind to spiritual altitudes, where the lust of the eye and the longings of the flesh are left behind us in a lower region. Only a soul attuned to the same chord of intellectual rapture can breathe in that fiery atmosphere and feel the vibrations of its electricity.

XI

I have used Michelangelo's poems freely throughout this work as documents illustrative of his opinions and sentiments, and also in their bearing on the events of his life. I have made them reveal the man in his personal relations to Pope Julius II., to Vittoria Colonna, to Tommaso dei Cavalieri, to Luigi del Riccio, to Febo di Poggio. I have let them tell their own tale, when sorrow came upon him in the death of his father and Urbino, and when old age shook his lofty spirit with the thought of approaching death. I have appealed to them for lighter incidents: matters of courtesy, the completion of the Sistine vault, the statue of Night at S. Lorenzo, the subjection of Florence to the Medici, his heart-felt admiration for Dante's genius. Examples of his poetic work, so far as these can be applied to the explanation of his psychology, his theory of art, his sympathies, his feeling under several moods of passion, will consequently be found scattered up and down by volumes. Translation, indeed, is difficult to the writer, and unsatisfactory to the reader. But I have been at pains to direct an honest student to the original sources, so that he may, if he wishes, compare my versions with the text. Therefore I do not think it necessary to load this chapter with voluminous citations. Still, there remains something to be said about Michelangelo as poet, and about the place he occupies as poet in Italian literature.

The value of Michelangelo's poetry is rather psychological than purely literary. He never claimed to be more than an amateur, writing to amuse himself. His style is obscure, crabbed, ungrammatical. Expression only finds a smooth and flowing outlet when the man's nature is profoundly stirred by some powerful emotion, as in the sonnets to Cavalieri, or the sonnets on the deaths of Vittoria Colonna and Urbino, or the sonnets on the thought of his own death. For the most part, it is clear that he found great difficulty in mastering his thoughts and images. This we dis cover from the innumerable variants of the same madrigal or sonnet which he made, and his habit of returning to them at intervals long after their composition. A good fourth of the Codex Vaticanus consists of repetitions and *rifacimenti*. He was also wont to submit what he wrote to the judgment of his friends, requesting them to alter and improve. He often had recourse to Luigi del Riccio's assistance in such matters. I may here adduce an inedited letter from two friends in Rome, Giovanni Francesco Bini and Giovanni Francesco Stella, who returned a poem they had handled in this manner: "We have done our best to alter some things in your sonnet, but not to set it all to rights, since there was not much wanting. Now that it is changed or put in order, according as the kindness of your nature wished, the result will be more due to your own judgment than to ours, since you have the true conception of the subject in your mind. We shall be greatly pleased if you find yourself as well served as we earnestly desire that you should command us." It was the custom of amateur poets to have recourse to literary craftsmen before they ventured to circulate their compositions. An amusing instance of this will be found in Professor Biagi's monograph upon Tullia d'Aragona, all of whose verses passed through the crucible of Benedetto Varchi's revision.

The thoughts and images out of which Michelangelo's poetry is woven are characteristically abstract and arid. He borrows no illustrations from external nature. The beauty of the world and all that lives in it might have been non-existent so far as he was concerned. Nor do his octave stanzas in praise of rural life form an exception to this statement; for these are imitated from Poliziano, so far as they attempt pictures of the country, and their chief poetical feature is the masque of vices belonging to human nature in the city. His stock-in-trade consists of a few Platonic notions and a few Petrarchan antitheses. In the very large number of compositions which are devoted to love, this one idea predominates: that physical beauty is a direct beam sent from the eternal source of all reality, in order to elevate the lover's soul and lead him on the upward path toward heaven. Carnal passion he regards with the aversion of an ascetic. It is impossible to say for certain to whom these mystical love-poems were addressed. Whether a man or a woman is in the case (for both were probably the objects of his æsthetical admiration), the tone of feeling, the language, and the philosophy do not vary. He uses the same imagery, the same conceits, the same abstract ideas for both sexes, and adapts the leading motive which he had invented for a person of one sex to a person of the other when it suits his purpose. In our absolute incapacity to fix any amative connection upon Michelangelo, or to link his name with that of any contemporary beauty, we arrive at the conclusion, strange as this may be, that the greater part of his love-poetry is a scholastic exercise upon emotions transmuted into metaphysical and mystical conceptions. Only two pieces in the long series break this monotony by a touch of realism. They are divided by a period of more than thirty years. The first seems to date from an early epoch of his life:—

> *What joy hath yon glad wreath of flowers that is*
> *Around her golden hair so deftly twined,*
> *Each blossom pressing forward from behind,*
> *As though to be the first her brows to kiss!*
> *The livelong day her dress hath perfect bliss,*
> *That now reveals her breast, now seems to bind:*
> *And that fair woven net of gold refined*
> *Rests on her cheek and throat in happiness!*
> *Yet still more blissful seems to me the band,*
> *Gilt at the tips, so sweetly doth it ring,*
> *And clasp the bosom that it serves to lace:*
> *Yea, and the belt, to such as understand,*
> *Bound round her waist, saith: Here I'd ever cling!*
> *What would my arms do in that girdle's place?*

The second can be ascribed with probability to the year 1534 or 1535. It is written upon the back of a rather singular letter addressed to him by a certain Pierantonio, when both men were in Rome together:—

> *Kind to the world, but to itself unkind,*
> *A worm is born, that, dying noiselessly,*
> *Despoils itself to clothe fair limbs, and be*
> *In its true worth alone by death divined.*
> *Would I might die for my dear lord to find*
> *Raiment in my outworn mortality:*
> *That, changing like the snake, I might be free*
> *To cast the slough wherein I dwell confined!*
> *Nay, were it mine, that shaggy fleece that stays,*
> *Woven and wrought into a vestment fair,*
> *Around yon breast so beauteous in such bliss!*
> *All through the day thou'd have me! Would I were*
> *The shoes that bear that burden! when the ways*
> *Were wet with rain, thy feet I then should kiss!*

I have already alluded to the fact that we can trace two widely different styles of writing in Michelangelo's poetry. Some of his sonnets, like the two just quoted, and those we can refer with certainty to the Cavalieri series, together with occasional compositions upon the deaths of Cecchino and Urbino, seem to come straight from the heart, and their manuscripts offer few variants to the editor. Others, of a different quality, where he is dealing with Platonic subtleties or Petrarchan conceits, have been twisted into so many forms, and tortured by such frequent re-handlings, that it is difficult now to settle a final text. The Codex Vaticanus is peculiarly rich in examples of these compositions. Madrigal lvii. and Sonnet lx., for example, recur with wearisome reiteration. These laboured and scholastic exercises, unlike the more spontaneous utterances of his feelings, are worked up into different forms, and the same conceits are not seldom used for various persons and on divers occasions.

One of the great difficulties under which a critic labours in discussing these personal poems is that their chronology cannot be ascertained in the majority of instances. Another is that we are continually hampered by the false traditions invented by Michelangelo the younger. Books like Lannan Rolland's "Michel-Ange et Vittoria Colonna" have no value whatsoever, because they are based upon that unlucky grand-nephew's deliberately corrupted text. Even Wadsworth's translations, fine as they are, have lost a large portion of their interest since the publication of the autographs by Cesare Guasti in 1863. It is certain that the younger Michelangelo meant well to his illustrious ancestor. He was anxious to give his rugged compositions the elegance and suavity of academical versification. He wished also to defend his character from the imputation of immorality. Therefore he rearranged the order of stanzas in the longer poems, pieced fragments together, changed whole lines, ideas, images, amplified and mutilated, altered phrases which seemed to him suspicious. Only one who has examined the manuscripts of the Buonarroti Archives knows what pains he bestowed upon this ungrateful and disastrous task. But the net result of his meddlesome benevolence is that now for nearly three centuries the greatest genius of the Italian Renaissance has worn a mask concealing the real nature of his emotion, and that a false legend concerning his relations to Vittoria Colonna has become inextricably interwoven with the story of his life.

The extraordinary importance attached by Michelangelo in old age to the passions of his youth is almost sufficient to justify those psychological investigators who regard him as the subject of a nervous disorder. It does not seem to be accounted for by anything known to us regarding his stern and solitary life, his aloofness from the vulgar, and his self-dedication to study. In addition to the splendid devotional sonnets addressed to Vasari, which will appear in their proper place, I may corroborate these remarks by the translation of a set of three madrigals bearing on the topic.

Ah me, ah me! how have I been betrayed
By my swift-flitting years, and by the glass,
Which yet tells truth to those who firmly gaze!
Thus happens it when one too long delays,
As I have done, nor feels time fleet and fade:—
One morn he finds himself grown old, alas!
To gird my loins, repent, my path repass,
Sound counsel take, I cannot, now death's near;
Foe to myself, each tear,
Each sigh, is idly to the light wind sent,
For there's no loss to equal time ill-spent.

Ah me, ah me! I wander telling o'er
Past years, and yet in all I cannot view
One day that might be rightly reckoned mine.
Delusive hopes and vain desires entwine
My soul that loves, weeps, burns, and sighs full sore.
Too well I know and prove that this is true,
Since of man's passions none to me are new.
Far from the truth my steps have gone astray,
In peril now I stay,
For, lo! the brief span of my life is o'er.
Yet, were it lengthened, I should love once more

Ah me! I wander tired, and know not whither:
I fear to sight my goal, the years gone by
Point it too plain; nor will closed eyes avail.
Now Time hath changed and gnawed this mortal veil,
Death and the soul in conflict strive together
About my future fate that looms so nigh.
Unless my judgment greatly goes awry,
Which God in mercy grant, I can but see
Eternal penalty
Waiting my wasted will, my misused mind,
And know not, Lord, where health and hope to find.

After reading these lamentations, it is well to remember that Michelangelo at times indulged a sense of humour. As examples of his lighter vein, we might allude to the sonnet on the Sistine and the capitolo in answer to Francesco Berni, written in the name of Fra Sebastiano. Sometimes his satire becomes malignant, as in the sonnet against the people of Pistoja, which breathes the spirit of Dantesque invective. Sometimes the fierceness of it is turned against himself, as in the capitolo upon old age and its infirmities. The grotesqueness of this lurid descant on senility and death is marked by something rather Teutonic than Italian, a "Danse Macabre" intensity of loathing; and it winds up with the bitter reflections, peculiar to him in his latest years, upon the vanity of art. "My much-prized art, on which I relied and which brought me fame, has now reduced me to this. I am poor and old, the slave of others. To the dogs I must go, unless I die quickly."

A proper conclusion to this chapter may be borrowed from the peroration of Varchi's discourse upon the philosophical love-poetry of Michelangelo. This time he chooses for his text the second of those sonnets (No. lii.) which caused the poet's grand-nephew so much perplexity, inducing him to alter the word *amici* in the last line into *animi*. It runs as follows:—

I saw no mortal beauty with these eyes
  When perfect peace in thy fair eyes I found;
  But far within, where all is holy ground,
  My soul felt Love, her comrade of the skies:
For she was born with God in Paradise;
  Else should we still to transient love be bound;
  But, finding these so false, we pass beyond
  Unto the Love of loves that never dies.
Nay, things that die cannot assuage the thirst
  Of souls undying; nor Eternity
  Serves Time, where all must fade that flourisheth

Sense is not love, but lawlessness accurst:
This kills the soul; while our love lifts on high
Our friends on earth—higher in heaven through death.

"From this sonnet," says Varchi, "I think that any man possessed of judgment will be able to discern to what extent this angel, or rather archangel, in addition to his three first and most noble professions of architecture, sculpture, and painting, wherein without dispute he not only eclipses all the moderns, but even surpasses the ancients, proves himself also excellent, nay singular, in poetry, and in the true art of loving; the which art is neither less fair nor less difficult, albeit it be more necessary and more profitable than the other four. Whereof no one ought to wonder: for this reason; that, over and above what is manifest to everybody, namely that nature, desirous of exhibiting her utmost power, chose to fashion a complete man, and (as the Latins say) one furnished in all proper parts; he, in addition to the gifts of nature, of such sort and so liberally scattered, added such study and a diligence so great that, even had he been by birth most rugged, he might through these means have become consummate in all virtue: and supposing he were born, I do not say in Florence and of a very noble family, in the time too of Lorenzo the Magnificent, who recognised, willed, knew, and had the power to elevate so vast a genius; but in Scythia, of any stock or stem you like, under some commonplace barbarian chief, a fellow not disdainful merely, but furiously hostile to all intellectual ability; still, in all circumstances, under any star, he would have been Michelangelo, that is to say, the unique painter, the singular sculptor, the most perfect architect, the most excellent poet, and a lover of the most divinest. For the which reasons I (it is now many years ago), holding his name not only in admiration, but also in veneration, before I knew that he was architect already, made a sonnet; with which (although it be as much below the supreme greatness of his worth as

it is unworthy of your most refined and chastened ears) I
mean to close this present conference; reserving the discussion on the arts (in obedience to our Consul's orders) for
another lecture.

> *Illustrious sculptor, 'twas enough and more,*
> *Not with the chisel and bruised bronze alone,*
> *But also with brush, colour, pencil, tone,*
> *To rival, nay, surpass that fame of yore.*
> *But now, transcending what those laurels bore*
> *Of pride and beauty for our age and zone.*
> *You climb of poetry the third high throne,*
> *Singing love's strife and peace, love's sweet and*
> *sore.*
> *O wise, and dear to God, old man well born,*
> *Who in so many, so fair ways, make fair*
> *This world, how shall your dues be dully paid?*
> *Doomed by eternal charters to adorn*
> *Nature and art, yourself their mirror are,*
> *None, first before, nor second after, made."*

In the above translation of Varchi's peroration I have
endeavoured to sustain those long-winded periods of which
he was so perfect and professed a master. We must remember that he actually read this dissertation before the Florentine Academy on the second Sunday in Lent, in the year
1546, when Michelangelo was still alive and hearty. He
afterwards sent it to the press; and the studied trumpet-
tones of eulogy, conferring upon Michelangelo the quintuple
crown of pre-eminence in painting, sculpture, architecture,
poetry, and loving, sounded from Venice down to Naples.
The style of the oration may strike us as *rococo* now, but the
accent of praise and appreciation is surely genuine. Varchi's
enthusiastic comment on the sonnets xxx, xxxi, and lii,
published to men of letters, taste, and learning in Florence
and all Italy, is the strongest vindication of their innocence

against editors and scholars who in various ways have attempted to disfigure or to misconstrue them.

CHAPTER XIII

I

THE correspondence which I used in the eleventh chapter, while describing Michelangelo's difficulties regarding the final contract with the Duke of Urbino, proves that he had not begun to paint the frescoes of the Cappella Paolina in October 1542. They were carried on with interruptions during the next seven years. These pictures, the last on which his talents were employed, are two large subjects: the Conversion of S. Paul, and the Martyrdom of S. Peter. They have suffered from smoke and other injuries of time even more than the frescoes of the Sistine, and can now be scarcely appreciated owing to discoloration. Nevertheless, at no period, even when fresh from the master's hand, can they have been typical of his style. It is true that contemporaries were not of this opinion. Condivi calls both of them "stupendous not only in the general exposition of the histories but also in the details of each figure." It is also true that the technical finish of these large compositions shows a perfect mastery of painting, and that the great designer has not lost his power of dealing at will with the human body. But the frigidity of old age had fallen on his feeling and imagination. The faces of his saints and angels here are more inexpressive than those of the Last Judgment. The type of form has become still more rigidly schematic. All those figures in violent attitudes have been invented in the artist's brain without reference to nature; and the activity of movement which he means to suggest, is frozen, petrified, suspended. The suppleness, the elasticity, the sympathy with which Michelangelo handled the nude, when he began to paint in the Sistine Chapel, have disappeared. We cannot refrain from regretting that seven years of his energetic old age should have been devoted to work so obviously indicative of decaying faculties.

The Cappella Paolina ran a risk of destruction by fire during the course of his operations there. Michelangelo wrote to Del Riccio in 1545, reminding him that part of the roof had been consumed, and that it would be necessary to cover it in roughly at once, since the rain was damaging the frescoes and weakening the walls. When they were finished, Paul III. appointed an official guardian with a fixed salary, whose sole business it should be "to clean the frescoes well and keep them in a state of cleanliness, free from dust and other impurities, as also from the smoke of candles lighted in both chapels during divine service." This man had charge of the Sistine as well as the Pauline Chapel; but his office does not seem to have been continued after the death of the Farnese. The first guardian nominated was Buonarroti's favourite servant Urbino.

Vasari, after describing these frescoes in some detail, but without his customary enthusiasm, goes on to observe: "Michelangelo attended only, as I have elsewhere said, to the perfection of art. There are no landscapes, nor trees, nor houses; nor again do we find in his work that variety of movement and prettiness which may be noticed in the pictures of other men. He always neglected such decoration, being unwilling to lower his lofty genius to these details." This is indeed true of the arid desert of the Pauline frescoes. Then he adds: "They were his last productions in painting. He was seventy-five years old when he carried them to completion; and, as he informed me, he did so with great effort and fatigue—painting, after a certain age, and especially fresco-painting, not being in truth fit work for old men."

The first of two acute illnesses, which showed that Michelangelo's constitution was beginning to give way, happened in the summer of 1544. On this occasion Luigi del Riccio took him into his own apartments at the Casa

Strozzi; and here he nursed him with such personal devotion that the old man afterwards regarded Del Riccio as the saviour of his life. We learn this from the following pathetic sonnet:—

> *It happens that the sweet unfathomed sea*
> *Of seeming courtesy sometimes doth hide*
> *Offence to life and honour. This descried,*
> *I hold less dear the health restored to me.*
> *He who lends wings of hope, while secretly*
> *He spreads a traitorous snare by the wayside,*
> *Hath dulled the flame of love, and mortified*
> *Friendship where friendship burns most fervently.*
> *Keep then, my dear Luigi, clear and pure,*
> *That ancient love to which my life I owe,*
> *That neither wind nor storm its calm may mar.*
> *For wrath and pain our gratitude obscure;*
> *And if the truest truth of love I know,*
> *One pang outweighs a thousand pleasures far.*

Ruberto Strozzi, who was then in France, wrote anxiously inquiring after his health. In reply, Michelangelo sent Strozzi a singular message by Luigi del Riccio, to the effect that "if the king of France restored Florence to liberty, he was ready to make his statue on horseback out of bronze at his own cost, and set it up in the Piazza." This throws some light upon a passage in a letter addressed subsequently to Lionardo Buonarroti, when the tyrannous law, termed "La Polverina," enacted against malcontents by the Duke Cosimo de' Medici, was disturbing the minds of Florentine citizens. Michelangelo then wrote as follows: "I am glad that you gave me news of the edict; because, if I have been careful up to this date in my conversation with exiles, I shall take more precautions for the future. As to my having been laid up with an illness in the house of the Strozzi, I do not hold that I was in their house, but in the apartment of Messer Luigi del Riccio, who was my intimate friend; and after the death of Bartolommeo Angelini, I found no one better able to transact my affairs, or more faithfully, than he did. When he died, I ceased to frequent the house, as all Rome can bear me witness; as they can also with regard to the general tenor of my life, inasmuch as I am always alone, go little around, and talk to no one, least of all to Florentines. When I am saluted on the open street, I cannot do less than respond with fair words and pass upon my way. Had I knowledge of the exiles, who they are, I would not reply to them in any manner. As I have said, I shall henceforward protect myself with diligence, the more that I have so much else to think about that I find it difficult to live."

This letter of 1548, taken in connection with the circumstances of Michelangelo's illness in 1544, his exchange of messages with Ruberto degli Strozzi, his gift of the two Captives to that gentleman, and his presence in the house of the Strozzi during his recovery, shows the delicacy of the political situation at Florence under Cosimo's rule. Slight indications of a reactionary spirit in the aged artist exposed his family to peril. Living in Rome, Michelangelo risked nothing with the Florentine government. But "La Polverina" attacked the heirs of exiles in their property and persons. It was therefore of importance to establish his noncomplicity in revolutionary intrigues. Luckily for himself and his nephew, he could make out a good case and defend his conduct. Though Buonarroti's sympathies and sentiments inclined him to prefer a republic in his native city, and though he threw his weight into that scale at the crisis of the siege, he did not forget his early obligations to the House of Medici. Clement VII. accepted his allegiance when the siege was over, and set him immediately to work at the tasks he wished him to perform. What is more, the Pope took pains and trouble to settle the differences between him and the Duke of Urbino. The man had been no conspirator. The architect and sculptor was coveted by every pope and prince in Italy. Still there remained a discord between his political instincts, however prudently and privately indulged, and his sense of personal loyalty to the family at whose board he sat in youth, and to whom he owed his advancement in life. Accordingly, we shall find that, though the Duke of Tuscany made advances to win him back to Florence, Michelangelo always preferred to live and die on neutral ground in Rome. Like the wise man that he was, he seems to have felt through these troublous times that his own duty, the service laid on him by God and nature, was to keep his force and mental faculties for art; obliging old patrons in all kindly offices, suppressing republican aspirations—in one word, "sticking to his last," and steering clear of shoals on which the main raft of his life might founder.

From this digression, which was needful to explain his attitude toward Florence and part of his psychology, I return to the incidents of Michelangelo's illness at Rome in 1544. Lionardo, having news of his uncle's danger, came post-haste to Rome. This was his simple duty, as a loving relative. But the old man, rendered suspicious by previous trans-actions with his family, did not take the action in its proper light. We have a letter, indorsed by Lionardo in Rome as received upon the 11th of July, to this effect: "Lionardo, I have been ill; and you, at the instance of Ser Giovan Francesco (probably Fattucci), have come to make me dead, and to see what I have left. Is there not enough of mine at Florence to content you? You cannot deny that you are the image of your father, who turned me out of my own house in Florence. Know that I have made a will of such tenor that you need not trouble your head about what I possess at Rome. Go then with God, and do not present yourself before me; and do not write to me again, and act like the priest in the fable."

The correspondence between uncle and nephew during the next months proves that this furious letter wrought no diminution of mutual regard and affection. Before the end of the year he must have recovered, for we find him writing to Del Riccio: "I am well again now, and hope to live yet some years, seeing that God has placed my health under the care of Maestro Baccio Rontini and the trebbian wine of the Ulivieri." This letter is referred to January 1545, and on the 9th of that month he dictated a letter to his friend Del Riccio, in which he tells Lionardo Buonarroti: "I do not feel well, and cannot write. Nevertheless I have recovered from my illness, and suffer no pain now." We have reason to think that Michelangelo fell gravely ill again toward the close of 1545. News came to Florence that he was dying; and Lionardo, not intimidated by his experience on the last occasion, set out to visit him. His *ricordo* of the journey was as follows: "I note how on the 15th of January 1545 (Flor. style, *i.e.* 1546) I went to Rome by post to see Michelangelo, who was ill, and returned to-day, the 26th."

It is not quite easy to seperate the records of these two acute illnesses of Michelangelo, falling between the summer of 1544 and the early spring of 1546. Still, there is no doubt that they signalised his passage from robust old age into a period of physical decline. Much of life survived in the hero yet; he had still to mould S. Peter's after his own mind, and to invent the cupola. Intellectually he suffered no diminution, but he became subject to a chronic disease of the bladder, and adopted habits suited to decaying faculty.

II

We have seen that Michelangelo regarded Luigi del Riccio as his most trusty friend and adviser. The letters which he wrote to him during these years turn mainly upon business or poetical compositions. Some, however, throw light upon the private life of both men, and on the nature of their intimacy. I will select a few for special comment here. The following has no date; but it is interesting, because we may connect the feeling expressed in it with one of Michelangelo's familiar sonnets. "Dear Messer Luigi.

since I know you are as great a master of ceremonies as I am unfit for that trade, I beg you to help me in a little matter. Monsignor di Todi (Federigo Cesi, afterwards Cardinal of S. Pancrazio) has made me a present, which Urbino will describe to you. I think you are a friend of his lordship: will you then thank him in my name, when you find a suitable occasion, and do so with those compliments which come easily to you, and to me are very hard? Make me too your debtor for some tartlet."

The sonnet is No. ix of Signor Guasti's edition. I have translated it thus:—

> The sugar, candles, and the saddled mule,
>   Together with your cask of malvoisie,
>   So far exceed all my necessity
>   That Michael and not I my debt must rule.
> In such a glassy calm the breezes fool
>   My sinking sails, so that amid the sea
>   My bark hath missed her way, and seems to be
>   A wisp of straw whirled on a weltering pool.
> To yield thee gift for gift and grace for grace,
>   For food and drink and carriage to and fro,
>   For all my need in every time and place,
> O my dear lord, matched with the much I owe,
>   All that I am were no real recompense:
>   Paying a debt is not munificence.

In the chapter upon Michelangelo's poetry I dwelt at length upon Luigi del Riccio's passionate affection for his cousin, Cecchino dei Bracci. This youth died at the age of sixteen, on January 8, 1545. Michelangelo undertook to design "the modest sepulchre of marble" erected to his memory by Del Riccio in the church of Araceli. He also began to write sonnets, madrigals, and epitaphs, which were sent from day to day. One of his letters gives an explanation of the eighth epitaph: "Our dead friend speaks and says: if the heavens robbed all beauty from all other men on earth to make me only, as indeed they made me, beautiful; and if by the divine decree I must return at doomsday to the shape I bore in life, it follows that I cannot give back the beauty robbed from others and bestowed on me, but that I must remain for ever more beautiful than the rest, and they be ugly. This is just the opposite of the conceit you expressed to me yesterday; the one is a fable, the other is the truth."

Some time in 1545 Luigi went to Lyons on a visit to Ruberto Strozzi and Giuliano de' Medici. This seems to have happened toward the end of the year; for we possess a letter indorsed by him, "sent to Lyons, and returned upon the 22nd of December." This document contains several interesting details. "All your friends are extremely grieved to hear about your illness, the more so that we cannot help you; especially Messer Donato (Giannotti) and myself. However, we hope that it may turn out to be no serious affair, God willing. In another letter I told you that, if you stayed away long, I meant to come to see you. This I repeat; for now that I have lost the Piacenza ferry, and cannot live at Rome without income, I would rather spend the little that I have in hostelries, than crawl about here, cramped up like a penniless cripple. So, if nothing happens, I have a mind to go to S. James of Compostella after Easter; and if you have not returned, I should like to travel through any place where I shall hear that you are staying. Urbino has spoken to Messer Aurelio, and will speak again. From what he tells me, I think that you will get the site you wanted for the tomb of Cecchino. It is nearly finished, and will turn out handsome."

Michelangelo's project of going upon pilgrimage to Galicia shows that his health was then good. But we know that he soon afterwards had another serious illness; and the scheme was abandoned.

This long and close friendship with Luigi comes to a sudden termination in one of those stormy outbursts of petulant rage which form a special feature of Michelangelo's psychology. Some angry words passed between them about an engraving, possibly of the Last Judgment, which Buonarroti wanted to destroy, while Del Riccio refused to obliterate the plate:—

"Messer Luigi,—You seem to think I shall reply according to your wishes, when the case is quite the contrary. You give me what I have refused, and refuse me what I begged. And it is not ignorance which makes you send it me through Ercole, when you are ashamed to give it me yourself.

"One who saved my life has certainly the power to disgrace me; but I do not know which is the heavier to bear, disgrace or death. Therefore I beg and entreat you, by the true friendship which exists between us, to spoil that print (*stampa*), and to burn the copies that are already printed off. And if you choose to buy and sell me, do not so to others. If you hack me into a thousand pieces, I will do the same, not indeed to yourself, but to what belongs to you.

"MICHELANGELO BUONARROTI.

"Not painter, nor sculptor, nor architect, but what you will, but not a drunkard, as you said at your house."

Unfortunately, this is the last of the Del Riccio's letters. It is very probable that the irascible artist speedily recovered his usual tone, and returned to amity with his old friend. But Del Riccio departed this life toward the close of this year, 1546.

Before resuming the narrative of Michelangelo's art-work at this period, I must refer to the correspondence which passed between him and King Francis I. The King wrote an epistle in the spring of 1546, requesting some fine monument from the illustrious master's hand. Michelangelo replied upon the 26th of April, in language of simple and respectful dignity, fine, as coming from an aged artist to a monarch on the eve of death:—

"Sacred Majesty,—I know not which is greater, the favour, or the astonishment it stirs in me, that your Majesty should have deigned to write to a man of my sort, and still more to ask him for things of his which are all unworthy of the name of your Majesty. But be they what they may, I beg your Majesty to know that for a long while since I have desired to serve you; but not having had an opportunity, owing to your not being in Italy, I have been unable to do so. Now I am old, and have been occupied these many months with the affairs of Pope Paul. But if some space of time is still granted to me after these engagements, I will do my utmost to fulfil the desire which, as I have said above, has long inspired me: that is, to make for your Majesty one work in marble, one in bronze, and one in painting. And if death prevents my carrying out this wish, should it be possible to make statues or pictures in the other world, I shall not fail to do so there, where there is no more growing old. And I pray God that He grant your Majesty a long and a happy life."

Francis died in 1547; and we do not know that any of Michelangelo's works passed directly into his hands, with the exception of the Leda, purchased through the agency of Luigi Alamanni, and the two Captives, presented by Ruberto Strozzi.

III

The absorbing tasks imposed upon Buonarroti's energies by Paul III., which are mentioned in this epistle to the French king, were not merely the frescoes of the Cappella Paolina, but also various architectural and engineering schemes of some importance. It is clear, I think, that at this period of his hale old age, Michelangelo preferred to use what still survived in him of vigour and creative genius for things requiring calculation, or the exercise of meditative fancy. The time had gone by when he could wield the brush and chisel with effective force. He was tired of expressing his sense of beauty and the deep thoughts of his brain in sculptured marble or on frescoed surfaces. He had exhausted the human form as a symbol of artistic utterance. But the extraordinary richness of his vein enabled him still to deal with abstract mathematical proportions in the art of building, and with rhythms in the art of writing. His best work, both as architect and poet, belongs to the period when he had lost power as sculptor and painter. This fact is psychologically interesting. Up to the age of seventy, he had been working in the plastic and the concrete. The language he had learned, and used with overwhelming mastery, was man: physical mankind, converted into spiritual vehicle by art. His grasp upon this region failed him now. Perhaps there was not the old sympathy with lovely shapes. Perhaps he knew that he had played on every gamut of that lyre. Emerging from the sphere of the sensuous, where ideas take plastic embodiment, he grappled in this final stage of his career with harmonical ratios and direct verbal expression, where ideas are disengaged from figurative form. The men and women, loved by him so long, so wonderfully wrought into imperishable shapes, "nurslings of immortality," recede. In their room arise, above the horizon of his intellect, the cupola of S. Peter's and a few imperishable poems, which will live as long as Italian claims a place among the languages. There is no comparison to be instituted between his actual achievements as a builder and a versifier. The whole tenor of his life made him more competent to deal with architecture than with literature. Nevertheless, it is significant that the versatile genius of the man was hencefroth restricted to these two channels of expression, and that in both of them his last twenty years of existence produced bloom and fruit of unexpected rarity.

After writing this paragraph, and before I engage in the narrative of what is certainly the final manifestation of Michelangelo's genius as a creative artist, I ought perhaps to pause, and to give some account of those survivals from his plastic impulse, which occupied the old man's energies for several years. They were entirely the outcome of religious feeling; and it is curious to notice that he never approached so nearly to true Christian sentiment as in the fragmentary designs which we may still abundantly collect from this late autumn of his artist's life. There are countless drawings for some great picture of the Crucifixion, which was never finished: exquisite in delicacy of touch, sublime in conception, dignified in breadth and grand repose of style. Condivi tells us that some of these were made for the Marchioness of Pescara. But Michelangelo must have gone on producing them long after her death. With these phantoms of stupendous works to be, the Museums of Europe abound. We cannot bring them together, or condense them into a single centralised conception. Their interest consists in their divergence and variety, showing the continuous poring of the master's mind upon a theme he could not definitely grasp. For those who love his work, and are in sympathy with his manner, these drawings, mostly in chalk, and very finely handled, have a supreme interest. They show him, in one sense, at his highest and his best, not only as a man of tender feeling, but also as a mighty draughtsman. Their incompleteness testifies to something pathetic—the humility of the imperious man before a theme he found to be beyond the reach of human faculty.

The tone, the *Stimmung,* of these designs corresponds so exactly to the sonnets of the same late period, that I feel impelled at this point to make his poetry take up the tale. But, as I cannot bring the cloud of witnesses of all those drawings into this small book, so am I unwilling to load its pages with poems which may be found elsewhere. Those who care to learn the heart of Michelangelo, when he felt near to God and face to face with death, will easily find access to the originals.

Concerning the Deposition from the Cross, which now

stands behind the high altar of the Florentine Duomo, Condivi writes as follows: "At the present time he has in hand a work in marble, which he carries on for his pleasure, as being one who, teeming with conceptions, must needs give birth each day to some of them. It is a group of four figures larger than life. A Christ taken from the cross, sustained in death by his Mother, who is represented in an attitude of marvellous pathos, leaning up against the corpse with breast, with arms, and lifted knee. Nicodemus from above assists her, standing erect and firmly planted, propping the dead Christ with a sturdy effort; while one of the Maries, on the left side, though plunged in sorrow, does all she can to assist the afflicted Mother, failing under the attempt to raise her Son. It would be quite impossible to describe the beauty of style displayed in this group, or the sublime emotions expressed in those woe-stricken countenances. I am confident that the Pietà is one of his rarest and most difficult masterpieces; particularly because the figures are kept apart distinctly, nor does the drapery of the one intermingle with that of the others."

This panegyric is by no means pitched too high. Justice has hardly been done in recent times to the noble conception, the intense feeling, and the broad manner of this Deposition. That may be due in part to the dull twilight in which the group is plunged, depriving all its lines of salience and relief. It is also true that in certain respects the composition is fairly open to adverse criticism. The torso of Christ overweighs the total scheme; and his legs are unnaturally attenuated. The kneeling woman on the left side is slender, and appears too small in proportion to the other figures; though, if she stood erect, it is probable that her height would be sufficient.

The best way to study Michelangelo's last work in marble is to take the admirable photograph produced under artificial illumination by Alinari. No sympathetic mind will fail to feel that we are in immediate contact with the sculptor's

very soul, at the close of his life, when all his thoughts were
weaned from earthly beauty, and he cried—

> *Painting nor sculpture now can lull to rest*
> *My soul, that turns to his great love on high,*
> *Whose arms to clasp us on the cross were spread.*

As a French critic has observed: "It is the most intimately
personal and the most pathetic of his works. The idea of
penitence exhales from it. The marble preaches the sufferings of the Passion; it makes us listen to an act of bitter
contrition and an act of sorrowing love."

Michelangelo is said to have designed the Pietà for his
own monument. In the person of Nicodemus, it is he who
sustains his dead Lord in the gloom of the sombre Duomo.
His old sad face, surrounded by the heavy cowl, looks down
for ever with a tenderness beyond expression, repeating
mutely through the years how much of anguish and of
blood divine the redemption of man's soul hath cost.

The history of this great poem in marble, abandoned by
its maker in some mood of deep dejection, is not without
interest. We are told that the stone selected was a capital
from one of the eight huge columns of the Temple of
Peace. Besides being hard and difficult to handle, the material betrayed flaws in working. This circumstance annoyed
the master; also, as he informed Vasari, Urbino kept continually urging him to finish it. One of his reasons for
attacking the block had been to keep himself in health by
exercise. Accordingly he hewed away with fury, and bit so
deep into the marble that he injured one of the Madonna's
elbows. When this happened, it was his invariable practice to
abandon the piece he had begun upon, feeling that an incomplete performance was preferable to a lame conclusion.
In his old age he suffered from sleeplessness; and it was
his habit to rise from bed and work upon the Pietà, wearing
a thick paper cap, in which he placed a lighted candle made
of goat's tallow. This method of chiselling by the light of

one candle must have complicated the technical difficulties of his labour. But what we may perhaps surmise to have been his final motive for the rejection of the work, was a sense of his inability, with diminished powers of execution, and a still more vivid sense of the importance of the motive, to accomplish what the brain conceived. The hand failed. The imagination of the subject grew more intimate and energetic. Losing patience then at last, he took a hammer and began to break the group up. Indeed, the right arm of the Mary shows a fracture. The left arm of the Christ is mutilated in several places. One of the nipples has been repaired, and the hand of the Madonna resting on the breast above it is cracked across. It would have been difficult to reduce the whole huge block to fragments; and when the work of destruction had advanced so far, Michelangelo's servant Antonio, the successor to Urbino, begged the remnants from his master. Tiberio Calcagni was a good friend of Buonarroti's at this time. He heard that Francesco Bandini, a Florentine settled in exile at Rome, earnestly desired some relic of the master's work. Accordingly, Calgagni, with Michelangelo's consent, bought the broken marble from Antonio for 200 crowns, pieced it together, and began to mend it. Fortunately, he does not seem to have elaborated the surface in any important particular; for both the finished and unfinished parts bear indubitable marks of Michelangelo's own handling. After the death of Calcagni and Bandini, the Pietà remained for some time in the garden of Antonio, Bandini's heir, at Montecavallo. It was transferred to Florence, and placed among the marbles used in erecting the new Medicean Chapel, until at last, in 1722, the Grand Duke Cosimo III. finally set it up behind the altar of the Duomo.

Vasari adds that Michelangelo began another Pietà in marble on a much smaller scale. It is possible that this may have been the unfinished group of two figures (a dead Christ sustained by a bending man), of which there is a cast in the

Accademia at Florence. In some respects the composition of this fragment bears a strong resemblance to the puzzling Deposition from the Cross in our National Gallery. The trailing languor of the dead Christ's limbs is almost identical in the marble and the painting.

While speaking of these several Pietàs, I must not forget the medallion in high relief of the Madonna clasping her dead Son, which adorns the Albergo dei Poveri at Genoa. It is ascribed to Michelangelo, was early believed to be his, and is still accepted without hesitation by competent judges. In spite of its strongly marked Michelangelesque mannerism, both as regards feeling, facial type, and design, I cannot regard the bas-relief, in its present condition at least, as a genuine work, but rather as the production of some imitator, or the *rifacimento* of a restorer. A similar impression may here be recorded regarding the noble portrait-bust in marble of Pope Paul III. at Naples. This too has been attributed to Michelangelo. But there is no external evidence to support the tradition, while the internal evidence from style and technical manipulation weighs strongly against it. The medallions introduced upon the heavily embroidered cope are not in his style. The treatment of the adolescent female form in particular indicates a different temperament. Were the ascription made to Benvenuto Cellini, we might have more easily accepted it. But Cellini would certainly have enlarged upon so important a piece of sculpture in his Memoirs. If then we are left to mere conjecture, it would be convenient to suggest Guglielmo della Porta, who executed the Farnese monument in S. Peter's.

IV

While still a Cardinal, Paul III. began to rebuild the old palace of the Farnesi on the Tiber shore. It closes one end of the great open space called the Campo di Fiore, and stands opposite to the Villa Farnesina, on the right bank of the river. Antonio da Sangallo was the architect employe upon this work, which advanced slowly until Alessandro Farnese's elevation to the Papacy. He then determined to push the building forward, and to complete it on a scale of magnificence befitting the supreme Pontiff. Sangallo had carried the walls up to the second story. The third remained to be accomplished, and the cornice had to be constructed. Paul was not satisfied with Sangallo's design, and referred it to Michelangelo for criticism—possibly in 1544. The result was a report, which we still possess, in which Buonarroti, basing his opinion on principles derived from Vitruvius, severely blames Sangallo's plan under six separate heads. He does not leave a single merit, as regards either harmony of proportion, or purity of style, or elegance of composition, or practical convenience, or decorative beauty, or distribution of parts. He calls the cornice barbarous, confused, bastard in style, discordant with the rest of the building, and so ill suited to the palace as, if carried out, to threaten the walls with destruction. This document has considerable interest, partly as illustrating Michelangelo's views on architecture in general, and displaying a pedantry of which he was never elsewhere guilty, partly as explaining the bitter hostility aroused against him in Sangallo and the whole tribe of that great architect's adherents. We do not, unfortunately, possess the design upon which the report was made. But, even granting that it must have been defective, Michelangelo, who professed that architecture was not his art, might, one thinks, have spared his rival such extremity of adverse criticism. It exposed him to the taunts of rivals and ill-wishers; justified them in calling him presumptuous, and gave them a plausible excuse when they accused him of jealousy. What made it worse was, that his own large building, the Laurentian Library, glaringly exhibits all the defects he discovered in Sangallo's cornice.

I find it difficult to resist the impression that Michelangelo was responsible, to a large extent, for the ill-will of those artists whom Vasari calls "la setta Sangallesca." His life became embittered by their animosity, and his industry as Papal architect continued to be hampered for many years by their intrigues. But he alone was to blame at the beginning, not so much for expressing an honest opinion, as for doing so with insulting severity.

That Michelangelo may have been right in his condemnation of Sangallo's cornice is of course possible. Paul himself was dissatisfied, and eventually threw that portion of the building open to competition. Perino del Vaga, Sebastiano del Piombo, and the young Giorgio Vasari are said to have furnished designs. Michelangelo did so also; and his plan was not only accepted, but eventually carried out. Nevertheless Sangallo, one of the most illustrious professional architects then alive, could not but have felt deeply wounded by the treatment he received. It was natural for his followers to exclaim that Buonarroti had contrived to oust their aged master, and to get a valuable commission into his own grasp, by the discourteous exercise of his commanding prestige in the world of art.

In order to be just to Michelangelo, we must remember that he was always singularly modest in regard to his own performances, and severe in self-criticism. Neither in his letters nor in his poems does a single word of self-complacency escape his pen. He sincerely felt himself to be an unprofitable servant: that was part of his constitutional depression. We know, too, that he allowed strong temporary feelings to control his utterance. The cruel criticism of Sangallo may therefore have been quite devoid of malice; and if it was as well founded as the criticism of that builder's plan for S. Peter's, then Michelangelo stands acquitted. Sangallo's model exists; it is so large that you can walk inside it, and compare your own impressions with the following judgment:—

"It cannot be denied that Bramante's talent as an architect was equal to that of any one from the times of the ancients until now. He laid the first plan of S. Peter, not confused, but clear and simple, full of light and detached from surrounding buildings, so that it interfered with no part of the palace. It was considered a very fine design, and indeed any one can see now that it is so. All the architects who departed from Bramante's scheme, as Sangallo has done, have departed from the truth; and those who have unprejudiced eyes can observe this in his model. Sangallo's ring of chapels takes light from the interior as Bramante planned it; and not only this, but he has provided no other means of lighting, and there are so many hiding-places, above and below, all dark, which lend themselves to innumerable knaveries, that the church would become a secret den for harbouring bandits, false coiners, for debauching nuns, and doing all sorts of rascality; and when it was shut up at night, twenty-five men would be needed to search the building for rogues hidden there, and it would be difficult enough to find them. There is, besides, another inconvenience: the interior circle of buildings added to Bramante's plan would necessitate the destruction of the Paoline Chapel, the offices of the Piombo and the Ruota, and more besides. I do not think that even the Sistine would escape."

After this Michelangelo adds that to remove the outworks and foundations begun upon Sangallo's plan would not cost 100,000 crowns, as the sect alleged, but only 16,000. The material would be infinitely useful, the foundations important for the building, and the whole fabric would profit in something like 200,000 crowns and 300 years of time. "This is my dispassionate opinion; and I say this in truth, for to gain a victory here would be my own incalculable loss." Michelangelo means that, at the time when he wrote the letter in question, it was still in doubt whether Sangallo's design should be carried out or his own adopted; and, as usual, he looked forward with dread to undertaking a colossal architectural task.

Returning to the Palazzo Farnese, it only remains to be said that Michelangelo lived to complete the edifice. His

genius was responsible for the inharmonious window above
the main entrance. According to Vasari, he not only finished
the exterior from the second story upwards, but designed
the whole of the central courtyard above the first story,
"making it the finest thing of its sort in Europe." The
interior, with the halls painted by Annibale Caracci, owed
its disposition into chambers and galleries to his invention.
The cornice has always been reckoned among his indubitable successes, combining as it does salience and audacity
with a grand heroic air of grace. It has been criticised for
disproportionate projection; and Michelangelo seems to have
felt uneasy on this score, since he caused a wooden model
of the right size to be made and placed upon the wall, in
order to judge of its effect.

Taken as a whole, the Palazzo Farnese remains the
most splendid of the noble Roman houses, surpassing all
the rest in pomp and pride, though falling short of Peruzzi's
Palazzo Massimo in beauty.

V

The catastrophe of 1527, when Rome was taken by assault on the side of the Borgo without effective resistance
being possible, rendered the fortification of the city absolutely necessary. Paul III determined to secure a position
of such vital importance to the Vatican by bastions. Accordingly he convened a diet of notables, including his architect-
in-chief, Antonio da Sangallo. He also wished to profit by
Michelangelo's experience, remembering the stout resistance
offered to the Prince of Orange by his outworks at S.
Miniato. Vasari tells an anecdote regarding this meeting
which illustrates the mutual bad feeling of the two illustrious artists. "After much discussion, the opinion of Buonarroti was requested. He had conceived views widely differing
from those of Sangallo and several others, and these he
expressed frankly. Whereupon Sangallo told him that sculpture and painting were his trade, not fortification. He re-

plied that about them he knew but little, whereas the anxious thought he had given to city defences, the time he had spent, and the experience he had practically gained in constructing them, made him superior in that art to Sangallo and all the masters of his family. He proceeded to point out before all present numerous errors in the works. Heated words passed on both sides, and the Pope had to reduce the men to silence. Before long he brought a plan for the fortification of the whole Borgo, which opened the eyes of those in power to the scheme which was finally adopted. Owing to changes he suggested, the great gate of Santo Spirito, designed by Sangallo and nearly finished, was left incomplete."

It is not clear what changes were introduced into San-gallo's scheme. They certainly involved drawing the line of defence much closer to the city than he intended. This ap-proved itself to Pier Luigi Farnese, then Duke of Castro, who presided over the meetings of the military committee. It was customary in carrying out the works of fortification to associate a practical engineer with the architect who pro-vided designs; and one of these men, Gian Francesco Mon-temellino, a trusted servant of the Farnesi, strongly sup-ported the alteration. That Michelangelo agreed with Montemellino, and felt that they could work together, appears from a letter addressed to the Castellano of S. Angelo. It seems to have been written soon after the dispute recorded by Vasari. In it he states, that although he differs in many respects from the persons who had hitherto con-trolled the works, yet he thinks it better not to abandon them altogether, but to correct them, alter the superintendence, and put Montemellino at the head of the direction. This would prevent the Pope from becoming disgusted with such frequent changes. "If affairs took the course he indicated, he was ready to offer his assistance, not in the capacity of colleague, but as a servant to command in all things." Nothing is here said openly about Sangallo, who remained architect-in-chief until his death. Still the covert wish expressed that the superintendence might be altered, shows a spirit of hostility against him; and a new plan for the lines must soon have been adopted. A despatch written to the Duke of Parma in September 1545 informs him that the old works were being abandoned, with the exception of the grand Doric gateway of S. Spirito. This is described at some length in another despatch of January 1546. Later on, in 1557, we find Michelangelo working as architect-in-chief with Jacopo Meleghino under his direction, but the fortifications were eventually carried through by a more competent engineer, one Jacopo Fusto Castriotto of Urbino.

VI

Antonio da Sangallo died on October 3, 1546, at Terni, while engaged in engineering works intended to drain the Lake Velino. Michelangelo immediately succeeded to the offices and employments he had held at Rome. Of these, the most important was the post of architect-in-chief at S. Peter's. Paul III. conferred it upon him for life by a brief dated January 1, 1547. He is there named "commissary, prefect, surveyor of the works, and architect, with full authority to change the model, form, and structure of the church at pleasure, and to dismiss and remove the working-men and foremen employed upon the same." The Pope intended to attach a special stipend to the onerous charge, but Michelangelo declined this honorarium, declaring that he meant to labour without recompense, for the love of God and the reverence he felt for the Prince of the Apostles. Although he might have had money for the asking, and sums were actually sent as presents by his Papal master, he persisted in this resolution, working steadily at S. Peter's without pay, until death gave him rest.

Michelangelo's career as servant to a Pope began with the design of that tomb which led Julius II. to destroy the old S. Peter's. He was now entering, after forty-two years, upon the last stage of his long life. Before the end came, he gave final form to the main features of the great basilica, raising the dome which dominates the Roman landscape like a stationary cloud upon the sky-line. What had happened to the edifice in the interval between 1505 and 1547 must be briefly narrated, although it is not within the scope of this work to give a complete history of the building.

Bramante's original design had been to construct the church in the form of a Greek cross, with four large semi-circular apses. The four angles made by the projecting arms of the cross were to be filled in with a complex but well-ordered scheme of shrines and chapels, so that ex-ternally the edifice would have presented the aspect of a square. The central piers, at the point of junction between the arms of the cross, supported a broad shallow dome, modelled upon that of the Pantheon. Similar domes of lesser dimensions crowned the out-buildings. He began by erecting the piers which were intended to support the central dome; but working hastily and without due regard to solid strength, Bramante made these piers too weak to sustain the ponderous mass they had to carry. How he would have rectified this error cannot be conjectured. Death cut his labours short in 1514, and only a small portion of his work remains embedded at the present day within the mightier masses raised beneath Buonarroti's cupola.

Leo X. commissioned Raffaello da Urbino to continue his kinsman's work, and appointed Antonio da Sangallo to assist him in the month of January 1517. Whether it was judged impossible to carry out Bramante's project of the central dome, or for some other reason unknown to us, Raffaello altered the plan so essentially as to design a basilica upon the conventional ground-plan of such churches. He abandoned the Greek cross, and adopted the Latin form by adding an elongated nave. The central piers were left in their places; the three terminal apses of the choir and transepts were strengthened, simplified, reduced to commonplace. Bramante's ground-plan is lucid, luminous, and exquisitely ordered in its intricacy. The true creation of a builder-poet's brain, it illustrates Leo Battista Alberti's definition of the charm of architecture, *tutta quella musica*, that melody and music of a graceful edifice. We are able to understand what Michelangelo meant when he remarked that all subsequent designers, by departing from it, had gone wrong. Raffaello's plan, if carried out, would have been monotonous and tame inside and out.

After the death of Raffaello in 1520, Baldassare Peruzzi was appointed to be Sangallo's colleague. This genial architect, in whose style all the graces were combined with dignity and strength, prepared a new design at Leo's request. Vasari, referring to this period of Peruzzi's life, says: "The Pope, thinking Bramante's scheme too large and not likely to be in keeping, obtained a new model from Baldassare; magnificent and truly full of fine invention, also so wisely constructed that certain portions have been adopted by subsequent builders." He reverted to Bramante's main conception of the Greek cross, but altered the details in so many important points, both by thickening the piers and walls, and also by complicating the internal disposition of the chapels, that the effect would have been quite different. The ground-plan, which is all I know of Peruzzi's project, has always seemed to me by far the most beautiful and interesting of those laid down for S. Peter's. It is richer, more imaginative and suggestive, than Bramante's. The style of Bramante, in spite of its serene simplicity, had something which might be described as shallow clearness. In comparison with Peruzzi's style, it is what Gluck's melody is to Mozart's. The course of public events prevented this scheme from being carried out. First came the pontificate of Adrian VI., so sluggish in art-industry; then the pontificate of Clement VII., so disastrous for Italy and Rome. Many years elapsed before art and literature recovered from the terror and the torpor of 1527. Peruzzi indeed returned to his office at S.

Peter's in 1535, but his death followed in 1537, when Antonio da Sangallo remained master of the situation.

Sangallo had the good sense to preserve many of Peruzzi's constructive features, especially in the apses of the choir and transepts; but he added a vast vestibule, which gave the church a length equal to that of Raffaello's plan. Externally, he designed a lofty central cupola and two flanking spires, curiously combining the Gothic spirit with Classical elements of style. In order to fill in the huge spaces of this edifice, he superimposed tiers of orders one above the other. Church, cupola, and spires are built up by a succession of Vitruvian temples, ascending from the ground into the air. The total impression produced by the mass, as we behold it now in the great wooden model at S. Peter's, is one of bewildering complexity. Of architectural repose it possesses little, except what belongs to a very original and vast conception on a colossal scale. The extent of the structure is frittered by its multiplicity of parts. Internally, as Michelangelo pointed out, the church would have been dark, inconvenient, and dangerous to public morals.

VII

Whatever we may think of Michelangelo's failings as an architect, there is no doubt that at this period of his life he aimed at something broad and heroic in style. He sought to attain grandeur by greatness in the masses and by economy of the constituent parts. His method of securing amplitude was exactly opposite to that of Sangallo, who relied upon the multiplication rather than the simplification of details. A kind of organic unity was what Michelangelo desired. For this reason, he employed in the construction of S. Peter's those stupendous orders which out-soar the columns of Baalbec, and those grandiose curves which make the cupola majestic. A letter written to the Cardinal Ridolfo Pio of Carpi contains this explanation of his principles. The last two sentences are highly significant:—

"Most Reverend Monsignor,—If a plan has divers parts, those which are of one type in respect to quality and quantity have to be decorated in the same way and the same fashion. The like is true of their counterparts. But when the plan changes form entirely, it is not only allowable, but necessary, to change the decorative appurtenances, as also with their counterparts. The intermediate parts are always free, left to their own bent. The nose, which stands in the middle of the forehead, is not bound to correspond with either of the eyes; but one hand must balance the other, and one eye be like its fellow. Therefore it may be assumed as certain that the members of an architectural structure follow the laws exemplified in the human body. He who has not been or is not a good master of the nude, and especially of anatomy, cannot understand the principles of architecture."

It followed that Michelangelo's first object, when he became Papal architect-in-chief, was to introduce order into the anarchy of previous plans, and to return, so far as this was now possible, to Bramante's simpler scheme. He adopted the Greek cross, and substituted a stately portico for the long vestibule invented by Sangallo. It was not, however, in his nature, nor did the changed taste of the times permit him to reproduce Bramante's manner. So far as S. Peter's bears the mark of Michelangelo at all, it represents his own peculiar genius. "The Pope," says Vasari, "approved his model, which reduced the cathedral to smaller dimensions, but also to a more essential greatness. He discovered that four principal piers, erected by Bramante and left standing by Antonio da Sangallo, which had to bear the weight of the tribune, were feeble. These he fortified in part, constructing two winding staircases at the side, with gently sloping steps, up which beasts of burden ascend with building material, and one can ride on horseback to the level above the arches. He carried the first cornice, made of travertine, round the arches: a wonderful piece of work, full of grace, and very different from the others; nor could anything be better done in its kind. He began the two great apses of the transept; and whereas Bramante, Raffaello, and Peruzzi had designed eight tabernacles toward the Campo Santo, which arrangement Sangallo adhered to, he reduced them to three, with three chapels inside. Suffice it to say that he began at once to work with diligence and accuracy at all points where the edifice required alteration, to the end that its main features might be fixed, and that no one might be able to change what he had planned." Vasari adds that this was the provision of a wise and prudent mind. So it was; but it did not prevent Michelangelo's successors from defeating his intentions in almost every detail, except the general effect of the cupola. This will appear in the sequel.

Antonio da Sangallo had controlled the building of S. Peter's for nearly thirty years before Michelangelo succeeded to his office. During that long space of time he formed a body of architects and workmen who were attached to his person and interested in the execution of his plans. There is good reason to believe that in Sangallo's days, as earlier in Bramante's, much money of the Church had been misappropriated by a gang of fraudulent and mutually indulgent craftsmen. It was not to be expected that these people should tamely submit to the intruder who put their master's cherished model on the shelf, and set about, in his high-handed way, to refashion the whole building from the bottom to the top. During Sangallo's lifetime no love had been lost between him and Buonarroti, and after his death it is probable that the latter dealt severely with the creatures of his predecessor. The Pope had given him unlimited powers of appointing and dismissing subordinates, controlling operations, and regulating expenditure. He was a man who abhorred jobs and corruption. A letter written near the close of his life, when he was dealing only with persons nominated by himself, proves this. He addressed the Superintendents of the Fabric of S. Peter's as follows: "You know that I told Balduccio not to send his lime unless it were good. He has sent bad quality, and does not seem to think he will be forced to take it back; which proves that he is in collusion with the person who accepted it. This gives great encouragement to the men I have dismissed for similar transactions. One who accepts bad goods needed for the fabric, when I have forbidden them, is doing nothing else but making friends of people whom I have turned into enemies against myself. I believe there will be a new conspiracy. Promises, fees, presents, corrupt justice. Therefore I beg you from this time forward, by the authority I hold from the Pope, not to accept anything which is not suitable, even though it comes to you from heaven. I must not be made to appear, what I am not, partial in my dealings." This fiery despatch, indicating not only Michelangelo's probity, but also his attention to minute details at the advanced age of eighty-six, makes it evident that he must have been a stern overseer in the first years of his office, terrible to the "sect of Sangallo," who were bent, on their part, to discredit him.

The sect began to plot and form conspiracies, feeling the violent old man's bit and bridle on their mouths, and seeing the firm seat he took upon the saddle. For some reason, which is not apparent, they had the Superintendents of the Fabric (a committee, including cardinals, appointed by the Pope) on their side. Probably these officials, accustomed to Sangallo and the previous course of things, disliked to be stirred up and sent about their business by the masterful new-comer. Michelangelo's support lay, as we shall see, in the four Popes who followed Paul III. They, with the doubtful exception of Marcellus II., accepted him on trust as a thoroughly honest servant, and the only artist capable of conducting the great work to its conclusion. In the last resort, when he was driven to bay, he offered to resign, and was invariably coaxed back by the final arbiter. The disinterested spirit in which he fulfilled his duties, accepting no pay while he gave his time and energy to their performance, stood him in good stead. Nothing speaks better for his perfect probity than that his enemies were unable to bring the slightest charge of peculation or of partiality against him. Michelangelo's conduct of affairs at S. Peter's reflects a splendid light upon the tenor of his life, and confutes those detractors who have accused him of avarice.

The duel between Michelangelo and the sect opened in 1547. A letter written by a friend in Florence on the 14th of May proves that his antagonists had then good hopes of crushing him. Giovan Francesco Ughi begins by saying that he has been silent because he had nothing special to report. "But now Jacopo del Conte has come here with the wife of Nanni di Baccio Bigio, alleging that he has brought her because Nanni is so occupied at S. Peter's. Among other things, he says that Nanni means to make a model for the building which will knock yours to nothing. He declares that what you are about is mad and babyish. He means to fling it all down, since he has quite as much credit with the Pope as you have. You throw oceans of money away and work by night, so that nobody may see what you are doing. You follow in the footsteps of a Spaniard, having no knowledge of your own about the art of building, and he less than nothing. Nanni stays there in your despite: you did everything to get him removed; but the Pope keeps him, being convinced that nothing good can be done without him." After this Ughi goes on to relate how Michelangelo's enemies are spreading all kinds of reports against his honour and good fame, criticising the cornice of the Palazzo Farnese, and hoping that its weight will drag the walls down. At the end he adds, that although he knows one ought not to write about such matters, yet the man's "insolence and blackguardly shamelessness of speech" compel him to put his friend on his guard against such calumnies.

After the receipt of this letter, Michelangelo sent it to

one of the Superintendents of the Fabric, on whose sym‚
pathy he could reckon, with the following indorsement in
his own handwriting: "Messer Bartolommeo (Ferrantino)‚
please read this letter, and take thought who the two
rascals are who, lying thus about what I did at the Palazzo
Farnese, are now lying in the matter of the information
they are laying before the deputies of S. Peter's. It comes
upon me in return for the kindness I have shown them. But
what else can one expect from a couple of the basest
scoundrelly villains?"

Nanni di Baccio Bigio had, as it seems, good friends at
court in Rome. He was an open enemy of Michelangelo,
who, nevertheless, found it difficult to shake him off. In the
history of S. Peter's the man's name will frequently occur.

Three years elapsed. Paul III. died, and Michelangelo
wrote to his nephew Lionardo on the occasion: "It is true
that I have suffered great sorrow, and not less loss, by the
Pope's death. I received benefits from his Holiness, and
hoped for more and better. God willed it so, and we must
have patience. His passage from this life was beautiful, in
full possession of his faculties up to the last word. God
have mercy on his soul." The Cardinal Giovan Maria
Ciocchi, of Monte San Savino, was elected to succeed Paul,
and took the title of Julius III. This change of masters
was duly noted by Michelangelo in a letter to his "dearest
friend," Giovan Francesco Fattucci at Florence. It breathes
so pleasant and comradely a spirit, that I will translate more
than bears immediately on the present topic: "Dear friend,
although we have not exchanged letters for many months
past, still our long and excellent friendship has not been
forgotten. I wish you well, as I have always done, and love
you with all my heart, for your own sake, and for the num-
berless pleasant things in life you have afforded me. As
regards old age, which weighs upon us both alike, I should
be glad to know how yours affects you; mine, I must say,
does not make me very happy. I beg you, then, to write me

something about this. You know, doubtless, that we have a new Pope, and who he is. All Rome is delighted, God be thanked; and everybody expects the greatest good from his reign, especially for the poor, his generosity being so notorious."

Michelangelo had good reason to rejoice over this event, for Julius III. felt a real attachment to his person, and thoroughly appreciated both his character and his genius. Nevertheless, the enemies he had in Rome now made a strong effort to dislodge Buonarroti from his official position at S. Peter's. It was probably about this time that the Superintendents of the Fabric drew up a memorial expressive of their grievances against him. We possess a document in Latin setting forth a statement of accounts in rough. "From the year 1540, when expenditures began to be made regularly and in order, from the very commencement as it were, up to the year 1547, when Michelangelo, at his own will and pleasure, undertook partly to build and partly to destroy, 162,624 ducats were expended. Since the latter date on to the present, during which time the deputies have served like the pipe at the organ, knowing nothing, nor what, nor how moneys were spent, but only at the orders of the said Michelangelo, such being the will of Paul III. of blessed memory, and also of the reigning Pontiff, 136,881 ducats have been paid out, as can be seen from our books. With regard to the edifice, what it is going to be, the deputies can make no statement, all things being hidden from them, as though they were outsiders. They have only been able to protest at several times, and do now again protest, for the easement of their conscience, that they do not like the ways used by Michelangelo, especially in what he keeps on pulling down. The demolition has been, and to-day is so great, that all who witness it are moved to an extremity of pity. Nevertheless, if his Holiness be satisfied, we, his deputies, shall have no reason to complain." It is clear that Michelangelo was carrying on with a high hand at S. Peter's.

Although the date of this document is uncertain, I think it may be taken in connection with a general meeting called by Julius III., the incidents of which are recorded by Vasari. Michelangelo must have demonstrated his integrity, for he came out of the affair victorious, and obtained from the Pope a brief confirming him in his office of architect-in-chief, with even fuller powers than had been granted by Paul III.

VIII

Vasari at this epoch becomes one of our most reliable authorities regarding the life of Michelangelo. He corresponded and conversed with him continuously, and enjoyed the master's confidence. We may therefore accept the following narrative as accurate: "It was some little while before the beginning of 1551, when Vasari, on his return from Florence to Rome, found that the sect of Sangallo were plotting against Michelangelo; they induced the Pope to hold a meeting in S. Peter's, where all the overseers and workmen connected with the building should attend, and his Holiness should be persuaded by false insinuations that Michelangelo had spoiled the fabric. He had already walled in the apse of the King where the three chapels are, and carried out the three upper windows. But it was not known what he meant to do with the vault. They then, misled by their shallow judgment, made Cardinal Salviati the elder, and Marcello Cervini, who was afterwards Pope, believe that S. Peter's would be badly lighted. When all were assembled, the Pope told Michelangelo that the deputies were of opinion the apse would have but little light. He answered: 'I should like to hear these deputies speak.' The Cardinal Marcello rejoined: 'Here we are.' Michelangelo then remarked: 'My lord, above these three windows there will be other three in the vault, which is to be built of travertine.' 'You never told us anything about this,' said the Cardinal. Michelangelo responded: 'I am not, nor do I mean to be obliged to tell your lordship or anybody what I ought or wish to do. It is your business to provide money, and to see that it is not stolen. As regards the plans of the building, you have to leave those to me.' Then he turned to the Pope and said: 'Holy Father, behold what gains are mine! Unless the hardships I endure prove beneficial to my soul, I am losing time and labour.' The Pope, who loved him, laid his hands upon his shoulders and exclaimed: 'You are gaining both for soul and body, have no fear!' Michelangelo's spirited self-defence increased the Pope's love, and he ordered him to repair next day with Vasari to the Vigna Giulia, where they held long discourses upon art." It is here that Vasari relates how Julius III. was in the habit of seating Michelangelo by his side while they talked together.

Julius then maintained the cause of Michelangelo against the deputies. It was during his pontificate that a piece of engineering work committed to Buonarroti's charge by Paul III. fell into the hands of Nanni di Baccio Bigio. The old bridge of Santa Maria had long shown signs of giving way, and materials had been collected for rebuilding it. Nanni's friends managed to transfer the execution of this work to him from Michelangelo. The man laid bad foundations, and Buonarroti riding over the new bridge one day with Vasari, cried out: "George, the bridge is quivering beneath us; let us spur on, before it gives way with us upon it." Eventually, the bridge did fall to pieces, at the time of a great inundation. Its ruins have long been known as the Ponte Rotto.

On the death of Julius III. in 1555, Cardinal Cervini was made Pope, with the title of Marcellus II. This event revived the hopes of the sect, who once more began to machinate against Michelangelo. The Duke of Tuscany at this time was exceedingly anxious that he should take up his final abode at Florence; and Buonarroti, feeling he had now no strong support in Rome, seems to have entertained these proposals with alacrity. The death of Marcellus after a few weeks, and the election of Paul IV., who besought the great architect not to desert S. Peter's, made him change his mind. Several letters written to Vasari and the Grand Duke in this and the next two years show that his heart was set on finishing S. Peter's, however much he wished to please his friends and longed to end his days in peace at home. "I was set to work upon S. Peter's against my will, and I have served now eight years gratis, and with the utmost injury and discomfort to myself. Now that the fabric has been pushed forward and there is money to spend, and I am just upon the point of vaulting in the cupola, my departure from Rome would be the ruin of the edifice, and for me a great disgrace throughout all Christendom, and to my soul a grievous sin. Pray ask his lordship to give me leave of absence till S. Peter's has reached a point at which it cannot be altered in its main features. Should I leave Rome earlier, I should be the cause of a great ruin, a great disgrace, and a great sin." To the Duke he writes in 1557 that his special reasons for not wishing to abandon S. Peter's were, first, that the work would fall into the hands of thieves and rogues; secondly, that it might probably be suspended altogether; thirdly, that he owned property in Rome to the amount of several thousand crowns, which, if he left without permission, would be lost; fourthly, that he was suffering from several ailments. He also observed that the work had just reached its most critical stage (*i.e.*, the erection of the cupola), and that to desert it at the present moment would be a great disgrace.

The vaulting of the cupola had now indeed become the main preoccupation of Michelangelo's life. Early in 1557 a serious illness threatened his health, and several friends, including the Cardinal of Carpi, Donato Giannotti, Tommaso Cavalieri, Francesco Bandini, and Lottino, persuaded him that he ought to construct a large model, so that the execution of this most important feature of the edifice might not be impeded in the event of his death. It appears certain that up to this date no models of his on anything like a large intelligible scale had been provided for S. Peter's; and the only extant model attributable to Michelangelo's own period is that of the cupola. This may help to account for the fact that, while the cupola was finished much as he intended, the rest of his scheme suffered a thorough and injurious remodelling.

He wrote to his nephew Lionardo on the 13th of February 1557 about the impossibility of meeting the Grand Duke's wishes and leaving Rome. "I told his Lordship that I was obliged to attend to S. Peter's until I could leave the work there at such a point that my plans would not be subsequently altered. This point has not been reached; and in addition, I am now obliged to construct a large wooden model for the cupola and lantern, in order that I may secure its being finished as it was meant to be. The whole of Rome, and especially the Cardinal of Carpi, puts great pressure on me to do this. Accordingly, I reckon that I shall have to remain here not less than a year; and so much time I beg the Duke to allow me for the love of Christ and S. Peter, so that I may not come home to Florence with a pricking conscience, but a mind easy about Rome." The model took about a year to make. It was executed by a French master named Jean.

All this while Michelangelo's enemies, headed by Nanni di Baccio Bigio, continued to calumniate and backbite. In the end they poisoned the mind of his old friend the Cardinal of Carpi. We gather this from a haughty letter written on the 13th of February 1560: "Messer Francesco Bandini informed me yesterday that your most illustrious and reverend lordship told him that the building of S. Peter's could not possibly go on worse than it is doing. This has grieved me deeply, partly because you have not been informed of the truth, and also because I, as my duty is, desire more than all men living that it should proceed well. Unless I am much deceived, I think I can assure you that it could not possibly go on better than it now is doing. It may, however, happen that my own interests and old age expose me to self-deception, and consequently expose the fabric of S. Peter's to harm or injury against my will. I therefore intend to ask permission on the first occasion from his Holiness to resign my office. Or rather, to save time, I wish to request your most illustrious and reverend lordship by these present to relieve me of the annoyance to which I have been subject seventeen years, at the orders of the Popes, working without remuneration. It is easy enough to see what has been accomplished by my industry during this period. I conclude by repeating my request that you will accept my resignation. You could not confer on me a more distinguished favour."

Giovanni Angelo Medici, of an obscure Milanese family, had succeeded to Paul IV. in 1559. Pius IV. felt a true admiration for Michelangelo. He confirmed the aged artist in his office by a brief which granted him the fullest authority in life, and strictly forbade any departure from his designs for S. Peter's after death. Notwithstanding this powerful support, Nanni di Baccio Bigio kept trying to eject him from his post. He wrote to the Grand Duke in 1562, arguing that Buonarroti was in his dotage, and begging Cosimo to use his influence to obtain the place for himself. In reply the Grand Duke told Nanni that he could not think of doing such a thing during Michelangelo's lifetime, but that after his death he would render what aid was in his power. An incident happened in 1563 which enabled Nanni to give his enemy some real annoyance. Michelangelo was now so old that he felt obliged to leave the personal superintendence of the operations at S. Peter's to a clerk of the works. The man employed at this time was a certain Cesare da Castel Durante, who was murdered in August under the following circumstances, communicated by Tiberio Calcagni to Lionardo Buonarroti on the 14th of that month: "I have only further to speak about the death of Cesare, clerk of the works, who was found by the cook of the Bishop of Forlì with his wife. The man gave Cesare thirteen stabs with his poignard, and four to his wife. The old man (*i.e.*, Michelangelo) is in much distress, seeing that he wished to give the post to that Pier Luigi, and has been unable to do so owing to the refusal of the deputies." This Pier Luigi, surnamed Gaeta, had been working since November 1561 as subordinate to Cesare; and we have a letter from Michelangelo to the deputies recommending him very warmly in that capacity. He was also the house-servant and personal attendant of the old master, running errands for him and transacting ordinary business, like Pietro Urbano and Stefano in former years. The deputies would not consent to nominate Pier Luigi as clerk of the works. They judged him to be too young, and were, moreover, persuaded that Michelangelo's men injured the work at S. Peter's. Accordingly they appointed Nanni di Baccio Bigio, and sent in a report, inspired by him, which severely blamed Buonarroti. Pius IV., after the receipt of this report, had an interview with Michelangelo, which ended in his sending his own relative, Gabrio Serbelloni, to inspect the works at S. Peter's. It was decided that Nanni had been calumniating the great old man. Accordingly he was dismissed with indignity. Immediately after the death of Michelangelo, however, Nanni renewed his applications to the Grand Duke. He claimed nothing less than the post of architect-in-chief. His petition was sent to Florence under cover of a despatch from the Duke's envoy, Averardo Serristori. The ambassador related the events of Michelangelo's death, and supported Nanni as "a worthy man, your vassal and true servant."

IX

Down to the last days of his life, Michelangelo was thus worried with the jealousies excited by his superintendence of the building at S. Peter's; and when he passed to the majority, he had not secured his heart's desire, to wit, that the fabric should be forced to retain the form he had designed for it. This was his own fault. Popes might issue briefs to the effect that his plans should be followed; but when it was discovered that, during his lifetime, he kept the builders in ignorance of his intentions, and that he left no working models fit for use, except in the case of the cupola, a free course was opened for every kind of innovation. So it came to pass that subsequent architects changed the essential features of his design by adding what might be called a nave, or, in other words, by substituting the Latin for the Greek cross in the ground-plan. He intended to front the mass of the edifice with a majestic colonnade, giving externally to one limb of the Greek cross a rectangular salience corresponding to its three semicircular apses. From this decastyle colonnade projected a tetrastyle portico, which introduced the people ascending from a flight of steps to a gigantic portal. The portal opened on the church, and all the glory of the dome was visible when they approached the sanctuary. Externally, according to his conception, the cupola dominated and crowned the edifice when viewed from a moderate or a greater distance. The cupola was the integral and vital feature of the structure. By producing one limb of the cross into a nave, destroying the colonnade and portico, and erecting a huge façade of *barocco* design, his followers threw the interior effect of the cupola into a subordinate position, and externally crushed it out of view, except at a great distance. In like manner they dealt with every particular of his plan. As an old writer has remarked: "The cross which Michelangelo made Greek is now Latin; and if it be thus with the essential form, judge ye of the details!" It was not exactly their fault, but rather that of the master, who chose to work by drawings and small clay models, from which no accurate conception of his thought could be derived by lesser craftsmen.

We cannot, therefore, regard S. Peter's in its present state as the creation of Buonarroti's genius. As a building, it is open to criticism at every point. In spite of its richness and overwhelming size, no architect of merit gives it approbation. It is vast without being really great, magnificent without touching the heart, proudly but not harmoniously ordered. The one redeeming feature in the structure is the cupola; and that is the one thing which Michelangelo bequeathed to the intelligence of his successors. The curve which it describes finds no phrase of language to express its grace. It is neither ellipse nor parabola nor section of the circle, but an inspiration of creative fancy. It outsoars in vital force, in elegance of form, the dome of the Pantheon and the dome of Brunelleschi, upon which it was actually modelled. As a French architect, adverse to Michelangelo, has remarked: "This portion is simple, noble, grand. It is an unparalleled idea, and the author of this marvellous cupola had the right to be proud of the thought which controlled his pencil when he traced it." An English critic, no less adverse to the Italian style, is forced to admit that architecture "has seldom produced a more magnificent object" than the cupola, "if its bad connection with the building is overlooked." He also adds that, internally, "the sublime concave" of this immense dome is the one redeeming feature of S. Peter's.

Michelangelo's reputation, not only as an imaginative builder, but also as a practical engineer in architecture, depends in a very large measure upon the cupola of S. Peter's. It is, therefore, of great importance to ascertain exactly how far the dome in its present form belongs to his conception. Fortunately for his reputation, we still possess the wooden model constructed under his inspection by a man called Giovanni Franzese. It shows that subsequent architects, especially Giacomo della Porta, upon whom the task fell of raising the vaults and lantern from the point where Michelangelo left the building, that is, from the summit of the drum, departed in no essential particular from his design. Della Porta omitted one feature, however, of

Michelangelo's plan, which would have added greatly to the dignity and elegance of the exterior. The model shows that the entablature of the drum broke into projections above each of the buttresses. Upon these projections or consoles Buonarroti intended to place statues of saints. He also connected their pedestals with the spring of the vault by a series of inverted curves sweeping upwards along the height of the shallow attic. The omission of these details not only weakened the support given to the arches of the dome, but it also lent a stilted effect to the cupola by abruptly separating the perpendicular lines of the drum and attic from the segment of the vaulting. This is an error which could even now be repaired, if any enterprising Pope undertook to complete the plan of the model. It may, indeed, be questioned whether the omission was not due to the difficulty of getting so many colossal statues adequately finished at a period when the fabric still remained imperfect in more essential parts.

Vasari, who lived in close intimacy with Michelangelo, and undoubtedly was familiar with the model, gives a confused but very minute description of the building. It is clear from this that the dome was designed with two shells, both of which were to be made of carefully selected bricks, the space between them being applied to the purpose of an interior staircase. The dormer windows in the outer sheath not only broke the surface of the vault, but also served to light this passage to the lantern. Vasari's description squares with the model, now preserved in a chamber of the Vatican basilica, and also with the present fabric.

It would not have been necessary to dwell at greater length upon the vaulting here but for difficulties which still surround the criticism of this salient feature of S. Peter's. Gotti published two plans of the cupola, which were made for him, he says, from accurate measurements of the model taken by Cavaliere Cesare Castelli, Lieut.-Col. of Engineers. The section drawing shows three shells instead of two, the innermost or lowest being flattened out like the vault of the Pantheon. Professor Josef Durm, in his essay upon the Domes of Florence and S. Peter's, gives a minute description of the model for the latter, and prints a carefully executed copperplate engraving of its section. It is clear from this work that at some time or other a third semi-spherical vault, corresponding to that of the Pantheon, had been contemplated. This would have been structurally of no value, and would have masked the two upper shells, which at present crown the edifice. The model shows that the dome itself was from the first intended to be composed of two solid vaults of masonry, in the space between which ran the staircase leading to the lantern. The lower and flatter shell, which appears also in the model, had no connection with the substantial portions of the edifice. It was an addition, perhaps an afterthought, designed possibly to serve as a ground for surface-decoration, or to provide an alternative scheme for the completion of the dome. Had Michelangelo really planned this innermost sheath, we could not credit him with the soaring sweep upwards of the mighty dome, its height and lightness, luminosity and space. The roof that met the eye internally would have been considerably lower and tamer, superfluous in the construction of the church, and bearing no right relation to the external curves of the vaulting. There would, moreover, have been a long dark funnel leading to the lantern. Heath Wilson would then have been justified in certain critical conclusions which may here be stated in his own words. "According to Michelangelo's idea, the cupola was formed of three vaults over each other. Apparently the inner one was intended to repeat the curves of the Pantheon, whilst the outer one was destined to give height and majesty to the building externally. The central vault, more pyramidal in form, was constructed to bear the weight of the lantern, and approached in form the dome of the Cathedral at Florence by Brunelleschi. Judging by the model, he meant the outer dome to be of wood, thus anticipating the construction of Sir Christopher Wren."

Farther on, he adds that the architects who carried out the work "omitted entirely the inner lower vault, evidently to give height internally, and made the external cupola of brick as well as the internal; and, to prevent it expanding, had recourse to encircling chains of iron, which bind it at the weakest parts of the curve." These chains, it may be mentioned parenthetically, were strengthened by Poleni, after the lapse of some years, when the second of the two shells showed some signs of cracking.

From Dr. Durm's minute description of the cupola, there seems to be no doubt about the existence of this third vault in Michelangelo's wooden model. He says that the two outer shells are carved out of one piece of wood, while the third or innermost is made of another piece, which has been inserted. The sunk or hollow compartments, which form the laquear of this depressed vault, differ considerably in shape and arrangement from those which were adopted when it was finally rejected. The question now remains, whether the semi-spherical shell was abandoned during Michelangelo's lifetime and with his approval. There is good reason to believe that this may have been the case: first, because the tambour, which he executed, differs from the model in the arching of its windows; secondly, because Fontana and other early writers on the cupola insist strongly on the fact that Michelangelo's own plans were strictly followed, although they never allude to the third or innermost vault. It is almost incredible that if Della Porta departed in so vital a point from Michelangelo's design, no notice should have been taken of the fact. On the other hand, the tradition that Della Porta improved the curve of the cupola by making the spring upward from the attic more abrupt, is due probably to the discrepancy between the internal aspects of the model and the dome itself. The actual truth is that the cupola in its curve and its dimensions corresponds accurately to the proportions of the double outer vaulting of the model.

Taking, then, Vasari's statement in conjunction with the

silence of Fontana, Poleni, and other early writers, and duly observing the care with which the proportions of the dome have been preserved, I think we may safely conclude that Michelangelo himself abandoned the third or semi-spherical vault, and that the cupola, as it exists, ought to be ascribed entirely to his conception. It is, in fact, the only portion of the basilica which remains as he designed it.

CHAPTER XIV

I

THERE is great difficulty in dealing chronologically with the last twenty years of Michelangelo's life. This is due in some measure to the multiplicity of his engagements, but more to the tardy rate at which his work, now almost wholly architectural, advanced. I therefore judged it best to carry the history of his doings at S. Peter's down to the latest date; and I shall take the same course now with regard to the lesser schemes which occupied his mind between 1545 and 1564, reserving for the last the treatment of his private life during this period.

A society of gentlemen and artists, to which Buonarroti belonged, conceived the plan of erecting buildings of suitable size and grandeur on the Campidoglio. This hill had always been dear to the Romans, as the central point of urban life since the foundation of their city, through the days of the Republic and the Empire, down to the latest Middle Ages. But it was distinguished only by its ancient name and fame. No splendid edifices and majestic squares reminded the spectator that here once stood the shrine of Jupiter Capitolinus, to which conquering generals rode in triumph with the spoils and captives of the habitable world behind their laurelled chariots. Paul III. approved of the design, and Michelangelo, who had received the citizenship of Rome on March 20, 1546, undertook to provide a scheme for its accomplishment. We are justified in believing that the disposition of the parts which now compose the Capitol is due to his conception: the long steep flight of steps leading up from the Piazza Araceli; the irregular open square, flanked on the left hand by the Museum of Sculpture, on the right by the Palazzo dei Conservatori, and closed at its farther end by the Palazzo del Senatore. He also placed the equestrian statue of Marcus Aurelius Antoninus on its noble pedestal, and suggested the introduction of other antique specimens of sculpture into various portions of the architectural plan. The splendid double staircase leading to the entrance hall of the Palazzo del Senatore, and part of the Palazzo dei Conservatori, were completed during Michelangelo's lifetime. When Vasari wrote in 1568, the dead sculptor's friend, Tommaso dei Cavalieri, was proceeding with the work. There is every reason, therefore, to assume that the latter building, at any rate, fairly corresponds to his intention. Vignola and Giacomo della Porta, both of them excellent architects, carried out the scheme, which must have been nearly finished in the pontificate of Innocent X. (1644-1655).

Like the cupola of S. Peter's, the Campidoglio has always been regarded as one of Michelangelo's most meritorious performances in architecture. His severe critic, M. Charles Garnier, says of the Capitol: "The general composition of the edifice is certainly worthy of Buonarroti's powerful conception. The balustrade which crowns the façade is indeed bad and vulgar; the great pilasters are very poor in invention, and the windows of the first story are extremely mediocre in style. Nevertheless, there is a great simplicity of lines in these palaces; and the porticoes of the ground-floor might be selected for the beauty of their leading motive. The opposition of the great pilasters to the little columns is an idea at once felicitous and original. The whole has a fine effect; and though I hold the proportions of the ground-floor too low in relation to the first story, I consider this façade of the Capitol not only one of Michelangelo's best works, but also one of the best specimens of the building of that period. Deduction must, of course, be made for heaviness and improprieties of taste, which are not rare."

Next to these designs for the Capitol, the most important architectural work of Michelangelo's old age was the plan he made of a new church to be erected by the Florentines in Rome to the honour of their patron, S. Giovanni. We find him writing to his nephew on the 15th of July 1559: "The Florentines are minded to erect a great edifice—that is to say, their church; and all of them with one accord put pressure on me to attend to this. I have answered that I am living here by the Duke's permission for the fabric of S. Peter's, and that unless he gives me leave, they can get nothing from me." The consul and counsellors of the Florentine nation in Rome wrote upon this to the Duke, who entered with enthusiasm into their scheme, not only sending a favourable reply, but also communicating personally upon the subject with Buonarroti. Three of Michelangelo's letters on the subject to the Duke have been preserved. After giving a short history of the project, and alluding to the fact that Leo X. began the church, he says that the Florentines had appointed a building committee of five men, at whose request he made several designs. One of these they selected, and according to his own opinion it was the best. "This I will have copied and drawn out more clearly than I have been able to do it, on account of old age, and will send it to your Most Illustrious Lordship." The drawings were executed and carried to Florence by the hand of Tiberio Calcagni. Vasari, who has given a long account of this design, says that Calcagni not only drew the plans, but that he also completed a clay model of the whole church within the space of two days, from which the Florentines caused a larger wooden model to be constructed. Michelangelo must have been satisfied with his conception, for he told the building-committee that "if they carried it

out, neither the Romans nor the Greeks ever erected so fine
an edifice in any of their temples. Words the like of which
neither before nor afterwards issued from his lips; for he
was exceedingly modest." Vasari, who had good opportunities for studying the model, pronounced it to be "superior
in beauty, richness and variety of invention to any temple
which was ever seen." The building was begun, and 5000
crowns were spent upon it. Then money or will failed.
The model and drawings perished. Nothing remains for
certain to show what Michelangelo's intentions were. The
present church of S. Giovanni dei Fiorentini in Strada Giulia
is the work of Giacomo della Porta, with a façade by Alessandro Galilei.

Of Tiberio Calcagni, the young Florentine sculptor and
architect, who acted like a kind of secretary or clerk to
Michelangelo, something may here be said. The correspondence of this artist with Lionardo Buonarroti shows him to
have been what Vasari calls him, "of gentle manners and
discreet behaviour." He felt both veneration and attachment
for the aged master, and was one of the small group of
intimate friends who cheered his last years. We have seen
that Michelangelo consigned the shattered Pietà to his care;
and Vasari tells us that he also wished him to complete the
bust of Brutus, which had been begun, at Donato Giannotti's
request, for the Cardinal Ridolfi. This bust is said to have
been modelled from an ancient cornelian in the possession of
a certain Giuliano Ceserino. Michelangelo not only blocked
the marble out, but brought it nearly to completion, working
the surface with very fine-toothed chisels. The sweetness of
Tiberio Calcagni's nature is proved by the fact that he would
not set his own hand to this masterpiece of sculpture. As
in the case of the Pietà, he left Buonarroti's work untouched,
where mere repairs were not required. Accordingly we still
can trace the fine-toothed marks of the chisel alluded to by
Vasari, hatched and cross-hatched with right and left handed
strokes in the style peculiar to Michelangelo. The Brutus

remains one of the finest specimens of his creative genius. It must have been conceived and executed in the plenitude of his vigour, probably at the time when Florence fell beneath the yoke of Alessandro de' Medici, or rather when his murderer Lorenzino gained the name of Brutus from the exiles (1539). Though Vasari may be right in saying that a Roman intaglio suggested the stamp of face and feature, yet we must regard this Brutus as an ideal portrait, intended to express the artist's conception of resolution and uncompromising energy in a patriot eager to sacrifice personal feelings and to dare the utmost for his country's welfare. Nothing can exceed the spirit with which a violent temperament, habitually repressed, but capable of leaping forth like sudden lightning, has been rendered. We must be grateful to Calcagni for leaving it in its suggestively unfinished state.

II

During these same years Michelangelo carried on a correspondence with Ammanati and Vasari about the completion of the Laurentian Library. His letters illustrate what I have more than once observed regarding his unpractical method of commencing great works, without more than the roughest sketches, intelligible to himself alone, and useless to an ordinary craftsman. The Florentine artists employed upon the fabric wanted very much to know how he meant to introduce the grand staircase into the vestibule. Michelangelo had forgotten all about it. "With regard to the staircase of the library, about which so much has been said to me, you may believe that if I could remember how I had arranged it, I should not need to be begged and prayed for information. There comes into my mind, as in a dream, the image of a certain staircase; but I do not think this can be the one I then designed, for it seems so stupid. However, I will describe it." Later on he sends a little clay model of a staircase, just enough to indicate his general conception, but not to determine details. He suggests that the work would look better if carried out in walnut. We have every reason to suppose that the present stone flight of steps is far from being representative of his idea.

He was now too old to do more than furnish drawings when asked to design some monument. Accordingly, when Pius IV. resolved to erect a tomb in Milan Cathedral to the memory of his brother, Giangiacomo de' Medici, Marquis of Marignano, commonly called Il Medeghino, he requested Michelangelo to supply the bronze-sculptor Leone Leoni of Menaggio with a design. This must have been insufficient for the sculptor's purpose—a mere hand-sketch not drawn to scale. The monument, though imposing in general effect, is very defective in its details and proportions. The architectural scheme has not been comprehended by the sculptor, who enriched it with a great variety of figures, excellently wrought in bronze, and faintly suggesting Michelangelo's manner.

The grotesque *barocco* style of the Porta Pia, strong in its total outline, but whimsical and weak in decorative detail, may probably be ascribed to the same cause. It was sketched out by Michelangelo during the pontificate of Pius IV., and can hardly have been erected under his personal supervision. Vasari says: "He made three sketches, extravagant in style and most beautiful, of which the Pope selected the least costly; this was executed much to his credit, as may now be seen." To what extent he was responsible for the other sixteenth-century gates of Rome, including the Porta del Popolo, which is commonly ascribed to him, cannot be determined; though Vasari asserts that Michelangelo supplied the Pope with "many other models" for the restoration of the gates. Indeed it may be said of all his later work that we are dealing with uncertain material, the original idea emanating perhaps from Buonarroti's mind, but the execution having devolved upon journeymen.

Pius IV. charged Michelangelo with another great undertaking, which was the restoration of the Baths of Diocletian in the form of a Christian church. Criticism is reduced to silence upon his work in this place, because S. Maria degli Angeli underwent a complete remodelling by the architect Vanvitelli in 1749. This man altered the ground-plan from the Latin to the Greek type, and adopted the decorative style in vogue at the beginning of the eighteenth century. All that appears certain is that Michelangelo had very considerable remains of the Roman building to make use of. We may also perhaps credit tradition, when it tells us that the vast Carthusian cloister belongs to him, and that the three great cypress-trees were planted by his hand.

Henri the Second's death occurred in 1559; and his widow, Catherine de' Medici, resolved to erect an equestrian statue to his memory. She bethought her of the aged sculptor, who had been bred in the palace of her great-grandfather, who had served two Pontiffs of her family, and who had placed the mournful image of her father on the tomb at San Lorenzo. Accordingly she wrote a letter on the 14th of November in that year, informing Michelangelo of her intention, and begging him to supply at least a design upon which the best masters in the realm of France might work. The statue was destined for the courtyard of the royal château at Blois, and was to be in bronze. Ruberto degli Strozzi, the Queen's cousin, happened about this time to visit Rome. Michelangelo having agreed to furnish a sketch, it was decided between them that the execution should be assigned to Daniele da Volterra. After nearly a year's interval, Catherine wrote again, informing Michelangelo that she had deposited a sum of 6000 golden crowns at the bank of Gianbattista Gondi for the work, adding: "Consequently, since on my side nothing remains to be done, I entreat you by the affection you have always shown to my family, to our Florence, and lastly to art, that you will use all diligence and assiduity, so far as your years permit, in pushing forward this noble work, and making it a living likeness of my lord, as well as worthy of your own unrivalled genius. It is true that this will add nothing to the fame you now enjoy; yet it will at least augment your reputation for most acceptable and affectionate devotion toward myself and my ancestors, and prolong through centuries the memory of my lawful and sole love; for the which I shall be eager and liberal to reward you." It is probable that by this time (October 30, 1560) Michelangelo had forwarded his sketch to France, for the Queen criticised some details relating to the portrait of her husband. She may have remembered with what idealistic freedom the statues of the Dukes of Nemours and Urbino had been treated in the Medicean Sacristy. Anyhow, she sent a picture, and made her agent, Baccio del Bene, write a postscript to her letter, ordering Michelangelo to model the King's head without curls, and to adopt the rich modern style for his armour and the trappings of his charger. She particularly insisted upon the likeness being carefully brought out.

Michelangelo died before the equestrian statue of Henri II. was finished. Cellini, in his Memoirs, relates that Daniele da Volterra worked slowly, and caused much annoyance to the Queen-mother of France. In 1562 her agent, Baccio del Bene, came to Florence on financial business with the Duke. He then proposed that Cellini should return to Paris and undertake the ornamental details of the tomb. The Duke would not consent, and Catherine de' Medici did not choose to quarrel with her cousin about an artist. So this arrangement, which might have secured the completion of the statue on a splendid scale, fell through. When Daniele died in 1566, only the horse was cast; and this part served finally for Biard's statue of Louis XIII.

III

The sculptor Leone Leoni, who was employed upon the statue of Giangiacomo de' Medici in Milan, wrote frequently to Michelangelo, showing by his letters that a warm friendship subsisted between them, which was also shared by Tommaso Cavalieri. In the year 1560, according to Vasari, Leoni modelled a profile portrait of the great master, which he afterwards cast in medal form. This is almost the most interesting, and it is probably the most genuine contemporary record which we possess regarding Michelangelo's appearance in the body. I may therefore take it as my basis for inquiring into the relative value of the many portraits said to have been modelled, painted, or sketched from the hero in his lifetime. So far as I am hitherto aware, no claim has been put in for the authenticity of any likeness, except Bonasoni's engraving, anterior to the date we have arrived at. While making this statement, I pass over the prostrate old man in the Victory, and the Nicodemus of the Florentine Pietà, both of which, with more or less reason, have been accepted as efforts after self-portraiture.

After making due allowance for Vasari's too notorious inaccuracies, deliberate misstatements, and random jumpings at conclusions, we have the right to accept him here as a first-rate authority. He was living at this time in close intimacy with Buonarroti, enjoyed his confidence, plumed himself upon their friendship, and had no reason to distort truth, which must have been accessible to one in his position. He says, then: "At this time the Cavaliere Leoni made a very lively portrait of Michelangelo upon a medal, and to meet his wishes, modelled on the reverse a blind man led by a dog, with this legend round the rim: DOCEBO INIQUOS VIAS TUAS, ET IMPII AD TE CONVERTENTUR. It pleased Michelangelo so much that he gave him a wax model of a Hercules throttling Antæus, by his own hand, together with some drawings. Of Michelangelo there exist no other portraits, except two in painting—one by Bugiardini, the other by Jacopo del Conte; and one in bronze, in full relief, made by Daniele da Volterra: these, and Leoni's medal, from which (in the plural) many copies have been made, and a great number of them have been seen by me in several parts of Italy and abroad."

Leoni's medal, on the obverse, shows the old artist's head in profile, with strong lines of drapery rising to the neck and gathering around the shoulders. It carries this legend: MICHELANGELUS BUONARROTUS, FLO. R. A.E.T.S. ANN. 88, and is signed LEO. Leoni then assumed that Michelangelo was eighty-eight years of age when he cast the die. But if this was done in 1560, the age he had then attained was eighty-five. We possess a letter from Leoni in Milan to Buonarroti in Rome, dated March 14, 1561. In it he says: "I am sending to your lordship, by the favour of Lord Carlo Visconti, a great man in this city, and beloved by his Holiness, four medals of your portrait: two in silver, and two in bronze. I should have done so earlier but for my occupation with the monument (of Medeghino), and for the certainty I feel that you will excuse my tardiness, if not a sin of ingratitude in me. The one enclosed within the little box has been worked up to the finest polish. I beg you to accept and keep this for the love of me. With the other three you will do as you think best. I say this because ambition has prompted me to send copies into Spain and Flanders, as I have also done to Rome and other places. I call it ambition, forasmuch as I have gained an overplus of benefits by acquiring the good-will of your lordship, whom I esteem so highly. Have I not received in little less than three months two letters written to me by you, divine man; and couched not in terms fit for a servant of good heart and will, but for one beloved as a son? I pray you to go on loving me, and when occasion serves, to favour me; and to Signor Tomao dei Cavalieri say that I shall never be unmindful of him."

It is clear, then, I think, that Leoni's model was made at Rome in 1560, cast at Milan, and sent early in the spring of 1561 to Michelangelo. The wide distribution of the medals, two of which exist still in silver, while several in bronze may be found in different collections, is accounted for by what Leoni says about his having given them away to various parts of Europe. We are bound to suppose that AET. 88 in the legend on the obverse is due to a misconception concerning Michelangelo's age. Old men are often ignorant or careless about the exact tale of years they have performed.

There is reason to believe that Leoni's original model of the profile, the likeness he shaped from life, and which he afterwards used for the medallion, is extant and in excellent preservation. Mr. C. Drury E. Fortnum (to whose monographs upon Michelangelo's portraits, kindly communicated by himself, I am deeply indebted at this portion of my work), tells us how he came into possession of an exquisite cameo, in flesh-coloured wax upon a black oval ground. This fragile work of art is framed in gilt metal and glazed, carrying upon its back an Italian inscription, which may be translated: "Portrait of Michelangelo Buonarroti, taken from the life, by Leone Aretino, his friend." Comparing the relief in wax with the medal, we cannot doubt that both represent the same man; and only cavillers will raise the question whether both were fashioned by one hand. Such discrepancies as occur between them are just what we should expect in the work of a craftsman who sought first to obtain an accurate likeness of his subject, and then treated the same subject on the lines of numismatic art. The wax shows a lean and subtly moulded face—the face of a delicate old man, wiry and worn with years of deep experience. The hair on head and beard is singularly natural; one feels it to be characteristic of the person. Transferring this portrait to bronze necessitated a general broadening of the masses, with a coarsening of outline to obtain bold relief. Something of the purest truth has been sacrificed to plastic effect by thickening the shrunken throat; and this induced a corresponding enlargement of the occiput for balance. Writing with photographs of these two models before me,

I feel convinced that in the wax we have a portrait from the life of the aged Buonarroti as Leoni knew him, and in the bronze a handling of that portrait as the craftsman felt his art of metal-work required its execution. There was a grand manner of medallion-portraiture in Italy, deriving from the times of Pisanello; and Leoni's bronze is worthy of that excellent tradition. He preserved the salient features of Buonarroti in old age. But having to send down to posterity a monumental record of the man, he added, insensibly or wilfully, both bulk and mass to the head he had so keenly studied. What confirms me in the opinion that Mr. Fornum's cameo is the most veracious portrait we possess of Michelangelo in old age, is that its fragility of structure, the tenuity of life vigorous but infinitely refined, reappears in the weak drawing made by Francesco d'Olanda of Buonarroti in hat and mantle. This is a comparatively poor and dreamy sketch. Yet it has an air of veracity; and what the Flemish painter seized in the divine man he so much admired, was a certain slender grace and dignity of person—exactly the quality which Mr. Fortnum's cameo possesses.

Before leaving this interesting subject, I ought to add that the blind man on the reverse of Leoni's medal is clearly a rough and ready sketch of Michelangelo, not treated like a portrait, but with indications sufficient to connect the figure with the highly wrought profile on the obverse.

Returning now to the passage cited from Vasari, we find that he reckons only two authentic portraits in painting of Michelangelo, one by Bugiardini, the other by Jacopo del Conte. He has neglected to mention two which are undoubtedly attempts to reproduce the features of the master by scholars he had formed. Probably Vasari overlooked them, because they did not exist as easel-pictures, but were introduced into great compositions as subordinate adjuncts. One of them is the head painted by Daniele da Volterra in his picture of the Assumption at the church of the Trinità de' Monti in Rome. It belongs to an apostle, draped in red, stretching arms aloft, close to a column, on the right hand of the painting as we look at it. This must be reckoned among the genuine likenesses of the great man by one who lived with him and knew him intimately. The other is a portrait placed by Marcello Venusti in the left-hand corner of his copy of the Last Judgment, executed, under Michelangelo's direction, for the Cardinal Farnese. It has value for the same reasons as those which make us dwell upon Daniele da Volterra's picture. Moreover, it connects itself with a series of easel-paintings. One of these, ascribed to Venusti, is preserved in the Museo Buonarroti at Florence; another at the Capitol in Rome. Several repetitions of this type exist: they look like studies taken by the pupil from his master, and reproduced to order when death closed the scene, making friends wish for mementoes of the genius who had passed away. The critique of such works will always remain obscure.

What has become of the portrait of Del Conte mentioned by Vasari cannot now be ascertained. We have no external evidence to guide us.

On the other hand, certain peculiarities about the portrait in the Uffizi, especially the exaggeration of one eye, lend some colouring to the belief that we here possess the picture ascribed by Vasari to Bugiardini.

Michelangelo's type of face was well accentuated, and all the more or less contemporary portraits of him reproduce it. Time is wasted in the effort to assign to little men their special part in the creation of a prevalent tradition. It seems to me, therefore, the function of sane criticism not to be particular about the easel-pictures ascribed to Venusti, Del Conte, and Bugiardini.

The case is different with a superb engraving by Giulio Bonasoni, a profile in a circle, dated 1546, and giving Buonarroti's age as seventy-two. This shows the man in fuller vigour than the portraits we have hitherto been deal-

ing with. From other prints which bear the signature of
Bonasoni, we see that he was interested in faithfully reproducing Michelangelo's work. What the relations between
the two men were remains uncertain, but Bonasoni may
have had opportunities of studying the master's person. At
any rate, as a product of the burin, this profile is comparable
for fidelity and veracity with Leoni's model, and is executed
in the same medallion spirit.

So far, then, as I have yet pursued the analysis of Michelangelo's portraits, I take Bonasoni's engraving to be decisive
for Michelangelo's appearance at the age of seventy;
Leoni's model as of equal or of greater value at the age
of eighty; Venusti's and Da Volterra's paintings as of some
importance for this later period; while I leave the attribution of minor easel-pictures to Del Conte or to Bugiardini
open.

It remains to speak of that "full relief in bronze made
by Daniele da Volterra," which Vasari mentions among the
four genuine portraits of Buonarroti. From the context we
should gather that this head was executed during the lifetime of Michelangelo, and the conclusion is supported by
the fact that only a few pages later on Vasari mentions
two other busts modelled after his death. Describing the
catafalque erected to his honour in S. Lorenzo, he says that
the pyramid which crowned the structure exhibited within
two ovals (one turned toward the chief door, and the other
toward the high altar) "the head of Michelangelo in relief,
taken from nature, and very excellently carried out by Santi
Buglioni." The words *ritratta dal naturale* do not, I think,
necessarily imply that it was modelled from the life. Owing
to the circumstances under which Michelangelo's obsequies
were prepared, there was not time to finish it in bronze or
stone; it may therefore have been one of those Florentine
terra-cotta effigies which artists elaborated from a cast taken
after death. That there existed such a cast is proved by what
we know about the monument designed by Vasari in S.

Croce. "One of the statues was assigned to Battista Lorenzi, an able sculptor, together with the head of Michelangelo." We learn from another source that this bust in marble "was taken from the mask cast after his death."

The custom of taking plaster casts from the faces of the illustrious dead, in order to perpetuate their features, was so universal in Italy, that it could hardly have been omitted in the case of Michelangelo. The question now arises whether the bronze head ascribed by Vasari to Daniele da Volterra was executed during Michelangelo's lifetime or after his decease, and whether we possess it. There are eight heads of this species known to students of Michelangelo, which correspond so nicely in their measurements and general features as to force the conclusion that they were all derived from an original moulded by one masterly hand. Three of these heads are unmounted, namely, those at Milan, Oxford, and M. Piot's house in Paris. One, that of the Capitoline Museum, is fixed upon a bust of *bigio morato* marble. The remaining four examples are executed throughout in bronze as busts, agreeing in the main as to the head, but differing in minor details of drapery. They exist respectively in the Museo Buonarroti, the Accademia, and the Bargello at Florence, and in the private collection of M. Cottier of Paris. It is clear, then, that we are dealing with bronze heads cast from a common mould, worked up afterwards according to the fancy of the artist. That this original head was the portrait ascribed to Daniele da Volterra will be conceded by all who care to trace the history of the bust; but whether he modelled it after Michelangelo's death cannot be decided. Professional critics are of the opinion that a mask was followed by the master; and this may have been the case. Michelangelo died upon the 17th of February 1564. His face was probably cast in the usual course of things, and copies may have been distributed among his friends in Rome and Florence. Lionardo Buonarroti showed at once a great anxiety to obtain his uncle's bust from Daniele da Volterra. Possibly he ordered it while resident in Rome, engaged in winding up Michelangelo's affairs. At any rate, Daniele wrote on June 11 to this effect: "As regards the portraits in metal, I have already completed a model in wax, and the work is going on as fast as circumstances permit; you may rely upon its being completed with due despatch and all the care I can bestow upon it." Nearly four months had elapsed since Michelangelo's decease, and this was quite enough time for the wax model to be made. The work of casting was begun, but Daniele's health at this time became so wretched that he found it impossible to work steadily at any of his undertakings. He sank slowly, and expired in the early spring of 1566.

What happened to the bronze heads in the interval between June 1564 and April 1566 may be partly understood from Diomede Leoni's correspondence. This man, a native of San Quirico, was Daniele's scholar, and an intimate friend of the Buonarroti family. On the 9th of September 1564 he wrote to Lionardo: "Your two heads of that sainted man are coming to a good result, and I am sure you will be satisfied with them." It appears, then, that Lionardo had ordered two copies from Daniele. On the 21st of April 1565 Diomede writes again: "I delivered your messages to Messer Daniele, who replies that you are always in his mind, as also the two heads of your lamented uncle. They will soon be cast, as also will my copy, which I mean to keep by me for my honour." The casting must have taken place in the summer of 1565, for Diomede writes upon the 6th of October: "I will remind him (Daniele) of your two heads; and he will find mine well finished, which will make him wish to have yours chased without further delay." The three heads had then been cast; Diomede was polishing his up with the file; Daniele had not yet begun to do this for Lionardo's. We hear nothing more until the death of Daniele da Volterra. After this event occurred, Lionardo Buonarroti received a letter from Jacopo del Duca, a Sicilian bronze-caster of high merit, who had enjoyed Michelangelo's confidence and friendship. He was at present employed upon the metal-work for Buonarroti's monument in the Church of the SS. Apostoli in Rome, and on the 18th of April he sent important information respecting the two heads left by Daniele. "Messer Danielo had cast them, but they are in such a state as to require working over afresh with chisels and files. I am not sure, then, whether they will suit your purpose; but that is your affair. I, for my part, should have liked you to have the portrait from the hand of the lamented master himself, and not from any other. Your lordship must decide: appeal to some one who can inform you better than I do. I know that I am speaking from the love I bear you; and perhaps, if Danielo had been alive, he would have had them brought to proper finish. As for those men of his, I do not know what they will do." On the same day, a certain Michele Alberti wrote as follows: "Messer Jacopo, your gossip, has told me that your lordship wished to know in what condition are the heads of the late lamented Michelangelo. I inform you that they are cast, and will be chased within the space of a month, or rather more. So your lordship will be able to have them; and you may rest assured that you will be well and quickly served." Alberti, we may conjecture, was one of Daniele's men alluded to by Jacopo del Duca. It is probable that just at this time they were making several *replicas* from their deceased master's model, in order to dispose of them at an advantage while Michelangelo's memory was still fresh. Lionardo grew more and more impatient. He appealed again to Diomede Leoni, who replied from San Quirico upon the 4th of June: "The two heads were in existence when I left Rome, but not finished up. I imagine you have given orders to have them delivered over to yourself. As for the work of chasing them, if you can wait till my return, we might intrust them to a man who succeeded very well with my own copy." Three years later, on September 17, 1569, Diomede wrote once again about his copy of Da Volterra's model: "I enjoy the continual contemplation of his effigy in bronze, which is now perfectly finished and set up in my garden, where you will see it, if good fortune favours me with a visit from you."

The net result of this correspondence seems to be that certainly three bronze heads, and probably more, remained unfinished in Daniele da Volterra's workship after his death, and that these were gradually cleaned and polished by different craftsmen, according to the pleasure of their purchasers. The strong resemblance of the eight bronze heads at present known to us, in combination with their different states of surface-finish, correspond entirely to this conclusion. Mr. Fortnum, in his classification, describes four as being not chased, one as "rudely and broadly chased," three as "more or less chased."

Of these variants upon the model common to them all, we can only trace one with relative certainty. It is the bust at present in the Bargello Palace, whither it came from the Grand Ducal villa of Poggio Imperiale. By the marriage of the heiress of the ducal house of Della Rovere with a Duke of Tuscany, this work of art passed, with other art treasures, notably with a statuette of Michelangelo's Moses, into the possession of the Medici. A letter written in 1570 to the Duke of Urbino by Buonarroti's house-servant, Antonio del Franzese of Castel Durante, throws light upon the matter. He begins by saying that he is glad to hear the Duke will accept the little Moses, though the object is too slight in value to deserve his notice. Then he adds: "The head of which your Excellency spoke in the very kind letter addressed to me at your command is the true likeness of Michelangelo Buonarroti, my old master; and it is of bronze, designed by himself. I keep it here in Rome, and now present it to your Excellency." Antonio then, in all probability, obtained one of the Daniele da Volterra bronzes; for it is wholly incredible that what he writes about its having been made by Michelangelo should be the truth. Had Michelangelo really modelled his own portrait and cast it in bronze, we must have heard of this from other sources. Moreover, the Medicean bust of Michelangelo which is now placed in the Bargello, and which we believe to have come from Urbino, belongs indubitably to the series of portraits made from Daniele da Volterra's model.

To sum up this question of Michelangelo's authentic portraits: I repeat that Bonasoni's engraving represents him at the age of seventy; Leoni's wax model and medallions at eighty; the eight bronze heads, derived from Daniele's model, at the epoch of his death. In painting, Marco Venusti and Daniele da Volterra helped to establish a traditional type by two episodical likenesses, the one worked into Venusti's copy of the Last Judgment (at Naples), the other into Volterra's original picture of the Assumption (at Trinità de' Monti, Rome). For the rest, the easel-pictures, which abound, can hardly now be distributed, by any sane method of criticism, between Bugiardini, Jacopo del Conte, and Venusti. They must be taken *en masse*, as contributions to the study of his personality; and, as I have already said, the oil-painting of the Uffizi may perhaps be ascribed with some show of probability to Bugiardini.

IV

Michelangelo's correspondence with his nephew Lionardo gives us ample details concerning his private life and interests in old age. It turns mainly upon the following topics: investment of money in land near Florence, the purchase of a mansion in the city, Lionardo's marriage, his own illnesses, the Duke's invitation, and the project of making a will, which was never carried out. Much as Michelangelo loved his nephew, he took frequent occasions of snubbing him. For instance, news reached Rome that the landed property of a certain Francesco Corboli was going to be sold. Michelangelo sent to Lionardo requesting him to make inquiries; and because the latter showed some alacrity in doing so, his uncle wrote him the following querulous epistle: "You have been very hasty in sending me information regarding the estates of the Corboli. I did not think you were yet in Florence. Are you afraid lest I should change my mind, as some one may perhaps have put it into your head? I tell you that I want to go slowly in this affair, because the money I must pay has been gained here with toil and trouble unintelligible to one who was born clothed and shod as you were. About your coming post-haste to Rome, I do not know that you came in such a hurry when I was a pauper and lacked bread. Enough for you to throw away the money that you did not earn. The fear of losing what you might inherit on my death impelled you. You say it was your duty to come, by reason of the love you bear me. The love of a woodworm! If you really loved me, you would have written now: 'Michelangelo, spend those 3000 ducats there upon yourself, for you have given us enough already: your life is dearer to us than your money.' You have all of you lived forty years upon me, and I have never had from you so much as one good word. 'Tis true that last year I scolded and rebuked you so that for very shame you sent me a load of trebbiano. I almost wish you hadn't! I do not write this because I am unwilling to buy. Indeed I have a mind to do so, in order to obtain an income for myself, now that I cannot work more. But I want to buy at leisure, so as not to purchase some annoyance. Therefore do not hurry."

Lionardo was careless about his handwriting, and this annoyed the old man terribly.

"Do not write to me again. Each time I get one of your letters, a fever takes me with the trouble I have in reading it. I do not know where you learned to write. I think that if you were writing to the greatest donkey in the world you would do it with more care. Therefore do not add to the annoyances I have, for I have already quite enough of them."

He returns to the subject over and over again, and once declares that he has flung a letter of Lionardo's into the fire unread, and so is incapable of answering it. This did not prevent a brisk interchange of friendly communications between the uncle and nephew.

Lionardo was now living in the Buonarroti house in Via Ghibellina. Michelangelo thought it advisable that he should remove into a more commodious mansion, and one not subject to inundations of the basement. He desired, however, not to go beyond the quarter of S. Croce, where the family had been for centuries established. The matter became urgent, for Lionardo wished to marry, and could not marry until he was provided with a residence. Eventually, after rejecting many plans and proffers of houses, they decided to enlarge and improve the original Buonarroti mansion in Via Ghibellina. This house continued to be their town-mansion until the year 1852, when it passed by testamentary devise to the city of Florence. It is now the Museo Buonarroti.

Lionardo was at this time thirty, and was the sole hope of the family, since Michelangelo and his two surviving brothers had no expectation of offspring. His uncle kept reminding the young man that, if he did not marry and get children, the whole property of the Buonarroti would go to the Hospital or to S. Martino. This made his marriage imperative; and Michelangelo's letters between March 5, 1547, and May 16, 1553, when the desired event took place, are full of the subject. He gives his nephew excellent advice as to the choice of a wife. She ought to be ten years younger than himself, of noble birth, but not of a very rich or powerful family; Lionardo must not expect her to be too handsome, since he is no miracle of manly beauty; the great thing is to obtain a good, useful, and obedient helpmate, who will not try to get the upper hand in the house, and who will be grateful for an honourable settlement in life. The following passages may be selected, as specimens of Michelangelo's advice: "You ought not to look for a dower, but only to consider whether the girl is well brought up, healthy, of good character and noble blood. You are not yourself of such parts and person as to be worthy of the first beauty of Florence." "You have need of a wife who would stay with you, and whom you could command, and who would not want to live in grand style or to gad about every day to marriages and banquets. Where a court is, it is easy to become a woman of loose life; especially for one who has no relatives."

Numerous young ladies were introduced by friends or matrimonial agents. Six years, however, elapsed before the suitable person presented herself in the shape of Cassandra, daughter of Donato Ridolfi. Meanwhile, in 1548, Michelangelo lost the elder of his surviving brothers. Giovan Simone died upon the 9th of January; and though he had given but little satisfaction in his lifetime, his death was felt acutely by the venerable artist. "I received news in your last of Giovan Simone's death. It has caused me the greatest sorrow; for though I am old, I had yet hoped to see him before he died, and before I died. God has willed it so. Patience! I should be glad to hear circumstantially what kind of end he made, and whether he confessed and communicated with all the sacraments of the Church. If he did so, and I am informed of it, I shall suffer less." A few days after the date of this letter, Michelangelo writes again, blaming Lionardo pretty severely for negligence in giving particulars of his uncle's death and affairs. Later on, it seems that he was satisfied regarding Giovan Simone's manner of departure from this world. A grudge remained against Lionardo because he had omitted to inform him about the property. "I heard the details from other persons before you sent them, which angered me exceedingly."

V

The year 1549 is marked by an exchange of civilities between Michelangelo and Benedetto Varchi. The learned man of letters and minute historiographer of Florence probably enjoyed our great sculptor's society in former years: recently they had been brought into closer relations at Rome. Varchi, who was interested in critical and academical problems, started the question whether sculpture or painting could justly claim a priority in the plastic arts. He conceived the very modern idea of collecting opinions from practical craftsmen, instituting, in fact, what would now be called a "Symposium" upon the subject. A good number of the answers to his query have been preserved, and among them is a letter from Michelangelo. It contains the following passage, which proves in how deep a sense Buonarroti was by temperament and predilection a sculptor: "My opinion is that all painting is the better the nearer it approaches to relief, and relief is the worse in proportion as it inclines to painting. And so I have been wont to think that sculpture is the lamp of painting, and that the difference between them might be likened to the difference between the sun and moon. Now that I have read your essay, in which you maintain that, philosophically speaking, things which fulfil the same purpose are essentially the same, I have altered my view. Therefore I say that, if greater judgment and difficulty, impediment and labour, in the handling of material do not constitute higher nobility, then painting and sculpture form one art. This being granted, it follows that no painter should underrate sculpture, and no sculptor should make light of painting. By sculpture I understand an art which operates by taking away superfluous material; by painting, one that attains its result by laying on. It is enough that both emanate from the same human intelligence, and consequently sculpture and painting ought to live in amity together, without these lengthy disputations. More time is wasted in talking about the problem than would go to the making of figures in both species. The man who wrote that painting was superior to sculpture, if he understood the other things he says no better, might be called a writer below the level of my maid-servant. There are infinite points not yet expressed which might be brought out regarding these arts; but, as I have said, they want too much time; and of time I have but little, being not only old, but almost numbered with the dead. Therefore, I pray you to have me excused. I recommend myself to you, and thank you to the best of my ability for the too great honour you have done me, which is more than I deserve."

Varchi printed this letter in a volume which he published at Florence in 1549, and reissued through another firm in 1590. It contained the treatise alluded to above, and also a commentary upon one of Michelangelo's sonnets, "Non ha l'ottimo artista alcun concetto." The book was duly sent to Michelangelo by the favour of a noble Florentine gentleman, Luca Martini. He responded to the present in a letter which deserves here to be recited. It is an eminent example of the urbanity observed by him in the interchange of these and similar courtesies:—

"I have received your letter, together with a little book containing a commentary on a sonnet of mine. The sonnet does indeed proceed from me, but the commentary comes from heaven. In truth it is a marvellous production; and I say this not on my own judgment only, but on that of able men, especially of Messer Donato Giannotti, who is never tired of reading it. He begs to be remembered to you. About the sonnet, I know very well what that is worth. Yet be it what it may, I cannot refrain from piquing myself a little on having been the cause of so beautiful and learned a commentary. The author of it, by his words and praises, shows clearly that he thinks me to be other than I am; so I beg you to express me to him in terms corresponding to so much love, affection, and courtesy. I entreat you to do this, because I feel myself inadequate, and one who has gained golden opinions ought not to tempt fortune; it is better to keep silence than to fall from that height. I am old, and death has robbed me of the thoughts of my youth. He who knows not what old age is, let him wait till it arrives: he cannot know beforehand. Remember me, as I said, to Varchi, with deep affection for his fine qualities, and as his servant wherever I may be."

Three other letters belonging to the same year show how deeply Michelangelo was touched and gratified by the distinguished honour Varchi paid him. In an earlier chapter of this book I have already pointed out how this correspondence bears upon the question of his friendship with Tommaso dei Cavalieri, and also upon an untenable hypothesis advanced by recent Florentine students of his biography. The incident is notable in other ways because Buonarroti was now adopted as a poet by the Florentine Academy. With a width of sympathy rare in such bodies, they condoned the ruggedness of his style and the uncouthness of his versification in their admiration for the high quality of his meditative inspiration. To the triple crown of sculptor, painter, architect, he now added the laurels of the bard; and this public recognition of his genius as a writer gave him well-merited pleasure in his declining years.

While gathering up these scattered fragments of Buonarroti's later life, I may here introduce a letter addressed to Benvenuto Cellini, which illustrates his glad acceptance of all good work in fellow-craftsmen:—

"My Benvenuto,—I have known you all these years as the greatest goldsmith of whom the world ever heard, and now I am to know you for a sculptor of the same quality. Messer Bindo Altoviti took me to see his portrait bust in bronze, and told me it was by your hand. I admired it much, but was sorry to see that it has been placed in a bad light. If it had a proper illumination, it would show itself to be the fine work it is."

VI

Lionardo Buonarroti was at last married to Cassandra, the daughter of Donato Ridolfi, upon the 16th of May 1553. One of the dearest wishes which had occupied his uncle's mind so long, came thus to its accomplishment. His letters are full of kindly thoughts for the young couple, and of prudent advice to the husband, who had not arranged all matters connected with the settlements to his own satisfaction. Michelangelo congratulated Lionardo heartily upon his happiness, and told him that he was minded to send the bride a handsome present, in token of his esteem. "I have not been able to do so yet, because Urbino was away. Now that he has returned, I shall give expression to my sentiments. They tell me that a fine pearl necklace of some value would be very proper. I have sent a goldsmith, Urbino's friend, in search of such an ornament, and hope to find it; but say nothing to her, and if you would like me to choose another article, please let me know." This letter winds up with a strange admonition: "Look to living, reflect and weigh things well; for the number of widows in the world is always larger than that of the widowers." Ultimately he decided upon two rings, one a diamond, the other a ruby. He tells Lionardo to have the stones valued in case he has been cheated, because he does not understand such things; and is glad to hear in due course that the jewels are genuine. After the proper interval, Cassandra expected her confinement, and Michelangelo corresponded with his nephew as to the child's name in case it was a boy. "I shall be very pleased if the name of Buonarroto does not die out of our family, it having lasted three hundred years with us." The child was born upon the 16th of May 1544, turned out a boy, and received the name of Buonarroto. Though Lionardo had seven other children, including Michelangelo the younger (born November 4, 1568), this Buonarroto alone continued the male line of the family. The old man in

Rome remarked resignedly during his later years, when he heard the news of a baby born and dead, that "I am not surprised; there was never in our family more than one at a time to keep it going."

Buonarroto was christened with some pomp, and Vasari wrote to Michelangelo describing the festivities. In the year 1554, Cosimo de' Medici had thrown his net round Siena. The Marquis of Marignano reduced the city first to extremities by famine, and finally to enslavement by capitulation. These facts account for the tone of Michelangelo's answer to Vasari's letter: "Yours has given me the greatest pleasure, because it assures me that you remember the poor old man; and more perhaps because you were present at the triumph you narrate, of seeing another Buonarroto reborn. I thank you heartily for the information. But I must say that I am displeased with so much pomp and show. Man ought not to laugh when the whole world weeps. So I think that Lionardo has not displayed great judgment, particularly in celebrating a nativity with all that joy and gladness which ought to be reserved for the decease of one who has lived well." There is what may be called an Elizabethan note— something like the lyrical interbreathings of our dramatists —in this blending of jubilation and sorrow, discontent and satisfaction, birth and death thoughts.

We have seen that Vasari worked for a short time as pupil under Michelangelo, and that during the pontificate of Paul III. they were brought into frequent contact at Rome. With years their friendship deepened into intimacy, and after the date 1550 their correspondence forms one of our most important sources of information. Michelangelo's letters begin upon the 1st of August in that year. Vasari was then living and working for the Duke at Florence; but he had designed a chapel for S. Pietro a Montorio in Rome, where Julius III. wished to erect tombs to the memory of his ancestors; and the work had been allotted to Bartolommeo Ammanati under Michelangelo's direction.

This business, otherwise of no importance in his biography, necessitated the writing of despatches, one of which is interesting, since it acknowledges the receipt of Vasari's celebrated book:—

"Referring to your three letters which I have received, my pen refuses to reply to such high compliments. I should indeed be happy if I were in some degree what you make me out to be, but I should not care for this except that then you would have a servant worth something. However, I am not surprised that you, who resuscitate the dead, should prolong the life of the living, or that you should steal the half-dead from death for an endless period."

It seems that on this occasion he also sent Vasari the sonnet composed upon his Lives of the Painters. Though it cannot be called one of his poetical masterpieces, the personal interest attaching to the verses justifies their introduction here:—

With pencil and with palette hitherto
  You made your art high Nature's paragon;
  Nay more, from Nature her own prize you won,
  Making what she made fair more fair to view.
Now that your learned hand with labour new
  Of pen and ink a worthier work hath done,
  What erst you lacked, what still remained her own,
  The power of giving life, is gained for you.
If men in any age with Nature vied
  In beauteous workmanship, they had to yield
  When to the fated end years brought their name.
You, re-illuming memories that died,
  In spite of Time and Nature have revealed
  For them and for yourself eternal fame.

Vasari's official position at the ducal court of Florence brought him into frequent and personal relations with Cosimo de' Medici. The Duke had long been anxious to lure the most gifted of his subjects back to Florence; but Michelangelo, though he remained a loyal servant to the Medicean family, could not approve of Cosimo's despotic rule. Moreover, he was now engaged by every tie of honour, interest, and artistic ambition to superintend the fabric of S. Peter's. He showed great tact, through delicate negotiations carried on for many years, in avoiding the Duke's overtures without sacrificing his friendship. Wishing to found his family in Florence and to fund the earnings of his life there, he naturally assumed a courteous attitude. A letter written by the Bishop Tornabuoni to Giovanni Francesco Lottini in Rome shows that these overtures began as early as 1546. The prelate says the Duke is so anxious to regain "Michelangelo, the divine sculptor," that he promises "to make him a member of the forty-eight senators, and to give him any office he may ask for." The affair was dropped for some years, but in 1552 Cosimo renewed his attempts, and now began to employ Vasari and Cellini as ambassadors. Soon after finishing his Perseus, Benvenuto begged for leave to go to Rome; and before starting, he showed the Duke Michelangelo's friendly letter on the bust of Bindo Altoviti. "He read it with much kindly interest, and said to me: 'Benvenuto, if you write to him, and can persuade him to return to Florence, I will make him a member of the Forty-eight.' Accordingly I wrote a letter full of warmth, and offered in the Duke's name a hundred times more than my commission carried; but not wanting to make any mistake, I showed this to the Duke before I sealed it, saying to his most illustrious Excellency: 'Prince, perhaps I have made him too many promises.' He replied: 'Michel Agnolo deserves more than you have promised, and I will bestow on him still greater favours.' To this letter he sent no answer, and I could see that the Duke was much offended with him."

While in Rome, Cellini went to visit Michelangelo, and renewed his offers in the Duke's name. What passed in that interview is so graphically told, introducing the rustic personality of Urbino on the stage, and giving a hint of Michelangelo's reasons for not returning in person to Florence, that the whole passage may be transcribed as opening a little window on the details of our hero's domestic life:—

"Then I went to visit Michel Agnolo Buonarroti, and repeated what I had written from Florence to him in the Duke's name. He replied that he was engaged upon the fabric of S. Peter's, and that this would prevent him from leaving Rome. I rejoined that, as he had decided on the model of that building, he could leave its execution to his man Urbino, who would carry out his orders to the letter. I added much about future favours, in the form of a message from the Duke. Upon this he looked me hard in the face, and said with a sarcastic smile: 'And you! to what extent are you satisfied with him?' Although I replied that I was extremely contented and was very well treated by his Excellency, he showed that he was acquainted with the greater part of my annoyances, and gave as his final answer that it would be difficult for him to leave Rome. To this I added that he could not do better than to return to his own land, which was governed by a prince renowned for justice, and the greatest lover of the arts and sciences who ever saw the light of this world. As I have remarked above, he had with him a servant of his who came from Urbino, and had lived many years in his employment, rather as valet and housekeeper than anything else; this indeed was obvious, because he had acquired no skill in the arts. Consequently, while I was pressing Michel Agnolo with arguments he could not answer, he turned round sharply to Urbino, as though to ask him his opinion. The fellow began to bawl out in his rustic way: 'I will never leave my master Michel Agnolo's side till I shall have flayed him or he shall have flayed me.' These stupid words forced me to laugh, and without saying farewell, I lowered my shoulders and retired."

This was in 1552. The Duke was loth to take a refusal, and for the next eight years he continued to ply Michelangelo with invitations, writing letters by his own hand, employing his agents in Rome and Florence, and working through Vasari. The letters to Vasari during this period are full of the subject. Michelangelo remains firm in his intention to remain at Rome and not abandon S. Peter's. As years went on, infirmities increased, and the solicitations of the Duke became more and more irksome to the old man. His discomfort at last elicited what may be called a real cry of pain in a letter to his nephew:—

"As regards my condition, I am ill with all the troubles which are wont to afflict old men. The stone prevents me passing water. My loins and back are so stiff that I often cannot climb upstairs. What makes matters worse is that my mind is much worried with anxieties. If I leave the conveniences I have here for my health, I can hardly live three days. Yet I do not want to lose the favour of the Duke, nor should I like to fail in my work at S. Peter's, nor in my duty to myself. I pray God to help and counsel me; and if I were taken ill by some dangerous fever, I would send for you at once."

Meanwhile, in spite of his resistance to the Duke's wishes, Michelangelo did not lose the favour of the Medicean family. The delicacy of behaviour by means of which he contrived to preserve and strengthen it, is indeed one of the strongest evidences of his sincerity, sagacity, and prudence. The Cardinal Giovanni, son of Cosimo, travelled to Rome in March 1560, in order to be invested with the purple by the Pope's hands. On this occasion Vasari, who rode in the young prince's train, wrote despatches to Florence which contain some interesting passages about Buonarroti. In one of them (March 29) he says: "My friend Michelangelo is so old that I do not hope to obtain much from him." Beside the reiterated overtures regarding a return to Florence, the Church of the Florentines was now in progress, and Cosimo also required Buonarroti's advice upon the decoration of the Great Hall in the Palazzo della Signoria. In a second letter (April 8) Vasari tells the Duke: "I reached Rome, and immediately after the most reverend and illustrious Medici had made his entrance and received the hat from our lord's hands, a ceremony which I wished to see with a view to the frescoes in the Palace, I went to visit my friend, the mighty Michelangelo. He had not expected me, and the tenderness of his reception was such as old men show when lost sons unexpectedly return to them. He fell upon my neck with a thousand kisses, weeping for joy. He was so glad to see me, and I him, that I have had no greater pleasure since I entered the service of your Excellency, albeit I enjoy so many through your kindness. We talked about the greatness and the wonders which our God in heaven has wrought for you, and he lamented that he could not serve you with his body, as he is ready to do with his talents at the least sign of your will. He also expressed his sorrow at being unable to wait upon the Cardinal, because he now can move about but little, and is grown so old that he gets small rest, and is so low in health I fear he will not last long, unless the goodness of God preserves him for the building of S. Peter's." After some further particulars, Vasari adds that he hopes "to spend Monday and Tuesday discussing the model of the Great Hall with Michelangelo, as well as the composition of the several frescoes. I have all that is necessary with me, and will do my utmost, while remaining in his company, to extract useful information and suggestions." We know from Vasari's Life of Michelangelo that the plans for decorating the Palace were settled to his own and the Duke's satisfaction during these colloquies at Rome.

Later on in the year, Cosimo came in person to Rome, attended by the Duchess Eleonora. Michelangelo immediately waited on their Highnesses, and was received with special marks of courtesy by the Duke, who bade him to be seated at his side, and discoursed at length about his own designs for Florence and certain discoveries he had made in the method of working porphyry. These interviews, says Vasari, were repeated several times during Cosimo's sojourn in Rome; and when the Crown-Prince of Florence, Don Francesco, arrived, this young nobleman showed his high respect for the great man by conversing with him cap in hand.

The project of bringing Buonarroti back to Florence was finally abandoned; but he had the satisfaction of feeling that, after the lapse of more than seventy years, his long connection with the House of Medici remained as firm and cordial as it had ever been. It was also consolatory to know that the relations established between himself and the reigning dynasty in Florence would prove of service to Lionardo, upon whom he now had concentrated the whole of his strong family affection.

In estimating Michelangelo as man, independent of his eminence as artist, the most singular point which strikes us is this persistent preoccupation with the ancient house he desired so earnestly to rehabilitate. He treated Lionardo with the greatest brutality. Nothing that this nephew did, or did not do, was right. Yet Lionardo was the sole hope of the Buonarroti-Simoni stock. When he married and got children, the old man purred with satisfaction over him, but only as a breeder of the race; and he did all in his power to establish Lionardo in a secure position.

VII

Returning to the history of Michelangelo's domestic life, we have to relate two sad events which happened to him at the end of 1555. On the 28th of September he wrote to Lionardo: "The bad news about Gismondo afflicts me deeply. I am not without my own troubles of health, and have many annoyances besides. In addition to all this, Urbino has been ill in bed with me three months, and is so still, which causes me much trouble and anxiety." Gismondo, who had been declining all the summer, died upon the 13th of November. His brother in Rome was too much taken up with the mortal sickness of his old friend and servant Urbino to express great sorrow. "Your letter informs me of my brother Gismondo's death, which is the cause to me of serious grief. We must have patience; and inasmuch as he died sound of mind and with all the sacraments of the Church, let God be praised. I am in great affliction here. Urbino is still in bed, and very seriously ill. I do not know what will come of it. I feel this trouble as though he were my own son, because he has lived in my service twenty-five years, and has been very faithful. Being old, I have no time to form another servant to my purpose; and so I am sad exceedingly. If then, you know of some devout person, I beg you to have prayers offered up to God for his recovery."

The next letter gives a short account of his death:—

"I inform you that yesterday, the 3rd of December, at four o'clock, Francesco called Urbino passed from this life, to my very great sorrow. He has left me sorely stricken and afflicted; nay, it would have been sweeter to have died with him, such is the love I bore him. Less than this love he did not deserve; for he had grown to be a worthy man, full of faith and loyalty. So, then, I feel as though his death had left me without life, and I cannot find heart's ease. I should be glad to see you, therefore; only I cannot think how you can leave Florence because of your wife."

To Vasari he wrote still more passionately upon this occasion:—

"I cannot write well; yet, in answer to your letter, I will say a few words. You know that Urbino is dead. I owe the greatest thanks to God, at the same time that my own loss is heavy and my sorrow infinite. The grace He gave me is that, while Urbino kept me alive in life, his death taught me to die without displeasure, rather with a deep and real desire. I had him with me twenty-six years, and found him above measure faithful and sincere. Now that I had made him rich, and thought to keep him as the staff and rest of my old age, he has vanished from my sight; nor have I hope left but that of seeing him again in Paradise. God has given us good foundation for this hope in the exceedingly happy ending of his life. Even more than dying, it grieved him to leave me alive in this treacherous world, with so many troubles; and yet the better part of me is gone with him, nor is there left to me aught but infinite distress. I recommend myself to you, and beg you, if it be not irksome, to make my excuses to Messer Benvenuto (Cellini) for omitting to answer his letter. The trouble of soul I suffer in thought about these things prevents me from writing. Remember me to him, and take my best respects to yourself."

How tenderly Michelangelo's thought dwelt upon Urbino appears from this sonnet, addressed in 1556 to Monsignor Lodovico Beccadelli:—

> God's grace, the cross, our troubles multiplied,
>   Will make us meet in heaven, full well I know:
>   Yet ere we yield our breath on earth below,
>   Why need a little solace be denied?
> Though seas and mountains and rough ways divide
>   Our feet asunder, neither frost nor snow
>   Can make the soul her ancient love forego;
>   Nor chains nor bonds the wings of thought have tied.
> Borne by these wings, with thee I dwell for aye,
>   And weep, and of my dead Urbino talk,
>   Who, were he living, now perchance would be—
> For so 'twas planned—thy guest as well as I.
>   Warned by his death, another way I walk
>   To meet him where he waits to live with me.

By his will, dated November 24, 1555, Urbino, whose real name was Francesco degli Amadori of Castel Durante, appointed his old friend and master one of his executors and the chief guardian of his widow and children. A certain Roso de Rosis and Pietro Filippo Vandini, both of Castel Durante, are named in the trust; and they managed the estate. Yet Michelangelo was evidently the principal authority. A voluminous correspondence preserved in the Buonarroti Archives proves this; for it consists of numerous letters addressed by Urbino's executors and family from Castel Durante and elsewhere to the old sculptor in Rome. Urbino had married a woman of fine character and high intelligence, named Cornelia Colonnelli. Two of her letters are printed by Gotti, and deserve to be studied for the power of their style and the elevation of their sentiments. He has not made use, however, of the other documents, all of which have some interest as giving a pretty complete view of a private family and its vexations, while they illustrate the conscientious fidelity with which Michelangelo discharged his duties as trustee. Urbino had a brother, also resident at Castel Durante, Raffaello's celebrated pupil in fresco-painting, Il Fattorino. This man and Vandini, together with Cornelia and her parents and her second husband, Giulio Brunelli, all wrote letters to Rome about the welfare of the children and the financial affairs of the estate. The coexecutor Roso de Rosis did not write; it appears from one of Cornelia's despatches that he took no active interest in the trust, while Brunelli even complains that he withheld moneys which were legally due to the heirs. One of Michelangelo's first duties was to take care that Cornelia got a proper man for her second husband. Her parents were eager to see her married, being themselves old, and not liking to leave a comparatively young widow alone in the world with so many children to look after. Their choice fell first upon a very undesirable person called Santagnolo, a young man of dissolute habits, ruined constitution, bad character, and no estate. She refused, with spirit, to sign the marriage contract; and a few months later wrote again to inform her guardian that a suitable match had been found in the person of Giulio Brunelli of Gubbio, a young doctor of laws, then resident at Castel Durante in the quality of podestà. Michelangelo's suspicions must have been aroused by the unworthy conduct of her parents in the matter of Santagnolo; for we infer that he at first refused to sanction this second match. Cornelia and the parents wrote once more, assuring him that Brunelli was an excellent man, and entreating him not to open his ears to malignant gossip. On the 15th of June Brunelli himself appears upon the scene, announcing his marriage with Cornelia, introducing himself in terms of becoming modesty to Michelangelo, and assuring him that Urbino's children have found a second father. He writes again upon the 29th of July, this time to announce the fact that Il Fattorino has spread about false rumours to the effect that Cornelia and himself intend to leave Castel Durante and desert the children. Their guardian must not credit such idle gossip, for they are both sincerely attached to the children, and intend to do the best they can for them. Family dissensions began to trouble their peace. In the course of the next few months Brunelli discovers that he cannot act with the Fattorino or with Vandini; Cornelia's dowry is not paid; Roso refuses to refund money due to the heirs; Michelangelo alone can decide what ought to be done for the estate and his wards. The Fattorino writes that Vandini has renounced the trust, and that all Brunelli's and his own entreaties cannot make him resume it. For himself, he is resolved not to bear the burden alone. He has his own shop to look after, and will not let himself be bothered. Unluckily, none of Michelangelo's answers have been preserved. We possess only one of his letters to Cornelia, which shows that she wished to place her son and his godson, Michelangelo, under his care at Rome. He replied that he did not feel himself in a position to accept the responsibility. "It would not do to send Michelangelo, seeing that I have nobody to manage the house and no female servants; the boy is still of tender age, and things might happen which would cause me the utmost annoyance. Moreover, the Duke of Florence has during the last month been making me the greatest offers, and putting strong pressure upon me to return home. I have begged for time to arrange my affairs here and leave S. Peter's in good order. So I expect to remain in Rome all the summer; and when I have settled my business, and yours with the Monte della Fede, I shall probably remove to Florence this winter and take up my abode there for good. I am old now, and have not the time to return to Rome. I will travel by way of Urbino; and if you like to give me Michelangelo, I will bring him to Florence, with more love than the sons of my nephew Lionardo, and will teach him all the things which I know that his father desired that he should learn."

VIII

The year 1556 was marked by an excursion which took Michelangelo into the mountain district of Spoleto. Paul IV.'s anti-Spanish policy had forced the Viceroy of Naples to make a formidable military demonstration. Accordingly the Duke of Alva, at the head of a powerful force, left Naples on the 1st of September and invaded the Campagna. The Romans dreaded a second siege and sack; not without reason, although the real intention of the expedition was to cow the fiery Pope into submission. It is impossible, when we remember Michelangelo's liability to panics, not to connect his autumn journey with a wish to escape from trouble in Rome. On the 31st of October he wrote to Lionardo that he had undertaken a pilgrimage to Loreto, but feeling tired, had stopped to rest at Spoleto. While he was there, a messenger arrived post-haste from Rome, commanding his immediate return. He is now once more at home there, and as well as the troublous circumstances of the times permit.

Later on he told Vasari: "I have recently enjoyed a great pleasure, though purchased at the cost of great discomfort and expense, among the mountains of Spoleto, on a visit to those hermits. Consequently, I have come back less than half myself to Rome; for of a truth there is no peace to be found except among the woods." This is the only passage in the whole of Michelangelo's correspondence which betrays the least feeling for wild nature. We cannot pretend, even here, to detect an interest in landscape or a true appreciation of country life. Compared with Rome and the Duke of Alva, those hermitages of the hills among their chestnut-groves seemed to him haunts of ancient peace. That is all; but when dealing with a man so sternly insensible to the charm of the external world, we have to be contented with a little.

In connection with this brief sojourn at Spoleto I will introduce two letters written to Michelangelo by the Archbishop of Ragusa from his See. The first is dated March 28, 1557, and was sent to Spoleto, probably under the impression that Buonarroti had not yet returned to Rome. After lamenting the unsettled state of public affairs, the Archbishop adds: "Keep well in your bodily health; as for that of your soul, I am sure you cannot be ill, knowing what prudence and piety keep you in perpetual companionship." The second followed at the interval of a year, April 6, 1558, and gave a pathetic picture of the meek old prelate's discomfort in his Dalmatian bishopric. He calls Ragusa "this exceedingly ill-cultivated vineyard of mine. Often-times does the carnal man in me revolt and yearn for Italy, for relatives and friends; but the spirit keeps desire in check, and compels it to be satisfied with that which is the pleasure of our Lord." Though the biographical importance of these extracts is but slight, I am glad, while recording the outlines of Buonarroti's character, to cast a side-light on his amiable qualities, and to show how highly valued he was by persons of the purest life.

IX

There was nothing peculiarly severe about the infirmities of Michelangelo's old age. We first hear of the dysuria from which he suffered, in 1548. He writes to Lionardo thanking him for pears: "I duly received the little barrel of pears you sent me. There were eighty-six. Thirty-three of them I sent to the Pope, who praised them as fine, and who enjoyed them. I have lately been in great difficulty from dysuria. However, I am better now. And thus I write to you, chiefly lest some chatterbox should scribble a thousand lies to make you jump." In the spring of 1549 he says that the doctors believe he is suffering from calculus: "The pain is great, and prevents me from sleeping. They propose that I should try the mineral waters of Viterbo; but I cannot go before the beginning of May. For the rest, as concerns my bodily condition, I am much the same as I was at thirty. This mischief has crept upon me through the great hardships of my life and heedlessness." A few days later he writes that a certain water he is taking, whether mineral or medicine, has been making a beneficial change. The following letters are very cheerful, and at length he is able to write: "With regard to my disease, I am greatly improved in health, and have hope, much to the surprise of many; for people thought me a lost man, and so I believed. I have had a good doctor, but I put more faith in prayers than I do in medicines." His physician was a very famous man, Realdo Colombo. In the summer of the same year he tells Lionardo that he has been drinking for the last two months water from a fountain forty miles distant from Rome. "I have to lay in a stock of it, and to drink nothing else, and also to use it in cooking, and to observe rules of living to which I am not used."

Although the immediate danger from the calculus passed away, Michelangelo grew feebler yearly. We have already seen how he wrote to Lionardo while Cosimo de' Medici was urging him to come to Florence in 1557. Passages in his correspondence with Lionardo like the following are frequent: "Writing is the greatest annoyance to my hand, my sight, my brains. So works old age!" "I go on enduring old age as well as I am able, with all the evils and discomforts it brings in its train; and I recommend myself to Him who can assist me." It was natural, after he had passed the ordinary term of life and was attacked with a disease so serious as the stone, that his thoughts should take a serious tone. Thus he writes to Lionardo: "This illness has made me think of setting the affairs of my soul and body more in order than I should have done. Accordingly, I have drawn up a rough sketch of a will, which I will send you by the next courier if I am able, and you can tell me what you think." The will provided that Gismondo and Lionardo Buonarroti should be his joint-heirs, without the power of dividing the property. This practically left Lionardo his sole heir after Gismondo's life-tenancy of a moiety. It does not, however, seem to have been executed, for Michelangelo died intestate. Probably, he judged it simplest to allow Lionardo to become his heir-general by the mere course of events. At the same time, he now displayed more than his usual munificence in charity. Lionardo was frequently instructed to seek out a poor and gentle family, who were living in decent distress, *poveri vergognosi*, as the Italians called such persons. Money was to be bestowed upon them with the utmost secrecy; and the way which Michelangelo proposed, was to dower a daughter or to pay for her entrance into a convent. It has been suggested that this method of seeking to benefit the deserving poor denoted a morbid tendency in Michelangelo's nature; but any one who is acquainted with Italian customs in the Middle Ages and the Renaissance must be aware that nothing was commoner than to dower poor girls or to establish them in nunneries by way of charity. Urbino, for example, by his will bound his executors to provide for the marriage of two honest girls with a dowry of twenty florins apiece within the space of four years from his death.

The religious sonnets, which are certainly among the finest of Michelangelo's compositions, belong to this period. Writing to Vasari on the 10th of September 1554, he begins: "You will probably say that I am old and mad to think of writing sonnets; yet since many persons pretend that I am in my second childhood, I have thought it well to act accordingly." Then follows this magnificent piece of verse, in which the sincerest feelings of the pious heart are expressed with a sublime dignity:—

> Now hath my life across a stormy sea,
>   Like a frail bark, reached that wide port where all
>   Are bidden, ere the final reckoning fall
>   Of good and evil for eternity.
> Now know I well how that fond phantasy
>   Which made my soul the worshipper and thrall
>   Of earthly art is vain; how criminal
>   Is that which all men seek unwillingly.
> Those amorous thoughts which were so lightly dressed,
>   What are they when the double death is nigh?
>   The one I know for sure, the other dread.
> Painting nor sculpture now can lull to rest
>   My soul, that turns to His great love on high,
>   Whose arms to clasp us on the cross were spread.

A second sonnet, enclosed in a letter to Vasari, runs as follows:—

> The fables of the world have filched away
>   The time I had for thinking upon God;
>   His grace lies buried 'neath oblivion's sod,
>   Whence springs an evil crop of sins alway.

What makes another wise, leads me astray,
    Slow to discern the bad path I have trod:
Hope fades, but still desire ascends that God
    May free me from self-love, my sure decay.
Shorten half-way my road to heaven from earth!
    Dear Lord, I cannot even half-way rise
    Unless Thou help me on this pilgrimage.
Teach me to hate the world so little worth,
    And all the lovely things I clasp and prize,
    That endless life, ere death, may be my wage.

While still in his seventieth year, Michelangelo had edu-
cated himself to meditate upon the thought of death as a
prophylactic against vain distractions and the passion of love.
"I may remind you that a man who would fain return unto
and enjoy his own self ought not to indulge so much in
merrymakings and festivities, but to think on death. This
thought is the only one which makes us know our proper
selves, which holds us together in the bond of our own
nature, which prevents us from being stolen away by kinsmen, friends, great men of genius, ambition, avarice, and
those other sins and vices which filch the man from himself,
keep him distraught and dispersed, without ever permitting
him to return unto himself and reunite his scattered parts.
Marvellous is the operation of this thought of death, which,
albeit death, by his nature, destroys all things, preserves and
supports those who think on death, and defends them from
all human passions." He supports this position by reciting a
madrigal he had composed, to show how the thought of
death is the greatest foe to love:—

Not death indeed, but the dread thought of death
    Saveth and severeth
    Me from the heartless fair who doth me slay:
And should, perchance, some day

The fire consuming blaze o'er measure bright,
I find for my sad plight
No help but from death's form fixed in my heart;
Since, where death reigneth, love must dwell apart.

In some way or another, then, Michelangelo used the thought of death as the mystagogue of his spirit into the temple of eternal things—τὰ ἀίδια, *die bleibenden Verhält-nisse*—and as the means of maintaining self-control and self-coherence amid the ever-shifting illusions of human life. This explains why in his love-sonnets he rarely speaks of carnal beauty except as the manifestation of the divine idea, which will be clearer to the soul after death than in the body.

When his life was drawing toward its close, Michelangelo's friends were not unnaturally anxious about his condition. Though he had a fairly good servant in Antonio del Franzese, and was surrounded by well-wishers like Tommaso Cavalieri, Daniele da Volterra, and Tiberio Calcagni, yet he led a very solitary life, and they felt he ought to be protected. Vasari tells us that he communicated privately with Averardo Serristori, the Duke's ambassador in Rome, recommending that some proper housekeeper should be appointed, and that due control should be instituted over the persons who frequented his house. It was very desirable, in case of a sudden accident, that his drawings and works of art should not be dispersed, but that what belonged to S. Peter's, to the Laurentian Library, and to the Sacristy should be duly assigned. Lionardo Buonarroti must have received similar advice from Rome, for a furious letter is extant, in which Michelangelo, impatient to the last of interference, literally rages at him:—

"I gather from your letter that you lend credence to certain envious and scoundrelly persons, who, since they cannot manage me or rob me, write you a lot of lies. They are a set of sharpers, and you are so silly as to believe what they say about my affairs, as though I were a baby. Get rid of them, the scandalous, envious, ill-lived rascals. As for my suffering the mismanagement you write about, I tell you that I could not be better off, or more faithfully served and attended to in all things. As for my being robbed, to which I think you allude, I assure you that I have people in my house whom I can trust and repose on. Therefore, look to your own life, and do not think about my affairs, because I know how to take care of myself if it is needful, and am not a baby. Keep well."

This is the last letter to Lionardo. It is singular that Michelangelo's correspondence with his father, with Luigi del Riccio, with Tommaso dei Cavalieri, and with his nephew, all of whom he sincerely loved, should close upon a note of petulance and wrath. The fact is no doubt accidental. But it is strange.

x

We have frequently had occasion to notice the extreme pain caused to Michelangelo's friends by his unreasonable irritability and readiness to credit injurious reports about them. These defects of temper justified to some extent his reputation for savagery, and they must be reckoned among the most salient features of his personality. I shall therefore add three other instances of the same kind which fell under my observation while studying the inedited documents of the Buonarroti Archives. Giovanni Francesco Fattucci was, as we well know, his most intimate friend and trusted counsellor during long and difficult years, when the negotiations with the heirs of Pope Julius were being carried on; yet there exists one letter of unaffected sorrow from this excellent man, under date October 14, 1545, which shows that for some unaccountable reason Michelangelo had suddenly chosen to mistrust him. Fattucci begins by declaring that he is wholly guiltless of things which his friend too credulously believed upon the strength of gossip. He ex-

presses the deepest grief at this unjust and suspicious treatment. The letter shows him to have been more hurt than
resentful. Another document signed by Francesco Sangallo
(the son of his old friend Giuliano), bearing no date, but
obviously written when they were both in Florence, and
therefore before the year 1535, carries the same burden of
complaint. The details are sufficiently picturesque to warrant the translation of a passage. After expressing astonishment at Michelangelo's habit of avoiding his society, he
proceeds: "And now, this morning, not thinking that I
should annoy you, I came up and spoke to you, and you received me with a very surly countenance. That evening,
too, when I met you on the threshold with Granacci, and
you left me by the shop of Pietro Osaio, and the other fore-
noon at S. Spirito, and to-day, it struck me as extremely
strange, especially in the presence of Piloto and so many
others. I cannot help thinking that you must have some
grudge against me; but I marvel that you do not open out
your mind to me, because it may be something which is
wholly false." The letter winds up with an earnest protest
that he has always been a true and faithful friend. He begs
to be allowed to come and clear the matter up in conversation, adding that he would rather lose the good-will of the
whole world than Michelangelo's.

The third letter is somewhat different in tone, and not
so personally interesting. Still it illustrates the nervousness
and apprehension under which Michelangelo's acquaintances
continually lived. The painter commonly known as Rosso
Fiorentino was on a visit to Rome, where he studied the
Sistine frescoes. They do not appear to have altogether pleased
him, and he uttered his opinion somewhat too freely in
public. Now he pens a long elaborate epistle, full of adula-
tion, to purge himself of having depreciated Michelangelo's
works. People said that "when I reached Rome, and entered
the chapel painted by your hand, I exclaimed that I was not
going to adopt that manner." One of Buonarroti's pupils

had been particularly offended. Rosso protests that he rather likes the man for his loyalty; but he wishes to remove any impression which Michelangelo may have received of his own irreverence or want of admiration. The one thing he is most solicitous about is not to lose the great man's good-will.

It must be added, at the close of this investigation, that however hot and hasty Michelangelo may have been, and however readily he lent his ear to rumours, he contrived to renew the broken threads of friendship with the persons he had hurt by his irritability.

CHAPTER XV

I

DURING the winter of 1563-64 Michelangelo's friends in Rome became extremely anxious about his health, and kept Lionardo Buonarroti from time to time informed of his proceedings. After New Year it was clear that he could not long maintain his former ways of life. Though within a few months of ninety, he persisted in going abroad in all weathers, and refused to surround himself with the comforts befitting a man of his eminence and venerable age. On the 14th of February he seems to have had a kind of seizure. Tiberio Calcagni, writing that day to Lionardo, gives expression to his grave anxiety: "Walking through Rome to-day, I heard from many persons that Messer Michelangelo was ill. Accordingly I went at once to visit him, and although it was raining I found him out of doors on foot. When I saw him, I said that I did not think it right and seemly for him to be going about in such weather. 'What do you want?' he answered; 'I am ill, and cannot find rest anywhere.' The uncertainty of his speech, together with the look and colour of his face, made me feel extremely uneasy about his life. The end may not be just now, but I fear greatly that it cannot be far off." Michelangelo did not leave the house again, but spent the next four days partly reclining in an arm-chair, partly in bed. Upon the 15th following, Diomede Leoni wrote to Lionardo, enclosing a letter by the hand of Daniele da Volterra, which Michelangelo had signed. The old man felt his end approaching, and wished to see his nephew. "You will learn from the enclosure how ill he is, and that he wants you to come to Rome. He was taken ill yesterday. I therefore exhort you to come at once, but do so with sufficient prudence. The roads are bad now, and you are not used to travel by post. This being so, you would run some risk if you came posthaste. Taking your own time upon the way, you may feel at ease when you remember that Messer Tommaso dei Cavalieri, Messer Daniele, and I are here to render every possible assistance in your absence. Beside us, Antonio, the old and faithful servant of your uncle, will be helpful in any service that may be expected from him." Diomede reiterates his advice that Lionardo should run no risks by travelling too fast. "If the illness portends mischief, which God forbid, you could not with the utmost haste arrive in time. . . . I left him just now, a little after 8 P.M., in full possession of his faculties and quiet in his mind, but oppressed with a continued sleepiness. This has annoyed him so much that, between three and four this afternoon, he tried to go out riding, as his wont is every evening in good weather. The coldness of the weather and the weakness of his head and legs prevented him; so he returned to the fireside, and settled down into an easy chair, which he greatly prefers to the bed." No improvement gave a ray of hope to Michelangelo's friends, and two days later, on the 17th, Tiberio Calcagni took up the correspondence with Lionardo: "This is to beg you to hasten your coming as much as possible, even though the weather be unfavourable. It is certain now that our dear Messer Michelangelo must leave us for good and all, and he ought to have the consolation of seeing you." Next day, on the 18th, Diomede Leoni wrote again: "He died without making a will, but in the attitude of a perfect Christian, this evening, about the Ave Maria. I was present, together with Messer Tommaso dei Cavalieri and Messer Daniele da Volterra, and we put everything in such order that you may rest with a tranquil mind. Yesterday Michelangelo sent for our friend Messer Daniele, and besought him to take up his abode in the house until such time as you arrive, and this he will do."

It was at a little before five o'clock on the afternoon of February 18, 1564, that Michelangelo breathed his last. The physicians who attended him to the end were Federigo Donati, and Gherardo Fidelissimi, of Pistoja. It is reported by Vasari that, during his last moments, "he made his will in three sentences, committing his soul into the hands of God, his body to the earth, and his substance to his nearest relatives; enjoining upon these last, when their hour came, to think upon the sufferings of Jesus Christ."

On the following day, February 19, Averardo Serristori, the Florentine envoy in Rome, sent a despatch to the Duke, informing him of Michelangelo's decease: "This morning, according to an arrangement I had made, the Governor sent to take an inventory of all the articles found in his house. These were few, and very few drawings. However, what was there they duly registered. The most important object was a box sealed with several seals, which the Governor ordered to be opened in the presence of Messer Tommaso dei Cavalieri and Maestro Daniele da Volterra, who had been sent for by Michelangelo before his death. Some seven or eight thousand crowns were found in it, which have now been deposited with the Ubaldini bankers. This was the command issued by the Governor, and those whom it concerns will have to go there to get the money. The people of the house will be examined as to whether anything has been carried away from it. This is not supposed to have been the case. As far as drawings are concerned, they say that he burned what he had by him before he died. What there is shall be handed over to his nephew when he comes, and this your Excellency can inform him."

The objects of art discovered in Michelangelo's house were a blocked-out statue of S. Peter, an unfinished Christ with another figure, and a statuette of Christ with the cross, resembling the Cristo Risorto of S. Maria Sopra Minerva. Ten original drawings were also catalogued, one of which (a Pietà) belonged to Tommaso dei Cavalieri; another (an Epiphany) was given to the notary, while the rest came into the possession of Lionardo Buonarroti. The cash-box, which had been sealed by Tommaso dei Cavalieri and Diomede Leoni, was handed over to the Ubaldini, and from them it passed to Lionardo Buonarroti at the end of February.

II

Lionardo travelled by post to Rome, but did not arrive until three days after his uncle's death. He began at once to take measures for the transport of Michelangelo's remains to Florence, according to the wish of the old man, frequently expressed and solemnly repeated two days before his death. The corpse had been deposited in the Church of the SS. Apostoli, where the funeral was celebrated with becoming pomp by all the Florentines in Rome, and by artists of every degree. The Romans had come to regard Buonarroti as one of themselves, and, when the report went abroad that he had expressed a wish to be buried in Florence, they refused to believe it, and began to project a decent monument to his memory in the Church of the SS. Apostoli. In order to secure his object, Lionardo was obliged to steal the body away, and to despatch it under the guise of mercantile goods to the custom-house of Florence. Vasari wrote to him from that city upon the 10th of March, informing him that the packing-case had duly arrived, and had been left under seal until his, Lionardo's, arrival at the custom-house.

About this time two plans were set on foot for erecting monuments to Michelangelo's memory. The scheme started by the Romans immediately after his death took its course, and the result is that tomb at the SS. Apostoli, which undoubtedly was meant to be a statue-portrait of the man. Vasari received from Lionardo Buonarroti commission to erect the tomb in S. Croce. The correspondence of the latter, both with Vasari and with Jacopo del Duca, who superintended the Roman monument, turns for some time upon these tombs. It is much to Vasari's credit that he wanted to place the Pietà which Michelangelo had broken, above the S. Croce sepulchre. He writes upon the subject in these words: "When I reflect that Michelangelo asserted, as is well known also to Daniele, Messer Tommaso dei Cavalieri, and many other of his friends, that he was making the Pietà of five figures, which he broke, to serve for his own tomb, I think that his heir ought to inquire how it came into the possession of Bandini. Besides, there is an old man in the group who represents the person of the sculptor. I entreat you, therefore, to take measures for regaining this Pietà, and I will make use of it in my design. Pierantonio Bandini is very courteous, and will probably consent. In this way you will gain several points. You will assign to your uncle's sepulchre the group he planned to place there, and you will be able to hand over the statues in Via Mozza to his Excellency, receiving in return enough money to complete the monument." Of the marbles in the Via Mozza at Florence, where Michelangelo's workshop stood, I have seen no catalogue, but they certainly comprised the Victory, probably also the Adonis and the Apollino. There had been some thought of adapting the Victory to the tomb in S. Croce. Vasari, however, doubted whether this group could be applied in any forcible sense allegorically to Buonarroti as man or as artist.

Eventually, as we know, the very mediocre monument designed by Vasari, which still exists at S. Croce, was erected at Lionardo Buonarroti's expense, the Duke supplying a sufficiency of marble.

III

It ought here to be mentioned that, in the spring of 1563, Cosimo founded an Academy of Fine Arts, under the title of "Arte del Disegno." It embraced all the painters, architects, and sculptors of Florence in a kind of guild, with privileges, grades, honours, and officers. The Duke condescended to be the first president of this academy. Next to him, Michelangelo was elected unanimously by all the members as their uncontested principal and leader, "inasmuch as this city, and peradventure the whole world, hath not a master more excellent in the three arts." The first great work upon which the Duke hoped to employ the guild was the completion of the sacristy at S. Lorenzo. Vasari's letter to Michelanglo shows that up to this date none of the statues had been erected in their proper places, and that it was intended to add a great number of figures, as well as to adorn blank spaces in the walls with frescoes. All the best artists of the time, including Gian Bologna, Cellini, Bronzino, Tribolo, Montelupo, Ammanati, offered their willing assistance, "forasmuch as there is not one of us but hath learned in this sacristy, or rather in this our school, whatever excellence he possesses in the arts of design." We know already only too well that the scheme was never carried out, probably in part because Michelangelo's rapidly declining strength prevented him from furnishing these eager artists with the necessary working drawings. Cosimo's anxiety to gain possession of any sketches left in Rome after Buonarroti's death may be ascribed to this project for completing the works begun at S. Lorenzo.

Well then, upon the news of Michelangelo's death, the academicians were summoned by their lieutenant, Don Vincenzo Borghini, to deliberate upon the best way of paying him honour, and celebrating his obsequies with befitting

pomp. It was decided that all the leading artists should con-
tribute something, each in his own line, to the erection of a
splendid catafalque, and a sub-committee of four men was
elected to superintend its execution. These were Angelo
Bronzino and Vasari, Benvenuto Cellini and Ammanati,
friends of the deceased, and men of highest mark in the two
fields of painting and sculpture. The church selected for the
ceremony was S. Lorenzo; the orator appointed was Benedetto Varchi. Borghini, in his capacity of lieutenant or
official representative, obtained the Duke's assent to the plan,
which was subsequently carried out, as we shall see in due
course.

Notwithstanding what Vasari wrote to Lionardo about
his uncle's coffin having been left at the Dogana, it seems
that it was removed upon the very day of its arrival, March
11, to the Oratory of the Assunta, underneath the church
of S. Pietro Maggiore. On the following day the painters,
sculptors, and architects of the newly founded academy met
together at this place, intending to transfer the body secretly
to S. Croce. They only brought a single pall of velvet, embroidered with gold, and a crucifix, to place upon the bier.
When night fell, the elder men lighted torches, while the
younger crowded together, vying one with another for the
privilege of carrying the coffin. Meantime the Florentines,
suspecting that something unusual was going forward at S.
Pietro, gathered round, and soon the news spread through
the city that Michelangelo was being borne to S. Croce. A
vast concourse of people in this way came unexpectedly together, following the artists through the streets, and doing
pathetic honour to the memory of the illustrious dead. The
spacious church of S. Croce was crowded in all its length and
breadth, so that the pall-bearers had considerable difficulty
in reaching the sacristy with their precious burden. In that
place Don Vincenzo Borghini, who was lieutenant of the
academy, ordered that the coffin should be opened. "He
thought he should be doing what was pleasing to many of

those present; and, as he afterwards admitted, he was personally anxious to behold in death one whom he had never seen in life, or at any rate so long ago as to have quite forgotten the occasion. All of us who stood by expected to find the corpse already defaced by the outrage of the sepulchre, inasmuch as twenty-five days had elapsed since Michelangelo's death, and twenty-one since his consignment to the coffin; but, to our great surprise, the dead man lay before us perfect in all his parts, and without the evil odours of the grave; indeed, one might have thought that he was resting in a sweet and very tranquil slumber. Not only did the features of his countenance bear exactly the same aspect as in life, except for some inevitable pallor, but none of his limbs were injured, or repulsive to the sight. The head and cheeks, to the touch, felt just as though he had breathed his last but a few hours since." As soon as the eagerness of the multitude calmed down a little, the bier was carried into the church again, and the coffin was deposited in a proper place behind the altar of the Cavalcanti.

When the academicians decreed a catafalque for Michelangelo's solemn obsequies in S. Lorenzo, they did not aim so much at worldly splendour or gorgeous trappings as at an impressive monument, combining the several arts which he had practised in his lifetime. Being made of stucco, woodwork, plaster, and such perishable materials, it was unfortunately destined to decay. But Florence had always been liberal, nay, lavish, of her genius in triumphs, masques, magnificent street architecture, evoked to celebrate some ephemeral event. A worthier occasion would not occur again; and we have every reason to believe that the superb structure, which was finally exposed to view upon the 14th of July, displayed all that was left at Florence of the grand style in the arts of modelling and painting. They were decadent indeed; during the eighty-nine years of Buonarroti's life upon earth they had expanded, flourished, and flowered with infinite variety in rapid evolution. He lived to watch their decline; yet the sunset of that long day was still splendid to the eyes and senses.

The four deputies appointed by the academy held frequent sittings before the plan was fixed, and the several parts had been assigned to individual craftsmen. Ill health prevented Cellini from attending, but he sent a letter to the lieutenant, which throws some interesting light upon the project in its earlier stages. A minute description of the monument was published soon after the event. Another may be read in the pages of Vasari. Varchi committed his oration to the press, and two other panegyrical discourses were issued, under the names of Leonardo Salviati and Giovan Maria Tarsia. Poems composed on the occasion were collected into one volume, and distributed by the Florentine firm of Sermatelli. To load these pages with the details of allegorical statues and pictures which have long passed out of existence, and to cite passages from funeral speeches, seems to me useless. It is enough to have directed the inquisitive to sources where their curiosity may be gratified.

IV

It would be impossible to take leave of Michelangelo without some general survey of his character and qualities. With this object in view I do not think I can do better than to follow what Condivi says at the close of his biography, omitting those passages which have been already used in the body of this book, and supplementing his summary with illustrative anecdotes from Vasari. Both of these men knew him intimately during the last years of his life; and if it is desirable to learn how a man strikes his contemporaries, we obtain from them a lively and veracious, though perhaps a slightly flattered, picture of the great master whom they studied with love and admiration from somewhat different points of view. This will introduce a critical examination of the analysis to which the psychology of Michelangelo has recently been subjected.

Condivi opens his peroration with the following paragraphs:—

"Now, to conclude this gossiping discourse of mine, I say that it is my opinion that in painting and sculpture nature bestowed all her riches with a full hand upon Michelangelo. I do not fear reproach or contradiction when I repeat that his statues are, as it were, inimitable. Nor do I think that I have suffered myself to exceed the bounds of truth while making this assertion. In the first place, he is the only artist who has handled both brush and mallet with equal excellence. Then we have no relics left of antique paintings to compare with his; and though many classical works in statuary survive, to whom among the ancients does he yield the palm in sculpture? In the judgment of experts and practical artists, he certainly yields to none; and were we to consult the vulgar, who admire antiquity without criticism, through a kind of jealousy toward the talents and the industry of their own times, even here we shall find none who say the contrary; to such a height has this great man soared above the scope of envy. Raffaello of Urbino, though he chose to strive in rivalry with Michelangelo, was wont to say that he thanked God for having been born in his days, since he learned from him a manner very different from that which his father, who was a painter, and his master, Perugino, taught him. Then, too, what proof of his singular excellence could be wished for, more convincing and more valid, than the eagerness with which the sovereigns of the world contended for him? Beside four pontiffs, Julius, Leo, Clement, and Paul, the Grand Turk, father of the present Sultan, sent certain Franciscans with letters begging him to come and reside at his court. By orders on the bank of the Gondi at Florence, he provided that whatever sums were asked for should be disbursed to pay the expenses of his journey; and when he should have reached Cossa, a town near Ragusa, one of the greatest nobles of the realm was told off to conduct him in most honourable fashion to Constantinople. Francis of Valois, King of France, tried to get him by many devices, giving instructions that, whenever he chose to travel, 3000 crowns should be told out to him in Rome. The Signory of Venice sent Bruciolo to Rome with an invitation to their city, offering a pension of 600 crowns if he would settle there. They attached no conditions to this offer, only desiring that he should honour the republic with his presence, and stipulating that whatever he might do in their service should be paid as though he were not in receipt of a fixed income. These are not ordinary occurrences, or such as happen every day, but strange and out of common usage; nor are they wont to befall any but men of singular and transcendent ability, as was Homer, for whom many cities strove in rivalry, each desirous of acquiring him and making him its own.

"The reigning Pope, Julius III., holds him in no less esteem than the princes I have mentioned. This sovereign, distinguished for rare taste and judgment, loves and promotes all arts and sciences, but is most particularly devoted to painting, sculpture, and architecture, as may be clearly seen in the buildings which his Holiness has erected in the Vatican and the Belvedere, and is now raising at his Villa Giulia (a monument worthy of a lofty and generous nature, as indeed his own is), where he has gathered together so many ancient and modern statues, such a variety of the finest pictures, precious columns, works in stucco, wall-painting, and every kind of decoration, of the which I must reserve a more extended account for some future occasion, since it deserves a particular study, and has not yet reached completion. This Pope has not used the services of Michelangelo for any active work, out of regard for his advanced age. He is fully alive to his greatness, and appreciates it, but refrains from adding burdens beyond those which Michelangelo himself desires; and this regard, in my opinion, confers more honour on him than any of the great undertakings which former pontiffs exacted from his genius. It is true that his Holiness almost always consults him on works of painting or of architecture he may have in progress, and very often sends the artists to confer with him at his own house. I regret, and his Holiness also regrets, that a certain natural shyness, or shall I say respect or reverence, which some folk call pride, prevents him from having recourse to the benevolence, goodness, and liberality of such a pontiff, and one so much his friend. For the Pope, as I first heard from the Most Rev. Monsignor of Forlì, his Master of the Chamber, has often observed that, were this possible, he would gladly give some of his own years and his own blood to add to Michelangelo's life, to the end that the world should not so soon be robbed of such a man. And this, when I had access to his Holiness, I heard with my own ears from his mouth. Moreover, if he happens to survive him, as seems reasonable in the course of nature, he has a mind to embalm him and keep him ever near to his own person, so that his body in death shall be as everlasting as his works. This he said to Michelangelo himself at the commencement of his reign, in the presence of many persons. I know not what could be more honourable to Michelangelo than such words, or a greater proof of the high account in which he is held by his Holiness.

"So then Michelangelo, while he was yet a youth, devoted himself not only to sculpture and painting, but also to all those other arts which to them are allied or subservient, and this he did with such absorbing energy that for a time he almost entirely cut himself off from human society, conversing with but very few intimate friends. On this account some folk thought him proud, others eccentric and capricious, although he was tainted with none of these defects; but, as hath happened to many men of great abilities, the love of study and the perpetual practice of his art rendered him solitary, being so taken up with the pleasure and delight of these things that society not only afforded him no solace, but even caused him annoyance by diverting him from meditation, being (as the great Scipio used to say) never less alone than when he was alone. Nevertheless, he very willingly embraced the friendship of those whose learned and cultivated conversation could be of profit to his mind, and in whom some beams of genius shone forth: as, for example, the most reverend and illustrious Monsignor Pole, for his rare virtues and singular goodness; and likewise the most reverend, my patron, Cardinal Crispo, in whom he discovered, beside his many excellent qualities, a distinguished gift of acute judgment; he was also warmly attached to the Cardinal of S. Croce, a man of the utmost gravity and wisdom, whom I have often heard him name in the highest terms; and to the most reverend Maffei, whose goodness and learning he has always praised: indeed, he loves and honours all the dependants of the house of Farnese, owing to the lively memory he cherishes of Pope Paul, whom he invariably mentions with the deepest reverence as a good and holy old man; and in like manner the most reverend Patriarch of Jerusalem, sometime Bishop of Cesena, has lived for some time in close intimacy with him, finding peculiar pleasure in so open and generous a nature. He was also on most friendly terms with my very reverend patron the Cardinal Ridolfi, of blessed memory, that refuge of all men of parts and talent. There are several others whom I omit for fear of being prolix, as Monsignor Claudio Tolomei, Messer Lorenzo Ridolfi, Messer Donato Giannotti, Messer Lionardo Malespini, Lottino, Messer Tommaso dei Cavalieri, and other honoured gentlemen. Of late years he has become deeply attached to Annibale Caro, of whom he told me that it grieves him not to have come to know him earlier, seeing that he finds him much to his taste."

"In like manner as he enjoyed the converse of learned men, so also did he take pleasure in the study of eminent writers, whether of prose or verse. Among these he particularly admired Dante, whose marvellous poems he hath almost all by heart. Nevertheless, the same might perhaps be said about his love for Petrarch. These poets he not only delighted in studying, but he also was wont to compose from time to time upon his own account. There are certain sonnets among those he wrote which give a very good notion of his great inventive power and judgment. Some of them have furnished Varchi with the subject of Discourses. It must be rememberd, however, that he practised poetry for his amusement, and not as a profession, always depreciating his own talent, and appealing to his ignorance in these matters. Just in the same way he has perused the Holy Scriptures with great care and industry, studying not merely the Old Testament, but also the New, together with their commentators, as, for example, the writings of Savonarola, for whom he always retained a deep affection, since the accents of the preacher's living voice rang in his memory.

"He has given away many of his works, the which, if he had chosen to sell them, would have brought him vast sums of money. A single instance of this generosity will suffice— namely, the two statues which he presented to his dearest friend, Messer Ruberto Strozzi. Nor was it only of his handiwork that he has been liberal. He opened his purse readily to poor men of talent in literature or art, as I can testify, having myself been the recipient of his bounty. He never showed an envious spirit toward the labours of other masters in the crafts he practised, and this was due rather to the goodness of his nature than to any sense of his own superiority. Indeed, he always praised all men of excellence without exception, even Raffaello of Urbino, between whom and himself there was of old time some rivalry in painting. I have only heard him say that Raffaello did not derive his mastery in that art so much from nature as from prolonged study. Nor is it true, as many persons assert to his discredit, that he has been unwilling to impart instruction. On the contrary, he did so readily, as I know by personal experience, for to me he unlocked all the secrets of the arts he had acquired. Ill-luck, however, willed that he should meet either with subjects ill adapted to such studies, or else with men of little perseverance, who, when they had been working a few months under his direction, began to think themselves past-masters. Moreover, although he was willing to teach, he did not like it to be known that he did so, caring more to do good than to seem to do it. I may add that he always attempted to communicate the arts to men of gentle birth, as did the ancients, and not to plebeians."

V

To this passage about Michelangelo's pupils we may add the following observation by Vasari: "He loved his workmen, and conversed with them on friendly terms. Among these I will mention Jacopo Sansovino, Rosso, Pontormo, Daniele da Volterra, and Giorgio Vasari. To the last of these men he showed unbounded kindness, and caused him to study architecture, with the view of employing his services in that art. He exchanged thoughts readily with him, and discoursed upon artistic topics. Those are in the wrong who assert that he refused to communicate his stores of knowledge. He always did so to his personal friends, and to all who sought his advice. It ought, however, to be mentioned that he was not lucky in the craftsmen who lived with him, since chance brought him into contact with people unfitted to profit by his example. Pietro Urbano of Pistoja was a man of talent but no industry. Antonio Mini had the will but not the brains, and hard wax takes a bad impression. Ascanio dalla Ripa Transone (*i.e.*, Condivi) took great pains, but brought nothing to perfection either in finished work or in design. He laboured many years upon a picture for which Michelangelo supplied the drawing. At last the expectations based upon this effort vanished into smoke. I remember that Michelangelo felt pity for his trouble, and helped him with his own hand. Nothing, however, came of it. He often told me that if he had found a proper subject he should have liked, old as he was, to have recommended anatomy, and to have written on it for the use of his work-men. However, he distrusted his own powers of expressing what he wanted in writing, albeit his letters show that he could easily put forth his thoughts in a few brief words."

About Michelangelo's kindness to his pupils and servants there is no doubt. We have only to remember his treatment of Pietro Urbano and Antonio Mini, Urbino and Condivi, Tiberio Calcagni and Antonio del Franzese. A curious letter from Michelangelo to Andrea Quarantesi, which I have quoted in another connection, shows that people were eager to get their sons placed under his charge. The inedited correspondence in the Buonarroti Archives abounds in instances illustrating the reputation he had gained for goodness. We have two grateful letters from a certain Pietro Bettino in Castel Durante speaking very warmly of Michelangelo's attention to his son Cesare. Two to the same effect from Amilcare Anguissola in Cremona acknowledge services rendered to his daughter Sofonisba, who was studying design in Rome. Pietro Urbano wrote twenty letters between the years 1517 and 1525, addressing him in terms like "carissimo quanto padre." After recovering from his illness at Pistoja, he expresses the hope that he will soon be back again at Florence (September 18, 1519): "Dearest to me like the most revered of fathers, I send you salutations, announcing that I am a little better, but not yet wholly cured of that flux; still I hope before many days are over to find myself at Florence." A certain Silvio Falcone, who had been in his service, and who had probably been sent away because of some misconduct, addressed a letter from Rome to him in Florence, which shows both penitence and warm affection. "I am and shall always be a good servant to you in every place where I may be. Do not remember my stupidity in those past concerns, which I know that, being a prudent man, you will not impute to malice. If you were to do so, this would cause me the greatest sorrow; for I desire nothing but to remain in your good grace, and if I had only this in the world, it would suffice me." He begs to be remembered to Pietro Urbano, and requests his pardon if he has offended him. Another set of letters, composed in the same tone by a man who signs himself Silvio di Giovanni da Cepparello, was written by a sculptor honourably mentioned in Vasari's Life of Andrea da Fiesole for his work at S. Lorenzo, in Genoa, and elsewhere. They show how highly the fame of having been in Michelangelo's employ was valued. He says that he is now working for Andrea Doria, Prince of Melfi, at Genoa. Still he should like to return, if this were possible, to his old master's service: "For if I lost all I had in the world, and found myself with you, I should think myself the first of men." A year later Silvio was still at work for Prince Doria and the Fieschi, but he again begs earnestly to be taken back by Michelangelo. "I feel what obligations I am under for all the kindness received from you in past times. When I remember the love you bore me while I was in your service, I do not know how I could repay it; and I tell you that only through having been in your service, wherever I may happen now to be, honour and courtesy are paid me; and that is wholly due to your excellent renown, and not to any merit of my own."

The only letter from Ascanio Condivi extant in the Buonarroti Archives may here be translated in full, since its tone does honour both to master and servant:—

"Unique lord and my most to be observed patron,—I have already written you two letters, but almost think you cannot have received them, since I have heard no news of you. This I write merely to beg that you will remember to command me, and to make use not of me alone, but of all my household, since we are all your servants. Indeed, my most honoured and revered master, I entreat you deign to dispose of me and do with me as one is wont to do with the least of servants. You have the right to do so, since I owe more to you than to my own father, and I will prove my desire to repay your kindness by my deeds. I will now end this letter, in order not to be irksome, recommending myself humbly, and praying you to let me have the comfort of knowing that you are well: for a greater I could not receive. Farewell."

It cannot be denied that Michelangelo sometimes treated his pupils and servants with the same irritability, suspicion, and waywardness of temper as he showed to his relatives and friends. It is only necessary to recall his indignation against Lapo and Lodovico at Bologna, Stefano at Florence, Sandro at Serravalle, all his female drudges, and the anonymous boy whom his father sent from Rome. That he was a man "gey ill to live with" seems indisputable. This may in part account for the fact that, unlike other great Italian masters, he formed no school. The *frescanti* who came from Florence to assist him in the Sistine Chapel were dismissed with abruptness, perhaps even with brutality. Montelupo and Montorsoli, among sculptors, Marcello Venusti and Pontormo, Daniele da Volterra and Sebastiano del Piombo, among painters, felt his direct influence. But they did not stand in the same relation to him as Raffaello's pupils to their master. The work of Giulio Romano, Giovanni da Udine, Francesco Penni, Perino del Vaga, Primaticcio, at Rome, at Mantua, and elsewhere, is a genial continuation of Raffaello's spirit and manner after his decease. Nothing of the sort can be maintained about the statues and the paintings which display a study of the style of Michelangelo. And this holds good in like manner of his imitators in architecture. For worse rather than for better, he powerfully and permanently affected Italian art; but he did not create a body of intelligent craftsmen, capable of carrying on his inspiration, as Giulio Romano expanded the Loggie of the Vatican into the Palazzo del Te. I have already expressed my opinions regarding the specific quality of the Michelangelo tradition in a passage which I may perhaps be here permitted to resume:—

"Michelangelo formed no school in the strict sense of

the word; yet his influence was not the less felt on that account, nor less powerful than Raffaello's. During his manhood a few painters endeavoured to add the charm of oil-
colouring to his designs, and long before his death the
seduction of his mighty mannerism began to exercise a fatal
charm for all the schools of Italy. Painters incapable of
fathoming his intention, unsympathetic to his rare type of
intellect, and gifted with less than a tithe of his native
force, set themselves to reproduce whatever may be justly
censured in his works. To heighten and enlarge their style
was reckoned a chief duty of aspiring craftsmen, and it was
thought that recipes for attaining to this final perfection of
the modern arts might be extracted without trouble from
Michelangelo's masterpieces. Unluckily, in proportion as his
fame increased, his peculiarities became with the advance
of age more manneristic and defined, so that his imitators
fixed precisely upon that which sober critics now regard as
a deduction from his greatness. They failed to perceive that
he owed his grandeur to his personality, and that the audacities which fascinated them became mere whimsical extrava-
gances when severed from his *terribilità*, and sombre
simplicity of impassioned thought. His power and his spirit
were alike unique and incommunicable, while the admiration of his youthful worshippers betrayed them into imitating
the externals of a style that was rapidly losing spontaneity.
Therefore they fancied they were treading in his footsteps
and using the grand manner when they covered church-
roofs and canvases with sprawling figures in distorted
attitudes. Instead of studying nature, they studied Michelangelo's cartoons, exaggerating by their unintelligent
discipleship his wilfulness and arbitrary choice of form.

"Vasari's and Cellini's criticisms of a master they both
honestly revered may suffice to illustrate the false method
adopted by these mimics of Michelangelo's ideal. To charge
him with faults proceeding from the weakness and blindness
of the Decadence—the faults of men too blind to read his

art aright, too weak to stand on their own feet without him
—would be either stupid or malicious. If at the close of the
sixteenth century the mannerists sought to startle and entrance the world by empty exhibitions of muscular anatomy
misunderstood, and by a braggadocio display of meaningless
effects—crowding their compositions with studies from the
nude, and painting agitated groups without a discernible
cause for agitation—the crime surely lay with the patrons
who liked such decoration, and with the journeymen who
provided it. Michelangelo himself always made his manner
serve his thought. We may fail to appreciate his manner
and may be incapable of comprehending his thought, but
only insincere or conceited critics will venture to gauge the
latter by what they feel to be displeasing in the former.
What seems lawless in him follows the law of a profound
and peculiar genius, with which, whether we like it or not,
we must reckon. His imitators were devoid of thought, and
too indifferent to question whether there was any law to
be obeyed. Like the jackass in the fable, they assumed the
dead lion's skin, and brayed beneath it, thinking they could
roar."

VI

Continuing these scattered observations upon Michelangelo's character and habits, we may collect what Vasari
records about his social intercourse with brother-artists. Being himself of a saturnine humour, he took great delight
in the society of persons little better than buffoons. Writing
the Life of Jacopo surnamed L'Indaco, a Florentine painter
of some merit, Vasari observes: "He lived on very familiar
terms of intimacy with Michelangelo; for that great artist,
great above all who ever were, when he wished to refresh
his mind, fatigued by studies and incessant labours of the
body and the intellect, found no one more to his liking and
more congenial to his humour than was Indaco." Nothing is
recorded concerning their friendship, except that Buonarroti

frequently invited Indaco to meals; and one day, growing tired of the man's incessant chatter, sent him out to buy figs, and then locked the house-door, so that he could not enter when he had discharged his errand. A boon-companion of the same type was Menighella, whom Vasari describes as "a mediocre and stupid painter of Valdarno, but extremely amusing." He used to frequent Michelangelo's house, "and he, who could with difficulty be induced to work for kings, would lay aside all other occupations in order to make drawings for this fellow." What Menighella wanted was some simple design or other of S. Rocco, S. Antonio, or S. Francesco, to be coloured for one of his peasant patrons. Vasari says that Michelangelo modelled a very beautiful Christ for this humble friend, from which Menighella made a cast, and repeated it in papier-mâché, selling these crucifixes through the country-side. What would not the world give for one of them, even though Michelangelo is said to have burst his sides with laughing at the man's stupidity! Another familiar of the same sort was a certain stone-cutter called Domenico Fancelli, and nicknamed Topolino. From a letter addressed to him by Buonarroti in 1523 it appears that he was regarded as a "very dear friend." According to Vasari, Topolino thought himself an able sculptor, but was in reality extremely feeble. He blocked out a marble Mercury, and begged the great master to pronounce a candid opinion on its merits. "You are a madman, Topolino," replied Michelangelo, "to attempt this art of statuary. Do you not see that your Mercury is too short by more than a third of a cubit from the knees to the feet? You have made him a dwarf, and spoiled the whole figure." "Oh, that is nothing! If there is no other fault, I can easily put that to rights. Leave the matter to me." Michelangelo laughed at the man's simplicity, and went upon his way. Then Topolino took a piece of marble, and cut off the legs of his Mercury below the knees. Next he fashioned a pair of buskins of the right height, and joined these on to the truncated limbs in such wise that the tops of the boots concealed the lines of juncture. When Buonarroti saw the finished statue, he remarked that fools were gifted with the instinct for rectifying errors by expedients which a wise man would not have hit upon.

Another of Michelangelo's buffoon friends was a Florentine celebrity, Piloto, the goldsmith. We know that he took this man with him when he went to Venice in 1530; but Vasari tells no characteristic stories concerning their friendship. It may be remarked that Il Lasca describes Piloto as a "most entertaining and facetious fellow," assigning him the principal part in one of his indecent novels. The painter Giuliano Bugiardini ought to be added to the same list. Messer Ottaviano de' Medici begged him to make a portrait of Michelangelo, who gave him a sitting without hesitation, being extremely partial to the man's company. At the end of two hours Giuliano exclaimed: "Michelangelo, if you want to see yourself, stand up; I have caught the likeness." Michelangelo did as he was bidden, and when he had examined the portrait, he laughed and said: "What the devil have you been about? You have painted me with one of my eyes up in the temple." Giuliano stood some time comparing the drawing with his model's face, and then remarked: "I do not think so; but take your seat again, and I shall be able to judge better when I have you in the proper pose." Michelangelo, who knew well where the fault lay, and how little judgment belonged to his friend Bugiardini, resumed his seat, grinning. After some time of careful contemplation, Giuliano rose to his feet and cried: "It seems to me that I have drawn it right, and that the life compels me to do so." "So then," replied Buonarroti, "the defect is nature's, and see you spare neither the brush nor art."

Both Sebastiano del Piombo and Giorgio Vasari were appreciated by Michelangelo for their lively parts and genial humour. The latter has told an anecdote which illustrates the old man's eccentricity. He was wont to wear a cardboard hat at night, into which he stuck a candle, and then worked by its light upon his statue of the Pietà. Vasari observing this habit, wished to do him a kindness by sending him 40 lbs. of candles made of goat's fat, knowing that they gutter less than ordinary dips of tallow. His servant carried them politely to the house two hours after nightfall, and presented them to Michelangelo. He refused, and said he did not want them. The man answered: "Sir, they have almost broken my arms carrying them all this long way from the bridge, nor will I take them home again. There is a heap of mud opposite your door, thick and firm enough to hold them upright. Here then I will set them all up, and light them." When Michelangelo heard this, he gave way: "Lay them down; I do not mean you to play pranks at my house-door." Vasari tells another anecdote about the Pietà. Pope Julius III. sent him late one evening to Michelangelo's house for some drawing. The old man came down with a lantern, and hearing what was wanted, told Urbino to look for the cartoon. Meanwhile, Vasari turned his attention to one of the legs of Christ, which Michelangelo had been trying to alter. In order to prevent his seeing, Michelangelo let the lamp fall, and they remained in darkness. He then called for a light, and stepped forth from the enclosure of planks behind which he worked. As he did so, he remarked, "I am so old that oftentimes Death plucks me by the cape to go with him, and one day this body of mine will fall like the lantern, and the light of life will be put out." Of death he used to say, that "if life gives us pleasure, we ought not to expect displeasure from death, seeing it is made by the hand of the same master."

Among stories relating to craftsmen, these are perhaps worth gleaning. While he was working on the termini for the tomb of Julius, he gave directions to a certain stone-cutter: "Remove such and such parts here to-day, smooth out in this place, and polish up in that." In course of time, without being aware of it, the man found that he had produced a statue, and stared astonished at his own performance. Michelangelo asked, "What do you think of it?" "I think it very good," he answered, "and I owe you a deep debt of gratitude." "Why do you say that?" "Because you have caused me to discover in myself a talent which I did not know that I possessed."—A certain citizen, who wanted a mortar, went to a sculptor and asked him to make one. The fellow, suspecting some practical joke, pointed out Buonarroti's house, and said that if he wanted mortars, a man lived there whose trade it was to make them. The customer accordingly addressed himself to Michelangelo, who, in his turn suspecting a trick, asked who had sent him. When he knew the sculptor's name, he promised to carve the mortar, on the condition that it should be paid for at the sculptor's valuation. This was settled, and the mortar turned out a miracle of arabesques and masks and grotesque inventions, wonderfully wrought and polished. In due course of time the mortar was taken to the envious and suspicious sculptor, who stood dumbfounded before it, and told the customer that there was nothing left but to carry this masterpiece of carving back to him who fashioned it, and order a plain article for himself.—At Modena he inspected the terra-cotta groups by Antonio Begarelli, enthusiastically crying out, "If this clay could become marble, woe to antique statuary." —A Florentine citizen once saw him gazing at Donatello's statue of S. Mark upon the outer wall of Orsanmichele. On being asked what he thought of it, Michelangelo replied, "I never saw a figure which so thoroughly represents a man of probity; if S. Mark was really like that, we have every reason to believe everything which he has said." To the S. George in the same place he is reported to have given the word of command, "March!"—Some one showed him a set of medals by Alessandro Cesari, upon which he exclaimed, "The death hour of art has struck; nothing more perfect can be seen than these."—Before Titian's portrait of Duke Alfonso di Ferrara he observed that he had not thought art could perform so much, adding that Titian alone deserved the name of painter.—He was wont to call Cronaca's church of S. Francesco al Monte "his lovely peasant girl," and Ghiberti's doors in the Florentine Baptistery "the Gates of Paradise."—Somebody showed him a boy's drawings, and excused their imperfection by pleading that he had only just begun to study: "That is obvious," he answered. A similar reply is said to have been made to Vasari, when he excused his own frescoes in the Cancelleria at Rome by saying they had been painted in a few days.—An artist showed him a Pietà which he had finished: "Yes, it is indeed a *pietà* (pitiful object) to see."—Ugo da Carpi signed one of his pictures with a legend declaring he had not used a brush on it: "It would have been better had he done so."—Sebastiano del Piombo was ordered to paint a friar in a chapel at S. Pietro a Montorio. Michelangelo observed, "He will spoil the chapel." Asked why, he answered, "When the friars have spoiled the world, which is so large, it surely is an easy thing for them to spoil such a tiny chapel."—A sculptor put together a number of figures imitated from the antique, and thought he had surpassed his models. Michelangelo remarked, "One who walks after another man, never goes in front of him; and one who is not able to do well by his own wit, will not be able to profit by the works of others."—A painter produced some notably poor picture, in which only an ox was vigorously drawn: "Every artist draws his own portrait best," said Michelangelo.—He went to see a statue which was in the sculptor's studio, waiting to be exposed before the public. The man bustled about altering the lights, in order to show his work off to the best advantage: "Do not take this trouble; what really matters will be the light of the piazza;" meaning that the people in the long-run decide what is good or bad in art.—Accused of want of spirit in his rivalry with Nanni di Baccio Bigio, he retorted, "Men who fight with folk of little worth win nothing."—A priest who was a friend of his said, "It is a pity that you never married, for you might have had many children, and would have left them all the profit and honour of your labours." Michelangelo answered, "I have only too much of a wife in this art of mine. She has always kept me struggling on. My children will be the works I leave behind me. Even though they are worth naught, yet I shall live awhile in them. Woe to Lorenzo Ghiberti if he had not made the gates of S. Giovanni! His children and grandchildren have sold and squandered the substance that he left. The gates are still in their places."

VII

This would be an appropriate place to estimate Michelangelo's professional gains in detail, to describe the properties he acquired in lands and houses, and to give an account of his total fortune. We are, however, not in the position to do this accurately. We only know the prices paid for a few of his minor works. He received, for instance, thirty ducats for the Sleeping Cupid, and 450 ducats for the Pietà of S. Peter's. He contracted with Cardinal Piccolomini to furnish fifteen statues for 500 ducats. In all of these cases the costs of marble, workmen, workshop, fell on him. He contracted with Florence to execute the David in two years, at a salary of six golden florins per month, together with a further sum when the work was finished. It appears that 400 florins in all (including salary) were finally adjudged to him. In these cases all incidental expenses had been paid by his employers. He contracted with the Operai del Duomo to make twelve statues in as many years, receiving two florins a month, and as much as the Operai thought fit to pay him when the whole was done. Here too he was relieved from incidental expenses. For the statue of Christ at S. Maria sopra Minerva he was paid 200 crowns.

These are a few of the most trustworthy items we possess, and they are rendered very worthless by the impossibility of reducing ducats, florins, and crowns to current values. With regard to the bronze statue of Julius II. at Bologna, Michelangelo tells us that he received in advance 1000 ducats, and when he ended his work there remained only 4½ ducats to the good. In this case, as in most of his great operations, he entered at the commencement into a contract with his patron, sending in an estimate of what he thought it would be worth his while to do the work for. The Italian is "pigliare a cottimo;" and in all of his dealings with successive Popes Michelangelo evidently preferred this method. It must have sometimes enabled the artist to make large profits; but the nature of the contract prevents his biographer from forming even a vague estimate of their amount. According to Condivi, he received 3000 ducats for the Sistine vault, working at his own costs. According to his own statement, several hundred ducats were owing at the end of the affair. It seems certain that Julius II. died in Michelangelo's debt, and that the various contracts for his tomb were a source of loss rather than of gain.

Such large undertakings as the sacristy and library of S. Lorenzo were probably agreed for on the contract system. But although there exist plenty of memoranda recording Michelangelo's disbursements at various times for various portions of these works, we can strike no balance showing an approximate calculation of his profits. What renders the matter still more perplexing is, that very few of Michelangelo's contracts were fulfilled according to the original intention of the parties. For one reason or another they had to be altered and accommodated to circumstances.

It is clear that, later on in life, he received money for drawings, for architectural work, and for models, the execution of which he bound himself to superintend. Cardinal Grimani wrote saying he would pay the artist's own price for a design he had requested. Vasari observes that the sketches he gave away were worth thousands of crowns. We know that he was offered a handsome salary for the superintendence of S. Peter's, which he magnanimously and piously declined to touch. But what we cannot arrive at is even a rough valuation of the sums he earned in these branches of employment.

Again, we know that he was promised a yearly salary from Clement VII., and one more handsome from Paul III. But the former was paid irregularly, and half of the latter depended on the profits of a ferry, which eventually failed him altogether. In each of these cases, then, the same circumstances of vagueness and uncertainty throw doubt on all investigation, and render a conjectural estimate impossible. Moreover, there remain no documents to prove what he may have gained, directly or indirectly, from succeeding Pontiffs. That he felt the loss of Paul III., as a generous patron, is proved by a letter written on the occasion of his death; and Vasari hints that the Pope had been munificent in largesses bestowed upon him. But of these occasional presents and emoluments we have no accurate information; and we are unable to state what he derived from Pius IV., who was certainly one of his best friends and greatest admirers.

At his death in Rome he left cash amounting to something under 9000 crowns. But, since he died intestate, we have no will to guide us as to the extent and nature of his whole estate. Nor, so far as I am aware, has the return of his property, which Lionardo Buonarroti may possibly have furnished to the state of Florence, been yet brought to light.

That he inherited some landed property at Settignano from his father is certain; and he added several plots of ground to the paternal acres. He also is said to have bought a farm in Valdichiana (doubtful), and other pieces of land in Tuscany. He owned a house at Rome, a house and workshop in the Via Mozza at Florence, and he purchased the Casa Buonarroti in Via Ghibellina. But we have no means of determining the total value of these real assets.

In these circumstances I feel unable to offer any probable opinion regarding the amount of Michelangelo's professional earnings, or the exact way in which they were acquired. That he died possessed of a considerable fortune, and that he was able during his lifetime to assist his family with large donations, cannot be disputed. But how he came to command so much money does not appear. His frugality, bordering upon penuriousness, impressed contemporaries. This, considering the length of his life, may account for not contemptible accumulations.

VIII

We have seen that Michelangelo's contemporaries found fault with several supposed frailties of his nature. These may be briefly catalogued under the following heads: A passionate violence of temper (*terribilità*), expressing itself in hasty acts and words; extreme suspiciousness and irritability; solitary habits, amounting to misanthropy or churlishness; eccentricity and melancholy bordering on madness; personal timidity and avarice; a want of generosity in imparting knowledge, and an undue partiality for handsome persons of his own sex. His biographers, Condivi and Vasari, thought these charges worthy of serious refutation, which proves that they were current. They had no difficulty in showing that his alleged misanthropy, melancholy, and madness were only signs of a studious nature absorbed in profound meditations. They easily refuted the charges of avarice and want of generosity in helping on young artists. But there remained a great deal in the popular conception which could not be dismissed, and which has recently been corroborated by the publication of his correspondence. The opinion that Michelangelo was a man of peculiar, and in some respects not altogether healthy nervous temperament, will force itself upon all those who have fairly weighed the evidence of the letters in connection with the events of his life. It has been developed in a somewhat exaggerated form, of late years, by several psychologists of the new school (Parlagreco and Lombroso in Italy, Nisbet in England), who attempt to prove that Michelangelo was the subject of neurotic disorder. The most important and serious essay in this direction is a little book of great interest and almost hypercritical acumen published recently at Naples. Signor Parlagreco lays great stress upon Michelangelo's insensibility to women, his "strange and contradictory feeling about feminine beauty." He seeks to show, what is indeed, I think, capable of demonstration, that the man's intense devotion to art and study, his solitary habits and constitutional melancholy, caused him to absorb the ordinary instincts and passions of a young man into his æsthetic temperament; and that when, in later life, he began to devote his attention to poetry, he treated love from the point of view of mystical philosophy. In support of this argument Parlagreco naturally insists upon the famous friendship with Vittoria Colonna, and quotes the Platonising poems commonly attributed to this emotion. He has omitted to mention, what certainly bears upon the point of Michelangelo's frigidity, that only one out of the five Buonarroti brothers, sons of Lodovico, married. Nor does he take into account the fact that Raffaello da Urbino, who was no less devoted and industrious in art and study, retained the liveliest sensibility to female charms. In other words, the critic appears to neglect that common-sense solution of the problem, which is found in a cold and physically sterile constitution as opposed to one of greater warmth and sensuous activity.

Parlagreco attributes much value to what he calls the religious terrors and remorse of Michelangelo's old age; says that "his fancy became haunted with doubts and fears; every day discovering fresh sins in the past, inveighing against the very art which made him famous among men, and seeking to propitiate Paradise for his soul by acts of charity to dowerless maidens." The sonnets to Vasari and some others are quoted in support of this view. But the question remains, whether it is not exaggerated to regard pious aspirations, and a sense of human life's inadequacy at its close, as the signs of nervous malady. The following passage sums up Parlagreco's theory in a succession of pregnant sentences. "An accurate study, based upon his correspondence in connection with the events of the artist's life and the history of his works, has enabled me to detect in his character a persistent oscillation. Continual contradictions between great and generous ideas upon the one side, and puerile ideas upon the other; between the will and the word, thought and action; an excessive irritability and the highest degree of susceptibility; constant love for others, great activity in doing good, sudden sympathies, great outbursts of enthusiasm, great fears; at times an unconsciousness with respect to his own actions; a marvellous modesty in the field of art, an unreasonable vanity regarding external appearances:—these are the diverse manifestations of psychical energy in Buonarroti's life; all which makes me believe that the mighty artist was affected by a degree of neuropathy bordering closely upon hysterical disease." He proceeds to support this general view by several considerations, among which the most remarkable are Michelangelo's asseverations to friends: "You will say that I am old and mad to make sonnets, but if people assert that I am on the verge of dotage, I have wished to act up to my character:" "You will say that I am old and mad; but I answer that there is no better way of keeping sane and free from anxiety, than by being mad:" "As regards the madness they ascribe to me, it does harm to nobody but myself:" "I enjoyed last evening, because it drew me out of my melancholy and mad humour."

Reviewing Parlagreco's argument in general, I think it may be justly remarked that if the qualities rehearsed above constitute hysterical neuropathy, then every testy, sensitive, impulsive, and benevolent person is neuropathically hysterical. In particular we may demur to the terms "puerile ideas," "unreasonable vanity regarding external appearances." It would be difficult to discover puerility in any of Buonarroti's utterances; and his only vanity was a certain pride in the supposed descent of his house from that of Canossa. The frequent allusions to melancholy and madness do not constitute a confession of these qualities. They express Michelangelo's irritation at being always twitted with unsociability and eccentricity. In the conversations recorded by Francesco d'Olanda he quietly and philosophically exculpates men of the artistic temperament from such charges, which were undoubtedly brought against him, and which the recluse manner of his life to some extent accounted for.

It may be well here to resume the main points of the indictment brought against Michelangelo's sanity by the neo-psychologists. In the first place, he admired male more than female beauty, and preferred the society of men to that of women. But this peculiarity, in an age and climate which gave larger licence to immoderate passions, exposed him to no serious malignancy of rumour. Such predilections were not uncommon in Italy. They caused scandal when they degenerated into vice, and rarely failed in that case to obscure the good fame of persons subject to them. Yet Michelangelo, surrounded by jealous rivals, was only very lightly touched by the breath of calumny in his lifetime. Aretino's malicious insinuation and Condivi's cautious vindication do not suffice to sully his memory with any dark suspicion. He lived with an almost culpable penuriousness in what concerned his personal expenditure. But he was generous towards his family, bountiful to his dependants, and liberal in charity. He suffered from constitutional depression, preferred solitude to crowds, and could not brook the interference of fashionable idlers with his studious leisure. But, as he sensibly urged in self-defence, these eccentricities, so frequent with men of genius, ought to have been ascribed to the severe demands made upon an artist's faculties by the problems with which he was continually engaged; the planning of a Pope's mausoleum, the distribution of a score of histories and several hundreds of human figures on a chapel-vaulting, the raising of S. Peter's cupola in air: none of which tasks can be either lightly undertaken or carried out with ease. At worst, Michelangelo's melancholy might be ascribed to that *morbus eruditorum* of which Burton speaks. It never assumed the form of hypochondria, hallucination, misogyny, or misanthropy. He was irritable, suspicious, and frequently unjust, both to his friends and relatives on slight occasions. But his relatives gave him good reason to be fretful by their greediness, ingratitude, and stupidity; and when he lost his temper he recovered it with singular ease. It is also noticeable that these paroxysms of crossness on which so much stress has been laid, came upon him mostly when he was old, worn out with perpetual mental and physical fatigue, and troubled by a painful disease of the bladder. There is nothing in their nature, frequency, or violence to justify the hypothesis of more than a hyper-sensitive nervous temperament; and without a temperament of this sort how could an artist of Michelangelo's calibre and intensity perform his life-work? In old age he dwelt upon the thought of death, meditated in a repentant spirit on the errors of his younger years, indulged a pious spirit, and clung to the cross of Christ. But when a man has passed the period allotted for the average of his race, ought not these preoccupations to be reckoned to him rather as appropriate and meritorious? We must not forget that he was born and lived as a believing Christian, in an age of immorality indeed, but one which had not yet been penetrated with scientific conceptions and materialism. There is nothing hysterical or unduly ascetic in the religion of his closing years. It did not prevent him from taking the keenest interest in his family, devoting his mind to business and the purchase of property, carrying on the Herculean labour of building the mother-church of Latin Christendom. He was subject, all through his career, to sudden panics, and suffered from a constitutional dread of assassination. We can only explain his flight from Rome, his escape from Florence, the anxiety he expressed about his own and his family's relations to the Medici, by supposing that his nerves were sensitive upon this point. But, considering the times in which he lived, the nature of the men around him, the despotic temper of the Medicean princes, was there anything morbid in this timidity? A student of Cellini's Memoirs, of Florentine history, and of the dark stories in which the private annals of the age abound, will be forced to admit that imaginative men of acute nervous susceptibility, who loved a quiet life and wished to keep their mental forces unimpaired for art and thought, were justified in feeling an habitual sense of uneasiness in Italy of the Renaissance period. Michelangelo's timidity, real as it was, did not prevent him from being bold upon occasion, speaking the truth to popes and princes, and making his personality respected. He was even accused of being too "terrible," too little of a courtier and time-server.

When the whole subject of Michelangelo's temperament has been calmly investigated, the truth seems to be that he did not possess a nervous temperament so evenly balanced as some phlegmatic men of average ability can boast of. But who could expect the creator of the Sistine, the sculptor of the Medicean tombs, the architect of the cupola, the writer of the sonnets, to be an absolutely normal individual? To identify genius with insanity is a pernicious paradox. To recognise that it cannot exist without some inequalities of nervous energy, some perturbations of nervous function, is reasonable. In other words, it is an axiom of physiology that the abnormal development of any organ or any faculty is balanced by some deficiency or abnormality elsewhere in the individual. This is only another way of saying that the man of genius is not a mediocre and ordinary personality: in other words, it is a truism, the statement of which appears superfluous. Rather ought we, in Michelangelo's case, to dwell upon the remarkable sobriety of his life, his sustained industry under very trying circumstances, his prolonged intellectual activity into extreme old age, the toughness of his constitution, and the elasticity of that nerve-fibre which continued to be sound and sane under the enormous and varied pressure put upon it over a period of seventy-five laborious years.

If we dared attempt a synthesis or reconstitution of this unique man's personality, upon the data furnished by his poems, letters, and occasional utterances, all of which have been set forth in their proper places in this work, I think we must construct him as a being gifted, above all his other qualities and talents, with a burning sense of abstract beauty and an eager desire to express this through several forms of art—design, sculpture, fresco-painting, architecture, poetry. The second point forced in upon our mind is that the same man vibrated acutely to the political agitation of his troubled age, to mental influences of various kinds, and finally to a persistent nervous susceptibility, which made him exquisitely sensitive to human charm. This quality rendered him irritable in his dealings with his fellow-men, like an instrument of music, finely strung, and jangled on a slight occasion. In the third place we discover that, while accepting the mental influences and submitting to the personal attractions I have indicated, he strove, by indulging solitary tastes, to maintain his central energies intact for art—joining in no rebellious conspiracies against the powers that be, bending his neck in silence to the storm, avoiding pastimes and social diversions which might have called into activity the latent sensuousness of his nature. For the same reason, partly by predilection, and partly by a deliberate wish to curb his irritable tendencies, he lived as much alone as possible, and poorly. At the close of his career, when he condescended to unburden his mind in verse and friendly dialogue, it is clear that he had formed the habit of recurring to religion for tranquillity, and of combating dominant desire by dwelling on the thought of inevitable death. Platonic speculations upon the eternal value of beauty displayed in mortal creatures helped him always in his warfare with the flesh and roving inclination. Self-control seems to have been the main object of his conscious striving, not for its own sake, but as the condition necessary to his highest spiritual activity. Self-coherence, self-concentration, not for any mean or self-indulgent end, but for the best attainment of his intellectual ideal, was what he sought for by the seclusion and the renunciations of a lifetime.

The total result of this singular attitude toward human life, which cannot be rightly described as either ascetic or mystical, but seems rather to have been based upon some self-preservative instinct, bidding him sacrifice lower and keener impulses to what he regarded as the higher and finer purpose of his being, is a certain clash and conflict of emotions, a certain sense of failure to attain the end proposed, which excuses, though I do not think it justifies, the psychologists, when they classify him among morbid subjects. Had he yielded at any period of his career to the ordinary customs of his easy-going age, he would have presented no problem to the scientific mind. After consuming the fuel of the passions, he might have subsided into common calm, or have blunted the edge of inspiration, or have finished in some phase of madness or ascetical repentance. Such are the common categories of extinct volcanic temperaments. But the essential point about Michelangelo is that he never burned out, and never lost his manly independence, in spite of numerous nervous disadvantages. That makes him the unparalleled personality he is, as now revealed to us by the impartial study of the documents at our disposal.

IX

It is the plain duty of criticism in this age to search and probe the characters of world-important individuals under as many aspects as possible, neglecting no analytical methods, shrinking from no tests, omitting no slight details or faint shadows that may help to round a picture. Yet, after all our labour, we are bound to confess that the man himself eludes our insight. "The abysmal deeps of personality" have never yet been sounded by mere human plummets. The most that microscope and scalpel can perform is to lay bare tissue and direct attention to peculiarities of structure. In the long-run we find that the current opinion formed by successive generations remains true in its grand outlines. That large collective portrait of the hero, slowly emerging from sympathies and censures, from judgments and panegyrics, seems dim indeed and visionary, when compared with some sharply indented description by a brilliant literary craftsman. It has the vagueness of a photograph produced by superimposing many negatives of the same face one upon the other. It lacks the pungent piquancy of an etching. Yet this is what we must abide by; for this is spiritually and generically veracious.

At the end, then, a sound critic returns to think of Michelangelo, not as Parlagreco and Lombroso show him, nor even as the minute examination of letters and of poems proves him to have been, but as tradition and the total tenor of his life display him to our admiration. Incalculable, incomprehensible, incommensurable: yes, all souls, the least and greatest, attack them as we will, are that. But definite in solitary sublimity, like a supreme mountain seen from a vast distance, soaring over shadowy hills and misty plains into the clear ether of immortal fame.

Viewed thus, he lives for ever as the type and symbol of a man, much-suffering, continually labouring, gifted with keen but rarely indulged passions, whose energies from boyhood to extreme old age were dedicated with unswerving purpose to the service of one master, plastic art. On his death-bed he may have felt, like Browning, in that sweetest of his poems, "other heights in other lives, God willing." But, for this earthly pilgrimage, he was contented to leave the ensample of a noble nature made perfect and completed in itself by addiction to one commanding impulse. We cannot cite another hero of the modern world who more fully and with greater intensity realised the main end of human life, which is self-effectuation, self-realisation, self-manifestation in one of the many lines of labour to which men may be called and chosen. Had we more of such individualities, the symphony of civilisation would be infinitely glorious; for nothing is more certain than that God and the world cannot be better served than by each specific self pushing forward to its own perfection, sacrificing the superfluous or hindering elements in its structure, regardless of side issues and collateral considerations.

Michelangelo, then, as Carlyle might have put it, is the Hero as Artist. When we have admitted this, all dregs and sediments of the analytical alembic sink to the bottom, leaving a clear crystalline elixir of the spirit. About the quality of his genius opinions may, will, and ought to differ. It is so pronounced, so peculiar, so repulsive to one man, so attractive to another, that, like his own dread statue of Lorenzo de' Medici, "it fascinates and is intolerable." There are few, I take it, who can feel at home with him in all the length and breadth and dark depths of the regions that he traversed. The world of thoughts and forms in which he lived habitually is too arid, like an extinct planet, tenanted by mighty elemental beings with little human left to them but visionary Titan-shapes, too vast and void for common minds to dwell in pleasurably. The sweetness that emerges from his strength, the beauty which blooms rarely, strangely, in unhomely wise, upon the awful crowd of his conceptions, are only to be apprehended by some innate sympathy or by long incubation of the brooding intellect. It is probable, therefore, that the deathless artist through long centuries of glory will abide as solitary as the simple old man did in his poor house at Rome. But no one, not the dullest, not the weakest, not the laziest and lustfullest, not the most indifferent to ideas or the most tolerant of platitudes and paradoxes, can pass him by without being arrested, quickened, stung, purged, stirred to uneasy self-examination by so strange a personality expressed in prophecies of art so pungent.

Each supreme artist whom God hath sent into the world

with inspiration and a particle of the imperishable fire, is a law to himself, an universe, a revelation of the divine life under one of its innumerable attributes. We cannot therefore classify Michelangelo with any of his peers throughout the long procession of the ages. Of each and all of them it must be said in Ariosto's words, "Nature made him, and then broke the mould." Yet, if we seek Michelangelo's affinities, we find them in Lucretius and Beethoven, not in Sophocles and Mozart. He belongs to the genus of deep, violent, colossal, passionately striving natures; not, like Raffaello, to the smooth, serene, broad, exquisitely finished, calmly perfect tribe. To God be the praise, who bestows upon the human race artists thus differing in type and personal quality, each one of whom incarnates some specific portion of the spirit of past ages, perpetuating the traditions of man's soul, interpreting century to century by everlasting hieroglyphics, mute witnesses to history and splendid illustrations of her pages.

THE END

Modern Library of the World's Best Books

COMPLETE LIST OF TITLES IN

THE MODERN LIBRARY

For convenience in ordering use number at right of title